Praise for

# DISRUPTING QUALITATIVE INQUIRY

"Love. Truth. Stouthearted. Intuition and hope, not exempt from struggle, controversy, and tensions, where love for infinite possibilities offset conflicts. *Disrupting Qualitative Inquiry* is a refreshing and timely dialogue, engaging new and old generations of critical qualitative researchers in an ongoing, ever-flowing discussion on the challenges and hope for a framework and methodology in education that does the risky, dirty, but ever-so-needed work of disruption. This energetic collection disrupts static norms of inquiry, teaching, and research practices to energize and move educational inquiry onward."

—*Blair E. Smith, Doctoral Student, Syracuse University*

"In this edited collection of methodological disruption, Ruth Nicole Brown, Rozana Carducci, and Candace R. Kuby have assembled a new generation of qualitative researchers who exhibit a healthy disregard for tradition, and a willingness to explore unchartered methodological territory. The research exemplars and theoretical discussions presented in this text are sure to serve as a model for both emerging, and established scholars looking for fresh examples of how such disruptive practices work."

—*Lisa A. Mazzei, Associate Professor, University of Oregon*

# DISRUPTING QUALITATIVE INQUIRY

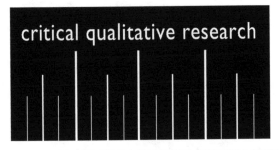

critical qualitative research

CRITICAL ISSUES FOR LEARNING AND TEACHING

Shirley R. Steinberg and Gaile S. Cannella
*Series Editors*

Vol. 10

---

The Critical Qualitative Research series
is part of the Peter Lang Education list.
Every volume is peer reviewed and meets
the highest quality standards for content and production.

---

PETER LANG
New York • Bern • Frankfurt • Berlin
Brussels • Vienna • Oxford • Warsaw

# DISRUPTING QUALITATIVE INQUIRY

*Possibilities and Tensions in Educational Research*

### Edited by
## Ruth Nicole Brown, Rozana Carducci, and Candace R. Kuby

PETER LANG
New York • Bern • Frankfurt • Berlin
Brussels • Vienna • Oxford • Warsaw

Library of Congress Cataloging-in-Publication Data

Disrupting qualitative inquiry: possibilities and tensions in educational research /
edited by Ruth Nicole Brown, Rozana Carducci, Candace R. Kuby.
pages cm. — (Critical qualitative research; v. 10)
Includes bibliographical references and index.
1. Education—Research—Methodology.
I. Brown, Ruth Nicole. II. Carducci, Rozana. III. Kuby, Candace R.
LB1028.D545    370.72—dc23    2013041729
ISBN 978-1-4331-2312-2 (hardcover)
ISBN 978-1-4331-2311-5 (paperback)
ISBN 978-1-4539-1268-3 (e-book)
ISSN 1947-5993


Bibliographic information published by **Die Deutsche Nationalbibliothek.**
**Die Deutsche Nationalbibliothek** lists this publication in the "Deutsche
Nationalbibliografie"; detailed bibliographic data are available
on the Internet at http://dnb.d-nb.de/.

Cover art by Teri Holbrook and Nicole M. Pourchier


The paper in this book meets the guidelines for permanence and durability
of the Committee on Production Guidelines for Book Longevity
of the Council of Library Resources.

© 2014 Peter Lang Publishing, Inc., New York
29 Broadway, 18th floor, New York, NY 10006
www.peterlang.com

Printed in the United States of America

# Dedications

To my parents, Lawrence and Evelyn Brown, for making a way when there was not one and expecting me to do the same for those I love.—Ruth Nicole Brown

To Melissa Contreras-McGavin, a dear friend whose courage and conviction serve as constant sources of inspiration and motivation. Thank you for helping me realize the power, possibility, and necessity of disrupting educational organizations.—Rozana Carducci

To Nick, who inspires and supports me in living-out disruptively.—Candace Kuby

And collectively we dedicate this book to all those who seek to live as disruptive scholars and educators, and work for social change and justice.

# Table of Contents

By series editor Gaile S. Cannella

By editors Ruth Nicole Brown, Rozana Carducci, and Candace R. Kuby

## Section 1 Doing Disruptive Qualitative Inquiry: Methodologies, Politics, and Practices

Ruth Nicole Brown

Rosario Carrillo

## Section 2 Living it Out: Disrupting Politics and Practices in the Academy

# List OF Figures

# Acknowledgments

Disruption and I go way back. Mariama Sesay and Tiffany Davis have been my best friends since forever, and together we became skilled in rule-breaking and resistance. I received superior training in positivist, interpretivist, and arts-based methods from masters of their craft, including political scientist/methodologist Martha Feldman, political scientist/organizer Greg Markus, filmmaker Carol Jacobsen, anthropologist Ruth Behar, playwright OyamO, director Glenda Dickerson, and drama professor Mbala Soka Di Nkanga. Charlie Vanover and I took many courses together, and it's been an honor to remain friends and colleagues as we continue to write and perform our research. I am thankful to those who give me support and mentorship, Chantal Nadeau, Siobhan Somerville, Yoon Pak, Adrienne Dixson, Mary Weems, James Anderson, and Chris Span. I would not be able to bare the cost of doing disruptive methods if it were not for my colleagues and friends, Christina DeNicolo, Aisha Durham, Melynda Price, Mimi Nguyen, Fiona Ngô, Dustin Allred, Soo Ah Kwon, Lisa Cacho, David Coyoca, Isabel Molina-Guzmán, Ian Sprandel, Steve Hocker, Zenzele Isoke, Karen Flynn, Will Mitchell, Bettina Love, Roxana Marachi, Michelle Tellez, Dorian Warren, Ferentz LaFargue, Robin Hayes, Amy Cabrera Rasmussen, and K. Nicola Williams. I am full of gratitude for those who have done, continue to do, and will do SOLHOT! Chamara Kwayke and Candy Taaffe thank you for walking the talk with me. To every student who has taken my Revolutionary Acts course, thank you for breaking routine to engage fully disruptive inquiry. May the next level disruptors, Dominique C. Hill, Durell Callier,

Dean Ivory Berry, CC Suarez, April Warren-Grice, Blair Smith, and Grenita Hall, have their say. Jessica Robinson and Porshe Garner thank you for being so critical to the resurrection. My your work extend the Black blues hip hop woman tradition, "revelations, bag lady ..." Certainly, I will continue to innovate, because Getu delivers inspiration and stability, Maya Sanaa embodies creative genius, Addis reminds me how to be really willful, and Kaleb gives hugs and smiles that restore weariness. A very special thank you goes to Bryana French—your generosity inspires, and I'm deeply appreciative for all that you do, especially for inviting me to perform at the University of Missouri and introducing me to my co-authors. Candace and Rozana, this has been such an intellectually fun, rewarding, and generative project. I'm so glad to have shared this experience with you, and I look forward to continued collaborations!

—Ruth Nicole

Peter Magolda, professor of Student Affairs in Higher Education at Miami University, played an important role in nurturing my fascination with and passion for qualitative inquiry. In addition to helping me understand the difference between methodology and method, Peter's cultural inquiry courses opened my eyes to a new way of seeing, studying, and practicing higher education. I am a better writer and thinker for knowing Peter, and I will be forever grateful for the gifts of his wisdom, mentorship, and expert editing skills. Penny A. Pasque, Aaron M. Kuntz, and Ryan E. Gildersleeve provided excellent company on my initial explorations of disruptive inquiry. Frustrated with the narrow conceptualizations of qualitative research advanced in our doctoral programs and the field of higher education, Penny, Aaron, Ryan, and I engaged in a series of disruptive methodological dialogues that spanned seven years, significantly shaping my perspectives on the nature, aims, and possibilities of educational research. I dedicated my contribution to this book to my dear friend and colleague Melissa Contreras-McGavin. To put it simply, I am a better person for knowing and collaborating with Melissa, an exceptional mother, scholar, and friend who inspires me to live life to the fullest and reach my disruptive potential. Casandra Harper helped keep me sane during this editing project, reminding me to laugh and put life in perspective. The unconditional love and support of my husband and best friend, Seth, makes each day better than the last; I know I am lucky to have him as a partner. I would also like to thank my co-editors, Candace and Ruth Nicole, for their intellectual energy, patience, and grace during our collaborative endeavor. It has been a true joy to work with you.

—Rozana

Being disruptive is not always easy. In fact, usually it is met with resistance. Therefore, it is important to acknowledge those who have supported my work as a disruptive scholar. I believe that living disruptively is both a personal and professional way of being. From a young age, my parents encouraged me, not necessarily with words, but in how they raised me to be independent as a woman. I was encouraged to color outside of the lines, literally and figuratively. Nick, my partner in life, has challenged me to disrupt normalized ways of being a woman, teacher, Christian, wife, and so forth. Professionally, when I think of one mentor scholar who modeled and encouraged me to disrupt, it is Barbara Dennis. While at Indiana University, her courses on feminist methodologies and narrative inquiry as well as conversations on critical theory and poststructuralism, fed my soul as a researcher and opened my eyes to endless possibilities. The readings and learning engagements in her courses gave me the space to think about the tensions and possibilities of disrupting qualitative inquiry. Thank you for teaching me what it means to research *with* people, not *on* people. Many thanks to each of you for encouraging me (whether or not you realized it) to disrupt. And finally, I remember sitting in a coffee shop with Rozana discussing the idea and vision for this book and then us meeting Ruth Nicole and thinking she was just the right match for a third editor. I learned so much from you both—thank you for sharing your beauty as humans, passion for justice and change, and savvy skills as editors. Thanks for making this journey so pleasurable.

—Candace

The visioning, organizing, writing, and editing of this book have not happened in isolation. The three of us are grateful for the support we have received, not only in editing this book, but also in our lives beyond this project that led us to the point of collaboration.

Collectively, we are also grateful for the support and wisdom of Gaile Cannella, the series editor, and the editorial and production team at Peter Lang. We are thrilled that Teri Holbrook and Nicole Pourchier accepted our invitation to live out their artist/researcher/teacher identities in creating the art for the cover of the book. Finally, we would like to acknowledge the hard work and inspirational disruption of the scholars contributing chapters to this book. Individually and collectively these authors offer an exciting vision of methodological possibility, helping advance the disruptive potential of qualitative educational inquiry.

# Foreword

As we are now well into the twenty-first century, a new generation of critical qualitative researchers have entered academia. As graduate students, most of these early career scholars have had the opportunity to work with older colleagues who have spent their careers practicing qualitative, feminist, poststructural, postcolonial, or other forms of research that have never been valued broadly in the academy either epistemologically or methodologically. This earlier generation dealt with faculties who were, most commonly, powerful senior-level white males, who believed in scientific truth and method. These faculty members, who were also predominately post-positivist and believers in inferential statistics/measurement, often dismissed and disrespected those who conducted qualitative research of any type. Further, the work of women and people of color has for the past 30 years often been treated with disdain and disregarded as if it were not legitimate, even when it did follow traditional, post-positivist structures and practices. This earlier generation stood up literally every day of their careers for diversity in research, even arguing for basic introductory qualitative research courses, as well as for the acceptance of feminist, critical, and postcolonial dissertations. At this point, many books (and book series) have been constructed and published, as well as qualitative and critical scholarly journals that serve as outlets for scholarly work that literally did not exist for the first generation.

We are now at a moment in history in which scholars who would be qualitative, critical, disruptive, and transformative have a generation before them who have attempted to change the academic environment, to open doors and opportunities that would center diversity, multiplicity, and issues of social/environmental justice. Further, calls for a critical social science have emanated from multiple locations for 20-plus years. However, the postpositivist power structure remains strong for a range of reasons. Faculty from some disciplines and academic institutions never accepted qualitative research in any form; in these locations, no coursework was offered, and no tenure has ever been granted for qualitative or critical work. Additionally, and more broadly, both obvious and veiled forms of backlash against the successes of qualitative research are now impacting life in academia, from patriarchal challenges to diverse perspectives such as feminism, to the construction of hegemonic discourses that co-opt and reinscribe such as mixed methods and evidence-based practices. Underlying all of this are both local and global neoliberalism that locks one into forms of governmentality through which all aspects of human functioning are interpreted as related to capital, as privileging production (e.g., test scores, audit culture, funding), and as entrepreneurial (e.g., research/teaching that produces capital).

The authors in this volume are dealing with these complexities: higher education that has opened doors to diverse qualitative forms of research; backlashes against much of this research as diverse ways of being have gained attention; an increasingly neoliberal, corporatized, managerial, and self-interested academic environment; and, the intellectual, emotional, and bodily struggles and pressures of being a critical researcher who wants to survive in, while transforming, a society (and institution) that has, despite the work of previous generation scholars, remained patriarchal, oppressive, capitalist, and competitive. In different ways, the chapters in *Disrupting Qualitative Inquiry: Possibilities & Tensions in Educational Research* represent the complex struggles that we all face as critical qualitative research scholars, as researchers who hope to make changes that address injustices of all types. The reader is invited to interact with this text in multiple and diverse ways as the authors share their constructions of both disruptive inquiry and disruptive teaching.

Gaile S. Cannella, Series Editor
Critical Qualitative Research

# Introduction

RUTH NICOLE BROWN, ROZANA CARDUCCI,
AND CANDACE R. KUBY

*The best method to use is the one that answers the research question. I was taught this as a graduate student and now, as a professor, I teach the same lesson to my students. It succinctly ends unproductive conversations about shopping for "methods" like one does for clothes. Should I go with what is trendy? Designer? Second-hand? Clearance? Which method will cost me less (time, stress, coursework), I am often asked? Methods are controversial; sometimes methods are rendered inconsequential, taught strictly within a disciplinary tradition, and/or chosen according to market demand. Some methods are stereotyped as threatening, and even if it is the best method for the question, students may resist because of what they've heard about a "qualitative" or "quantitative" project. Fear looms large, and it shows up in unexpected ways—even in conversations about methods.*

—REFLECTION, RUTH NICOLE

As the opening reflection illustrates, decisions concerning the selection of research methodologies and methods remain a contested terrain, studded with assumptions, ideologies, and fears regarding the proper and/or most efficient way to conduct research. It is now acknowledged (at least by researchers anchored in critical, feminist, and postmodern schools of thought) that the process of inquiry is not a neutral activity (Brown & Strega, 2005); it is a highly political endeavor with significant implications for the researcher as well as the individuals and contexts that serve as the focus of study. While the opening reflection from Ruth Nicole sheds light on a particular strategy for shaping the methodological choices of graduate students beginning their socialization as educational researchers (i.e., teaching them to let the question guide the selection of method[ology]),[1] it is important to recognize that Ruth Nicole's counsel is only one of the many ideologically anchored discourses influencing the development of researcher identities and methodological preferences. In addition to the guidance of mentors and educational inquiry instructors like Ruth Nicole, who themselves teach from a particular, although often unnamed, political point of view, the research beliefs and practices of emerging scholars are also shaped by global, national, disciplinary, and organizational discourses that delimit the parameters of legitimate inquiry and exert subtle (and occasionally overt) pressure to conform to particular prescriptions for what counts as research. The National Research Council's (NRC) (2002) treatise, *Scientific Research in Education*, American Educational Research Association's (AERA) (2006) *Standards for Reporting on Empirical Social Science Research in AERA Publications*, and institutional review board protocols predicated on the medical model of research (Koro-Ljungberg, Gemignani, Brodeur, & Kmiec, 2007) are three common examples of national and organizational discourses that seek to govern the practice of educational research.

Unfortunately, despite the proliferation of qualitative research methodologies over the last 20 years—Denzin and Lincoln (2005) asserted that "an embarrassment of choices now characterizes the field of qualitative research" (p. 20)—educational research continues to be dominated by discourses that extol postpositivist and constructivist assumptions of data, analysis, representation, and knowledge production (Pasque, Carducci, Kuntz, & Gildersleeve, 2012) that serve to constrain methodological imagination and perpetuate the inequitable status quo in our schools and communities. Innovative ways of being a researcher and doing qualitative research are often met with resistance in the advising meeting, dissertation proposal defense, peer review process for publication, funding, or promotion and tenure. Whether in actual conversations with mentors, instructors, and colleagues or through subtle, nonverbal cues communicated via actions, educational researchers seeking to engage in new ways of producing and disseminating knowledge often hear, "*This isn't how we do things in academia. This is not how educational research has been done before.*"

Perhaps you have heard this refrain or something similar when discussing a research idea with an advisor, colleague, or reviewer. How did you respond to this challenge in the moment? How did the normalizing statements of your colleague shape your research decisions moving forward? Did you change your research plan to conform to dominant inquiry norms or opt to move forward with your "disruptive" study? Where do you think these disciplining messages come from and how might they be contested?

In the process of reflecting on, and sharing, our individual responses to the preceding questions, we discovered the inspiration and strategic value derived from exchanging stories of disruption. As we compared notes and anecdotes, we realized that despite our frustration with the discourses of methodological conservatism (Denzin & Giardiana, 2006; Lincoln & Cannella, 2004a, 2004b), which characterize the contemporary era of educational inquiry, we could identify mentors, colleagues, and, most importantly, early career peers, who were successfully engaging in innovative qualitative studies of educational contexts and phenomena. The idea for this book emerged from these deeply personal and empowering conversations. *Disrupting Qualitative Inquiry: Possibilities and Tensions in Educational Research* aims to interrupt prevailing postpositivist and constructivist approaches to qualitative research, challenging established norms of inquiry and illuminating ways of disrupting research practices, dissertating, teaching, and disseminating research in order to *move educational inquiry forward.* Forward in innovative ways of doing research *with* others, in questions we ask and method(ologie)s chosen, in how we choose to (re)present research, in disrupting life within academia, and in sharing how our disruptive paths have been shaped. Our hope is that emerging and established scholars (and those in between) derive energy, support, and respite from this book.

We want to begin with a strategic disruption. Think back to the time before you found yourself entrenched in graduate school and department politics, constrained by the norms of academic dress and vocabulary, and weighted down with the formal and informal advice of colleagues. Remember the research questions and educational issues that captured your mind and heart before you were told, "while it sounds promising, it's better to wait to do that project until you get a tenure-track job and have tenure." It is those questions and issues, those unmentionable projects that will not let you go even as they lay buried underneath the scripted elevator spiel you have prepared about who you are and what you study, that we would like you to focus on as you read this volume. To fully receive the gift of what we aim to offer in this book, we need you the reader to abandon any and all messages about the "right" way to do research, "appropriate questions," and "best methods and methodologies." This is the regularly scheduled program we aim to disrupt with this suggestive: where there is passion, there is possibility; where there is a haunting (longing), there is a research question begging to be spoken. If you dare speak the project, a methodology and method can be devised. As the research examples and personal narratives compiled in this book attest, disrupting qualitative research norms in educational inquiry is both challenging and possible. It requires conviction, a healthy disregard for tradition, and a willingness to explore unchartered methodological territory. To be sure, there are tensions associated with disruptive work (e.g., navigating disciplinary politics, maintaining resilience despite the inevitable fatigue associated with repeatedly explaining and defending your work); however, for us and the authors who contributed to this book, the possibilities far outweigh the tensions. Rather than distancing you from the academy, engaging in disruptive scholarship may bring you closer to others similarly interested in transforming stale academic routines, innovating both what we know and how we know, contributing diverse ideas to old and new questions while at the very least charting new fields of study made possible because you stayed with what was uncomfortable, different, and disruptive.

## FRAMING DISRUPTIVE INQUIRY

When brainstorming potential titles for this book we considered the terms critical, non-dominant, and untraditional qualitative research. We selected the term "disrupting" for several reasons. First, critical is a loaded word in educational research often tied to critical social theory. While some of the chapters in the book draw on critical theories, not all research that disrupts aligns with the tenets of critical social thought. We also struggled with our intent in using words like non-dominant or untraditional. While at this time, many of the methodologies and methods described in the book might be considered non-dominant and untraditional, our conversations about potential book titles challenged us to carefully reflect on and articulate the overarching goals driving our collaborative work. Do we want non-dominant (or untraditional or critical) method(ologie)s to become dominant and traditional, replacing or at least expanding the postpositivist and constructivist discourses that currently frame the parameters of educational inquiry? After a series of discussions and email exchanges, we reached consensus that methodological dominance is not the aim of this book; rather, we seek to engage in methodological advocacy, calling attention to the new forms of knowledge and social change made possible by embracing a wider repertoire of method(ologie)s than are currently acknowledged by the disciplinary powers that be. Ultimately, we came to a consensus on a title that centers on a verb that we feel best captures our aim in editing this volume: disrupting. The chapters in this book are actively disrupting ways of being, researching, writing, advising, and teaching qualitative inquiry in academia.

Having reached agreement on the goal of disruption, we next turned our attention to elaborating on the nature of the disruption we hoped to incite. For the purposes of this book, we identified five specific ways scholars may disrupt qualitative method(ologie)s in educational research. Each of these focal disruptive practices is described below. It is important to note first, however, that our disruptive framework is by no means fixed or complete. It is a fluid and evolving framework intended to illustrate the possibilities and tensions embedded within disruptive qualitative educational inquiry. We hope this discussion will spark your methodological imagination and encourage you to extend our framework by reflecting on and enacting your own notions of disruptive research principles, processes, and practices. Disruptive qualitative educational research:

*Disrupts dominant notions of research roles and relationships*—Disruptive qualitative researchers redefine the nature of what it means to participate in research and by whom. These relationships enact new approaches to recognizing and negotiating power within the research site as well as the education scholarly community.

*Disrupts dominant approaches to the collection and analysis of data*—Disruptive qualitative researchers seek alternative ways of collecting and analyzing data. In doing so, expanded ways of knowing and being are valued, and perspectives that are not always valued in educational research are foregrounded.

*Disrupts dominant notions of (re)presenting and disseminating research findings*—Disruptive qualitative researchers intentionally seek alternative publication formats and venues. They realize that research journals are not the only, or even the best, venue for work to be shared if the goals are to create change and honor the stories of co-researchers/collaborators. Disruptive researchers ask, to what end do I research? And how best can I share with co-researchers? And why and with whom do we wish to engage in dialogue?

*Disrupts rigid epistemological and methodological boundaries*—Disruptive qualitative researchers view theories as malleable and encourage the application of non-traditional theories in educational research. They understand that new theories and ways of researching are needed to examine current educational practices and policies. Disruptive researchers also understand that theoretical readings are not fixed, canonical, and rigid, but can be interpreted in various ways by various people.

*Disrupts disciplinarily boundaries and assumptive frameworks of how to do educational research*— Disruptive qualitative researchers interrogate how knowledge is produced and organized, challenging rigid and unproductive disciplinary boundaries. Utilizing knowledge situated across and beyond the academy, they seek to intervene and create new ways of doing research that disrupt the status quo in educational research.

Drawing upon research examples and personal reflection, the educational scholars featured in this book bring our disruptive framework to life. Their narratives illustrate the potential for theoretical and methodological disruption to improve educational practice and policy in the interest of fostering more socially just schools and communities. Our hope is that directing attention to the nuances of disruptive qualitative inquiry will open up spaces to think through the promises, limits, privileges, and shortcomings of research approaches that are typically overlooked or dismissed within the field of education.

## DISRUPTION AS BEING AND DOING

As evidenced in the personal reflections of the authors contributing to this volume, for some educational researchers, disruption is a way of being; it is who they are as people, as scholars. Disruptive researchers often feel they do not have a choice with respect to the work they do. On many occasions, the research emerges from the researcher's personal biography and lived experience, which is used to inform how they review previously written academic literature, the ways in which they go about gaining access and building relationships with those who they do not see as "data" but rather as peoples and partners in research. Skills and talents that lie outside of the traditional purview of researchers, say, for example, those who identity as artists may also argue that how they present their research grows as much from who they are as it does from the research question posed (see Chapter 5 by Pourchier and Holbrook). Much of what we understand as disruptive relies on the individual, which begs a valuation of diversity and embrace of fluid identities (see Chapter 10 by Nicolazzo and Chapter 11 by Pasque).

For other disruptive scholars, disruption is more about what they do, the practices and actions that intentionally work against the academy's collusion with militarization, violence, privatization, and elitism. The kinds of disruptive actions taken often depend on the context in which they labor, their location in hierarchies of power, position, and prestige, and the resources they have access to. Disruption as practice is dynamic, and they act in ways both small and large to transform processes and productions of knowledge to become accessible and accountable to the minoritized and marginalized. Disruption as being and doing is not easy, but it nourishes us and, hopefully, the people we humbly and respectfully call collaborators in research.

To acknowledge methodological disruption as a way of being and doing, we asked the authors contributing to this volume to include personal reflections on their methodological disruptions. Authors were encouraged to write about the ways in which multiple and fluid identities shaped their guiding research questions, methodological perspectives, and career decisions. The inclusion of personal narratives is intended to help readers recognize the personal in the politics of inquiry and gain insight from others' lessons learned.

## THE ORIGINS OF OUR DISRUPTIVE WORK

3019. What will disruption look like in the future? Who will remember this book? What will be laughable? What will seem ancient? What problems will endure? I dream of a music studio in a comfortable office that emits no dangerous smells and is spacious, safe, and fun enough for collective meetings, children, and theatrical performances. It would be supplied with materials for doing our best work, which includes a free-of-charge working copier and printer for students and professors alike who will not take for granted their dreams, and who do recognize the full humanity of those they work with. We will not struggle to make ends meet. We undo boundaries that construct "the university" and "the community" as false binaries. My kind of music plays as loud as I want and so does yours.

Surprise. Profound revelation. When I create the space for students to ask questions that sincerely motivate them, when I spend the necessary hours (a no-deadline kind of time) to converse, share ideas, name a life's work, divulge secret yearnings, un-taboo topics, make profound observations, interrogate personal experiences, claim individual gifts and talents, plot, plan, write, and conduct the dream of researchable projects, while sensing us all being, there is an awful lot of freezing up. Changing of the mind. Blame. Guilt. Resistance. Circling back and forth. Reduction. Retreating. Playing small. I mean, when I say, "yeah let's create this playground from the ground up ... bringing only those things we most want and desire, and I mean let's really get free, and not just free for ourselves, but for those who did not make it, for those we've left behind, for those yet to come"—fear shows up where I was looking for love.

Long sigh. Deep breath. Transformation. I remember wanting to perform, to create, to be an artist that was well-versed in the science of politics. How naïve I was to the ways knowledge is managed and organized in the academy! I do know now that feeling my blackness, feminism, body, penchant for the wild and the performative, working class values, unparalleled optimism, Midwestern pleasantness, and deep desire to create what does not exist, disrupts more than I initially imagined. My struggle sometimes looks like being overly defensive, hyper-supportive of students, and unresponsive to my own humanness. But struggle is no match for my fearlessness. Perhaps, "soft," "fluff," and "indecisive" are code for interdisciplinary scholarship. I remember. Let's change it all.

—RUTH NICOLE

****

I was a first-year doctoral student in 2002 eager to embed myself in my new academic home, the UCLA Graduate School of Education and Information Sciences (GSEIS). When I received an email notice of a brown bag meeting to discuss the newly published National Research Council's (2002) methodological manifesto, Scientific Research in Education, I saw an opportunity to expand my social and scholarly network. It was at this informal lunchtime gathering that I first learned about the politics of inquiry—global, national, disciplinary, organizational, and individual efforts to discipline (educational) scholars who engage in research that disrupts the normative principle and practices of postpositivism. Although I was in the early stages of formulating my scholarly identity and commitments, I had long ago discovered my preference for qualitative research and was disheartened to learn of a movement to marginalize qualitative perspectives within the educational research community.

The politics of inquiry became personal during my second year of doctoral work as I completed the three-course qualitative research sequence (222 A—B—C) offered by the GSEIS Social Research Methodology unit. Qualitative research was narrowly conceptualized in the 222 sequence as participant observation. The core texts were ethnographies (Jay MacLeod's, 1995, *Ain't No Making It*, and William Foot Whyte's, 1943, *Street Corner Society*). Class assignments focused on learning the steps of drafting a standard research proposal (Maxwell, 1996) and practicing the skills of participant observation data collection and analysis. As I was relatively new to the study and practice of qualitative research, I did not realize the sequence was providing me with a rather limited introduction to the world of qualitative educational inquiry. I did not know what I was missing as I had not yet heard of performance ethnography, autoethnography, a/r/tography, critical race theory counterstorytelling, poetic narratives, or photovoice. Thankfully, Carla (a pseudonym), a student in my 222B seminar opened my eyes.

Carla was a doctoral student studying indigenous epistemologies and education. We had taken 222A together and were enrolled in the same section of 222B, the field methods class. On the first day of the methods seminar, the professor explained the aims of the class and the nature of the semester-long participant observation project. Each student was required to propose and carry out a mini-ethnography of a site of our choosing, spending a minimum of five hours a week engaging in participant observation. At the end of the course overview, Carla raised her hand, and when called on by the professor, politely articulated the concern that the class's exclusive focus on ethnographic data collection methods was at odds with her indigenous epistemological and methodological commitments. She asked if there was a possibility of modifying the project so that she could carry out a research project informed by her evolving understanding of indigenous educational inquiry—a research paradigm that emphasized conducting research with, not on, "others." Although the professor acknowledged Carla's epistemological and methodological dilemma, she quickly denied the request, stating that this was a participant observation seminar and everyone needed to complete a traditional participant observation project. Carla opted to remain enrolled in the seminar but quietly resisted the professor's attempt to discipline her research agenda by designing and carrying out a class project that reflected her indigenous beliefs and values (i.e., her study did not include participant observation). The professor penalized Carla for her disobedience by deducting points from her final project grade. To my knowledge, Carla did not contest the lower grade because, for Carla, the grade wasn't the point—methodological congruence and intellectual freedom were more important.

Although I can no longer recall the specific focus of Carla's project, I can tell you her study had a profound influence in shaping my beliefs about the nature and purpose of educational research. Carla opened my eyes to the possibility—indeed the necessity—of disrupting the politics of inquiry that seek to narrowly define what counts as legitimate educational research. Carla taught me that the threat of methodological discipline and punishment is not solely embedded in the global neoliberal discourse that informs research policy documents such as those that the NRC report. The threat is also local and personal and can come from those you least expect, like the instructor of your qualitative research seminar, the same person who co-sponsored the brown bag on resisting the narrow inquiry parameters imposed by the science-based educational research movement.

—ROZANA

**** 

Shocked. Confused. Blind-sided. Unsure how to respond. These are descriptions for how I felt when I left my dissertation defense. While I thought I had worked closely with committee members on the theories and methods of analysis for my research (even sought their review of research talks for job interviews), this is not what materialized in the meeting. In studying emotions as a verb (as a performance) I sought to create a new method for analysis bricolaging three theoretical perspectives: critical sociocultural, performative aspects of narrative, and rhizomatic. My memory from the defense meeting conversation was that I could not use critical sociocultural theory without using an activity theory approach to analysis and I could not claim to use rhizomatic theory without visually mapping-out analysis. I was asked to take out these two perspectives from the description of theories and methodology sections and move them to a last chapter on future directions of research.

I was frustrated because I did not understand these requests. My reading of critical sociocultural theory (Lewis, Enciso, & Moje, 2007) did not dictate one approach for analysis. Not all studies I read that applied rhizomatic analysis created a visual mapping (Alvermann, 2000; Hagood, 2009; Kamberelis, 2004). I knew it was risky to create a new method of analysis for emotions, but, felt that being asked to remove these two aspects was not reflective of the thinking, analyzing, and writing up of research that I did for my dissertation. After much discerning (and little sleep) and seeking advice, I did what the committee requested, in a sense, to jump through the hoop and graduate. I submitted a letter to the committee expressing my concerns along with the revised dissertation.

Since then, I have published peer-reviewed articles that I believe truly reflect my dissertation process (Kuby, 2013a; in press). From a faculty position now, I understand how and why these requests might have surfaced from my committee members. Having served on dissertation committees, I know that the chemistry and dynamics of committee members materialize behind closed doors, and graduate students are not always privy to that knowledge. While I view theories as malleable and intentionally seek for ways to create new understandings with innovative method(ologie)s, I understand that not all faculty are socialized in this way, and it can be perplexing. I have the utmost respect for all of my committee members and value their support in writing a non-traditional dissertation (i.e., structure of chapters), and as a teacher/researcher using autoethnographic methods. They each encouraged me to think about moving forward with a book publication, which has now come to fruition (Kuby, 2013b). I look back at the defense meeting (several years later) as a defining moment and fissure in my career that served as a catalyst for embracing disruptive qualitative inquiry.

—CANDACE

\*\*\*\*

As the vignettes illustrate, we have each experienced moments in our work as educational researchers that prompted us to find alternative ways of being in the academy. We have each encountered tensions with educational inquiry and processes of inquiry socialization. Research and writing are not neutral; therefore it is important for us to share the previous vignettes as a way to invite readers into our lives and how we embody disruptive educational research—these were pivotal moments in our lives that prompted us to be and do disruptive inquiry. We came together because of our unifying interest in making public the tensions and possibilities of disrupting qualitative research.

We also feel that readers need to understand our story of collaboration—how we found each other, so to speak. As many of the authors in this book share, being and doing disruptive research happens in relationships with others. Specially, seeking out like-minded colleagues is necessary, as disruptive researchers (see Chapter 12 by Hughes and Vagle and Chapter 13 by Osei-Kofi). We share how our collaboration developed in order to encourage readers to seek out people, in a grassroots sort of way, as collaborators of disruptive inquiry. This organic movement is needed to sustain, support, and encourage us as researchers, and the projects and people we choose to collaborate with as educators. We see grassroots partnerships as a way to deliberately disrupt macro, meso, and self-policing micro ways of doing traditional, normalized, and/or accepted research.

Candace and Rozana were both part of an organic collaboration of faculty at the University of Missouri (QuaRC: Qualitative Research Consortium) that sought to support graduate students who were interested in approaches to qualitative research (e.g., seminar and panel discussions, schedule of advanced qualitative research classes, help with writing proposals for conferences, and so forth), and to support other faculty members in their research and advising. The larger aim was to develop a culture of valuing qualitative research within our College of Education, something that was not evident in practices, discourses, and policies. Candace and Rozana had conversations sharing the frustrations and hopes of disruptive qualitative approaches. We had a vision for creating an edited book but wanted a third editor to embark on the journey with us. One of the QuaRC seminar sessions was on performance ethnography. Ruth Nicole and doctoral students from the University of Illinois came to Missouri to share about their experiences in SOLHOT (see Chapters 2 and 10) and to perform ethnographically from their collaborative research. It was at this meeting that Candace and Rozana—somewhat synchronously—thought that Ruth Nicole would be a perfect editor! We sensed a passion and vision in the work Ruth Nicole shared and invited her to join us in this endeavor. The friendship and professional relationship began.

While we each have varied disciplinary homes—Candace is an early childhood literacy researcher; Ruth Nicole is trained as a political scientist with a joint appointment in women and gender studies and educational policy, organization, and leadership, whose scholarship is dedicated to Black girlhood and youth culture; and Rozana studies higher education organizations and leadership—we find energy and solace in a desire to question the established ways of doing research and encourage innovate ways of researching. It is our hope that the experience readers have with this book will provide inspiration and information about methodological disruption. Our focus is on several different levels of inquiry including structural (the disciplinary norms which govern research), technical (exploration of disruptive methods), and personal (the experience of engaging in disruptive research). These different levels are meant to highlight the complex possibilities of doing intellectual labor that challenge hegemonic norms of academic inquiry. Our desire is for this book to continue and mediate conversations about the politics and possibility of departing from disciplinary norms on methods as well as critiques of newer methods and disruptive approaches.

## THE TIME IS NOW FOR DISRUPTIVE QUALITATIVE INQUIRY

As described in the previous section, this book was born out of a shared interest in advancing disruptive approaches to qualitative inquiry in educational research. We have been wrestling with this project for years as doctoral students and assistant professors in disparate educational specialties, confronting and resisting within our own work the disciplining politics of inquiry embedded within the science- and evidence-based research movements (National Research Council, 2002) that have dominated education scholarship over the last 10 years (Baez & Boyles, 2009; Pasque, Carducci, Kuntz, & Gildersleeve, 2012). Social scientists in general, and educational scholars in particular, continue to be mired in an era of methodological conservatism (Denzin & Giardina, 2006; Lincoln & Cannella, 2004a, 2004b), which frames large-scale, random-sample, (quasi)-experimental designs as the gold standard in educational research. Through the demarcation of "legitimate" educational inquiry parameters (e.g., rigid publication formatting guidelines, postpositivist institutional review board protocols), agents of methodological conservatism (for example, journal editors, funding boards, doctoral committees, government agencies) seek to discredit and marginalize what the National Research Council (2002) described as "extreme epistemological perspectives" (p. 25)—postmodern, critical, queer, indigenous, etc., approaches to knowledge production that challenge the possibility (and indeed the necessity) of identifying and disseminating objective, generalizable, and reliable educational "Truths."

An impromptu conversation over bagels at the 2012 International Congress of Qualitative Inquiry included a collective observation that in spite of the increasing prominence of the disciplining discourses and practices of methodological conservatism, disruption abounds within the educational research community as scholars and their collaborators advance innovative forms of data collection, analysis, representation, engagement, and knowledge dissemination that reflect new ways of being, doing, and knowing within the educational research community. As we swept up the crumbs from our conference breakfast, we began to envision a book that placed these disruptive qualitative methodological perspectives and practices at the center rather than at the margins of educational scholarship. We were particularly interested in shining a spotlight on the cadre of emerging educational scholars (graduate students and assistant professors) engaged in disruptive work. Our aim was to build on the critical commentary of methodological conservatism previously written by prominent senior scholars (Bloch, 2004; Denzin, 2009; Dillard, 2009; Locke, Golden-Biddle, & Feldman, 2008; Lincoln & Cannella, 2004a; St. Pierre, 2004; Yanow & Schwartz-Shea, 2006). With this book we wanted to make central the unique risks, tensions, and opportunities encountered by emerging scholars seeking to disrupt the methodological status quo. We felt the time was ripe for compiling this collection of disruptive methodological narratives, as we do not foresee an end to the era of methodological conservatism in the near future—the principles and practices of neopositivism are too deeply entrenched within the organizations that govern the production and dissemination of educational research. Thus, it is imperative that we cultivate a new generation of educational scholars capable of, and committed to, disrupting disciplining methodological norms that seek to silence new approaches to understanding educational phenomena and addressing inequity.

Inextricably intertwined with the aim of cultivating a new generation of disruptive educational scholars is our belief that disruptive inquiry is a powerful vehicle for diversifying the academy—an essential and timely goal. Disruptive inquiry diversifies everything, including what is researched, how it is researched, and who does the researching. Drawing upon the "disruption as being" argument advanced earlier in this chapter, the expanded recognition and practice of disruptive research perspectives within the academy will not only contribute to the diversification of epistemological and methodological perspectives brought to bear on the examination and resolution of complex educational challenges, it will also create a more welcoming and productive space for scholars of diverse backgrounds. When diversity is embraced as more than a buzzword or strategic initiative, it requires radical attention to categories of difference as signified by race, class, sexuality, nation, and gender, but also by the kinds of questions considered researchable and opportunities afforded to practice disruptive inquiry. We believe diversifying our profession in terms of who conducts research, and how they go about the process of inquiry will not only benefit educational scholars and the communities they work with, but also the broader public, as disruptive educational scholarship makes a lasting, more sustained impact than we currently are capable of achieving.

The third justification we offer for the timeliness of our disruptive methodological advocacy is our belief that disruptive research practices are needed and necessary in order to better understand and address the complex, contemporary global historical/political/economic/social contexts, phenomena, and relationships that undermine the achievement of equitable educational access and outcomes. We ask what is left out or what is missing in educational research dominated by postpositivist and constructivist research norms? While researchers use critical, poststructural, and feminist theoretical frameworks in studies, critical methodological approaches and methods that disrupt assumptions and traditions of postpositivist perspectives remain marginalized. In today's multifaceted educational contexts, we claim that disruptive inquiries are needed to better understand the lives of students and educators as well as policies at national, state, local, and institutional levels. For example, innovative approaches to inquiry are crucial in helping educators explore affect, emotions, and the personal (see chapters by Kuby, Brown, Taaffe, Pourchier & Holbrook, and Giles & Hughes); places and contexts (Quigley & Beeman-Cadwallader, and Pourchier & Holbrook); complexities of relationships (Carillo, Quigley & Beeman-Cadwallader, Nicolazzo, Taaffe, Brown, Kuby, & Stovall); teaching and learning (Pasque, Nicolazzo, and Hughes & Vagle); and power and institutional practices (Giles & Hughes, Osei-Kofi, Hughes & Vagle, Nicolazzo, Pasque, & Childers). We argue, conceptualizing disruption as being and doing offers specific insight about "how not to reproduce what we inherit" (Ahmed, 2012, p. 182), a concern shared by many of us contributing to this book.

As we have attempted to make clear in this section, we believe the time is now for the expansion of disruptive qualitative inquiry perspectives. We are not advocating methodological disruption for the sake of disruption. Rather, we believe methodological disruption serves several critical, time-sensitive, and interconnected purposes—cultivating the next generation of diverse educational scholars capable of resolving complex educational challenges and fostering positive social change.

## DISRUPTING THE POLITICS OF INQUIRY

The verb "disrupt" means to interrupt, disorder, and rupture (merriam-webster. com). In the chapters that follow, the contributing authors share their unique stories of disruption, illustrating both the possibilities and tensions embedded in efforts to interrupt dominant educational inquiry discourses, disorder research norms, and rupture traditional methodological practices that serve to perpetuate the inequitable status quo in our schools, colleges, and communities. Although displaying tremendous diversity in their disruptive aims and strategies (e.g., a/r/tography, promiscuous deployments of theory and methodology, wreckless theatrics, the valuing of local knowledge in science education research, rethinking approaches to teaching qualitative inquiry), the 18 scholars featured in this volume are collectively engaged in a movement to contest global, national, and local attempts to narrowly define the parameters of legitimate educational research. They are disrupting the politics of inquiry.

In order to contextualize and establish connections across the resistance efforts described in chapters 1 through 13, we feel it is important to synthesize contemporary scholarship on the politics of inquiry, specifically disciplining regimes of truth (Foucault, 1980), such as the National Research Council's (2002) *Scientific Research in Education* and campus institutional review board protocols that govern educational research through the prescription of inquiry discourses, structures, norms, and practices. These regimes of truth work individually and collectively to cement rigid disciplinary boundaries, reify power differentials between researchers and their "subjects," narrowly delimit acceptable data collection and analysis procedures, and reject knowledge production and representation efforts informed by critical, postmodern, and poststructural epistemological and methodological perspectives. Accordingly, a central argument of this book is that within the contemporary era of methodological conservatism, disrupting qualitative educational research requires a knowledge of, and a willingness to engage in, the politics of inquiry—the overlapping constellation of macro- (global), meso-(organizational), and micro-level (individual) forces that establish and reproduce disciplining educational inquiry norms.

At the macro level, the global movement of methodological conservatism (Denzin, 2009; Denzin & Giardina, 2006; Lincoln & Cannella, 2004a, 2004b), anchored in the tenets of neoliberalism and neoconservatism, is embodied in the science- and evidence-based research discourses that literally seek to govern the production and dissemination of knowledge (Baez & Boyles, 2009). For example, in the United States, the adoption and enforcement of national policy efforts such as the *No Child Left Behind Act of 2001, Education Sciences Reform Act of 2002,* and the 2002 National Research Council's, *Scientific Research in Education* have resulted in the construction of a national educational research agenda that prioritizes large-scale, random-sample, experimental-design studies and the development and application of quantitative quality and accountability metrics (e.g., journal impact factors). Unapologetically tethered to postpositivist notions of inquiry and knowledge in the illusive pursuit of "what works," these national policy documents narrowly define the hallmarks of science-based educational inquiry, explicitly excluding from the national knowledge regime humanities-based research perspectives (history, philosophy, arts) and research that draws upon postmodernism, critical race theory, queer theory, etc. (Baez & Boyles, 2009). As Pasque, Carducci, Kuntz and Gildersleeve (2012) asserted, one consequence of national policy efforts to reaffirm the distinct borders of humanities and science-based inquiry is that "turning scholarly attention to issues of academic discipline and the demarcation of disciplinary methods effectively serves to silence the voices of educational scholars who locate their research across, betwixt, and/or outside disciplinary walls" (p. 55). Similarly, given that inquiry anchored in critical and postmodern paradigms seeks to honor local knowledge and the unique experiences of historically marginalized populations as a means of disrupting systemic oppression, excluding these disruptive epistemological and methodological perspectives from consideration as legitimate forms of educational inquiry contributes to the production and dissemination of knowledge that privileges the voices and interests of those in power.

Far from confined to the United States, methodological conservatism and the discourse on science-based research is a global movement, as evidenced in the adoption of the Australian Research Quality Framework (Cheek, 2007), the Research Assessment Exercise in the UK (Broadhead & Howard, 1998; Hare, 2003; Morgan, 2004), and New Zealand's Performance Based Research Fund (Curtis, 2008; Waitere, Wright, Tremaine, Brown, & Pause, 2011). Cumulatively, these national policy efforts have constructed a "regime of truth" (Foucault, 1980), which serves to legitimate some knowledge claims and silence others.

A second example of the politics of inquiry operating at the macro level is the global academic capitalism knowledge/learning regime (Slaughter & Rhoades, 2004), a disciplining discourse that explains and supports the expanded market engagement of higher education institutions. Guided by the market-driven principles and priorities of neoliberalism, universities entrenched in academic capitalism are establishing institutional policies and practices that reward faculty for individual economic achievement (e.g., technology transfer, extramural research funding, commercialization of instructional materials). Macro-level efforts to frame research as a market activity hold powerful implications for educational scholars who are increasingly incentivized to pursue research agendas and adopt research method(ologie)s that reflect market values, rather than student, school, and community needs. Cheek (2005) elaborated:

> It is the market, not necessarily peers, that determine the worth of research, and even what research will be done. Furthermore, this marketplace is tightly regulated in terms of the means of obtaining funding, what is actually funded, the way research performance is assessed, and the reporting that researchers must do both about their research and the way that they use their time in general. (p. 405)

As described by Cheek, the academic capitalism knowledge/learning regime is a powerful discourse that disciplines the practice of inquiry by demanding compliance with the market. Educational scholars interested in disrupting the macro force of academic capitalism must find ways to negotiate or overturn escalating expectations for extramural funding.

In addition to observations of the politics of inquiry operating at macro political and economic levels, we can also see (and perhaps have experienced) the meso-level manifestations of the politics of inquiry through such organizational and institutional efforts as peer review processes for grant funding and publication (Cheek, 2007; Denzin, 2009; Greenwood & Levin, 2000; Stanley, 2007; Torrance, 2008, 2011), institutional review board evaluation and censure of research proposals (Koro-Ljungberg, Germignani, Brodeur, & Kmiec, 2007; Lincoln & Tierney, 2004; Tierney & Corwin, 2007), and promotion and tenure practices heavily influenced by neoliberal metrics of quality and productivity (Osei-Kofi, 2012). Although the particular nature of the disciplining policies, practices, and procedures varies across context, within the modern era of methodological conservatism, these meso-level processes frequently serve to discredit disruptive educational inquiry and/or require scholars to conform to postpositivist research evaluation criteria in order to gain recognition and/or professional rewards. For example, Institutional Review Boards may withhold approval until applicants modify their research designs and language in compliance with the medical model of research upon which IRB protocols were developed (Koro-Ljungberg, Germignani, Brodeur, & Kmiec, 2007; Lincoln & Tierney, 2004; Tierney & Corwin, 2007).

Several authors in this volume offer additional compelling examples of confronting the politics of inquiry at the meso-level. In Chapter 12, Hilary Hughes and Mark Vagle discuss their efforts to challenge their university's rigid dissertation formatting guidelines that prevented Hilary from filing the original version of her dissertation, a teen magazine that reflected her disruptive epistemological and methodological commitments. In Chapter 7, Cassie Quigley describes the obstacles she and her co-researchers confronted in their attempt to publish findings from a project that disrupted disciplinary norms concerning what counts as science education research.

As is evident in these examples of institutional and organizational efforts to govern the nature of knowledge production and dissemination, a great deal is at stake for education scholars who decide to adopt disruptive methodological perspectives (e.g., research approval, degree attainment, publication opportunities). Bloch (2004) eloquently described the professional punishments meted out to researchers who opt to resist disciplining educational inquiry regimes operating at macro and meso levels:

> This governing of those who are abnormal in the conduct of research—or the understanding of rigor—or the interpretation or use of science—creates a disciplinary margin. Researchers who choose other ways of knowing, looking, or reflecting critically on knowledge construction, selection, and reproduction are positioned as in this margin. Although the margin is not a bad place to be, this particular circumstance creates a group of scholars who are always identified as less legitimate, and/or oppositional, and not as fully accepting of the norms of good science as others who, in fact become established as abnormal in the real science of research in education. (p. 102)

Confronted with the dangerous consequences associated with conforming to and/or resisting the macro and meso forces of methodological conservatism, disruptive educational scholars must carefully navigate the daily micro practices of inquiry (e.g., research relationships, data collection, analysis, writing) that serve to reinforce and potentially contest dominant knowledge production discourses.

Chapters 1 through 13 include numerous powerful examples of disrupting the politics of inquiry at the micro level. For example, Ruth Nicole Brown (Chapter 1) and Penny Pasque (Chapter 11) both share stories of how they disrupted the micro practices of teaching qualitative research methodology, reimagining both curriculum and pedagogy in the interest of helping their students understand and experience diverse epistemological and methodological perspectives. Z Nicolazzo (Chapter 10) and Hilary Hughes and Mark Vagle (Chapter 12) describe strategies for disrupting the micro practices of advising and mentoring emerging educational scholars in the interest of nurturing disruptive scholarship. Nana Osei-Kofi (Chapter 13) eloquently shares the multiple micro practices she adopted to remain true to her social justice commitments while pursuing tenure (for example, seeking out the company of like-minded scholars who "fed her soul as a scholar and as a human being").

When considering the micro-level politics of inquiry, we think it is particularly important for researchers to reflect on and engage in dialogue with others concerning the extent to which the threat of censure from peers, advisors and committee members, reviewers, or funding agencies contributes to self-disciplining behavior (Baez & Boyles, 2009; Foucault, 1977) that undermines the transformative potential of disruptive qualitative inquiry. More specifically, we must consider the ways in which global and organizational inquiry regimes are fulfilling the role of Foucault's (1977) panopticon, fostering a fear of observation and punishment among educational scholars that contributes to the self-disciplining decision to adopt and perpetuate postpositivist and constructivist qualitative inquiry principles and practices. As Foucault (1977) explained, "the major effect of the Panopticon [is] to induce in the inmate a state of conscious and permanent visibility that assures the automatic functioning of power" (p. 201). When applied to the politics of inquiry framework advanced in this book, the escalating prominence of macro and meso disciplining regimes of methodological truth (e.g., science-based educational research, academic capitalism, IRB protocols, promotion and tenure standards) induces in educational researchers (the inmates in Foucault's explanation) a state of perpetual visibility and observation. As Foucault explained, "he [sic] who is subject to a field of visibility, and who knows it, assumes responsibility for the constraints of power; he makes them play spontaneously upon himself" (p. 202). Again returning to the context of educational inquiry, confronted with the threat of constant observation by promotion and tenure committee members, journal editors, and/or advisors, educational researchers are likely exercising the constraints of power over themselves, electively conforming to the principles and practices of methodological conservatism.

Our hope is that the facilitation of reflective and candid dialogues on the nature and implications of the macro, meso, and micro political forces shaping educational inquiry will contribute to the exchange of ideas and the enactment of collective strategies for interrogating and overturning knowledge production regimes that dismiss the contribution of disruptive scholars who seek to realize the transformative potential of educational research. Unfortunately, the politics of inquiry are rarely given comprehensive consideration in graduate education research programs (most qualitative inquiry coursework focuses on delineating methodologies and practicing data collection and analysis techniques). The politics of inquiry are, however, frequently explored informally within schools of education as emerging and seasoned scholars seek guidance from mentors, advisors, and peers on how to advance their scholarship (i.e., secure IRB approval, funding, publication, tenure, etc.) within increasingly narrow frameworks of legitimate inquiry. The power and promise of mentorship, supportive advising relationships, and peer networks when navigating the politics of inquiry are eloquently described by the authors contributing to Section Two of this volume.

## ORGANIZATION OF BOOK

In concert with the book's aims, we intentionally solicited chapters from authors who represent diverse social and academic identities. We also sought to include people with various levels of experience in the use of disruptive method(ologie)s. Specifically, the authors contributing to this book represent diverse perspectives and advocate for a wide range of disruptive practices with respect to educational research disciplines (e.g., education policy, early childhood, gender studies, elementary, higher education, science education), gender (male, female, transgender), race and ethnicity (Latina, African American, Caucasian), and academic rank (doctoral students, tenure-track faculty, and tenured scholars). The voices and perspectives featured in this book exemplify the rich diversity that characterizes the education scholarly community.

Individually and collectively, each chapter of this book highlights the possibilities, strategies, and pitfalls of adopting disruptive qualitative methodological perspectives within the educational research community. In the interest of establishing connections across the methodological disruptions and innovations discussed, we organized the book into two sections: 1) Doing Disruptive Qualitative Inquiry: Methodologies, Politics, and Practices and 2) Living It Out: Disrupting Politics and Practices in the Academy. Below, we discuss the aims of both sections and describe the chapters within each.

### Section 1—Doing Disruptive Qualitative Inquiry: Methodologies, Politics, and Practices

The chapters in Section One illustrate various disruptive methods and/or methodologies. Using an illustrative research example, the authors discuss the politics, practices, tensions, and possibilities they experienced. Guided by the framework of disruptive inquiry articulated earlier, the authors developed essays that not only provide insight into how they conduct educational research that disrupts dominant inquiry norms and processes, but also illustrates their efforts with excerpts and examples from their work. We also asked authors to discuss the material, psychological, social, metaphysical, etc., tensions that they have had to navigate as a result of their decision to engage in this type of paradigm shift. We also invited authors to provide a list of resources (theoretical and empirical pieces, exemplary work, relevant scholarly associations, professional conferences, media recommendations, etc.) that may be of value to readers interested in learning more about their particular approach to educational inquiry. These lists appear after the reference sections in chapters.

Chapter 1, "*She Came at Me Wreckless!" Wreckless Theatrics as Disruptive Methodology*, by Ruth Nicole Brown, introduces wreckless theatrics as a methodology with a promise of reframing Black girlhood as a perpetual encounter of Black girl genius. Attuned to Black girl expressive cultures, Brown interrogates the nuances of a deviant Black girlhood idiom, "She came at me wreckless," to name the disruptive possibilities of performance inquiry. Based on a theatrical performance she co-authored and directed, Brown includes the scene, "Hoochies," in its entirety and analyzes the performance to show how it re-presents a different image of Black girlhood that counters mainstream characterizations of Black girl rebelliousness. This chapter concludes with an explicitly personal exploration of the possibilities, obstacles, and tensions Brown has encountered in engaging performance as a symbolic, imagined, and practitioner of wreckless theatrics for the purpose of encouraging scholars of performance, valuing the politically resistant possibilities of deviance, and reminding herself and others that doing differently should not mean death, but rather quite the opposite, as a way to sustain life in spite of struggle.

Chapter 2, *Reports of Illegal Activities by Research Participants: Meaning-Making Through Reflexivity, Dis-Order and Mexican American Studies*, by Rosario Carrillo, explores how an educational project led Maya Montanez, a young Mexican-American woman, to report her involvement in four types of "illegal" practices involving a guage (an unlicensed after-hours speakeasy), the smuggling of goods (la fayuca), dumpster-diving, and undocumented migrant status. For Carrillo, this required her to realign the traditional researcher reflexivity exercise to its purpose of questioning inequitable power relations. As such, young Mexican-American women involved with illegal activities might be dismissed or condemned from a white androcentric and middle-class perspective, whose power is validated through law and tradition. However, Mexican American Studies (MAS) disrupts the biases of dominant ideology and its views on officialdom, propriety, and citizenship. As Carrillo explains, MAS signals the inherited and legendary practices as disorderly maneuvers in the interruption of whiteness and exposes the political interests behind whiteness and the stratification of Mexicans and Mexican Americans in socio-economic hierarchies. Providing an interdisciplinary academic and socio-political intervention, this chapter discerns between enforced inalienable rights set against presumed rightless status of people of color.

Chapter 3, *Promiscuous Methodology: Breaching the Limits of Theory and Practice for a Social Science We Can Live With,* is authored by Sara Childers. In this chapter, Childers discusses how feminist policy analysis and policy ethnography in and through poststructural and critical race theories disrupt the methodological boundaries of traditional policy analysis. Childers conducted and analyzed data from an 18-month ethnographic case study of a high-achieving, high-poverty high school in Ohio. The goal of the project was to understand how this school negotiated educational policy "as practice" to subvert the constraining effects of NCLB and promote success. While initially the methodological approach aimed to disrupt traditional policy analysis, it also became apparent that diverse critical perspectives that were paradigmatically distinct were needed to get at the complications and disruptions of what success meant at this school. This notion of disrupting policy analysis is not new (see Marshall, 1997; Scheurich, 1994; Pillow, 2004). What is potentially different about what Childers does as a policy researcher is to confront the unavoidable tensions of placing methodologies up against each other. She offers a reflexive cross-methodological critique, which enables the researcher to wrestle with the disruptions rather than exclude them in favor of a more coherent analysis.

Chapter 4, *CRiT Walking for Disruption of Educational Master Narratives,* is co-authored by Mark Giles and Robin Hughes. This chapter reviews the predominance of white, middle-class norms, mythical colorblindness, and culturally deficit paradigms of darker complexioned "others" as central tropes in the master narratives of American education. Many progressive educators often seek alternative epistemological and methodological ways of seeing, thinking, and acting, which results in the disruption of oppressive political-corporate-factory models of knowledge construction and dissemination, and toward equitable learning experiences for students across the K-20 continuum. Critical Race Theory (CRT) and CRiT walking (Hughes & Giles, 2010) offer a theoretical framework through which to view and challenge hegemonic policies and practices, which makes racialized educational settings potential sites of empowering counter-narratives and more honest discourses on several deeply systemic problems that plague the educational enterprise.

Nicole Pourchier and Teri Holbrook co-author Chapter 5, *Always Already Inquiry: A/r/tography as a Disruptive Methodology.* Troubled by knowledge that is lost in the research process, the authors question the privileged status of traditional forms of qualitative research that claim to produce valid, generalizable, and replicable results. As researchers who also identify as practicing artists and teachers, Pourchier and Holbrook work through a/r/tography (Irwin & Springgay, 2008)—an arts-based approach to living inquiry—to theorize and articulate their discomfort with qualitative research-as-usual. In this chapter, they explain that although a/r/tography defies a concise definition or a scripted process that can be picked up and followed, there are several theoretical underpinnings that encourage a/r/tographic inquiry. From these theoretical positions—relationality, embodiment, and contingency—a/r/tography issues a call "to provoke, to generate, and to un/do meaning" (Springgay, 2008, p. 161). The authors use this discussion to describe how a/r/tography disrupts traditional research concepts such as measurability, objectivity, and validity. Such concepts trouble them, and they share how this disquiet, along with their artistic experiences, draws them to a/r/tography. Holbrook and Pourchier offer no procedures for others to do a/r/tography, but instead, share pieces of an ongoing "story" about how they are coming to know a/r/tography.

Chapter 6, *Crystallization as a Methodology: Disrupting Traditional Ways of Analyzing and (Re)presenting through Multiple Genres,* is written by Candace Kuby. Crystallization, as discussed by Richardson and St. Pierre (2005), deconstructs traditional views of validity and (post)positivist notions of triangulation. Richardson and St. Pierre argue what we see in research depends on our angle of repose each time we approach data. Crystallization as a methodology (Ellingson, 2009) embraces a multigenre approach to analysis and (re)presentation that blurs the boundaries of art and science. The focus of this chapter is crystallization as a methodology in an educational study of critical inquiry in an early childhood classroom (Kuby, 2010). To demonstrate how crystallization disrupts traditional processes of research, Kuby discusses three fluid and recursive aspects of the study: 1) autoethnography to unpack ideologies that influenced teaching/researching; 2) practitioner inquiry while teaching children; and 3) a critical performative analysis of emotion. She also discusses the tensions and possibilities of disrupting qualitative research traditions in the academy. This chapter demonstrates how multiple genres can be used for analysis and (re)presentation (e.g., multi-voice poetry, pro/epilogues of narrative vignettes, images and embodied conversations).

Cassie Quigley and Nicole Beeman-Cadwallader co-author Chapter 7, *Beyond Scientific "Facts": Choosing to Honor and Make Visible a Variety of Knowledge Systems.* The goal of this chapter is to expose the methodological *choices* Quigley and Beeman-Cadwallader made for disrupting science education research, choices which confront scholarly principles and standards for conducting meaningful research in science education settings. Through cross-cultural research projects, the authors turn the discussion inward towards the researcher to expose methodological choices they made to show evidence of their awareness of the influence/imposition/interpretation of research projects on participants, the field of science education research, and themselves. Quigley and Beeman-Cadwallader posit that if the current trajectory of methodological choices continues in the field of science education, as a science education community, educators will only permit a certain way of knowing in science classrooms. They challenge the reader to consider *what* and *whose* knowledge and ways of knowing are left out. By disrupting methodologies in science education research, Quigley and Beeman-Cadwallader are not proposing new data sources, rather providing disruptive methodological processes or frameworks to collect and analyze data.

David Stovall authors Chapter 8, *"Bringing a Little Bit of Heaven to Humanity": Raising Hell While Interrupting Traditional Methods for the Purpose of Justice*. The quote in the title of this chapter is taken from a conversation with a colleague of Stovall on the intention of interrupting the status quo in community-based research. During their interaction, Stovall mentioned how "raising hell" is often a precondition in the radical tradition of engaged, activist research. The colleague responded by stating that we are not raising hell but are instead "bringing a little bit of heaven to humanity." Through the conversation, the interpretation is that our interruption of traditional methods is the "heaven" the humanity of researchers need to engage to refute the colonial relationship often engendered in traditional research methods. Integral to the process is realizing that despite the unpopularity of authentic community engagement, it has the inverse effect as a recruitment tool for students and like-minded faculty at the university level. Using the city of Chicago as the site, the chapter highlights the author's experience in a local public school as central office attempted to close the institution. In moving towards the future, the chapter engages in the truth-telling of what is needed to understand our work in higher education institutions as intentional and uncompromisingly political. Despite perceived and real limitations, such work remains necessary if we are to make any claims towards justice.

Claudine Candy Taaffe writes Chapter 9, *Picture This: Using Photography to Tell a Black Girl's Truth*. Taaffe positions herself within Saving Our Lives, Hear Our Truths (SOLHOT), a site of praxis, where she conducted research in both of her roles of Black woman researcher and Black girl participant. In SOLHOT, Black girls share their life stories, using the camera as a tool for interrogating notions of power, voice, and representation as articulated within the images and stereotypes of Black girls. In this chapter, Taaffe discusses the disruptive data collection and analysis processes of a visual ethnography, exploring how photography is used to document the counter-narratives of Black girls, where a value is placed upon collective voice and analysis over the construct of individually produced research within the academy. This process of collective data analysis adds a unique construct to visual analysis in the tradition of Black women's self-determination work.

## Section 2—Living it Out: Disrupting Politics and Practices in the Academy

This section focuses specifically on how disruptive method(ologie)s are taught, learned, and implemented in higher education and academia. Grounded in the lived experience of graduate students and professors (both tenured and pre-tenured), the chapters in this section address the following questions: How do faculty support graduate students who desire to embark on disruptive dissertation journeys? How might emerging scholars participate in disruptive inquiry and still work towards promotion and tenure? How can faculty disrupt norms or dominant approaches in teaching qualitative research? Written as firsthand accounts, authors articulate tangible and specific practices they have adopted in the interest of advancing disruptive qualitative research perspectives via their teaching, mentoring, and advising roles and relationships. The chapters in Section Two offer narratives of resistance and resilience.

Z Nicolazzo authors Chapter 10, *Identity as Inquiry: Living and Researching from the Borderlands.* As a white, queer, able-bodied, culturally Jewish, atheist, middle-class, transgender individual, Z lives in, and researches from, the borderlands (Anzaldúa, 2007) of identity. In this chapter, Z explores the connections between the dimensions of personal identity and the scope, methodologies(s), and representation of research as a doctoral student. Utilizing an autoethnographic approach—itself a disruptive form of data collection and knowledge representation—Z examines how living in the borderlands has influenced who ze is personally *and* professionally. Specifically, Z explores concerns encountered in hir doctoral program about how ze presents both hirself and hir research in a higher education environment that is increasingly ambivalent to disruptive formations of identity and inquiry. Z describes advising and mentoring relationships that encouraged hir to explore alternative issues, methodologies, and representations of research as a way to counteract assimilationist research practices. Z closes by advocating for the proliferation of research agendas and lines of inquiry situated intimately in one's personal identities and experiences. Although such an approach is laced with tensions related to issues of power and privilege, it has the potential to expand who we are, whom we come to know, and the populations and communities who become known to us.

Penny Pasque describes her journey as an instructor of qualitative research methodologies in Chapter 11, *Advancing Disruptive Methodological Perspectives in Educational Qualitative Research Through Teaching and Learning.* Colleges and universities are positioned to play an instrumental role in researching and addressing educational and economic inequities, yet often they fail to foster needed change (Pasque, 2010). One way institutions may intentionally work toward social justice is through the education of the researchers, practitioners, and policy makers of tomorrow. Yet, if graduate students are taught only dominant notions of qualitative inquiry, then dominant research paradigms, findings, and recommendations will continue to perpetuate the status quo—with tangible implications for our schools, colleges and universities, policies and programs. In this chapter, Pasque explores the ways in which instructors may include non-dominant critical research methodologies in qualitative inquiry courses in order to expand student knowledge production (Cheek, 2008). She provides specific examples from her teaching of qualitative inquiry courses, including the use of performative autoethnography (Spry, 2011) with a new graduate student researcher to interrogate socioeconomic and rural student inequities during the transition from high school to college.

Hilary Hughes and Mark Vagle co-author Chapter 12, *Disrupting the Dissertation, Phenomenologically Speaking: A Reflexive Dialogue between Advisor-Advisee.* This chapter offers a dialogic multigenre text between advisee and advisor to explore some of the tensions and possibilities when graduate students use alternative dissertation formats. Hilary's story hinges on her phenomenological dissertation, written in the format of a teen magazine, and her stuck places when relying on writing as a method of inquiry: those moments when her writing-as-thinking (Hughes-Decatur & Bridges-Rhoades, 2013) quickly morphed into writing paralysis and she could no longer write about/through her phenomenon of interest, because she did not know *how* she would present the animating, evocative story she wanted to tell. Hughes describes specific moments, for example, when she physically had to walk away from the computer for hours (or days) at a time in order to create some distance between her and the phenomenon *on the page* so she could then read/think/talk her way back to writing about the intricate complexities of the phenomenon and how the Seventh Grade girls in her study experienced it.

As her advisor, Vagle then engages in a dialogic conversation with the text by weaving his observations and insights throughout Hughes' story. In some instances, he points to possibilities perhaps not yet visible to Hughes, and at other times actively attempts to get out of her way. All the while, Vagle aims to keep a core tenet of his post-intentional (Vagle, 2010a; 2010b) phenomenology in play—to remain committed to seeing all knowledge and intentional relations (and in turn the dissertation's "form" and the "pedagogical advice" he gave in relation to the dissertation) as tentative and fleeting. For instance, as Hughes searched for possible ways she might tell her evocative story, Vagle needed to actively and persistently try to question his knowledge of how a dissertation should look, feel, and sound. He found that his "advising" had to be more fluid and responsive to Hughes's evolving understandings of the phenomenon under investigation.

Nana Osei-Kofi shares her story in Chapter 13, *Methodological Freedom: A Journey.* Captured in the form of an open letter to methodological conservatives in the field of education, in this narrative, Osei-Kofi discusses her journey to tenure as a scholar whose approaches to research as well as topics of research are typically viewed by traditionalists as failing to meet normative standards of the field. Recounting her decision-making process and experiences with the politics of engaging in arts-based inquiry, critical discourse analysis, as well as theoretical research, Osei-Kofi offers a candid discussion of the consequences of engaging in work that disrupts narrow and often highly anti-intellectual conceptions of what counts as research in the study of education. Building from this analysis, she speaks to what made it possible for her to achieve tenure as a disruptive scholar, and the structural changes she deemed necessary to rupture stifling contemporary knowledge production regimes in the field of education, in favor of diverse and innovative approaches that disrupt the status quo.

## A CALL FOR METHODOLOGICAL ADVOCACY AND CHANGE

In the process of developing the proposal for this book, we engaged in a number of conversations about our individual and collective aims for an edited volume on disruptive qualitative inquiry. What did we hope to accomplish with this project? What change did we wish to bring about in the nature and practice of educational research? Although we used different words to describe our individual motivations and goals, a common thread soon emerged, tying our transformational aspirations together—a desire for qualitative methodological perspectives, processes, and practices that disrupt the status quo and disturb current valuations of research legitimacy so often used to marginalize and manipulate researchers of educational transformation. We end the introduction with a discussion about advocacy and change, and a call to be and do disruptive work.

Methodological legitimacy often implies respect, positive recognition, and funding. As we re-envision all that it means to be legit, respect would manifest the fair treatment and consideration of disruptive qualitative educational scholarship in peer review processes encompassing, but certainly not limited to, institutional research board review, conference planning, funding panels, publication, as well as promotion and tenure evaluations. All too often, disruptive educational researchers seeking peer review of their work are subject to review processes characterized by the application of inappropriate evaluation criteria (Stanley, 2007). Nana Osei-Kofi (Chapter 13), Cassie Quigley and Nicole Beeman-Cadwallader (Chapter 7), and Hilary Hughes and Mark Vagle (Chapter 12), speak directly to the lack of respect they have encountered in the peer review and/or dissertation process, describing the receipt of feedback that denigrated their work on the basis of a perceived failure to attain universal (postpositivist) standards of rigor and excellence. With respect, peer reviews of disruptive qualitative scholarship should use evaluation criteria congruent with the author's stated methodological aims and principles to evaluate the quality and contribution of the research.

The inclusion of disruptive methodological perspectives in the socialization experiences of emerging educational researchers would certainly disrupt what is currently regarded as legitimate ways of knowing. When valued as a form of inquiry, disruptive qualitative methodological perspectives are fully integrated into research education efforts (e.g., coursework, advising, research apprenticeships), cultivating among the next generation of educational scholars an understanding of and respect for the full range of ontological, epistemological, and methodological principles that frame educational inquiry. Qualitative methodology instructors and research advisors ought to reflect on the ways their methodological commitments serve to expand and/or limit the research perspectives considered acceptable by graduate students. We concur with Pasque, Carducci, Kuntz, and Gildersleeve (2012) who note,

> Although it is naïve to expect all educational scholars to openly embrace the principles of critical [or disruptive] methodology (indeed, we recognize the right of educational researchers to formulate methodological commitments with a wide range of epistemological beliefs, including post/positivism), it is important for faculty to acknowledge that their scholarly identities shape, and in many ways, constrain, the methodological possibilities imagined by doctoral students engaged in the process of formulating research agendas on their own. To be sure, these same doctoral students are the faculty, journal reviewers, and teachers of qualitative research in the future; the epistemological and methodological impact of introductions to qualitative inquiry has the potential to expand or be reified across generations. (pp. 81–82)

If we hope to create a cadre of peer reviewers capable of providing fair and informed assessments of disruptive research, emerging educational scholars must be given opportunities to learn about, practice, and evaluate these methodological perspectives during their socialization to the educational research profession. Rather than giving brief attention to disruptive research assumptions and practices in introductory qualitative seminars (e.g., adding a critical methodology week at the end of the seminar), we call for disruptive research perspectives to take center stage in educational research programs, along with postpositivist and constructive approaches. In most cases, this will require radically rethinking the nature and content of qualitative inquiry coursework.

Within the contemporary era of academic capitalism (Slaughter & Rhoades, 2004), the procurement of extramural research funding is a key source of institutional prestige and professional legitimacy (Cheek, 2005). Accordingly, for disruptive educational research to be considered legitimate, it must be viewed as a worthy investment by government agencies and philanthropic foundations. While institutional pressure to secure extramural funding is certainly not a new phenomena (Slaughter & Leslie, 1997), the personal and professional stakes of garnering financial support are escalating as market-driven promotion and tenure criteria take center stage in faculty performance review processes (Osei-Kofi, 2012; Pasque, Carducci, Kuntz, & Gildersleeve, 2012). Given that funding agencies play an increasingly important role in determining the institutional and disciplinary legitimacy of educational research, garnering broader recognition and acceptance of disruptive qualitative educational inquiry will likely necessitate market engagement. On the one hand, disruptive educational researchers may find it beneficial to use the logic and discourses of the market (Kezar & Lester, 2011) to frame the contributions of their research. On the other hand, they may seek to aggressively expand the epistemological and methodological criteria agencies use to evaluate research quality through participation in funding panels and other forms of methodological activism. We do not see these options as mutually exclusive but rather productive strategies that may be used in concert to advance disruptive educational inquiry in the era of academic capitalism. While some disruptive researchers may prefer to forgo extramural funding, aligning with the view that "the revolution will not be funded" (INCITE! Women of Color against Violence, 2009), a perspective we share at times, we also recognize the important role the market plays in granting methodological legitimacy and we aspire to see disruptive qualitative research well represented in the requests for proposals and funding announcements.

To reevaluate the forms of legitimacy described above (i.e., respect, socialization, funding), educational research organizations—colleges of education, scholarly associations, funding agencies, journals, think tanks, etc.,—will need to undergo substantive ideological, structural, and cultural change, embracing diverse epistemological and methodological perspectives as well as enacting new norms, policies, practices that recognize and advance disruptive approaches to educational inquiry. Not only does change need to happen in graduate schools related to *how* and *what* content is taught in qualitative inquiry courses, ways of approaching the process of dissertation research and advisor/advisee relationships, but also with policies at the institutional levels and expectations in academia as whole. It is not enough to encourage graduate students to try out disruptive practices if the institutions they will work in, and larger policies that shape publications and tenure/promotion processes, do not also embrace change. It is also important that we interrogate the cultural assumptions embedded in our departments and institutions. What attitudes, code language, gossip, perceptions, and/or expectations circulate that constrain scholars from speaking aloud and practicing disruptive methods? We ask ourselves (and you) to consider, what is the call, response, and purpose of our research? To what end do we dedicate our lives researching? Is it only a means to an end for tenure and promotion? Or does it serve a greater humanitarian good of seeking to understand and change the lives of humans, which are complex, situated, and fluid? Not only tolerating, but also accepting and embracing disruptive research is necessary for education, broadly defined.

Without systemic change, too many experimental method(ologie)s and avant-garde approaches remain idiosyncratic and thus deidentified as a "scholarly contribution." Our excitement about the disruptive work we are engaged in and our call for research to disrupt is also about our desire to go deeper, to challenge the boundaries of disruption we have unknowingly conceived, and to have our work read and evaluated by communities of scholars and students literate in disruptive methodologies. The contributing authors to this volume point to a number of specific actions educational scholars and their organizations may take to initiate change. Collectively, the contributing authors make a compelling case for the value and possibility of disruptive qualitative educational research.

## NOTES

1. While some researchers use the terms method and methodology interchangeably, we were socialized to conceptualize these inquiry concepts as related but distinct aspects of the qualitative research process. Methodology refers to the set of guiding principles, assumptions, and procedures that frame a research design (e.g., case study, performance ethnography, participatory action research), while method refers to particular data collection and analysis tools (e.g., document analysis, observation) (Pasque, Carducci, Kuntz, & Gildersleeve, 2012).

## REFERENCES

Ahmed, S. (2012). *On being included: Racism and diversity in institutional life*. Durham, NC: Duke University Press.

Alvermann, D. E. (2000). Researching libraries, literacies, and lives: A rhizoanalysis. In E. St. Pierre & W. Pillow (Eds.), *Working the ruins: Feminist poststructural theory and methods in education*. New York, NY: Routledge.

American Educational Research Association. (2006). *Standards for reporting on empirical social science research in AERA publications*. Retrieved from http://www.sagepub.com/upm-data/13127_Standards_from_AERA.pdf

Anzaldúa, G. (2007). *Borderlands/La frontera: The new mestiza* (3rd ed.). San Francisco, CA: Aunt Lute Books.

Baez, B., & Boyles, D. (2009). *Politics of inquiry: Educational research and the "culture of science."* Albany, NY: State University of New York Press.

Bloch, M. (2004). A discourse that disciplines, governs, and regulates: The National Research Council's Report on Scientific Research in Education. *Qualitative Inquiry, 10*(1), 96–110.

Broadhead, L., & Howard, S. (1998). "The art of punishing": The research assessment exercise and the ritualisation of power in higher education. *Education Policy Analysis Archives, 6*(8), 1–11.

Brown, L., & Strega, S. (Eds.). (2005). Research as resistance: Critical, indigenous, and anti-oppressive approaches. Toronto, Canada: Canadian Scholars Press

Cheek, J. (2005). The practice and politics of funded qualitative research. *The Sage handbook of qualitative research* (3rd ed.) (pp. 387–409). Thousand Oaks, CA: Sage.

Cheek, J. (2007). Qualitative inquiry, ethics, and politics of evidence: Working within these spaces rather than being worked over by them. *Qualitative Inquiry, 13*(8), 1051–1059.

Cheek, J. (2008). A fine line: Positioning qualitative inquiry in the wake of the politics of evidence. *International Review of Qualitative Research, 1*(1), 19–32.

Curtis, B. (2008). The performance-based research fund: Research assessment and funding in New Zealand. *Globalisation, Societies and Education, 6*(2), 179–194.

Denzin, N. K. (2009). The elephant in the living room: Or extending the conversation about the politics of evidence. *Qualitative Research, 9*(2), 139–160.

Denzin, N. K., & Giardina, M. D. (2006). Introduction: Qualitative inquiry and the conservative challenge. In N. K. Denzin & M. D. Giardina (Eds.), *Qualitative inquiry and the conservative challenge.* Walnut Creek, CA: Left Coast Press.

Denzin, N. K., & Lincoln, Y. S. (2005). Introduction: The discipline and practice of qualitative research. In N. K. Denzin & Y. S. Lincoln (Eds.), *The SAGE handbook of qualitative research* (3rd ed.) (pp. 1–32). Thousand Oaks, CA: Sage.

Dillard, C. (2006). When the music changes, so should the dance: Cultural and spiritual considerations in paradigm "proliferation". *International Journal of Qualitative Studies in Education, 19*(1), 59–76.

Education Sciences Reform Act, 108 Cong. 2nd Sess. 48 (2002).

Ellingson, L. L. (2009). *Engaging in crystallization in qualitative research: An introduction.* Thousand Oaks, CA: Sage.

Foucault, M. (1977). *Discipline and punish: The birth of the prison.* New York, NY: Vintage.

Foucault, M. (1980). *Power/knowledge: Selected interviews & other writings 1972–1977* (C. Gordon, Trans., Ed.). New York, NY: Pantheon.

Greenwood, D. J., & Levin, M. (2000). Reconstructing the relationships between universities and society through action research. In N. K. Denzin & Y. S. Lincoln (Eds.), *Handbook of qualitative research* (2nd ed.) (pp. 85–106). Thousand Oaks, CA: Sage.

Hagood, M. C. (2009). Mapping a rhizome of 21st century language arts: Travel plans for research and practice. *Language Arts, 87*(1), 39–48.

Hare, P. G. (2003). The United Kingdom's education research assessment exercise: Impact on institutions, departments, individuals. *Higher Management and Policy, 15*(2), 43–62.

Hughes-Decatur, H. E., & Bridges-Rhoads, S. (2013). Beyond the scope of this paper: Troubling writing across paradigms in education dissertations. *International Review of Qualitative Research, 6*(1), 103–125.

Hughes, R. L., & Giles, M. S. (2010). CRiT walking in higher education: Activating critical race theory in the academy. *Race, Ethnicity & Education, 13*(1), 41–57.

INCITE! Women of Color against Violence (2009). The revolution will not be funded: Beyond the non-profit industrial complex. Cambridge, MA: South End Press.

Irwin, R. L., & Springgay, S. (2008). A/r/tography as practice-based research. In S. Springgay, R. Irwin, C. Leggo, & P. Gouzouasis (Eds.), *Being with a/r/tography (xix–xxxiii).* Rotterdam, The Netherlands: Sense.

Kamberelis, G. (2004). The rhizome and the pack: Liminal literacy formations with political teeth. In K. Leander, & M. Sheehy (Eds.), *Spatializing literacy research and practice* (pp. 161–197). New York, NY: Peter Lang.

Kezar, A. J., & Lester, J. (2011). *Enhancing campus capacity for leadership: An examination of grassroots leaders in higher education.* Stanford, CA: Stanford University Press.

Koro-Ljungberg, M., Gemignani. M., Brodeur, C. W., Kmiec, C. (2007). The technologies of normalization and self: Thinking about IRBs and extrinsic research ethics with Foucault. *Qualitative Inquiry, 13*(8), 1075–1094.

Kuby, C. R. (2010). *Understanding an early childhood inquiry curriculum through crystallizing autoethnography, practitioner research, and a performative analysis of emotion* (Doctoral dissertation,

Indiana University). Retrieved from Pro-Quest Dissertations & Theses database (UMI No. 3413651).

Kuby, C. R. (2013a). "OK this is hard": Doing emotions in social justice dialogue. *Education, Citizenship, and Social Justice, 8*(1), 29–42.

Kuby, C. R., (2013b). *Critical literacy in early childhood classrooms: Unpacking histories, unlearning privilege.* New York, NY: Teachers College Press.

Kuby, C. R. (in press). Understanding emotions as situated, embodied, and fissured: Thinking with theory to create an analytical tool. *International Journal for Qualitative Studies in Education.* On-line first version published October 14, 2013: http://dx.doi.org/10.1080/09518398.2013.834390.

Lewis, C., Enciso, P., & Moje, E. B. (Eds.). (2007). *Reframing sociocultural research on literacy.* Mahwah, NJ: Lawrence Erlbaum.

Lincoln, Y., & Cannella, G. S. (2004a). Dangerous discourses: Methodological conservativism and governmental regimes of truth. *Qualitative Inquiry, 10*(1), 5–14.

Lincoln, Y., & Cannella, G. S. (2004b). Qualitative research, power, and the radical right. *Qualitative Inquiry, 10*(2), 175–201.

Lincoln, Y. S., & Tierney, W. G. (2004). Qualitative research and institutional review boards. *Qualitative Inquiry, 10*(2), 219 –234.

Locke, K., Golden-Biddle, K., & Feldman, M. (2008). Making doubt generative: Rethinking the role of doubt in the research process. *Organization Science. 19*(6), 907–918.

MacLeod, J. (1995). *Ain't no making it.* Boulder, CO: Westview.

Maxwell, J. A. (1996). *Qualitative research design: An interactive approach.* Thousand Oaks, CA: Sage.

Morgan, K. J. (2004). The research assessment exercise in English universities, *2001. Higher Education: The International Journal of Higher Education and Educational Planning, 48*(4), 461–482.

National Research Council (NRC). (2002). Scientific research in education. Washington, DC: National Academy Press.

No Child Left Behind Act of 2001, Pub. L. No. 107–110, 115 Stat. 1425 (2002).

Osei-Kofi, N. (2012). Junior faculty of color in the corporate university: Implications of neoliberalism and neoconservativism on research, teaching and service. *Critical Studies in Education, 53*(2), 229–244.

Pasque, P. A. (2010). *American higher education, leadership, and policy: Critical issues and the public good.* New York, NY: Palgrave Macmillan.

Pasque, P. A., Carducci, R., Kuntz, A. M., & Gildersleeve, R. (2012). *Qualitative inquiry for equity in higher education: Methodological innovations, implications, and interventions. ASHE Higher Education Report, 37*(6). San Francisco, CA: Jossey-Bass.

Richardson, L., & St. Pierre, E. A. (2005). Writing: A method of inquiry. In N. K. Denzin & Y. S. Lincoln (Eds.), *The Sage handbook of qualitative research* (3rd ed.) (pp. 959–978). Thousand Oaks, CA: Sage.

Slaughter, S., & Leslie, L. L. (1997). *Academic capitalism: Politics, policies, and the entrepreneurial university.* Baltimore, MD: Johns Hopkins University Press.

Slaughter S., & Rhoades, G. (2004). *Academic capitalism and the new economy: Markets, state and higher education.* Baltimore, MD: Johns Hopkins University Press

Springgay, S. (2008). An ethics of embodiment. In S. Springgay, R. Irwin, C. Leggo, & P. Gouzouasis (Eds.), *Being with a/r/tography* (pp. 153–166). Rotterdam, The Netherlands: Sense.

Spry, T. (2011). *Body, paper, stage: Writing and performing autoethnography.* Walnut Creek, CA: Left Coast Press.

St. Pierre, E. A. (2004). Refusing alternatives: A science of contestation. *Qualitative Inquiry, 10*(1), 130–139.

Stanley, C. A. (2007). When counter narratives meet master narratives in the journal editorial-review process. *Educational Researcher, 36*(1), 14–24.

Tierney, W. G., & Corwin, Z. B. (2007). The tension between academic freedom and institutional review boards. *Qualitative Inquiry, 13*(3), 388–398.

Torrance, H. (2008). Building confidence in qualitative research: Engaging the demands of policy. *Qualitative Inquiry, 14*(4), 507–527.

Torrance, H. (2011). Qualitative research, science, and government: Evidence, criteria, policy, and politics. In N. K. Denzin & Y. S. Lincoln. (Eds.), *The Sage handbook of qualitative research* (4th ed.) (pp. 569–580). Thousand Oaks, CA: Sage.

Vagle, M. D. (2010a). Re-framing Schon's call for a phenomenology of practice: A "post-intentional approach." *Reflective Practice, 11*(3), 393–407.

Vagle, M. D. (2010b, May). A post-intentional phenomenological research approach. Paper presented at the annual meeting of the American Educational Research Association, Denver, CO.

Waitere, H. J., Wright, J., Tremaine, M., Brown, S., & Pause, C. J. (2011). Choosing whether to resist or reinforce the new managerialism: The impact of performance-based research funding on academic identity. *Higher Education Research and Development, 30*(2), 205–217.

Whyte, W. F. (1943). *Street corner society: The social structure of an Italian slum.* Chicago, IL: University of Chicago.

Yanow, D., & Schwartz-Shea, P. (Eds). (2006). *Interpretation and method: Empirical research methods and the interpretive turn.* Armonk, NY: M. E. Sharpe.

# Doing Disruptive Qualitative Inquiry: Methodologies, Politics, AND Practices

# CHAPTER ONE

# "She Came AT Me Wreckless!"

## Wreckless Theatrics as Disruptive Methodology

RUTH NICOLE BROWN

"She came at me wreckless!" said a 14-year-old master storyteller who often entertained and informed us with the random details of her particular school day. Similar to reckless, but spelled with a "wr" and spoken in Black-girl-to-Black-girl company, "wreckless" was understood in Saving Our Lives Hear Our Truths (SOLHOT)[1] to mean a particular approach that is dramatic, semi-confrontational, and passionately argued even in the case of inevitable defeat. As a performative idiomatic expression, "She came at me wreckless" is a useful point of reference to define the disruptive possibilities of what I call "wreckless theatrics"—a particular method of inquiry that makes possible the description, documentation, and demonstration of new images and meanings of Black girls while also reframing Black girlhood as a perpetual encounter of Black girl genius.

SOLHOT as a space of Black girlhood celebration supports the telling of many truths from diverse Black girls and those who love them. Often in partnership with local youth-serving institutions in the Midwest, SOLHOT engages topics relevant to those who attend and uses various arts to express our truths, individual, and collective. I started SOLHOT in 2006 with Black girls and women ages 11–40. It is important to note, in the doing of SOLHOT, we all consider ourselves students and teachers and do not rely on a hierarchal elitist leadership structure. However, for the purpose of this discussion of wreckless theatrics, when I use the terminology, *young people*, I am referring to the youngest of us, ages 11–18. When I use the term *students*, I am referring to the undergraduate and graduate students who have taken a class with me at the university and also organize SOLHOT.

In this chapter, I provide a beginning framework for thinking about wreckless theatrics as a methodology of disruption. I offer a definition, highlight key assumptions, outline significant characteristics, map its relationship to other performance methods, and articulate the disruptive possibilities it affords. To give a sense of what wreckless theatrics may look, feel, and sound like, I discuss the process and production of creating a performance titled "Check In!!" In an extended analysis of one scene, "Hoochies," I draw on Cathy Cohen's (2004) "Deviance and Resistance" to interrogate the political possibilities of "Hoochies" as a means of creating a new image of Black girlhood that disrupts mainstream perceptions about Black girl rebelliousness. Moving beyond the particulars of one production, I offer a meditation on the costs and joys of engaging wreckless theatrics and pursuing research questions that require disruptive methods more generally. Lastly, I offer advice to practitioners of disruptive methods and conclude with a wish of wellness for those who do research with Black girls about Black girlhood and rely on disruptive methodology.

## WRECKLESS THEATRICS: DEFINING A METHOD

Wreckless theatrics emerged from my research on Black girlhood and gains its motivation from organizing with young people. Working with others, in practice, often results in the revelations of an ancient wisdom, a new idea, and/or an act of resistance against oppression—all worthy of retelling because such revelations are personally transformative and have the potential to radically move others toward justice. Wreckless theatrics creates opportunities to tell the multiple truths of those typically unheard, and, when spoken out loud, the act of telling feels a lot like freedom. To represent through performance what was learned in practice came from a sincere desire to acknowledge the everyday people with whom time and space has been shared and the ideas we created. By performing our stories for a larger public, including those with whom we labored, we remember ourselves as we want to be seen, and it feels a lot like justice. Performing Black girls' stories that emerge from a collective practice, in the company of those who remain committed to organizing well after the performance, feels a lot like love.

Wreckless theatrics is in conversation with performance methodology (Denzin, 2003; Jones, 1997; Madison, 2011; Saldana, 2011), autoethnography (Boylorn, 2103; Durham, 2007; Jones, Adams, & Ellis, 2013; McClaurin, 2001), practice as research (Kershaw & Nicholson, 2011), hip hop theatre aesthetics (Chang, 2006; Osumare, 2008), hip hop feminist art and pedagogy (Brown & Kwakye, 2012; Pough, Richardson, Durham, & Raimist, 2007) and Black feminist performance

(Anderson, 2008; Goddard, 2007; Mahone, 1994). As authoethnography is described as "a way of being in the world, one that requires living consciously, emotionally, and reflexively" (Jones et al., 2013), so too it is with wreckless theatrics. Although wreckless theatrics shares many of the same attributes as the established methods mentioned above, it bears a necessary distinction that enables it to stand on its own: Wreckless theatrics is a method with a promise of attending to the nuances and complexities of Black girlhood. Importantly, many other methods make possible the production of knowledge about Black girls, and wreckless theatrics is not just beholden to the study of Black girlhood. However, it is a method that is derived from and informed by knowledge produced in conversation with Black girls. Black girlhood knowledge need no longer be colonized by traditional paradigms and manipulated to "fit," but rather the hope is that the naming of wreckless theatrics as method also inspires the proliferation of many more creative methods that disrupt preexisting ways of knowing by starting with altogether different genealogies and privileging different revolutionary thinkers and modes of thought.

As I have practiced it, wreckless theatrics bears certain characteristics that include the following:

1) It embraces the dramatic structuring of everyday life.
2) It highlights the motions and emotions of Black girls attempting to live their lives.
3) It values the cultural resources and performances of Black girlhood.
4) It disrupts/confronts academic and theatrical conventions.
5) It makes productive use of ambiguity, uncertainty, and disorientation.
6) It allows for the creation, presentation, and representations of culturally embodied knowledge of import to particular communities of practice.
7) It shares stories of Black girlhood as told by Black girls and those who love them as a means of collective action dedicated to the survival of Black girls everywhere.

Wreckless theatrics disrupts positivism in favor of experimentation and organic creativity. Wreckless theatrics disrupts the explicit and tacitly taught assumption of objectivity and the correlate practice of researchers disappearing themselves for the sake of data collection and analysis. It is a "live" thing and subject to all that happens in the present. Wreckless theatrics disrupts the very idea of who is valued or assumed to be a producer of knowledge, as Black girls are rarely constructed as experts on their own lives. Wreckless theatrics, like performance, is ephemeral and disrupts norms of research publication and circulation. Practicing a wreckless theatric method disrupts the idea of research as an individual project, in favor of collaboration and collective knowledge production. Wreckless theatrics is a paradigm shifter generated by the belief in the power of Black girls' stories to produce new knowledge and meanings that the world needs to move to a higher frequency of liberation for all.

## "CHECK IN!" AN EXAMPLE OF WRECKLESS THEATRICS

There is a whole range of performances that could be subsumed under and contributive to the cosmology of wreckless theatrics. To provide a detailed exemplar of the kind of work that gives meaning to wreckless theatrics, I discuss the process and production of "Check In!" To illustrate the more disruptive elements of "Check In!," I include an excerpt from the script featuring a scene called "Hoochies," which is followed by an analysis of how it matters for wreckless theatrics methodology and creating new images of Black girlhood.

### The Creative Process

"Check In!" was the result of an epic failure. The collective of university students with whom I worked to celebrate Black girlhood in SOLHOT had lost our way. Individual agendas, personal problems, and fatigue had gotten the best of us. Yet, it was still assumed that we would continue to go in the schools and do SOLHOT, in spite of the reality that we were not well, working with each other. Sensing little-to-weak commitment to do the work amongst ourselves that we expressed wanting to do with Black girls, I called a time out. Everyone was shocked. I announced that we needed to get our act together, at least more together than it was. As difficult as it would be, we would have to decide if our work together was more important than our individual agendas and personal shortcomings.

The time out lasted a semester. To facilitate discussion and reflection, I taught a course specifically dedicated to working out our issues. I assigned texts that I believed held the answer to our organizing dilemmas. I created assignments that enabled us to uncover and recognize each other's gifts, talents, and idiosyncrasies. To enlarge our vision, I assigned readings that placed our practice in a broader perspective and strengthened our political analysis. We wrote about experiences, connected them to the readings, and critically interrogated what we lived. There were big arguments and major disagreements. There was also forgiveness. Sometimes spirit moved. I remember once, a student shared a story of personal hardship she was going through, and, immediately after she spoke, another student responded with a hug and a couple of dollars. I use the term spirit intentionally; as there are a number of ways that example could read, but I felt it as a movement from indifference to kindness, solidarity, and grace that I recognize as spirit. Many students later confided that it was the hardest class they've ever taken and the course they least looked forward to attending. It was an education.

As the instructor or facilitator, I felt responsible for the messiness that showed up in our organizing. I worried about whether or not students were being harmed in a way they could not recover from. As the "visionary" of SOLHOT, I was anxious about where my vision was taking us. Students told me that they expected me to have the answers, but I did not always. I learned that some wanted out but felt obliged to participate. I was surprised to learn that my high expectations, mixed with my strong belief in our ability, paralyzed a few. I had to come to terms with my observation that, in some cases, I enabled more than I taught. Even still, the honest conversations and reflections motivated me. I was not threatened by our limitations spoken out loud, even as I was implicated.

We certainly benefitted from momentarily disengaging practice to prioritize reading, studying, and relationship-building.[2] I watched people work past each other's personalities and get unstuck. Celebrity was resisted, leadership shared, and conversations took place among peers, replacing top-down instruction. The studied person, the quiet student, the artist, and the facilitator were recognized as just as important as the critical, the charismatic, the vocal, and the inspirational. Advanced practitioners of wreckless theatrics demonstrated foresight and recognized how the political economy of the university structured our actions as students, professors, and workers. We recognized time to reflect on our practice as critically important for forward movement.

In the class, our writing and performing resolved issues. I prompted each student to create two choreopoems, or poems set to music, in the tradition of internationally renowned playwright, Ntozake Shange (1997). The subject matter had to relate to some aspect of our community work with Black girls, relationships with each other, the class itself, and/or the collective and individual insights that emerged during our shared time. We performed the choreopoems for each other. Those that moved the class to a place of deeper understanding, often signified by a visible affective response, were chosen for the final class project, a public performance titled, "Check In!"

After a semester of showcasing our drama in the classroom and on the stage, we proved to ourselves that not only could we do the organizing work, but we could also create an intentional performance. The performance was free, open to the public, well attended, and a success (by our own standards). The young people we were most accountable to shared their approval and enjoyed the show. After "Check In!," we continued to collectively organize, when just a semester before we were hopelessly falling apart and taking each other out.

## CHECK IN! A THEATRE OF THE WRECKLESS PRODUCTION

"Check In!" is more than the name of the performance. "Check In!" is firstly a SOLHOT ritual that gives everyone a turn to introduce themselves and share details of their day. In many ways, the performance represented our semester-long check in with each other. The title signaled to those familiar with the ritual of check in that this was a performance for them. Disrupting the theatrical convention of the fourth wall, we dedicated time in the performance for audience members to check in and therefore become a part of the show without the burden (and obstacles) of attending numerous rehearsals. Though we created a script with a specific order and sequence, the performance structure was forgiving and flexible. In the same way we center the voices of young Black girls in our organizing work, the script's flexibility and our ability to improvise made space for the stories and performances of Black girls who attended to be a valuable part of the show.

Beyond what happened off script, another way we made productive use of disorientation, ambiguity, and uncertainty in the performance itself was also documented in the material artifacts of "Check In!" For example, there was no one single narrative that defines what the show is about, and therefore the program included multiple synopses:

"Check In!" is a revolutionary act of collective storytelling of the lived experience of the co-authors, as well as those who matter most in their lives—friends, families, loved ones and the girls within SOLHOT. It is truth telling made live, where inconvenient truths—street harassment, Black female bodily surveillance, and the dehumanization of Black bodies in particular but Black girls specifically—are given preference. And no matter how uncomfortable the truth(s) may be, they are explored for all to witness. Moreover, it is in the discomfort that a hope exists. "Check In!" is a performative springboard of hope, where the realities of what is, are turned on their face to explore the realities of what could be—as imagined by Black girls and those who love them.

"Check In!" is the exploration of Black girlhood from the highest emotion to the very lowest and oppressed. Understanding what makes us different and all the while unique. Black girls are misunderstood (Ms. Understood), but they, we, continue to go forth and endure whatever life challenges are thrown our way.

"Check In!" is a presentation of a collection of artistic works featuring poetry, spoken word, music, and dance. "Check In!" celebrates the brilliance, endurance, uniqueness, creativity, and awesomeness of Black females.

"Check In!" is a performance that features the tensions of doing the work and putting in labor to a project that is utopian, ahead of its time, and relies more on intangible resources than money. This performance features stories about Black girls grounded in their lived experience. We present to you another complicated production showcasing everything from our flaws to our fabulousness!

The order and sequencing of individual choreopoems changed depending on the location, time, and space of each performance. The following is the order we used in the first performance:

Side A: Who We Are and Who We Roll With
Track 1: Black gurls dance
Track 2: Hey Girls, Tour Guide Welcome
Track 3: I NEED A BREAK!
Track 4: Work That
Track 5: Tour Guides, Check in
Track 6: Hoochies
Track 7: Batty Dance
Track 8: With Each Beat/The Almighty and Most Powerful/ I Got Nice Eyes
Track 9: Up Grade

Side B: Looking Back To Move Forward
Track 10: Window Seat
Track 11: Tour Guides, Check in
Track 12: Sweetheart
Track 13: Tour Guides, Check in
Track 14: Keep Ya Head Up
Track 15: Tour Guides, Check in
Track 16: Yemaya and Oya
Track 17: Choreopoem For Johnnie/ Libation
The End!

## "HOOCHIES": AN EXCERPT FROM THE SCRIPT OF "CHECK IN!"

| | |
|---|---|
| *Setting:* | *A high school classroom* |
| *Characters:* | |
| *Teacher* | |
| *Girl 1* | *"G" (G stands for Girls)* |
| *Girl 2* | *"W" (W stands for With)* |
| *Girl 3* | *"J" (J stands for J.U.I.C.E. which stands for Just Unique Individuals Checking Everybody!)* |
| G: | The year is 1994 and I am ... a Hoochie. |
| | *Cue music–Paradise: "Hoochies Need Love"* |
| G: | I'm a senior in high school and |
| | BIGGER to me than |
| | Rwanda |
| | South Africa |
| | North Korea |
| | Nancy Kerrigan |
| | Whitewater |
| | Friends |
| | NAFTA |
| | OJ |
| | And Susan Smith |

W:     *(raises hand and answers)* I knew she was lying!
       *Teacher passes out papers*
G:     Waz graduating high school. I know I'm gonna graduate because I'm
       an honor roll student. Always have been. For my crew, academic excel-
       lence was a given. Senior year waz about havin' a good time.
       A good time included boys. A good time included drinking. A good
       time included sex. A good time included everything Tupac.
ALL:   *(put on a bandana like Pac).*
G:     A good time was Hip Hop. Me and My acronymed crew. We wrote
       poetry/lyrics/& rhymes to document every exploit, accomplishment,
       and secret. The content of our letters was deeper than anything we
       were assigned; the precision of the pass, more skillful than any of our
       driving, at the time.
J:     *(passes me a note with style and flair)*
G:     I got this note from my S.F.L sista for life, my B/F/F best friend
       forever:
J:     "Isn't it funny how some songs can evoke more than just a memory…"
       the cars we rolled
       the dudes we played
       the liquor we drank
       the dudes we thought we played
       the kickin it we did
       the dudes who played us
       the rules we broke
       the secrets we kept
       the excitement
       the fun
       the feeling of a never ending summer…
       Hoochies Need Love Too!"
G:     Hoochies Need Love Too!
       From the Above the Rim soundtrack … the song by Paradise.
       I have never heard of another song she has done. Where is Paradise
       now?
       Hoochies Need Love Too completely defined 1994 for me.
W:     *(throws a piece of paper at the teacher's head, and raps loudly)* And
       you know a
       hoochie ain't a hizoe! That's why you gotta gizo
       *(Teacher reprimands GWJ, and gives W a Detention Tag)*
G:     To be exact, on a list of 59 reasons why "we are da bomb"
       "We're hoochies" was number five.
       So after reading a couple books, after teaching a class on hip hop fem-
       inism, after the critiques of the culture and the music making…
       I can't front.
       I was a hoochie.

G:    I consumed—in every sense that the critics fear—hip hop.
And when I'm working with Black girls in SOLHOT.
I know I was a hoochie.

G:    I also remember number three on the list:

W:    *(raises hand and answers affirmatively as if affirmatively responding correctly to an exam question).* We got 2 of the finest dudes in school to go to Chucky Cheeses with us and the mall afterwards!

G:    I remember number fourteen:

J:    *(raises hand and answers affirmatively as if affirmatively responding correctly to an exam question)* We got through history and thought of western man!

G:    I remember number twenty-four:

J:    *(raises hand and answers affirmatively as if affirmatively responding correctly to an exam question)* We regulated underclass hoes.

G:    I remember number thirty-three: We haven't gotten pregnant.
I love the girls in SOLHOT. I love how they come to us and how they leave us. I love the way they keep the traditions alive … like dressin' alike … like creating an entirely new language adults do not understand. "I know you ain't talking bout throwing dem hands" know dat! *(directed at W).*

G:    You remember … wondering who was going to be there or not … trying on curse words like new clothes … you remember your first time. Don't chu?
And even if I don't get Lil' Wayne. Okay, I confess. I don't get Lil' Wayne. Porsha is wayyyyyyyyy more talented than Lil' Wayne, but she loves him and thinks he's the icon when I know she is…. And my stanky leg is stank, and my bootie do-don't, but I can remember… when it did.

W:    Number seven?

G:    Our U of I weekend with Smokey and Daddy.

J:    Number nine?

G:    We've gone home many times under the influence and never got in trouble.

W:    Number sixteen?

J:    Dudes paged us and got jealous when our pagers blew up.

G:    So, in SOLHOT, when a girl says to me

W:    *(to teacher)* "get it right get it tight"

J:    *(to G)* "I'm the baddest bitch"

G:    or

W:    *(to audience)* "Lil' Wayne is wayyyy better than Tupac"

G:    I remember I was a hoochie.

J:    Number fifty-nine:
Because they didn't and still don't know what to do without our love.

L.Y.L.A.S! (Love you like a sister).
*School bell rings. Class is over. All exit and take stools off stage*
*The End!*

## THE DISRUPTIVE POSSIBILITIES OF HOOCHIES

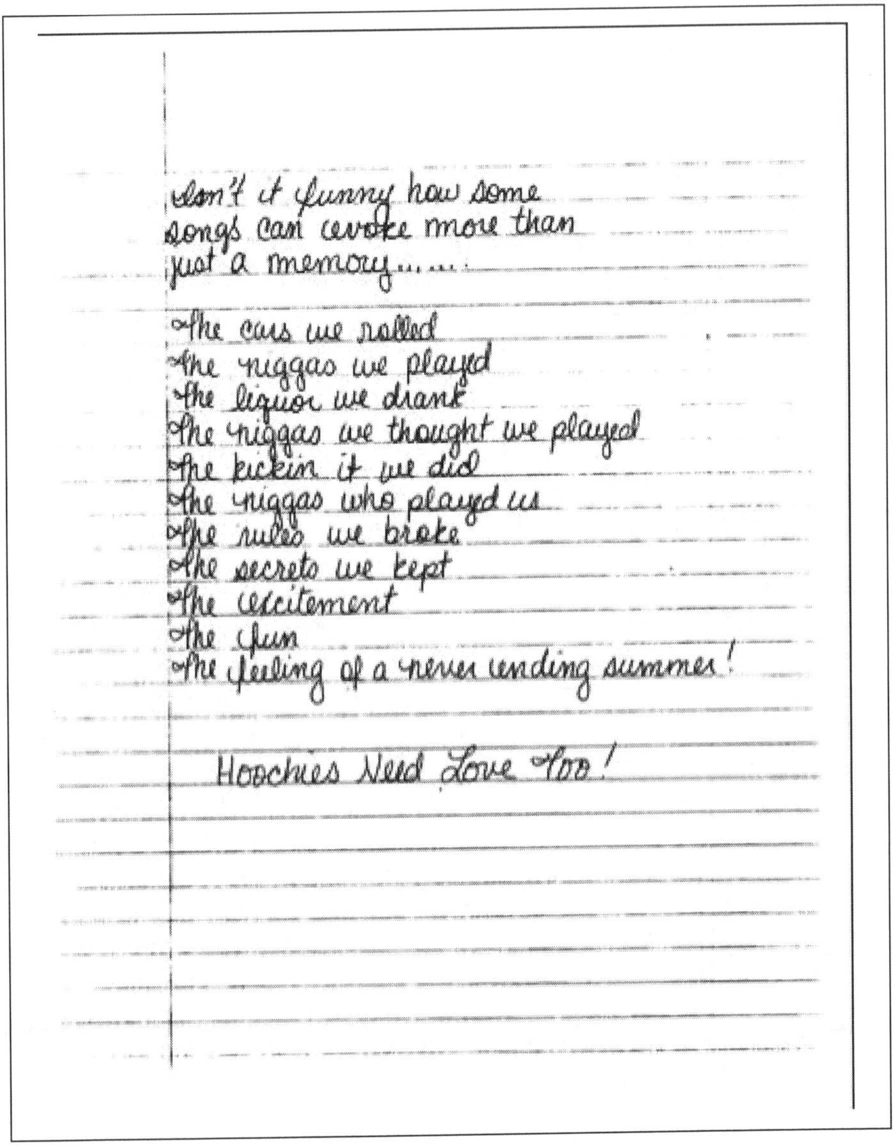

don't it funny how some
songs can evoke more than
just a memory......

-The cars we rolled
-The niggas we played
-The liquor we drank
-The niggas we thought we played
-The kickin it we did
-The niggas who played us
-The rules we broke
-The secrets we kept
-The excitement
-The fun
-The feeling of a never ending summer!

Hoochies Need Love Too!

Fig 1.1. B/F/F note[3].

Of the two choreopoems I personally wrote and contributed, the class insisted on performing "Hoochies," the one I was least excited about. "Hoochies" was based on a note I found written by my forever best friend. We traded notes all the time, at least since the start of sixth grade until we graduated high school in 1994, the year the note was written. Our social lives were well crafted. We wanted to be seen, we were concerned about setting trends, and we made trouble, usually without getting caught. The note listed 59 reasons why "we were da bomb." It documented our summertime accomplishments, our exploits, secrets, successes, and proudest moments. Number five on the list especially caught my attention. It simply read, "We're hoochies." Hoochies was how we identified ourselves, and I remember we did so at the time without reservation. "Hoochies Need Love Too," part plea, part anthem, was important to me because it served as a soundtrack to good times and teenage memories worthy of extracurricular documentation. We schemed day and night to make sure our weekends were memorable. If we were really 'bout it, our escapades would inspire a poem, to be passed on Monday through each other's hands that were too young to really know tired and still nimble from the thrill of it.

Paradise's hit "Hoochies Need Love Too," a song my friends and I repeatedly rewound, memorized, and sang out loud, was a part of the soundtrack from *Above the Rim* (Riley & Brown, 1994). In her groundbreaking book, *Check It While I Wreck It*, Gwendolyn Pough (2004) defined hoochie as "usually the down girl who hangs around the guys because she is cool, almost one of them. She gets very little respect, but her presence is tolerated" (p. 135); Pough noted that, in contrast to the chickenhead, "the hoochie is usually represented in a more positive light." Our senior year list confirmed Pough's assertion that the hoochie is a male dependent construct, as much of our list related to time spent with boys.

As a researcher of Black girlhood and youth advocate, my hoochie past haunts me. Initially, I wrote the choreopoem to disrupt a kind of respectability politics that often overdetermines perceptions about adults who work with and for young people, and young people who work with and for adults. Also, I wanted to challenge the ways Black girls are too easily pathologized as deviant. As Lisa Cacho (2007) rightly contended, deviancy and respectable domesticity is a binary maintained by intersecting, racialized, and gendered discourses that script attributes and denials of human value. The physical letter made the writing easy; memories flooded back, and I wrote them down, allowing me to flip the script. I shared the poem with the class, and I did not expect them to appreciate it as much as they did. The quickly reached consensus to include the choreopoem as a part of the final performance gave me pause. Judgment unsuspended, I worried. What about the girls? Was the content appropriate? What would parents think? What if someone wrongly interpreted the intent and our performance? Will I lose the respect of the school administrators? Might someone treat me differently? How quickly I became that "adult" who wanted to erase any sign of personal belligerence. I did not want them to know that I was not always a respectable adult. To own up to that list of fifty-nine reasons felt dangerous.

More than anything, our teenage identification as hoochies was a sign of our power and ability to express desire and pleasure and to create situations we controlled. Hoochies exhibited a hip hop feminist embodiment of the erotic as power, which Audre Lorde (1984) defined "as an assertion of the lifeforce of women; of that creative energy empowered, the knowledge and use of which we are not reclaiming in our language, our history, our dancing, our loving, our work, our lives" (p. 55). Moreover, because our friendship fundamentally rejected the idea of the lone female surrounded by men, hoochies plural represented to us a hip hop kind of Black girlhood solidarity.

Unexpectedly, the poem I wrote served useful for the class because, out of all the choreopoems, "Hoochies" made us laugh the hardest. Our organizing dilemmas, semester-long analysis, and the creative process of building a performance, required a good laugh. Our performance embodied the kind of humor necessary for greater cultural understanding of ourselves and each other (Carrillo, 2006). Our laughter upstaged the recited lines and minimally scripted stage directions. Everyone wanted to be "the hoochie" and had their own special something they brought to the role based on where they were from, where they now lived, and how old they imagined themselves to be. The fun of passing notes behind the teachers' back, flirting with classmates, fixating on appearance while simultaneously raising your hand to answer the teacher's question, which of course you answered correctly, was our display of being hoochies. We enjoyed playing unruly Black girls defiant to authority because, as we wrote the script, we knew these Black girls were gonna win, not be punished for speaking truth to power. In this scene, hoochies effectively transformed the power dynamics of a public school classroom experience. bell hooks (2000) wrote, "There can be no love without justice. Until we live in a culture that not only respects but also upholds basic civil rights for children, most children will not know love" (p. 19). Maybe a hoochie designation of defiance is no end goal, but a means to an unexpected end that recognizes a much wider and profound enjoying of life for Black girls previously categorized as unworthy. The story highlighted the agency of a self-defined hoochie—a hip-hop-loving Black girl—and disrupted the played-out narrative of Black girl with a bad attitude, duped by media, defeated by structural inequalities, and victimized by and of her own selfish irresponsibility.

Gilli Bush-Bailey with Jacky Bratton (Davis, Normington, Bush-Bailey, & Bratton, 2011) wrote,

> We need to explore and trust to the history carried in the body of the performer ... Working on our own established teaching procedure of "doing history backwards," we begin most fruitfully by starting where we are—in the present—and thinking backwards. (p. 102)

The performance enabled me to interrogate my own hoochie history. Now when I work with a girl who calls herself "a bad bitch," for example, I ask questions. I do not condemn. I wonder how her beloved affiliation produces what she feels as joy. I want to have those conversations that are made possible when Black girls do not attempt to make themselves legible for non-hoochies, ex-hoochies, or anti-hoochies. I think it's important for Black women and Black girls to be able to trade notes, secrets, and knowledge behind the back of the disciplinarian, so that the space we need for ourselves can be kept for our delight. It is quite possible that what made our performance of "Hoochies" successful is inexplicable to theatre critics, dissertation advisors, peer reviewers, or anyone else in a position to judge good from bad performance, and right and wrong methods. But I was there, and our performance worked.[4]

Cathy Cohen (2004) drew a useful distinction between defiant behavior and the radical political possibility of deviance that explains how "Hoochies" disrupted normative assumptions about Black girl behavior. Cohen argued that perceived acts of deviance by people who have been marginalized by dominant forms of state power must be rethought by social scientists as a form and exercise that is potentially politically radical. By understanding the motivations and decision-making strategies of those who subvert social norms, rules, and behavior, Cohen asks us to reconsider how their choices and agency may reveal political strategies that improve the lives of those most vulnerable in Black communities. What is needed, Cohen argued, are "intervening mechanisms" that can "transform deviant and defiant behavior into politically conscious acts that can be used as a point of entry into a mobilized political movement" (p. 38). The performance of "Hoochies" provided insight on the wreckless behavior I engaged in as a teenager. In the context of the entire performance of "Check In!," "Hoochies" was a scene that revealed how young Black girls with little access to formal structures of decision making governed their lives in such a way as to make fun and pleasure a part of their daily experience. As an intervening mechanism, the performance of "Check In!" created the space to rethink a range of experiences, behaviors, and issues as potentially political. I would argue that post-performance organizing with those who attended transformed individual interest into collective action.

## THE COSTS, MY JOY, AND SOME ADVICE ON DISRUPTION

I am uncertain if doing wreckless theatrics in and of itself bears any more costs than simply being a woman of color in the academy presumed incompetent (Gutierrez, Niemann, Gonzalez, & Harris, 2013) where death is argued as an occupational hazard of Black female intellectual life (Priest, 2008). For Black women who advance scholarship that disrupts the status quo, the details and particularities of the costs of doing so are often intimate and painful. I have certainly paid more than I should have to do this work. Some of the costs include sacrificing time with family and taking care of myself. Wreckless theatrics requires beyond teaching, researching, mentoring, advising, the additional time spent in rehearsal and performing on the road. At times, I have experienced resentment and succumbed to bitterness because it is quite possible to be taken for granted by those who claim to appreciate and love the work because it's something different, but then do not respect you for the same reason. I have known exhaustion. Access to formal theatre spaces is often denied or does not exist for non-formally trained thespians of color, so I have to make a way out of no way, and that is often stressful. The lack of courses in qualitative methods, especially those that are highly disruptive, means you become a one-woman department, expected to teach it all if you want your students to succeed, and that can be physically, emotionally, and spiritually taxing. There is also the misguided expectation that the professor knows it all, even though methodological experimentation requires one to find their way as they make it. The continuous cycle of mentally *quitting but not really* impacts the fun factor of doing disruptive methods. If one does not have a huge grant to support collaborative work (to pay people for their time and labor, to feed people, to support traveling and performances), then there are also financial costs. I have paid out of my pocket. There are those who resent you, perhaps because you make the labor of disruption look easier than it is. Then there are the myriads of ways stress physically shows up in the body to mean you no good.

If the joy did not overflow to offset the costs, I would do something different. But the goodness of wreckless theatrics has especially made every step of my journey worth it. First of all, I am doing the work that I have always wanted to do. I am working with young people, undergraduate and graduate students, and community leaders, attempting to build a more socially just world using performance and creative methods toward a political end. From the beginning of my academic journey, I have wanted to do this, and to live to see the day, when I did not think I would pass my qualifying exams, offers serious self satisfaction. I also know the joy of being in spaces dedicated to Black girls on a consistent basis. Usually because of something I heard and learned, I am challenged to think more deeply about the relationship between ideas and social change. Not to dwell on the obvious, but so much of the joy for me is connected to the truths Black girls have spoken out loud, giving me a gift and responsibility I try to honor in my research. Wreckless theatrics enables me to say, I heard you, I appreciate you, and I'm grateful to be with you and witness your genius. Wreckless theatrics means the new ideas and meanings we perform about Black girlhood circulate beyond traditional academic sites of the classroom, beyond the printed word, and go much further than a small group of elites. Though, to be clear, I am also wildly excited when research that implements disruptive methods is recognized and rewarded by all of the traditional academic measures of success. But much more of my joy is connected to people and the relationships that have formed because of the work I do. Being with other Black girls transforms the world and us. Watching students discover something about themselves and share their gifts with others is meaningful work to me. When someone you know well or someone whom you never met builds on the work and sends an email of appreciation, well, that's a beautiful call to joy. When a famous poet takes the time to read your work and write a foreword to your book, well, that kind of joy disrupts your whole universe.

Many privileges and circumstances allow me to use disruptive methods free from fear of physical violence and professional suicide. I have worked with amazingly talented students who have freely shared their talents and ideas. My colleague-friends are brilliant and push me toward disruption as "destroyers of the status quo" (Nguyen, 2012). I have witnessed and benefited from administrative leadership that has allowed me to teach courses of my design. The schools and community institutions I partner with welcome the work that I do without needing to rearrange us. When the struggle of doing this work seems permanent and fighting obligatory, I have a support system in my family that reminds me otherwise.

Considering the costs and the joys of disruptive methodology, I offer a bit of advice. First, grow your imagination as big as possible, and affirm everything that contributes to it. There are many ways my imagination was nurtured, particularly as a child whose mother insisted that I learn how to entertain myself. I continued to nurture my imagination into adulthood by engaging the arts (mostly of everyday life) and gaining a certificate in Performance Studies as a graduate student. Second, fight and resist the corporatizing of the university, for it negates, among many things, the imaginative capacity needed to disrupt. I encourage graduate students to think beyond bureaucratic categories, disciplines, and clusters that have no intellectual foundation. I would encourage students to organize, to collaborate, to partner with, and engage each other in collective knowledge production. In agreement with Dillard, Abdur-Rashid, and Tyson (2000, p. 447), it is necessary to challenge Eurocentric hegemony in the academy by offering alternative truths, reconceptualizing what it means to be human, and demystifying the value-free claims of social science. Follow your passion, resist professionalization, act and read, and read and act, all fearlessly.

## CONCLUSION

I envision myself an artist scholar interested in questions of Black girlhood as a potentially radical construct that requires disrupting what is called knowledge, how it is produced, and how it is engaged. As a visionary, I have imagined encounters of perpetual Black girl genius as an entirely appropriate and legitimate area of academic inquiry. For certain, it requires innovation including and extending beyond methodology, even beyond the method of wreckless theatrics. Especially, for those doing research on Black girlhood informed by practice, I am looking to all the ways disciplinarity will be demolished because of how we know. So I end with a wishful thought of new beginnings, where becoming wreckless does not instigate a fight, but a lesson in transforming relations of power so that Black girl genius reverberates in and outside of struggle.

## NOTES

1. For details of SOLHOT as an organizing effort dedicated to the celebration of Black girlhood see Brown, R. N. (2009). *Black girlhood celebration: Toward a hip hop feminist pedagogy.* New York, NY: Peter Lang.
2. At this time it was necessary to focus more on theory and each other than SOLHOT practice. Of course, it is all SOLHOT as there is no true "out there in the community" as university rhetoric and logics of civic engagement would have us believe. Within that logic, however, sometimes disengagement is just as, if not, more productive than engaging the community.
3. I recognize the n-word is highly controversial. As teenagers, we used the word among ourselves without consequence at the same time we knew that outside of our crew, the n-word held great consequences.
4. In this chapter, I do not address the limitations of wreckless theatrics explicitly. My hope is that the narrative provided troubles the idea of what is usually inferred by discussions of methodological limitations. In whatever ways we were "limited," we used it to our benefit. That said, I do not claim wreckless theatrics makes everything about Black girlhood known. Again, my hope is that this method complicates what it means to know, as unknowing, and that which we do not want known is equally valuable.

## REFERENCES

Anderson, L. M. (2008). *Black feminism in contemporary drama.* Champaign, IL: University of Illinois Press.

Boylorn, R. M. (2013). Blackgirl blogs, auto/ethnography and crunk feminism. *Liminalities: A Journal of Performance Studies, 9*(2), 73–82.

Brown, R. N. (2009). *Black girlhood celebration: Toward a hip-hop feminist pedagogy.* New York, NY: Peter Lang.

Brown, R. N., & Kwakye, C. J. (Eds.). (2012). *Wish to live: The hip-hop feminism pedagogy reader.* New York, NY: Peter Lang.

Cacho, L. M. (2007). "You just don't know how much he meant": Deviancy, death, and devaluation. *Latino Studies, 5*(2), 182–208.

Carrillo, R. (2006). Humor casero mujerista (womanist humor of the home): Laughing all the way to greater cultural understandings and social relations. In D. D. Bernal, C. A. Elenes,

F. E. Godinez, & S. Villenas (Eds.), *Chicana/Latina education in everyday life: Feminista perspectives on pedagogy and epistemology* (pp.162–181). New York, NY: SUNY Press.

Chang, J. (2006). *Total chaos: The art and aesthetics of hip hop.* New York, NY: Basic Civitas Books.

Cohen, C. J. (2004). Deviance as resistance: A new research agenda for the study of black politics. *Du Bois Review, 1*(1), 27–45.

Davis, J., Normington, K., Bush-Bailey, G., & Bratton, J. (2011). Researching theatre history and historiography. In B. Kershaw & H. Nicholson (Eds.), *Research methods in theatre and performance.* Edinburgh, Scotland: Edinburgh University Press.

Dillard, C., Abdur-Rashid, D., & Tyson, C. (2000). My soul is a witness: Affirming pedagogies of the spirit. *Qualitative Studies in Education, 13*(5), 447–462.

Denzin, N. K. (2003). *Performance ethnography: Critical pedagogy and the politics of culture.* Thousand Oaks, CA: Sage.

Durham, A. S. (2007). *Homegirl going home: Hip hop feminism and the representational politics of location.* Retrieved from ProQuest Dissertations and Theses. (AAT 304856923).

Goddard, L. (2007). *Staging black feminisms: Identity, politics, performance.* Basingstoke, England: Palgrave Macmillan.

Gutierrez, G. M., Niemann, Y, F., Gonzalez, C. G., & Harris, A. P. (Eds). (2013). *Presumed incompetent: The intersections of race and class for women in academia.* Logan, UT: Utah State University Press.

hooks, b. (2000). *All about love: New visions.* New York, NY: William Morrow.

Jones, J. L. (1997). sista docta: Performance as critique of the Academy. *TDR: The Drama Review: A Journal of Performance Studies, 41*(2[154]), 51–67.

Jones, S. H., Adams, T. E., Ellis, C. (Eds). (2013). *Handbook of authoethnography.* Walnut Creek, CA: Left Coast Press.

Kershaw, B., & Nicholson, H. (Eds). (2011). Research methods in theatre and performance. *Research methods for the Arts and the Humanities.* Edinburgh, Scotland: Edinburgh University Press.

Lorde, A. (1984). *Sister outsider: Essays and speeches.* Trumansburg, NY: Crossing Press.

Madison, D. S. (2011). *Critical ethnography: Method, ethics, and performance.* Thousand Oaks, CA: Sage.

Mahone, S. (1994). *Moon marked and touched by sun: Plays by African-American women.* New York, NY: Theatre Communications Group.

McClaurin, I. (2001). *Black feminist anthropology: Theory, politics, praxis, and poetics.* New Brunswick, NJ: Rutgers University Press.

Nguyen, M. T. (2012). Riot grrl, race, and revival. *Woman and Performance: A Journal of Feminist Theory. Punk Anteriors: Genealogy, Theory Performance, 22*(2–3), 173–196.

Osumare, H. (2008). *The Africanist aesthetic in global Hip-Hop: Power moves.* Hampshire, England: Palgrave Macmillan

Pough, G. D. (2004). *Check it while I wreck it: Black womanhood, hip-hop culture, and the public sphere.* Boston, MA: Northeastern University Press.

Pough, G. D., Richardson, E., Durham, A., & Raimist, R. (Eds). (2007). *Homegirls make some noise: Hip Hop feminist anthology.* Mira Loma, CA: Parker.

Priest, M. (2008). Salvation is the issue. *Meridians: Feminism, race, transnationalism, 8*(2), 116–122.

Riley, S., & Brown, S. (1994). Hoochies need love too [Recorded by Paradise]. On *Above the rim motion picture soundtrack* [CD]. Los Angeles, CA & Santa Monica, CA: Death Row Records & Interscope Records.

Saldana, J. (2011). *Ethnotheatre: Research from page to stage.* Walnut Creek, CA: Left Coast Press.

Shange, N. (1997). *For colored girls who have considered suicide, when the rainbow is enuf: A choreopoem.* New York, NY: Scribner Poetry.

## ADDITIONAL RESOURCES

These authors, artists, performers, conferences, and collectives have tremendously inspired me and have positively impacted my scholarship:

## Books

Boylorn, R. (2013). *Sweetwater: Black women and narratives of resilience.* New York, NY: Peter Lang.
Feldman, M. (1994). *Strategies for interpreting qualitative data.* Thousand Oaks, CA: Sage Publications.
Finney. N. (1998). *Rice.* Toronto, CA: Sister Vision Press.
Jocson. K. (2008). *Youth poets.* New York, NY: Peter Lang.
Morriseau. D. (2013). *Sunset baby.* London, England: Oberon Books.
Perkins, K. (Ed.). 2008. *African women playwrights.* Champaign, IL: University of Illinois Press.
Richardson, E. (2013). *PhD to Ph.D.: How education saved my life.* Anderson, SC: Parlor Press.
Saldaña, J. (Ed.) (2005). *Ethnodrama: An anthology of reality theatre.* Lanham, MD: AltaMira Press.
Shange, N. (1989). *For colored girls who have considered suicide/ When the rainbow is enuf.* New York, NY: Scribner.
Ulysse, G. (2008). *Downtown ladies: Informal commercial importers, A Haitian anthropologist and self-making in Jamaica.* Chicago, IL: University of Chicago Press.
Winn. M. (2011). *Girl time: Literacy, justice, and school-to-prison pipeline.* New York, NY: Teachers College Press.

## Artists

Invincible http://emergencemedia.org/
Lynnée Denise http://djlynneedenise.podomatic.com/
Marc Bamuthi Joseph http://livingwordproject.org/lwp_mbj.html
Sunni Patterson http://www.sunnipatterson.com/

## Academic Conferences

Ethnography in Education Research Forum (Graduate School of Education University of Pennsylvania)
International Congress of Qualitative Inquiry
Imagining America
National Women's Studies Association

## Collectives and Movements

Center for Art and Thought http://www.centerforartandthought.org/
Hemispheric Institute of Performance and Politics http://hemisphericinstitute.org/hemi/
Saving Our Lives Hear Our Truths http://solhot.weebly.com/
The BlackLight Project http://blacklightnewark.wordpress.com/

# CHAPTER TWO

# Reports OF Illegal Activities BY Research Participants

## Meaning-Making Through Reflexivity, Dis-Order, and Mexican American Studies

ROSARIO CARRILLO

Trained as a traditional educational researcher in a doctoral program, and as a faculty member in a Mexican American Studies (MAS) department, I embarked upon a research project about Maya Montanez, a Mexican American young woman, and her written, spoken, embodied, and performative practices. Upon recording and documenting her educational life history, I quickly realized that my training had not prepared me for addressing her reports of four types of illegal practices. These four types are carried out by her person and her family, as well as by other Mexicans and Mexican Americans. The practices involve a *guage* (an unlicensed after-hours speakeasy), the smuggling of goods (*la fayuca*), dumpster-diving, and undocumented status. To contemplate what to make of her reports of unlawfulness, I undertook a methodological rumination that I discuss in this chapter. I pinpoint unhelpful trends in traditional qualitative researcher reflexivity so as not to repeat them. I also identify and apply critical methodological strategies that focus more on ideology and less on training steps in how to conduct research (cf. Sheftel & Zembrzycki, 2010). Ideology involves political interests propagated through the stratification of people in socio-economic hierarchies. Social formations and cultural biases reinforce dominant ideology, through U.S. law and norms, as natural, proper, and ideal. I focus on making visible the four types of sanctionable practices as "strategies of intervention" (Ferguson, 2012, p. 17) that undermine the dominant ideology of whiteness and its power. This chapter, thus, reveals the political choices I assert as a scholar in the process of framing and writing about Maya's reports. For those of us researchers who do not want to reproduce inequitable power relations, I share how we might make sense of challenging narratives linked to seemingly illegal practices.

## TRADITIONAL REFLEXIVITY LITERATURE: OVERVIEW AND TENDENCIES

I began my journey of making meaning of Maya's reports of illegal activities by consulting scholarship on traditional qualitative researcher reflexivity (Bucholtz, 2001; Delgado Bernal, 1998; Dyrness, 2008; Ellwood, 2006; Ergun & Erdemir, 2010; Etherington, 2007; Kleinsasser, 2000; Roque Ramírez, 2007; Soto, Cervantes-Soon, Villarreal, & Campos, 2009; Soto, 2010; Takacs, 2002; Vagle, Hughes, & Durbin, 2009; Villenas, 1996; Wong, 2006). White male scholars founded and still dominate most disciplines and fields, including education. Their whitestream, androcentric, and middle-class ways of knowing prompted what is referred to as reflexive exercise, which over time has turned into a dysfunctional, cursory procedure in academia executed without in-depth interrogation of researcher subjectivity, power relations, and officialdom. Much of the reflexivity literature glosses over difficult matters and instead discloses "confessions" of researcher positionality (Macbeth, 2001) and documents what I call "perfunctory oaths to uphold social justice"—seemingly requisite statements in dissertations, research articles, or books.

With the goal of improving research practice, the reflexivity literature repeated calls for the researcher to examine his or her pre-existing meanings, identities, and representational practices.[1] The assumption is that if one is aware of one's subject positions, one will be less likely to reproduce inequitable power relations in the process of conducting the research. Reflexivity attempts to address how researchers (historically white, middle-class males) and research participants (often from vulnerable populations) can embody vastly different lived realities and privileges; and, how the research relationship, if left un-reflected upon, can exacerbate power differences and inequity between the researcher and the participants (Macbeth, 2001), as in a colonizing white male researcher who investigates a colonized "native" participant, where the former is often referred to as the "outsider" and the latter as the "insider" in the reflexivity literature (cf. Rosaldo, 1993; Villenas, 1996). The concept of the reflexive exercise is still viable because, as this chapter demonstrates, there is a sharp contrast between a dominant white and androcentric middle-class way of knowing, on the one hand, and an underclass Mexican and Mexican American way of knowing, on the other. Reflexivity is a space in which to call into question the production and re-production of inequitable power relations.

As an insider working with an insider, I culled the reflexivity literature to find out (a) what other scholars of color who undertake research with communities of color have to say about such difficult matters; (b) what moral or ethical compass I could employ in writing about her reports of illegality; (c) how I could best testify to what Maya shared with me for public circulation; and (d) what are some guiding posts for handling such matters?

In several reflexive accounts, researchers of color simply align themselves as insiders and with the interests of the insider group. The alignment or alliance is set against another group and/or disempowering idea. Historian Horacio Roque Ramírez (2007), a gay Salvadorian, aligned himself with queer Latinos living in San Francisco. Through music and the nightclub scene, this insider group created a feeling of community that was juxtaposed against white queers and straight people. Chicana scholar Sandra Soto (2010) aligned with her Chicana subject, Cherrie Moraga, as queers of color insiders, in contrast to queer theorists, many of whom are white and who often exclude or limit the documentation of the experiences of insiders. In Hong Kong, historian Day Wong (2006) aligned with the Women Who Love Women collective, whose purpose, among others, is to update conceptions of such insider women and to counteract the heterosexual/homosexual binary (Wong, 2006). In their introduction of educational youth participatory action research (YPAR) projects, Cammarota and Fine wrote that as researchers they, "are more or less 'insiders' in a given situation" (2008, p. 5) where they share with young people the multiple stakes involved with transformational change for social justice. The alignment as insiders with youth is set against "controlling interests ... meant to provide certain people with power at the expense of subordinating others" (p. 3). In a research study about immigrant Latinas in the Midwest, I aligned myself with these women as an insider and as a member of their humorous and political collective, *Unión de Viejas Argüenteras* (Union of Argumentative Broads; Carrillo, 2006, 2009). Together, we stood against xenophobia, sexism, and worker exploitation. The act of aligning oneself, as a researcher, with the insider group can be empowering in the sense that the historically disenfranchised insider group gains an ally in solidarity. This solidarity helps to offset some of the traditional power dynamics. However, simply by aligning with the insider group, we mask possible intra-group power dynamics and obfuscate the challenges of working as insiders with insiders. Worse, perhaps we perpetuate inequitable power relations by continuing the rote reflexive exercise marked by confessions, oaths, and convenient alignments.

Why have our tendencies been to confess, pledge oaths, and partner with insiders? Perhaps it is because (a) we keep getting trained in graduate school to do so, (b) the socialization in our academic professions reinforces us to continue to perform in these ways, and (c) we are trying to avoid the possible accusation that we are at times reproducing inequitable power relations with research participants, just as the traditional, colonial white male researcher outsider has been accused of on numerous occasions (cf. Rosaldo, 1993; Villenas, 1996). Some of us may be outright hesitant to take political stands against power. But, there is too much at stake. With the token confessions, pledges, and alignments, we do not get an opportunity to really reflect about how we are experiencing challenges during the data collection process. We do not get a chance to contemplate some of the meanings conveyed by the research participants—meanings that may or may not be part of the foci of the research. In this chapter, I examine how the four types of outlawed activities related to Maya's family's guage and fayuca, and her dumpster-diving and undocumented status, disorder and disrupt power and its ally in domination, whiteness. These activities are largely "off-the-radar" to most researchers and U.S. society and involve trading and ongoing migration linked to primeval customs of the ancestors of Mexicans and Mexican Americans.

## RESORTING TO MAS TO CATEGORICALLY DIS-ORDER POWER

Not served by the traditional reflexivity literature, I find guidance instead in my training in MAS. In doing so, I remind us that MAS[2] is indeed an interdisciplinary discipline (cf. Soldatenko, 2009) that serves as a localized form of activism. I acquired a Mexican American Studies perspective as an undergraduate at UCLA in the early 1990s, and I have honed this perspective in the Department of MAS at the University of Arizona as a faculty member. MAS has much to do with an embodied (Anzaldúa, 1987/2007) and relational (Thayer-Bacon, 2003) type of knowledge that is often indexed as Mexican, Mexican American, or Chican@. One acquires embodied knowledge through what the body experiences first-hand, the information the body receives through everyday living. One acquires relational knowledge through the social interactions in networks. The Mexican American or Chican@ self-identifications often signal politics through a sense of a shared set of experiences and/or recognition of certain objects, practices, symbols, sounds, or words that may or may not be associated with Mexican heritage. Majoritarian U.S. researchers often cannot "see" the lived realities of Mexicans and Mexican Americans because they have not been a part of them. Utilizing Ahmed's (2006) terminology, we can say that these researchers have not been "oriented" towards Mexican and Mexican American tendencies, objects, and ways of being.

In using a living MAS approach (González, 1998), it never occurred to me to judge Maya for any of her activities, including her sexuality.[3] MAS has taught me to question instead those who tend to criminalize marginalized people—those who, based on an "order of things," fall low or off the social totem pole.

Pérez (2007) underscored that in a "spirit of disorder ... we Chicanas/os have tenaciously dedicated ourselves, like other marginalized folk, to conversing with images that 'sane' folk don't see" (p. 39). I argue that poor Mexican Americans converse with signs that typically "sane" mainstream folk do not want to see or hear because "the dominant ruling order has disciplined them to have this reaction" (Carrillo, 2009, p. 130). To "proper," "law-abiding," "orderly," citizens, illegal practices are impolite, best left quiet.

Dis-order involves the disruption of officialdom (Bakhtin, 1968) such as U.S. and Mexican laws that seek to discipline bodies. It involves change and freedom from those imposed constrictions on the body, mind, and soul. "Popular behavior," that is unruly, Soldatenko (2009) reminded us, "overthrows normal social operations" (p. 19). Most of us Mexicans and Mexican Americans are poor and, regardless of country of residency, fall (a) outside of propriety (b) beyond the bounds of scientific "normal" standards, and (c) below decorum. We rejoice in our bawdy, naughty *rasquache*-ness (Carrillo, 2006, 2009). Officialdom is put on notice because it is highly capricious and biased. It benefits the ruling dominant class (Bourdieu, 1984). Our "lack of papers" and acts of *guageria, fayuqueria*, dumpster-*diveneria* constitute under-the-table practices that shake-up power. Disordering the power discrepancy between the disenfranchised and whiteness is what this chapter targets.

## Legally Empowering Whiteness

Terms such as "Mexican American" and "Chican@" are forms of signaling recognition, antagonism, and/or resistance to the role of whiteness in the brutal history of colonization. "Mexican American" also reifies whiteness, as it calls attention to the difference from white America as the U.S. center or mainstream/whitestream. The "Mexican" part provides distance for white America to be "the 'starting point'" (Ahmed, 2006, p. 121) for what counts as legitimate and quintessential in the currently marked territory. "Whiteness [has become through physical and ideological force and laws] what is 'here'" (p. 121) in this land. Whiteness encroached itself as "a line from which the [first] world unfolds, which also makes [or establishes] what is 'there' on 'the other side'" (p. 121). The other side has become the space of many Mexican and Mexican American families, a space marked by the U.S.-Mexico border and the new order.

I prefer the term whiteness, because it signals a space, not any one individual. Instead of an "individualized notion of power ... power as a complex and multisited social formation" (Ferguson, 2012, p. 7), which enables one to track it as an ongoing set of relations in institutions such as those concerning the law. Whiteness signals greed and corruption. Whiteness encompasses "physical objects ... styles, capacities, aspirations, techniques, even worlds" (Ahmed, 2006, p. 126), as well as tendencies, dispositions, and habits that sustain the inequitable distribution of power. For example, white, as a racial construct superior over indigenous or African races, was supercharged to facilitate the colonization or "taking-over" of much of the Americas and the exploitation of labor of non-whites (Quijano, 2007). Whiteness does attempt to embody itself in the consciousness of most people worldwide, whether of white skin or not, as it drowns out other cultures or ways of being, doing, communicating, believing, and valuing. Whiteness has facilitated domination globally and it continues to be served and protected by the U.S. legal system.

The U.S. constitution and legal system were created to protect the "white rights" of males as inalienable—rights that cannot be taken away. Cacho (2012) made clear that "whiteness has a legal history very different from racial difference" (p. 23). She added, "impoverished people of color, who occupy rightless statuses—such as gang members or illegal aliens—are more likely to be categorically criminalized without regard to their actions or intentions" (p. 23). Whiteness automatically has value and is righteous, while those of us who do not occupy white space are presumed abnormal deviants. Those of us not looking white or practicing whiteness by reproducing a patriarchal middle-class standard are asked to show "papers" for our conduct and being. In Arizona, Proposition 1070 has given police officers freedom to keep us brown-looking people in "check" more than usual. Working in tandem, Proposition 2281 forbids MAS in the K-12 school system, effectively disallowing the learning of Mexican American cultural practices, language, and ways of knowing and being.

In these ongoing times[4] of Mexican bashing and bullying of Mexican Americans, by dedicating my life's work to our community, as a scholar, I help shift and re-orient the powers-that-be. Instead of retreating from *Mexicanidad* or Mexicanness, with MAS, I affirm and re-claim it. By adjoining a MAS approach to traditional qualitative educational research, I set out to effect an academic and socio-political intervention. I blur disciplinary boundaries between MAS and education. Surely MAS has its share of contradictions of nationalism and patriarchy in its own history. Any concept has its tensions and limitations. For instance, the term "ethnic" in ethnic studies relegates all non-whites as Other. The term "women" in women's studies universalizes the non-male gender. In education, we have areas of research entitled "minority" and "urban" as if "minority" and "urban" are catch-all labels for investigations on socio-culturally deficient students of color. By infusing a MAS sensibility into traditional reflexive practice and educational research, I aim to disrupt and dis-order standard terminology and academic discourse that pay lip service to the categories of race, class, and gender/sexuality, and that treat grueling socioeconomic realities as a check-off box of whether students receive a free lunch or not. Inherited customs of Mexican Americans, such as informal economies, need to be understood from the lived and embodied knowledge that MAS provides.

## MAYA MONTANEZ

The data reported herein are a part of a larger project. I am the principal investigator of that project, which is an educational life and oral history about Maya Montanez—her lessons from in and out of school that have played a pivotal role in how she narrates who she is, where she comes from, and where she chooses to root her place of belonging. The data were collected in 2010 and 2011. The primary data are 26 hours of audio recordings, 700 printed, double-spaced pages. The secondary data are field notes and copies of Maya's written work. By 2011, the data were transcribed by Datalyst, a professional company, then re-transcribed by graduate student Lizette Opio Curiel. The final nuanced translations herein are my own.

When I met her, Maya was going to college and looking forward to embarking upon a doctoral program in MAS. She was born in northern Mexico and raised in Arizona. In order to protect her and her family and friends, as well as unforeseen parties, I create a composite portrait of Maya's life, and I use pseudonyms for her and those in her life.

Her great-grandparents are descendants of Europeans and people indigenous to Mexico. Living in various northern states of Mexico, they subsisted on corn grown next to their living quarters: makeshift shacks with dirt floors. One of her grandfathers was a *bracero*[5] working on and off in U.S. cotton and watermelon agribusinesses across several states. Maya's grandmothers migrated hundreds of miles by foot to find personal safety in towns near the U.S.-Mexico international border. As a young woman, Raquel, the paternal grandmother, "ran away from home, walked through a lot of fields and just fed off mangos and wild fruit." As a hired hand, she was beaten. She owned one dress that she washed in the river and put back on wet. She became a maid to a man who raped her, then had and lost her first child at 13 years of age.

Running away from physical, psychological, and sexual abuse, the grandmothers found ways to survive. The maternal grandmother, Alejandra, started a second-hand store. Raquel started a *guage*, what I translate for U.S. readers as an unlicensed after-hours speakeasy.

Maya's parents, Laura and Saul Sr., were born in a border town and met in a Catholic church. They had four children, Saul Jr., Alejandra, Elizabeth, and Maya, the youngest. Laura worked as a maid and a seamstress in a *maquiladora* (sweatshop) on the U.S. side of the border. She also took care of elders, and handmade corn tortillas sold in an informal economy of her local neighborhood in Arizona. After battling breast cancer, undergoing a mastectomy and chemotherapy, she now dedicates herself to her home, garden, and extended family, particularly her grandchildren. Saul Sr. works as a *fayuquero* (smuggler) of vehicles and as an owner of two Mexican *guajes*. His income provides for all the households in their extended network, particularly his son Saul Jr. and his wives and children, on both sides of the border.

## FOUR TYPES OF ALLEGED ILLEGALITIES

The concept of disorder enables me to re-view practices that are deemed "out of place" (Ahmed, 2006, p. 9) and subject to laws that are made and re-made to serve domination (Cacho, 2012). It helps me underscore how "criminals" have been historically "racialized in how [they] occupy space, just as space is, as it were, already occupied as an effect of racialization" (Ahmed, p. 24) and colonization. In fact, the practices reported by Maya disorder and disrupt the existing hegemonic power structures and status quo socio-economic hierarchies.

### The Guage and the Nana Pass

Maya was born into the family business of the guage. Regarding Raquel's practices, she recalls, "she had a restaurant and a cabaret when my papa was little." After closing both businesses people would still come to Raquel for alcohol, so she started a guage. Maya adds, "I really liked that about my grandmother. That, even when she was older, she had a lot of influence in this town."

When Maya and her family use the word guage, they are referring to an after-hours bar on the Mexican side of the U.S. international border. There are many such guages in multiple northern states of Mexico. Guage, also spelled *güaje*, is a large woody gourd from the calabash tree. Some in the Sonora desert believe this word comes from the Yaqui *bweja* or *bweja'e*. Bweja or bweja'e is *jícara* in Spanish for gourd (Fernández, Valenzuela, Camacho, Celaya, & Flores, 2004, p. 251). Linguists in Mexico have found that throughout the country people use the words jícara and guage, and the variations, including *güaje, guacal, huacal, tecomate, vaso, jarrita, vasija, jarro, bote, pocillo, chui, morro,* and *teconte* (Blanch, 2000). The gourd has been used for washing or drinking.

Maya has pleaded with her father and family to be next in line to manage the guage. She believes her brother Saul Jr. is a "useless bastard" who impregnates and abandons females and cannot be entrusted to run the guage. The guage is important to her as a beacon of light for migrants who pass through this border town. She states,

> Recently I found out that *a mi nana le decían "la tía"* [the migrants called my grand-mammy "the auntie"] and it was a migrant stop. People who were migrants back then would stop at my grandmother's. My grandmother would give them food and shelter ... I do remember hearing her being called *tía* or they would knock on the door because I would sleep there sometimes. *Decía, ¿ quién es?* [She'd ask, "who is it?"] Because selling alcohol [after-hours]

was still illegal. Well, it is still. *Decía, tía soy yo* [The voice on the other side of the door would say, "it is me auntie."] And I would say, "who is it?" And she would tell me, "no, go to sleep." And I would stay in bed and my grandma would get up.

I asked Maya to describe the physicality of the guage. She described Raquel's home that housed a convenience store. The kitchen led to an entrance where she would sell the beer. For quick access throughout the night, the kitchen area became Raquel's bedroom. In Raquel's life, the lines were blurred between the store, the kitchen and sleeping quarters, the under-the-counter selling of beer, and off-the-books social services to migrants. No red-tape here. She also utilized unconventional means to defend her guage activity.

> Raquel had one encounter with authorities in Mexico who police the guage. Young federal-level male *alcoholes* arrived at the guage to close it, take the beer, and arrest Raquel. Maya said, My nana told a soldier, "do you have a nana?" The man answered "Yes, I have a nana. But, you know she died." And my nana said, "Good thing she is dead because if she could see what you are doing to another poor nana, she would die a second time." The soldier says, "no doña [mam] Raquel, don't tell me that." So she used her older age to get around from it, because they're not going to take an old lady to jail. So she kind of used that emotional side of a grandmother and caregiver. "I have no one to take care of me and how will I eat." And they let her go. She kept the beer. Tecate.

Raquel pulls out her own kind of credentials to defend her livelihood. These are old age, her vulnerability as an elderly person, surviving challenges in life, and the reminder that there is a strong emotional connection to nanas that surpasses the proper ways of doing business. I call this type of credential the nana pass that disrupts officialdom. It discontinues, if only momentarily, the applicability of law—Mexican commerce law, in this case—by putting into question its credibility and power. The nana pass dis-orders the levels of jurisdiction, whereby nanas can over-rule the *federales*.

Research on guages is scarce. A study on the illegal alcohol market in Ontario, Canada, may shed some light. This study covers alcohol smuggling into Canada from the U.S., a northern border issue, similar to southern borders issues. Mcdonald, Wells, and Giesbrecht (1999) conducted a survey investigating any alcohol purchase from an unlicensed source. "Respondents who reported purchasing alcohol from an unlicensed source…reported drinking more drinks per drinking occasion…drinking significantly more often…[and] were more likely to be young…and male" (p. 27). Selling alcohol "under the table" (p. 27) carries "public health consequences" (p. 28) whereby "youth and heavier drinkers" (p. 28) can be "significantly more likely to obtain alcohol from unrecorded sources (p. 28). These vulnerable groups have "easier access to alcohol from unrecorded sources than mainstream distribution sources" (p. 28). In other words, this study about Canada suggests that guages have their limitations and contradictions. They run the risk of making vulnerable populations such as male migrants and under-aged people even more vulnerable by feeding any alcohol issues. The obscurity in the literature of gauges and their impact on communities alerted me to not dismiss Maya's report. Asking open-ended and follow-up questions facilitated me to learn about the guage as a multi-faceted practice, which provides subsistence for some and possible dangers for others.

## La Fayuca and the Petatero Pass

The smuggling activity of fayuqueros such as Maya's father also side-step laws, in this case importing and exporting laws of the United States and Mexico. Maya tells about her father's business activity,

> From my dad's side, they've always been part of an informal economy. They are called *fayuqueros*. I guess it comes from the verb buy-u-quiar, which just pretty much means that you buy something in the U.S. and then you bring it into Mexico and then you sell it, whether it be cards whether it be secondhand clothes. But, my dad didn't do that. He buys and resells cars. So, my dad kinda survived on that. We pretty much lived day by day....Part of my dad being a fayuquero is that he is always buying cars for $300, $500 and fixing them up, then selling them. And so he has various cars. In his hometown they look up at him. Not so much now, because of all the narco-trafficking.

O'Day and Lopez (2001) concurred with Maya that most of the smuggling is clothing. They wrote that in the latter part of the nineteenth century fayuqueros smuggled "30% of the textiles sold in Mexico" (p. 233). They added that "this tradition has continued down to the present day, with the dry goods of choice now being ready-to-wear used clothing" (p. 233).

In the film *El Embustero* (1983/2004), the term fayuquero does not appear. However, the root of this word "fayuca" does appear, when a man tries to sell the protagonist a "*lote de televisiones*" (a bundle of televisions) and the protagonist asks, "*¿autentica fayuca?*" to determine if the merchandise is authentic, not stolen. The protagonist, Chente, played by Vicente Fernández, is referred to as an embustero, which means a tale-teller who embellishes the truth to buy and sell his wares at good prices. Embustero is used interchangeably with *chapucero*, which is a shoddy botcher or someone who bungles and causes an unsatisfactory outcome. The 2004-released version of the film by Northridge-based Laguna Films in California summarizes the film on the DVD jacket as,

> *Un milagro que solo el amor puede lograr; la total regeneracion de un coyote en los billares, fayuquero y transa entre los transas del barrio quien todos conocen como "El embustero."* Only love can accomplish such a miracle; to turn somebody from a very likeable barrio crook into a respectable teacher of a small town [translation by Laguna Films].

The theme song includes the following lyrics, which I have translated:

> I am of that barrio where one loves poverty, where the people are pure heart, where dreams are our riches sometimes, where we cry but love with passion. Here the rich squabble over coins and I take their *pesos* in one quick swoop to redistribute among my people that I love the most. I am an embustero, but I have my reasons. They call me the embustero, the chapucero, the bacilador/trickster. But I feel proud that in being bad, I am the best. I come from a humble crib. I am also a good player of no bad intentions. But because of my bad circumstances, I am of the worst kind, of an ugly business.

Like Chente, Saul Sr. found himself in the predicament of being a fayuquero. He comes from a family of fayuqueros. That is the knowledge and means of livelihood that they passed down onto him. He in turn is exposing and socializing his daughter Maya into the business.

She shared that she has driven in some of her father's cars and has been harassed at immigration enforcement stops at U.S. border crossings. Intimidated into not using the cars her father can provide, her brown body and the extension of her self—her folk transportation as a "lifeline" (Ahmed, 2006, p. 18) in the desert—are interrogated and halted. Bodies that do not lengthen or transpire whiteness in spaces, such as those marked by U.S. enforcement, as Ahmed indicated, are "stopped" (p.139) for existing outside the lines, the rules, the regulations. But, where else is she to get a means of transportation in this "*herida abierta*" (Anzaldúa, 1987/2007, p. 25), this stretch of festering open wounds?

In the film, Chente is also referred to as *petatero*, which means indigenous seller who places his or her wares on a *petate*, or Indian woven rug. After colonization by Spaniards, Americans, and their descendants, the natives of Mexico took refuge in the hills and mountains and would come down to the lowlands to sell their wares. To this day, they still engage in the petatero practice. As descendants of white and indigenous peoples, Mexican *mestizos* like Chente and Maya's family continue the practice as an inherited, cultural, economic, and social means of survival. I call the justification of this informal economy the petatero pass as it has been bequeathed by our ancestors.

Like Chente, Saul Sr. and Maya realize that the fayuca practice has the possible unsavory ring of "lemon" cars. After decades of sales in the same Mexican towns, reputation builds itself. Furthermore, Saul Sr. would not knowingly put his daughter in broken "fixer-uppers." Providing a service, in some ways, Saul Sr. engages in civic action as best as he can.

## Dumpster-Diving and the Survivor Pass

Maya mentioned how during college it was hard to find work and that she eventually worked as a maid for a conservative and racist elderly white couple. She also began to occasionally dumpster-dive. She stated that it was challenging to "make ends meet." Dumpster-diving is considered to be the practice of raiding or quickly and illicitly searching dumpster(s) to find discarded items that are still useful, can be recycled, and have some value. When Maya uses the idiom "making-ends meet," she is referring to money and being able to stretch her money in order to pay her expenses for things such as rent, food, utility bills, and gasoline for her car. Dumpster-diving can also be referred to as skip diving or binning. Dumpster-divers may be in violation of several municipal laws including trespassing, invasion of privacy, environmental damage, or even in some cases theft.

Volz (2010) wrote online, "it's against the law in Phoenix, no matter how innocent your intent." Voltz also quoted Terry Gellenbeck, a solid waste administrative analyst for the city, "Once a resident puts something in a [trash] barrel, it becomes the property of the city of Phoenix....It's not legal to be scavenging." I concur with Volz when he stated that dumpster-diving is not something typically enforced. Dumpster-diving may be considered a misdemeanor civil offense depending on the year and municipality. Volz warned,

> Dumpster diving is a serious concern for law enforcement officials struggling to curb identity theft in the state. According to a Phoenix Business Journal article published in February, Arizona is no longer the nation's capital for identity theft—but it is second, slipping just behind Florida.

I include Volz's warning because I want to make clear that I am not under any circumstance recommending anyone try some of the practices Maya reports. There are legal, social, environmental, automotive, and health consequences. There are many germs and sharp edges in trash bins. One can get cut, infected, and become seriously ill. At the same time, it is important for us as researchers to document these types of practices and engender conversations in and outside of academia. Maya cannot be judged. From a lived perspective of severe poverty, like mine growing up in Mexico, eating dirt and Gansitos (Mexican chocolate-covered Twinkies) for dinner, one gains an appreciation of how the survivor pass comes to surface.

## Undocumented Status and the Migrant Pass

The last type of practice has to do with Maya's unapprehended, nondetained status as an undocumented immigrant from the age of seven to 18. While her mother gave birth to her three siblings on the Arizona side of the border, Maya was born early and had to be delivered at home. Maya reflects,

> I was born one week early and all tangled up...choking myself to death with my mama's umbilical cord. *Se le quebró el agua a mi mamá* [My mama's water broke]. Had me *en la casa* [at home]. *Y vino el doctor y vino una partera* [And the doctor came and a midwife came].

Labeled and treated as undocumented in the U.S. during her childhood, she found extracurricular activities targeting Mexican Americans and choreographed performance shows dealing with female empowerment. Upon graduating high school, she got her "green card" and embarked upon an undergraduate education. Through the passage of the Immigration Reform and Control Act (IRCA) of 1986, she got her temporary and permanent resident cards from the U.S. Department of Justice, Immigration and Naturalization Service. Maya and her family, like my family and I, are part of the 1,123,162 who have been legalized under IRCA (Fuchs, 1992).

The discourse of U.S. immigration and legislation displaces Others like Maya and her network as not naturally belonging, while keeping securely in place power. According to a U.S. Citizenship and Immigration Services (USCIS) website (2013a), IRCA "required employers to examine documentation from each newly hired employee to *prove his or her identity and eligibility* [my emphasis] to work in the United States." The ideology behind this immigration discourse is the "natural" white entitlement to resources and jobs. Cacho (2012) wrote, "When immigration opponents appeal to concerns [that for example] immigrants take jobs that belong to American citizens, they are appealing to the expectation of white entitlement" (p. 26).

Since 1986, there has been the Immigration Act of 1990 that has, among other things, "increased the limits on legal immigration…[and] authorized temporary protected status to aliens of designated countries" (USCIS, 2013b). To focus on "aliens of designated countries" and the topic of immigration is to skirt the question of U.S. occupation of the territory in question. The Illegal Immigration Reform and Immigrant Responsibility Act of 1996, along with the Antiterrorism and Effective Death Penalty Act, "are [additional] legal means for 'detecting' the abnormal, the immoral, and the criminal" (Cacho, 2012, p. 95)—essentially those Others who stand outside whiteness, like Maya. As Cacho reminded us, immigration laws "target [and discipline] races and world regions, developing nations, and non-Western cultures…[in effect] people and places [considered to be] still 'developing' [properly]" (p. 95).

Cornelius (1982) argued that there is feasibility and desirability of direct research on immigrants. While the trend in U.S. policy research on illegal immigrants "is frequently limited to the compilation of evidence in favor of closing or keeping open the immigration door" (Portes, 1982, p. 294), some call for research on immigrants' adaptation to American society. They raise questions about needing to know more about how immigrants and their children understand obligations of citizenship and what kinds of educational and other experiences generate interest in and commitment to civic activity, even before naturalization. But desire to understand obligations to citizenship presumes that the ideal should be white U.S. citizenship, not *citizenship of the world*. And, most humans, yes even those with ties to Mexico, already understand how to relate to fellow human beings, with kindness, generosity, and fellowship—principles the U.S. immigration discourse and regime often lack.

## ANALYSIS AND REMAINING THOUGHTS

Guageros, fayuqueros, dumpster-diveneros, and migrants reflect an industrious hardworking spirit and a sense of obligation in that their practices provide for themselves and their families. Their legendary practices have taken place before and after the concepts of colonization, U.S. citizenship, and naturalization. Whiteness, in the U.S. and Mexico, has disciplined and sanctioned these indigenous practices according to its own scheme. As "strategies of intervention" (Ferguson, 2012, p. 17) against the oppression of power, these practices have survived invasion and changing political climates. They may seem kitsch-like, but in their trickster rasquache-ness, they usurp officialdom, a major scaffold of power that threatens with imprisonment and even the loss of life.

Why did Maya tell me about these practices? I suspect that even though I am an educational researcher, a recorder for academia—a predominantly white institution—she felt safe with me. She knew I would provide an intervention to mitigate power inequity. She knows that my MAS affiliation and Mexicanidad serves as a safety net. I identified with her experiences and established empathy before the research project began. She realizes that her story exists in the service of greater understanding and treatment of Mexicans and Mexican Americans. MAS serves as a place of affiliation, receptivity, and "homecoming" that acknowledges her existence, her background, and her inherited practices. It aids in the restoration of her humanity and the equitable distribution of power—power to claim our stories, our practices, and being.

In being able to tell her story "freely," Maya relishes her grandmother Raquel's power with the statement "even when she was older, she had a lot of influence in this town." As a feminist and anti-hetero-normative being, Maya knows that Raquel's power as a woman and as an older person is significant. She recounts this moment of power in her family with pride and longing. She wants to be next in line to "run" the family guages. She wants to defy gender norms like Raquel did. She also knows that with a college education, she can have greater stability and socio-economic mobility to fulfill her own sense of family and migrant community obligations.

Part of Maya's genius is that she recognizes her nana Raquel's virtuous ways of knowing and doing—basically, don't screw around with nanas and what they do to get by in life. Their old age gives them a pass. Maya is becoming a nana, as well. At the age of 30, she has already been raped, and physically and psychologically beaten. So, she gets a nana pass, too, on the early-bird special.

I avail myself of humor in creating the nana, petatero, survivor, and migrant passes to expunge from my physical being excessive feelings of devastation, despair, sadness, and rage. I take cue from the disorderly carnivalesque ambiance (Limón, 1994) in our Mexicanidad, where we use our wits to fashion a meal, "to make ends meet." There is no disgrace in our survival tactics. As majoritarian Americans continue to live in *"Disneylandia"* (Urrea, 1996, p. 21), we continue to be "the object of the hostile [legal and moral] white gaze" (Ahmed, 2006, p. 110).

If you feel uncomfortable or not at ease as you read this chapter, it is working its magic. It portrays dis-ease. As scholartistry (Neilsen, 2006), it presents a conundrum as to what to make of discomfiting and unsettling reports. There are no conclusive statements or easy answers. Regarding research in migration and ethnic research, Portes (1982) envisioned, "Scholarly research may be defined as an activity oriented to gaining reliable knowledge of the origins of a particular phenomenon, its internal dynamics, and its likely future course" (p. 294). It is clear that as researchers, we ought to bring attention to how illegal practices have legal and public health consequences and how they might exacerbate problems for vulnerable groups of people. Werch and Anzalone (1995), for instance, found that inter-drug use progression among youth can involve a generally invariant, non-linear sequence. Youth may jump around in the following stages: nonuse, legal drug use, marijuana use, and illegal drug use. I wonder what dangers and vulnerabilities lay ahead for Maya and her network. Will being immersed in illegal practices predispose her to committing future ones? Will the nature of illegality and danger escalate? How can the practices be fashion for greater good?

In education and other fields and disciplines, how else but through critical in-depth reflections can we become sensitized to these matters? Reflexivity helps us put "in-check" fantasies about, among other things, a "level-playing field" in U.S. schooling. It also affords us opportunities to ruminate our role in the hyper-capitalistic and materialistic economy. When will we truly appreciate the value of the labor and civic actions that sustain the luxuries in the U.S. such as cheap *braceros, maquiladora* workers, caretakers, and housemaids? How do we stop to think about the exploited hands and bodies that put together our televisions, radios, and designer jeans and t-shirts on both sides of the U.S.-Mexico border? If we can terminate redundant tendencies to confess, pledge oaths, and only align with insiders, we can engage with signs, symbols, and embodiments that are typically considered improper and unwanted. Doing so enables us to reappropriate the meaning or status behind them and thus disrupt the order of how things are traditionally done.

## NOTES

1. Macbeth (2001) makes useful distinctions between positional reflexivity and textual reflexivity (although both serve similar purposes) as well as constitutive reflexivity. Still other scholars add types of reflexivity such as multiperspective, multivoicing, positioning, and destabilizing that can enhance the multiple ways in which researchers can reflect upon their practice as researchers (Alvesson, Hardy, & Harley, 2008).

2. As of January 2013, there are three doctoral programs in MAS at UC Santa Barbara, the University of Arizona, and UCLA. The flagship journals and academic associations include

*Aztlan: A Journal of Chicano Studies, Chicana/Latina Studies: The Journal of Mujeres Activas en Letras Y Cambio Social* (MALCS), the National Association of Chicana and Chicano Studies, and the MALCS organization. Some foundational and landmark texts in MAS include Rudolfo Acuña's (1972) *Occupied America* and Gloria Anzaldúa's (1987) *Borderlands/La Frontera.*

3. The U.S. has historically criminalized homosexuality. Currently in over half the states same-sex marriage is banned.

4. See also Proposition 187 in California and anti-bilingual (Spanish/English) propositions and legislation in almost every state.

5. The bracero program ended on December 31, 1964 (Fuchs, 1992, p. 1069).

# REFERENCES

Acuña, R. (1972). Occupied America: The Chicano's Struggle Toward Liberation. New York, New York: Harber and Row.

Ahmed, S. (2006). *Queer phenomenology: Orientations, objects and others.* Durham, NC: Duke Press.

Alvesson, M., Hardy, C., & Harley, B. (2008). Reflecting on reflexivity: Reflexive textual practices in organization and management theory. *Journal of Management Studies, 45*(3), 408–501.

Anzaldúa, G. (1987/2007). *Borderlands, La Frontera: The New Mestiza* (3rd ed.). San Francisco, CA: Aunt Lute Books.

Bakhtin, M. (1968). *Rabelais and his world.* Cambridge, MA: MIT Press.

Blanch, J. L. (2000). *Atlas lingüístico de México: Tomo III, Léxico, Volumen VI.* México, DF: El Colegio de Mexico, UNAM.

Bourdieu. P. (1984). *Distinctions: A Social critique of the judgment of taste* (R. Nice, Trans.). Cambridge, MA: Harvard University Press.

Bucholtz, M. (2001). Reflexivity and critique in discourse analysis. *Critique of Anthropology, 21*(2), 165–183.

Cacho, L. (2012). *Social death: Racialized rightlessness and the criminalization of the unprotected.* New York, NY: New York University Press.

Cammarota, J., & Fine, M. (2008). *Revolutionizing education: Youth participatory action research in motion.* New York, NY: Routledge.

Carrillo, R. (2006). *Humor casero mujerista* (womanist humor of the home): Laughing all the way to greater cultural understandings and social relations. In D. Delgado Bernal, A. C. Elenes, F. E. Godinez, & S. Villenas (Eds.), *Chicana/Latina education in everyday life: Feminista perspectives on pedagogy and epistemology.* New York, NY: SUNY Press.

Carrillo, R. (2009). Expressing Latina sexuality with *Vieja Argüentera* embodiments and rasquache language. *National Women Studies Association Journal, 21*(3), 121–142.

Cornelius, W. A. (1982). Interviewing undocumented immigrants: Methodological reflections based on fieldwork in Mexico and the U.S., *International Migration Review, 16*(2), 378–411.

Delgado Bernal, D. (1998). Using a Chicana feminist epistemology in educational research. *Harvard Educational Review 68*(4), 555–582.

Dyrness, A. (2008). Research for change versus research as change: Lessons from a mujerista participatory research team. *Anthropology & Education Quarterly, 39*(1), 23–44.

Ellwood, C. (2006). On coming out and coming undone: Sexualities and reflexivities in language education research. *Journal of Language, Identity & Education, 5*(1), 67–84.

Ergun, A., & Erdemir, A. (2010). Negotiating insider and outsider identities in the field: "Insider" in a foreign land; "outsider" in one's own land. *Field Methods, 22*(1), 16–38.

Etherington, K. (2007). Ethical research in reflexive relationships. *Qualitative Inquiry, 13*(5), 599–616.

Ferguson, R. A. (2012). *The re-order of things: The university and its pedagogies of minority difference.* Minneapolis, MN: The University of Minnesota Press.

Fernández, Z. E., Valenzuela, C. B., Camacho, A. E. G., Celaya, M. E. C., & Flores, A. C. (2004). *Diccionario yaqui-español y textos: Obra de preservación lingüística.* Hermosillo, Sonora: Universidad de Sonora.

Fuchs, L. H. (1992). Introduction: Migration research and immigration policy. *International Migration Review, 26*(4), 1069–1076.

González, D. (1998). Speaking secrets: Living Chicana theory. In C. Trujillo (Ed.), *Living Chicana theory* (pp. 46–77). Berkeley, CA: Third Woman Press.

Kleinsasser, A. M. (2000). Researchers, reflexivity, and good data: Writing to unlearn. *Theory into Practice, 39*(3), 155–162.

Limón, J. (1994). *Dancing with the Devil: Society and cultural poetics in Mexican-American South Texas.* Madison, WI: University of Wisconsin Press.

Macbeth, D. (2001). On "reflexivity" in qualitative research: Two readings, and a third. *Qualitative Inquiry, 7*(1), 35–68.

Mcdonald, S., Wells, S., & Giesbrecht, N. (1999). Unrecorded alcohol consumption in Ontario, Canada. *Drug and Alcohol Review, 18*(1), 21–29.

Neilsen, L. (2006). Playing for real: Texts and the performance of identity. In D. E. Alvermann, K. A. Hinchman, D. W. Moore, S. F. Phelps, D. R. Waff (Eds.), *Reconceptualizing the literacies in adolescents' lives* (pp. 5–27). Mahwah, NJ: Lawrence Erlbaum.

O'day, P., & Lopez, A. (2001). Organizing the underground NAFTA: Fayuqueros and el arreglo. *Journal of Contemporary Criminal Justice, 17*(3), 232–242.

Pérez, L. (2007). *Chicana art: The politics of spiritual and aesthetic altarities.* Durham, NC: Duke University Press.

Portes, A. (1982). Introduction. *International Migration Review, 16*(2), 292–297.

Quijano, A. (2007). Coloniality and modernity/rationality. *Cultural Studies, 21*(2–3), 168–178.

Roque Ramirez, H. N. (2007). "*Mira, yo soy boricua y estoy aquí*": Rafa Negrón´s Pan Dulce and the queer sonic latinaje of San Francisco. *Centro Journal, 19*(1), 274–313.

Rosaldo, R. (1993). *Culture and truth: The remaking of social analysis.* Boston, MA: Beacon Press.

Sheftel, A., & Zembrzycki, S. (2010). Only human: A reflection on the ethical and methodological challenges of working with "difficult" stories. *Oral History Review, 37*(2), 191–214.

Soldatenko, M. (2009). *Chicano studies: The genesis of a discipline.* Tucson, AZ: The University of Arizona Press.

Soto, L. D., Cervantes-Soon, C. G., Villarreal, E., & Campos, E. E. (2009). The Xicana sacred space: A communal circle of *compromiso* for educational researchers. *Harvard Educational Review, 79*(4), 755–775.

Soto, S. K. (2010). *Reading Chican@ like a queer: The de-mastery of desire.* Austin, TX: University of Texas Press.

Takacs, D. (2002). Positionality, epistemology, and social justice in the classroom. *Social Justice, 29*(4), 168–181.

Thayer-Bacon, B. (2003). *Relational "(E)pistemologies."* New York, NY: Peter Lang.

Urrea, L. A. (1996). *By the lake of the sleeping children: The secret life of the Mexican border.* New York, NY: Anchor Books.

U.S. Citizenship and Immigration Services. (2013a). History and milestones. Retrieved from http://www.uscis.gov/portal/site/uscis/menuitem.eb1d4c2a3e5b9ac89243c6a7543f6d1a/?vgnextoid=84979589cdb76210VgnVCM100000b92ca60aRCRD&vgnextchannel=84979589cdb76210VgnVCM100000b92ca60aRCRD

U.S. Citizenship and Immigration Services. (2013b). Immigration Act of 1990. Retrieved from http://www.uscis.gov/portal/site/uscis/menuitem.5af9bb95919f35e66f614176543f6d1a/?vgnextoid=84ff95c4f635f010VgnVCM1000000ecd190aRCRD&vgnextchannel=b328194d3e88d010VgnVCM10000048f3d6a1RCRD

Vagle, M. D., Hughes, H. E., & Durbin, D. J. (2009). Remaining skeptical: Bridling for and with one another. *Field Methods, 21*(4), 347–367.

Villenas, S. (1996). The colonizer/colonized Chicana ethnographer: Identity, marginalization, and co-optation in the field. *Harvard Educational Review, 66*(4), 711–731.

Volz, D. (2010). *Dumpster diving: For love, salvation or identity theft?* Retrieved from http://cronkitezine.asu.edu/spring2010/dumpsterdiving/laws.html

Werch, C. E., & Anzalone, D. (1995). Stage theory and research on tobacco, alcohol, and other drug use. *Journal of Drug Education, 25*(2), 81–98.

Wong, D. (2006). Beyond identity politics: The making of an oral history of Hong Kong women who love women. *Journal of Lesbian Studies, 10*(3), 29–48.

# ADDITIONAL RESOURCES

Here is a list of recommended sources for developing a disorderly approach to research:

The American Educational Studies Association (AESA) critically explores the foundations of education, such as educational equality and equity, from a variety of views including philosophy, history, politics, sociology, anthropology, and economics as well as comparative/international and cultural studies.

The Center of Study and Investigation for Global Dialogues hosts an annual decolonial school, *Decolonizing Knowledge And Power: Postcolonial Studies, Decolonial Horizons*, with scholars such as Emma Perez, Ramón Grosfoguel, Salman Sayyid, Chela Sandoval.

The Summer Institute at the Columbia Center for Oral History organized by director Mary Marshall Clark advocates politically oppressed and silenced voices and narratives.

The Council on Anthropology and Education (CAE), a section of the Anthropology Association of America, advances anti-oppressive education by examining socially equitable and racially just means.

The *Mujeres Activas en Letras y Cambio Social* (MALCS; Women Active in Letters and Social Change) hosts an annual Summer Institute. At the institute, the Writing Workshop spearheaded by Karen Mary Davalos utilizes a supportive feminist editorial process in order to help participants produce disruptive, un-traditional texts.

# CHAPTER THREE

# Promiscuous Methodology

## Breaching the Limits of Theory and Practice for a Social Science We Can Live With

SARA M. CHILDERS

This chapter takes on the concept of disruption to think about not only how researchers and educators can disrupt the taken-for-granted, but also how qualitative inquiry is always already a disruptive event that shakes up our thinking and ways of being in the world. Using data from a two-year ethnographic case study of a high-achieving, high-poverty high school, I discuss how I engaged what I came to think of as a promiscuous methodology. I argue that what brought about this promiscuous methodology was an affective engagement with my field site and participants, and that the materiality of research acted upon me in unexpected ways that pushed me to do my work differently, in ways that felt somehow against prescription, and therefore promiscuous. To explore this idea, I focus on how the entanglement of participants/field site/researcher/theories took on an energy of its own that affected my reading the data through two seemingly incommensurable theoretical perspectives, Critical Race Theory and Foucauldian theories of power/knowledge and discourse, to conduct a sociocultural policy analysis, or a study of policy as lived practice. The effects of analyzing the data simultaneously through these frameworks not only disrupted traditional approaches to policy analysis, but also disrupted what I perceived to be uncrossable methodological and theoretical boundaries.

Moving forward, I define promiscuity as a methodological concept and response to the incommensurability argument in qualitative research. Next, I look at how I promiscuously engaged Critical Race Theory (CRT) and Foucauldian theories of power/knowledge and discourse to analyze the data. I conclude the chapter with a discussion of how engaging promiscuity with intention and commitment to inhabiting the complex material engagements that are part and parcel of research holds promise for approaching our work. But first, some background about the study.

I conducted a two-year ethnographic case study[1] of Ohio Public High School (OPHS),[2] a nationally ranked high-achieving high-poverty urban[3] high school in Ohio. It received a great deal of attention from local and national media, not only for its high test scores and graduation rates, but also for its unique humanities curriculum. I wanted to better understand how curriculum and instruction practices embedded in the humanities program contributed to the school's ability to subvert what had been referred to in the literature as the constraining effects of the No Child Left Behind Act of 2001[4] to support the academic achievement of its students. It would be quite easy to assume that NCLB policy was responsible for the academic gains made by students in this school. Rather than looking at the presumed effectiveness of the policy as is done by traditional policy analysis, I was interested in how policy was lived at OPHS.

Upon beginning fieldwork, parents, faculty and administrators, and students discussed with me at length how they negotiated federal education policies. They attributed the huge gains in student achievement in part to the long-standing humanities curriculum and college-preparation environment that they felt enabled students to become academically engaged with the exploration and construction of knowledge. They perceived that this approach to learning therefore naturally led to improved test scores and graduation rates, though this was not the implicit goal. They struggled to protect the curriculum from federal policies that inspired local attempts to change or thwart it, because the faculty and parents felt strongly that a climate of high expectations coupled with an engaging curriculum was the key to the overwhelming success of its students. Because of their proven track record and high profile, they were able to protect their program from teaching to the test and other damaging consequences of NCLB. A traditional policy analysis would miss the complex ways in which actors negotiated the constraints of NCLB and were successful in spite of, rather than because of, the policy.

Taking an ethnographic approach to study "policy as practice" (Sutton & Levinson, 2001), I witnessed firsthand how students, teachers, parents, and administrators negotiated the constraints of federal policy, and I was able to document the subversive curriculum and instruction practices that had "real" tangible outcomes of academic success. OPHS had a 30-year history as an alternative school deeply invested in academic achievement and was nationally recognized as a "breakthrough school," "urban school of promise," and school of "excellence."[5] The demographics of the student body at OPHS closely mimicked the demographics of other schools; the high rate of academic achievement did not, which is why OPHS continued to be cited as an urban success story. For example, at the time of this study 65.5% of the students at OPHS were identified as African American,[6] 2.5% as Hispanic, and 3% as Asian or Pacific Islander backgrounds. OPHS graduated 99.3 % of its students in 2009 as compared to the district graduation rate of 72.7%. The school reported that 96% of its 2007 graduates attended two- or four-year colleges and earned nearly $7 million in scholarships to 50 schools, including top Ivy-League institutions.

Yet, held within the success of this school was how race[7] was implicated in the everyday practices of teaching and learning; how the very things they did to promote student success were "raced" or racialized in that their practices were differentially enacted along lines of race (and class). For example, access to educational resources and opportunities such as Advanced Placement (AP) and International Baccalaureate (IB) courses was unequally distributed. And, while to some participants that I interviewed those instances of diminished opportunity seemed coincidental and inconsequential to the larger gains all students made, when they coagulated in the data they could not be ignored.

Urban education gives meaning to race and is framed particularly as a democratic project concerned with equity and access for at-risk students. Though the generic term "urban" education is most often used, race functions in meaningful ways within and through the bodies of its students. Urban students, their raced bodies, and what they signify become useful in showcasing urban education and its transformative effects on "the disadvantaged." It capitalizes on and solidifies historic and racialized narratives[8] of the always failing, culturally deprived student of color (and, more specifically, the Black student), and excludes the history of Black education, the failures of integration, and the implications of these failures for urban education today.

Success at OPHS was deeply entwined with inequity. In fact, the identity of this "successful urban school" hinged on deficit notions of students of color as the always failing and at risk as opposed to educational agents who were responsible for their own achievement. What sustained the school's reputation was the surprise that such graduation and college-going rates were possible at an urban (i.e., Black and poor) school. Simultaneously, these deficit discourses subtly permeated academic advising and student scheduling in a ghostly counterbalance to the climate of high achievement that filled the school.

But this is not an either/or story. Students at this school were graduating and attending college at rates higher than any other school in the district, and this had huge implications for their futures. Students spoke at great length about how they were positively impacted by OPHS. They discussed how they felt challenged and supported in ways they would not have been at traditional schools in the district and how the climate of high expectations instilled in them a sense of pride. They were proud to be students at OPHS. And almost in the same breath, they would explain how they had been excluded or persuaded not to pursue an academic opportunity.

In spite of its best intentions to harness educational excellence as a way to promote and sustain educational equity, OPHS also perpetuated inequality even while its students were for all intents and purposes closing the achievement gap. While policy ethnography became my way into the complicated story of OPHS, I realized that a multi-methodological and theoretical approach was needed to work the disruptions of (un)success rather than forfeit them for the sake of cohesive findings (Childers, 2011). The data disrupted any one way of seeing, and the methodology needed to follow the disruptive energy rather than try to tame it.

What plagued me the most was that I found Critical Race and poststructural theories, when worked together, to be the most helpful in bringing forth the complexities of the data in spite of their assumed or prescribed incommensurability. No one theory, concept, or framework alone seemed able to get at the nuances of how race worked materially and discursively in this school, but when I thought about the data with these theories simultaneously the disruptions remained in play, because these theories were critical and disruptive of each other. Rather than fear what it meant to transgress methodological prescription, I began to think about promiscuity as a way to think through the dangers of incommensurability as well as how methodological and theoretical promiscuity might push the limits of knowing, make interventions, and help us to thrive on the tensions, complications, and losses of research in ways that might be productive.

## INCOMMENSURABILITY AND PROMISCUITY

In spite of 25 years of debate, the question of commensurability among paradigms continues to be an "unresolvable conundrum" in qualitative research (Lincoln, 2010, p. 6). Due to the ontological and epistemological disagreements as to the nature of knowledge, reality, and the role that power and language play in understanding the world, the biggest fissures have been between positivism on the one hand and interpretive-critical-poststructural paradigmatic standpoints on the other. If we look to the mixed methods debate, one response to the question of commensurability has been a pragmatic approach where the research question dictates methodology and in some cases asserts a blatant disregard for paradigmatic differences. Lincoln (2010) read this disregard as a failure to understand the importance of how knowing is deeply linked to our beliefs about knowledge and the world. There is a danger to mixing paradigms.

Though most discussions about incommensurability have been around the qualitative/quantitative divide, the question of incommensurability can also be extended to think about the implications of bringing diverse and seemingly incommensurable theoretical perspectives to bear on one project. I would like to discuss some general distinctions that I wrestled with in considering integrating poststructural theories of power and knowledge with CRT, and I emphasize that I am thinking big picture for a moment as opposed to the nuances of different poststructural theories or the branches of CRT.⁹ First, poststructuralism is generally a practice of constant deconstruction, never allowing any one way of seeing to take hold. According to MacLure (2013), "Theorists reject the idea of universal truth and objective knowledge, asserting that truths are always partial, and knowledge always situated .... Language ... is inextricably implicated in the fabrication of realities" (p. 167). Wary of fixed identities that posit the humanist subject, theorists instigate a subject fractured, situated, and decentered by language, culture, discourse, power, the unconscious, the body, history, and I could go on. The subject is produced and can be undone and reconfigured over and over.

On the other hand, in CRT, racism is recognized as endemic to United States society. It positions race as a salient and real category. Racial identity is established through social, historical, and cultural experiences of discrimination and forced oppression that are deeply tied to "being" a member of a racial group in the United States. The political project of identifying and responding to racial oppression requires an acknowledgement that race exists and people occupy particular standpoints based on their race, and these standpoints produce knowledge grounded in experience. Social justice is key to CRT research, whereas poststructuralism is suspicious of truth claims and how power shapes and potentially turns social justice into another tool of domination.

Might poststructuralism undermine the political efficacy of CRT by deconstructing its basic assumptions? And how is poststructural theory rendered impotent by its inability to directly respond to structural inequality and hold categories in suspension long enough to make legal claims? As argued by Lincoln (2010), mixing paradigms often disregards the ontological and epistemological differences and the dilemmas they produce. And there is the risk of being seen as misusing the work of scholars I greatly admire.

But as I have laid out these generalizations, I think it is their very generality that is the problem. It is far safer to assume that these theories "just don't mix" as opposed to intentionally inhabiting the counterintuitive moments and strange assemblages that seem to emerge from the very problems and complexities they bring to the fore.¹⁰ Incommensurability has a habit of shutting down borders, though what resides within it are strange becomings always already promiscuously feeding and circulating in our ways of seeing and being in the world. How might we see unresolvability as an invitation to meet incommensurability with intention to wrestle with and inhabit the intricacies and problems of their disruptions? How does promiscuity open up possibility?

The concept of promiscuous methodology that I use here was developed as part of a larger project on promiscuous feminisms for a special issue in the International Journal of Qualitative Studies in Education (Childers, Daza, & Rhee, 2013).

"Promiscuity" is a racy, sexy, pejorative and even punitive term denoting "bad" girls. Around 1600, "promiscuous" meant "mixed and indiscriminate," but it was not recorded as referring to sexual relations until 1900 (*Online Etymology Dictionary*; see also Voithofer, 2013). The use of the phrase "promiscuous" to describe methodology is not merely an attention-seeking oxymoron, though I do capitalize on the ability for promiscuity to send the reader on an imaginative foray. The sexism embedded in language is what makes the notion of promiscuous "feminists gone wild" tantalizing, but when I think of "promiscuous women," for example, I think of defying norms, boundaries, and the constraints of a heterosexist and masculinist gender system. I think about how defiance opens up a space for different living and that such promiscuity is not indiscriminate, but often quite deliberate.

I am interested in the intentionality of promiscuous deployments of theory and methodology, not so much in intentionally being promiscuous, but again being willing to give over to the productive possibilities that might come from the always already comingling of the world with our methodologies and theories that leave an indelible mark on our thinking and being. If we take seriously the idea that the world, and our research, is made up of a "network of 'distributed agency' that involves human and nonhuman 'actants'" that communicate collectively through promiscuous assemblages that really do not care about paradigms or theories, then our research is not a "purely human achievement" (Kirby, 2011, Chapter Four, Section Four, Paragraph Four), but more a result of "how we pack the world into words" (Latour, 1999, p. 24). I cannot deny the ways in which the materiality of the world acts on me, rubs up against me, and pushes me to think differently (Childers, 2013). I cannot *not* think in and through that with which I am already familiar, or deny how I am affectively propelled in my research to seek out new knowledge to respond to problems. I cannot turn off this active knowledge like a faucet, or pretend that it has no influence, but I can write as if that "madness" (Mishra Tarc, 2013) of knowledge does not exist, which is what I think incommensurability inspires. Promiscuity is a way to narrate the affective "madness, vulnerability, failure, collisions, betrayals, resistances, excess, loss, alienation, and isolation" (Childers, Rhee, & Daza, 2013) that feminist researchers may experience when they go against prescription, trends in the field, and long-standing debates about how research should be. So here, I try to write toward this madness, using promiscuity as a vehicle for thinking.

## FROM METHODOLOGICAL CERTAINTY TO PROMISCUITY

Disrupting traditional approaches to policy analysis is not new (see Marshall, 1997; Pillow, 2004; Scheurich, 1994, 1997). Researchers seeking to recognize the local complexities of policy have previously adopted methodological frameworks such as policy ethnography, feminist critical analysis, and poststructural policy analysis that could have provided methodological roadmaps for the OPHS analysis. It would have been much easier to follow a path already laid out before me, particularly to utilize a Foucauldian analysis as part of a policy as practice framework. It had been done before, done well, and was clearly recognized as a commensurable approach to policy analysis.

Foucauldian theories of power/knowledge and discourse were in many ways already embedded in a sociocultural approach to policy analysis. Sutton and Levinson (2001) called for a socio-cultural approach to educational policy that elucidates the "richness and complexity of the policy process" to see the way policy works as a cultural practice (p. 4), with particular attention paid to *"policy as a practice of power"* (p. 1). Michel Foucault's (1977) theories of the relationship between power and knowledge assert that,

> (p)ower produces knowledge; that Power and knowledge directly imply one another that there is no power relation without the correlative constitution of a field of knowledge, nor any knowledge that does not presuppose and constitute at the same time power relations. (p. 27)

This notion of power/knowledge as "everywhere ... unbalanced, heterogeneous, unstable, and tense ..." (Foucault, 1990, p. 93) is embedded in the sociocultural approach to policy analysis. Policies therefore are power/knowledge. Looking at policies as practices of power shifts the analysis from the macro-process of policy development and implementation planning to policy-on-the ground, the micro-level engagements of schooling actors with institutional policies, and the effects of these local practices of policy appropriation in schools. In effect, it shifts to consider policy as a discursive practice with limits and ruptures.

Socially theorized policy is multi-dimensional, and the taken-for-granted positioning of policy as mere mandate is disrupted by the recognition of policy as action, production, practice, discourse, and power. Policy is viewed as an "on-going social practice of normative cultural production constituted by diverse actors across diverse contexts" (Levinson, Sutton, & Winstead, 2009, p. 770). Much like Foucault's discursive practice, rather than a static thing or text, policy is a "practice" or "process" through which life and behavior become authorized by people or groups across social contexts. As such, policy can be authorized—somehow legally binding either by law or force—or unauthorized—developed informally in networks outside of institutions invested with the power of official policy-making. Policy therefore does not have to be a text or document; it can also exist as a form of practice and institutional memory. The writing of policy can itself be viewed as one of many policy practices. Power is located within the "will to policy," a set of conditions that make policy (authorized, unauthorized, as a practice, or a text) possible, and also the "will in policy," the matrix of competing and overlapping power relations that permeate the social field through which power as policy flows (Levinson, Sutton, & Winstead, 2009, pp. 770–778).

In relation to my study, the policy as practice framework worked synergistically with Foucauldian theory to elucidate how policy as power circulated in schools and was lived by participants, and also helped me to see how curriculum and instruction were discursive practices shaped by policy and social context. But utilizing only Foucauldian theories as an analytic framework reinforced a discursive analysis that was on its own insufficient to engage the way race produced structural inequalities for Black and other students of color. It was not that a policy as practice framework or Foucauldian analysis excluded attention to race, but it did not provide the explanatory power needed to directly address the complex lived experiences of participants. As I explore in the next section, in spite of concerns about incommensurability and breaching the limits of analytic approaches carefully developed by researchers, it was necessary to bring a critical race approach to this methodology.

## THE MISSING DISCOURSE OF RACE IN POLICY ANALYSIS

Early in the first months of fieldwork, I became aware of a disruption to the story of success and achievement—a pattern of racially stratified course enrollment. As a researcher entering a school that placed equity at the forefront of its mission, my expectation was that the three curriculum tracks that comprised the exclusive college preparatory school—Basic College Preparation, Advanced Placement (AP), and International Baccalaureate (IB)—would roughly reflect the demographic make-up of the school (i.e., 65% of each class would hypothetically be Black). To the contrary, students were racially stratified across the three curriculums; basic college-prep courses were perceived to be the lowest achieving level of coursework and were overrepresented by Black students and other students of color, while AP and IB courses served predominantly white students. It was apparent that the stratification of enrollment was not a result of student choice, but rather practices of academic advising and enrollment that were both material and discursive. Race was deeply entwined with how school staff counseled students on course enrollment and scheduled them for classes, contributing to persistent patterns of racial segregation and a limiting of access to educational opportunities for students of color, patterns that were mostly overlooked.

In a special issue of *Race Ethnicity and Education* (Leonardo, 2007), contributors argued that No Child Left Behind policy in and of itself is a racial project, not merely a set of policies aimed at closing the achievement gap, but policies heavily invested in the larger racial system of the United States. The editor boldly asserted,

Overtly, it implicates improvements for students of color .... Implicitly, NCLB is part of a racial project since it is enacted within a radicalized nation-state. As part of the racialized state apparatuses, schools bear the markings and carry the anxieties of US race relations. (Leonardo, 2007, p. 241)

These researchers asserted that NCLB ignores the structural inequalities of the education system perpetuated in and through the racial system of the United States. Furthermore, David Tyack argued "policy talk about questions of diversity in education today often ignores a long history of the social and political constructions of difference in American society and public schools" (1993, p. 8).

The policy as practice framework and Foucauldian theories did not directly address the anxieties of race relations or the material realities of Black students and other students of color at OPHS. My training in qualitative inquiry focused a great deal on the crisis of representation and the potential violences of research. The complications of "writing culture" (Clifford & Marcus, 1986), "racing research and researching race" (Twine & Warren, 2000), and extremely complex critiques of research and poststructuralism made by feminists of color such as Patricia Hill Collins (1990), Gloria Anzaldúa (1999/1987), bell hooks (1981), and many others forced me to consider the insufficiency and potential violence of using only Foucauldian theory to try address the materiality of students' lives.

Racialized enrollment at OPHS was not just a discursive practice to be analyzed. While this was a study of local policy in practice, the local policy was also a materiality sustained by, and further sustaining of, long-term historical and social structural inequalities based on race. It had material effects on students' ability to access opportunities, such as Black students' limited access to advanced placement and international baccalaureate courses in high school that could later offset college expenses and time-to-degree upon entering post-secondary education. To understand the process of policy negotiation at the local level, I needed to be accountable methodologically to directly addressing the "real" racial inequalities experienced by students, naming how white privilege present in the data was bound up in these inequalities, and rendering visible the logics of the practices. Critical Race Theory in Education (Ladson-Billings & Tate, 1995) provided a way to directly engage the missing discourse of race in policy analysis. In the next section, I trace how I used Critical Race Theory and the work of Foucault to think through an example of how course enrollment was a racialized practice of policy.

## PUTTING PROMISCUITY TO WORK: AN ANALYSIS

White parents[11] overwhelmingly talked about how the AP and IB courses made it possible for their students to leave the "troublemakers" behind. As one parent explained, "But as he got into his sophomore year and he could take AP art history and AP Euro, then the troublemakers were left behind. And now he's in IB and they're gone as far as I know," [Parent Focus Group, 1/6/09]. There was a perception that OPHS was attracting more and more students not interested in academics and also that it was attracting more Black students than it had in the past, because it was safe, or because parents were choosing OPHS in good faith hoping that the school would prepare their academically disinterested student for college. These students were perceived as negatively impacting the climate of the school, and AP and IB courses served to "weed out" the troublemakers. Parents, white and Black, perceived this weeding out process as beneficial for their own students.

In these conversations, parents did not make a connection between their white students' escape to AP and IB and how the "weeding out" process left behind predominantly Black students in the college prep courses. They also did not see a connection between the over-representation of Black students in the college prep track and the ways in which this track was defined as the place where the troublemakers and disinterested students remained. CRT helps us to see that the maintenance of the AP and IB programs as predominantly white, though school administrators argued that this occurred inadvertently due to student choice, served as a form of white privilege, or whiteness as property (Harris, 1995).

Whiteness as property (Harris, 1995) is a key concept in CRT. According to Harris (1995), United States society is based on a system of property rights located within racial subordination.

> Slavery as a system of property facilitated the merger of white identity and property. Because the system of slavery was contingent on and conflated with racial identity, it became crucial to be "white," to be identified as white, to have the property of being white. Whiteness was the characteristic, the attribute, the property of free human beings. (Harris, 1995, p. 279)

Through the slavery of blacks and the seizure of Native American lands, whiteness came to be a form of privilege to ownership and a form of protection from being owned:

> Whiteness became a shield from slavery, a highly volatile and unstable form of property.... Because whites could not be enslaved or held as slaves, the racial line between white and black was extremely critical; it became a line of threat of commodification, and it determined the allocation of benefits and burdens of this form of property. White identity and whiteness were sources of privilege and protection; their absence meant being an object of property. (Harris, 1995, p. 279)

A racially stratified enrollment across the three curriculums at OPHS was maintained through racialized power relations that make use of the property values of whiteness. Whiteness colored the enrollment process. The status and prestige associated with AP and IB constructed the privileges from which white students could benefit more often than students of color. White students and families, due to their access to middle school prerequisites and an early knowledge of requirements their students would need to meet to take advantage of advanced courses, maintained their rights to the use and enjoyment of the programs, while Black students were structurally excluded from this use and enjoyment. As predominantly white courses, they took on a positive reputation and status, one that was not bestowed on the predominantly Black college prep courses. The right to exclude, a component of white privilege, was inextricably bound up in the use of entrance applications and an emphasis on rigor over benefit to discourage college prep students, students with jobs, and students with disengaged parents from applying. The majority of Black students I interviewed reported these as factors that discouraged their enrollment in AP and IB.

This analysis brought race to the forefront and explicitly named how white privilege was undermining equity and opportunity for black students and other students of color in the school. I do not think, however, that such analysis alone does enough to render visible the logic of the system, a logic that needs to be understood to be destabilized. This is where Foucauldian concepts become most useful.

I used Foucault's definitions of discourse and analysis as a framework. According to Sara Mills (1997/2004) Foucault offers three different ways to think of discourse:

> utterances or texts which have meaning and which have some effects in the real world... discourses, that is groups of utterances which seem to be regulated in some way and which seem to have a coherence and a force to them in common...(and) the rules and structures which produce particular utterances and texts. (p. 6)

Elizabeth St. Pierre (2000) continued, "Foucault's theory of discourse illustrates how language gathers itself together according to socially constructed rules and regularities that allow certain statements to be made and not others" (p. 485). Because it looks for historical shifts when people do or say things differently, it also looks at the productive nature of discourse within fields of power/knowledge and possibilities for resistance. In these ways, Foucauldian theories become useful for tracing how discourses of urban schooling and students are produced in and through policy, and productive of the practices/effects documented in this study.

Using Foucauldian discourse analysis, the advising and enrollment practices that resulted in an overrepresentation of black students in college prep classes were justified in and through racialized discourses of urban students that constructed them as at-risk in school. For example, a counselor discussed at length how she used the large size of the AP Art History textbook as a way to deter students who, she felt, might not be suited for the rigors of the course, students who, she worried, might "crash and burn." Black students I interviewed also discussed how they felt pushed out and counseled away from AP and IB courses even though they argued they had the appropriate prerequisites, grades, and interest. While such practices may have been coming from a place of real concern—the counselor did not want students to fail, damage their grade point average, and therefore their college acceptance—this concern was hinged on deficit discourses that circulated about Black students.

Similarly, a discourse of colorblindness, the idea that the way to obliterate racism is to not "see" it, enabled the school to overlook structural issues that may have impeded students' desire to enroll. As an administrator told me during an interview, the fact that the curriculums were racially stratified was not about race, but about student desire and choice to enroll (Childers, 2011). The racialized discourses of deficit insidiously fed local discourses, perpetuated the idea that disinterested students "chose" college preparation rather than AP or IB, but elided the fact that these discourses were read on and through the bodies of Black students who populated these courses. These deficit discourses were in essence de-raced by other power/knowledge frameworks. Colorblind discourses and the local discourse of student choice were held up as explanations as to why Black students were overrepresented in the college prep program. These discourses maintained the absent presence of race, rendering race something visible yet inconsequential (i.e., we could see that classes had patterns along lines of race, yet these patterns were rendered insignificant). These articulations impaired any desire or need to look further, look structurally, or reflectively question practices that might be having an impact on Black students.

In summary, Critical Race Theory held me accountable to being explicit about the role of race materially, socially, and historically in my analysis, and I did not find this to be antithetical to a Foucauldian analysis. Combining Foucauldian discourse analysis with CRT enabled me to look at how practices such as whiteness as property not only sustained inequality, but also were produced in and through the persistence of deficit discourses that constructed urban students as at risk and culturally deprived. Similarly, discourses of colorblindness equally encouraged teachers to deny that their academic perceptions of students were raced, and therefore how such perceptions impacted how they counseled and enrolled students.

## CONCLUSION

Placing CRT into conversation with Foucault had the effect of tightening and loosening frameworks. CRT held me accountable to naming race and privilege; it tightened power/knowledge to be attentive to the materiality of urban students' experiences and bring structural inequality to bear on the analysis. As such, race mattered and was a privileged site of working Foucauldian analysis. Simultaneously, Foucault performed a loosening of CRT, reading structural inequalities along the lines of power/knowledge that are held within them, identifying both the limits and the productive possibilities, and using the loosened reading to locate how deficit discourses were read on the bodies of Black students.[12]

Putting incommensurable theoretical frameworks into conversation was anything but indiscriminate, merely pragmatic, or a blatant disregard for how my beliefs about the world shape my research. It was in part a methodological attempt to address the ethical issues inherent in doing research on race, and trying to not perpetuate the missing discourse in policy analysis by ignoring the effects of race materially and discursively on the lives of Black students at this school. Racism, white privilege, policy, and power coursed through this "urban" school and were activated through strange and violent assemblages that brought these separated methodologies together in my thinking in a way that was maddening, and I chose to write about it here.

In working on the special issue on promiscuous feminisms and thinking a great deal about how "the materiality of the field" (Childers, 2013) guided my research decisions and analytic choices, I have found promiscuity an apt way to think through my research engagements. By bringing together Foucault's theories of power and the conceptual apparatus of Critical Race Theory, I am in no way implying that these metaphysical positions are commensurable, that the epistemological and ontological differences are insignificant, or that they are merely methods or concepts that could be put to work. Rather, I wanted to speak to the madness that guided thinking and the tensions that productively pushed analysis. Writing about it seems riskier than experiencing its becoming. Transgressing these analytic boundaries could be read as indiscriminate. I argue that promiscuity as a methodological practice also calls on an intention to inhabit the complexities and see what happens. Promiscuity is not always about the racy, sexy side of difference. It is also about pushing limits of possibility and taking the risk to do research differently in the hopes of a social science we can live with.

## NOTES

1. This study included document analysis, nine consecutive months of classroom and school observations, and interviews and focus groups with 40 students, parents, teachers, and administrators, followed by analysis and writing that were simultaneous with return trips to the school for member checks and further research. A great deal of time was spent prior to the study building relationships and gaining access.

2. All names are pseudonyms assigned by the researcher to protect the confidentiality and anonymity of study participants.

3.  Ohio Public High School is designated an urban school within a Major Urban District by the Ohio Department of Education. It is a predominantly Black high school with a fluctuating percentage of students (as high as 90% in some years) receiving free and reduced lunch.

4.  Bizarre ironies, paradoxes, and contradictions characterize the current state of US education under NCLB. Testing culture promotes a narrowed curriculum, focused on low-level skills and high-stakes test "training." Rich critical inquiry and maximum potential have been replaced with rote memorization and minimum expectations governed by the testing regime that undermines teachers, students, and schools. Testing and accountability provide strong incentives to exclude or ignore low-performing students and have led to an increase, rather than decrease, in the drop out rate. Schools that serve the most disadvantaged students lose access to funding when they fail to improve or meet targets. This "diversity penalty" encourages them to push out, keep out, or drop out low-scoring students. Some of the neediest students, such as English language learners and special needs students, are held to inappropriate standards and expectations, and they simultaneously suffer from a lack of appropriate support to make academic progress, leading to increased dropping out. Public shaming, intimidation, and punishment experienced through the labeling of failing schools and the resulting reduction in funding and incentives to these needy programs not only demoralizes the teachers themselves but also reduces the ability of schools and districts to attract and retain high-quality educators, another intended goal of the bill (Darling-Hammond, 2007; Gay, 2007; Hursh, 2007).

5.  To preserve the identity of OPHS, citations for these recognitions are not included in the bibliography and the school website is not provided for reference.

6.  While the Ohio Department of Education used the phrase "African American" as an identity category, I found in my interviews that students often identified themselves as "Black," and this included African American as well as other backgrounds. I use the term "Black" for the remainder of the article for this reason.

7.  Michael Omi and Howard Winant (1986) conceptualized race "as an unstable and 'decentered' complex of social meanings constantly being transformed by political struggle" (p. 123) and defined it further *"as a concept which signifies and symbolizes social conflicts and interests by referring to different types of human bodies"* (p. 123, italics theirs). They clarified this contested term by arguing that "although the concept of race invokes biological based human characteristics...selection of these particular human features for purposes of racial signification is always and necessarily a social and historical process" (p. 123).

8.  We can locate tangible examples of these discourses in social science research conducted in the United States. The 1966 study by James Coleman entitled *Equality of Educational Opportunity*, also referred to as "The Coleman Report," equated lagging achievement in predominantly Black schools with deprivation produced by racial isolation, family background, and social composition. *The Negro Family: The Case for National Action* (1965), a report published by the Office of Policy Planning and Research at the United States Department of Labor, also known as "The Moynihan Report," argued that "the fundamental source of the weakness of the Negro community" and "of the fabric of Negro society is the deterioration of the Negro family" (p. 5). These high profile reports used "science" to shift responsibility for poor educational outcomes for Black students to their families and cultures and away from the structural inequalities inherent in the education system.

9.  Though no theory can be reduced to a set of unanimously agreed-upon characteristics, CRT is often identified by six unifying themes, and CRT in education also employs these principles. It is asserted that Critical Race Theory:

1. Recognizes racism as endemic to US life and society.
2. Challenges dominant legal claims of neutrality, objectivity, colorblindness, and meritocracy.
3. Argues against ahistoricism and insists that law must be analyzed within history and context.
4. Locates its analysis within the experiential knowledge of people of color and privileges this type of knowledge through the use of narrative and storytelling.
5. Is interdisciplinary.
6. Views activism and social change as requisite components of its work toward the elimination of racial oppression and the larger goal of ending all forms of oppression (Matsuda, Lawrence, Delgado, & Crenshaw, 1993, quoted in Dixson & Rousseau, 2006, p. 33).

10. The ideas here are loosely taken from Vicky Kirby's discussion of critique in *Quantum Anthropologies: Life at Large*, 2011.
11. Of the 11 parents that I interviewed, eight were white and three were Black. Of the parents, all but one of their students was participating in AP or IB programs. Of the three Black parents, one student was taking one AP course.
12. Other analysis not presented in this chapter move to unhinge and unfix these discourses from the bodies of urban students to think differently about them as educational agents on their own terms.

## REFERENCES

Anzaldúa, G. (1999/1987). *Borderlands, La frontera: The New mestiza* (2nd ed.). San Francisco, CA: Aunt Lute Books.

Childers, S. (2011). Getting in trouble: Feminist post-critical policy ethnography in an urban school. *Qualitative Inquiry, 17*(5), 345–354.

Childers, S. (2013). The materiality of fieldwork: Ontology of feminist becoming. *International Journal of Qualitative Studies in Education, 26*(5), p. 598–602.

Childers, S., Rhee, J., & Daza, S. (2013). Editors' introduction. *International Journal of Qualitative Studies in Education, 26*(5), p. 507–622.

Childers, S., Daza, S., & Rhee, J., (Eds.) (2013). Special Issue: Promiscuous feminisms: The dirty theory and messy practice of feminist educational research beyond gender. *International Journal of Qualitative Studies in Education, 26*(5).

Clifford, J., & Marcus, G. E. (1986). *Writing culture: The poetics and politics of ethnography*. Berkeley, CA: University of California Press.

Coleman, J. (1966). *Equality of educational opportunity*. Washington, DC: Government Printing Office.

Collins, P. H., (1990). *Black feminist thought: Knowledge, consciousness, and the politics of empowerment*. Minneapolis, MN: University of Minnesota Press.

Darling-Hammond, L. (2007). Race, inequality, and educational accountability: The irony of "No Child Left Behind." *Race, Ethnicity, and Education, 10*(3), 245–260.

Dixson, A. D., & Rousseau, C. K. (Eds.). (2006). Critical Race Theory in education: All God's children got a song. New York, NY: Routledge.

Foucault, M. (1977). *Discipline & punish: The birth of the prison*. New York, NY: Vintage Books.

Foucault, M. (1990). *The history of sexuality: An introduction* (Vol. 1, R. Hurley, Trans.). New York, NY: Vintage.

Gay, G. (2007). The rhetoric and reality of NCLB. *Race, Ethnicity, and Education, 10*(3), 279–293.

Harris, C. I. (1995). Whiteness as property. In K. Crenshaw, N. Gotanda, G. Peller, & K. Thomas (Eds.), *Critical Race Theory: The key writings that formed the movement* (pp. 276–291). New York, NY: The New Press.

hooks, b. (1981). *Ain't I a woman: Black women and feminism.* New York, NY: South End Press.

Hursh, D. (2007). Exacerbating inequality: The failed promise of the No Child Left Behind Act. *Race, Ethnicity, and Education, 10*(3), 295–308.

Kirby, V. (2011). *Quantum anthropologies: Life at large* [Kindle Version]. Durham, NC: Duke University Press.

Ladson-Billings, G., & Tate, W. F. (1995). Toward a Critical Race Theory of education. *Teachers College Record, 97*(1), p. 47–68.

Latour, B. (1994). *Pandora's hope: Essays on the reality of science studies.* Cambridge, MA: Harvard University Press.

Leonardo, Z. (Ed.). (2007). Special issue on No Child Left Behind. *Race Ethnicity and Education, 10*(3).

Levinson, B. A. U., Sutton, M., & Winstead, T. (2009). Education policy as a practice of power: Theoretical tools, ethnographic methods, democratic options. *Educational Policy, 23*(6), 767–795.

Lincoln, Y. S. (2010). "What a long, strange trip it's been…": Twenty-five years of qualitative and new paradigm research. *Qualitative Inquiry, 16*(1), 3–9.

MacLure, M. (2013). Classification or wonder? Coding as an analytic practice in qualitative research. In B. Coleman & J. Ringrose (Eds.), *Deleuze and research methodologies.* Edinburgh, Scotland: EUP.

Marshall, C. (Ed.). (1997). *Feminist critical policy analysis I: A perspective from primary and secondary schooling* (Vol. 1). London, England: The Falmer Press.

Matsuda, M., Lawrence, C., Delgado, R., & Crenshaw, K. (Eds.). (1993). Words that wound: Critical Race Theory, assaultive speech, and the first amendment. Boulder, CO: Westview.

Mills, S. (2004). *Discourse.* New York, NY: Routledge.

Mishra Tarc, A. (2013). Wild reading: This madness to our method. *International Journal of Qualitative Studies In Education, 26*(5), 537–552.

No Child Left Behind Act, 20 U.S.C. § 6301, (2001)

Office of Planning and Research, United States Department of Labor. (1965). The Negro family, the case for national action. Washington, DC: Government Printing Office.

Omi, M., & Winant, H. (1986). *Racial formation in the United States: From the 1960s to the 1990s.* New York, NY: Routledge.

Pillow, W. (2004). *Unfit subjects: Educational policy and the teen mother.* New York, NY: Routledge Falmer.

Scheurich, J. J. (1994). Policy archeology: A new policy studies methodology. *Educational Policy, 9*(4), 297–316.

Scheurich, J. J. (1997). *Research method in the postmodern.* London, England: Falmer.

St. Pierre, E. A. (2000). Poststructural feminism in education: An overview. *International Qualitative Studies in Education, 13*(5), 477–515.

Sutton, M., & Levinson, B. A. U. (Eds.). (2001). *Policy as practice: Toward a comparative sociocultural analysis of educational policy.* Westport, CT: Ablex.

Twine, F. W., & Warren, J. (Eds). (2000). *Racing research, researching race.* New York, NY: University Press.

Tyack, D. B. (1993). Constructing difference: Historical reflections on schooling and social diversity. *Teachers College Record, 95*(1), 8–34.

Voithofer, R. (2013). Promiscuous feminisms for troubling times. *International Journal of Qualitative Studies in Education, 26*(5), 524–536.

## ADDITIONAL RESOURCES

## Promiscuity

Childers, S., Daza, S., & Rhee, J., (Eds.). (2013). Special issue: Promiscuous feminisms: The dirty theory and messy practice of feminist educational research beyond gender. *International Journal of Qualitative Studies in Education, 26*(5).

## New Feminist Materialism

Alaimo, S., & Hekman, S. (2008). *Material feminisms*. Bloomington, IN: Indiana University Press.

Barad, K. 2007. *Meeting the universe halfway: Quantum physics and the entanglement of matter and meaning*. Durham, NC: Duke University Press.

Hekman, S. 2010. *The material of knowledge: Feminist disclosures*. Bloomington, IN: Indiana University Press.

Kirby, V. (2011). *Quantum anthropologies: Life at large* [Kindle Version]. Durham, NC: Duke University Press.

## Poststructural Theory

Jackson, A. Y., & Mazzei, L. (2012). *Thinking with theory in qualitative research: Using epistemological frameworks in the production of meaning*. London, England: Routledge.

## Critical Race Theory

Crenshaw, K., Gotanda, N., Peller, G., & Thomas, K. (Eds.). (1995). *Critical Race Theory: The key writings that formed the movement*. New York, NY: The New Press.

Taylor, E., Gillborn, D., & Ladson-Billings, G. (Eds.). (2009). *Foundations of Critical Race Theory in education*. New York, NY: Routledge.

## Policy

Hess, F. M. (Ed.). (2008). *When research matters: How scholarship influences education policy*. Cambridge, MA: Harvard Education Press.

Lather, P. (2010). *Engaging science policy: From the side of the messy*. New York, NY: Peter Lang.

Sutton, M., & Levinson, B. A. U. (Eds.). (2001). *Policy as practice: Toward a comparative sociocultural analysis of educational policy*. Westport, CT: Ablex.

# CHAPTER FOUR

# CRiT Walking FOR Disruption OF Educational Master Narratives

MARK S. GILES & ROBIN L. HUGHES

August 28, 2013 was the 50th anniversary of the 1963 March on Washington for Jobs and Freedom. That event is largely remembered as the setting where Dr. Martin Luther King, Jr., delivered his "I Have a Dream" speech. That historic moment, where more than a stirring speech by Dr. King occurred, contributed to many positive and sweeping national cultural changes, such as the mid-1960s civil rights and voting rights legislation. The ensuing events advanced the cause of human and citizenship rights for all, and led to vast improvements for interracial relationships. In addition, the era ushered in subsequent laws that challenged the practices of racial discrimination in the areas of housing, employment, and educational access, to name a few. However, in 2013, systemic racism (Feagin, 2006) remains alive and well. It lives in the disproportionate incarceration rates for black males (Alexander, 2010), the inequities in the healthcare system (Washington, 2008), and the ongoing disparities in our schools and post-secondary education institutions (Anderson, Attwood, & Howard, 2004; Darling-Hammond, 2010; Dixson & Rousseau, 2006; Hale, 2001; Kunjufu, 2005; Noguera, 2008; Obakeng-Mabokela & Green, 2001; Shabazz, 2004; Wise, 2005). The mainstream or traditional narrative of education and how it is often researched and understood exist within the contexts of a highly racialized, complex web of social, cultural, political, and economic systems.

In order to begin understanding any of these issues, along with other complex social dynamics, it is vital to have critical consciousness and paradigms through which to see and deconstruct certain pervasive problems while possessing useful tools for making change. Born out of critical legal studies, Critical Race Theory (CRT) offers a deconstructive paradigm, and conceptual, methodological tools to "understand how ostensibly race-neutral structures in education—knowledge, truth, merit, objectivity, and 'good education'—are in fact ways of forming and policing the racial boundaries of white supremacy and racism" (Roithmayr, 1999, p. 4). This chapter highlights CRT as a paradigm that informs the deconstruction work CRT scholarship performs and our naming that deconstructive process as CRiT walking (Hughes & Giles, 2010).

Our very presence as black faculty members in the academy represents a type of disruption of historical educational norms of who can and should be professional educators and scholars. We position ourselves within the academy as critical race studies and critical race theorist scholars who believe it is important to challenge traditional norms and interpretive frames of educational research that can perpetuate systemic injustice and racial bias in knowledge production, analysis, and distribution. We see this work as part of the larger equity and excellence, social and racial justice mission engaged in by many educators and scholars across the country and around the globe. Our positionality and argument for development of a CRT paradigm represents an essential entry point to understand this chapter and its ideas. What is CRT and why is it relevant to educational research? Richard Delgado and Jean Stefancic (2001) in their primer on Critical Race Theory stated:

> The Critical Race Theory (CRT) movement is a collection of activists and scholars interested in studying and transforming the relationship among race, racism, and power ... Critical Race Theory questions the very foundations of the liberal order, including equality theory, legal reasoning, Enlightenment rationalism, and neutral principals of constitutional law. Today, many in the field of education consider themselves critical race theorists who use CRT's ideas to understand issues of school discipline and hierarchy, tracking, controversies over curriculum and history, and IQ and achievement testing. (pp. 2–3)

We agree with Delgado and Stefancic regarding the notion that educational researchers cannot honestly hold totally neutral positions on issues such as race and racism, and we acknowledge paying attention to the centrality of race, the foregrounding of racial constructs, contexts, and systemic racism in our lenses on the American educational enterprise. Sylvia Lazos Vargas (2003) stated, "For Critical Race Theory, race is just not an additional variable in the equation; instead, it is at the center of the research enterprise" (p. 1). Our adoption of this type of positioning and paradigm results from our personal and professional experiences, CRT interpretative frameworks, and our individual, multiple identities. In addition, we agree with Melanie Carter (2003), who explained how the use of CRT in educational research "encourages researchers to trouble methodological rules that stipulate a particular dominant narrative...name and interpret realities that cannot or have not been understood using other methodologies" (p. 30). The act of questioning institutionalized and societal norms can represent danger to some faculty who desire to advance their careers yet face the constant risk of losing the support of those in power who might not share their ideological, epistemological, ontological, or political perspectives. This ever present danger can lead some faculty members to fear exercising their own authentic voices and research agendas. However, if those faculty members did not question certain norms such as deficit thinking or the myth of meritocracy, it would cut against their operational authenticity in these highly political, contested academic spaces. There is power in specifically naming and un-naming positionality for faculty of color who seek to advance an anti-racist pedagogy and challenge the norms of systemic racism in educational settings.

We claim positionality as interdisciplinary CRT activist scholars. Recognizing that activism can mean different things to different people, we attempt to exercise activism for social justice goals grounded in CRT principles through our teaching, writing, and work in various organizations. Our individual and collective teaching and research interests intentionally transgress several mainstream boundaries guided by a CRT paradigm, which by its very nature disrupts the traditional, dominant colorblind, race-neutral assumptions of not only educational research, but also of educational policies, politics, and practices. For example, Robin's main research interests focus on the intersectionality of race and sports across educational levels, yet she primarily teaches in a higher education/student affairs program that frequently directs the majority of its graduate students into traditional student affairs professional positions that often lay claim to social justice, but can represent a mainstay of institutional status quo replication. Mark's main research interests focus on African American leadership, spirituality, and twentieth-century U.S. history. At the same time, he is director of an African American Studies undergraduate minor program, regularly teaches across all levels of his university (i.e., undergraduate, master's, and doctoral), and across programmatic areas of his home department in Educational Leadership and Policy Studies (i.e., higher education, social foundations, educational administration/leadership). The audacity of trying to teach and write across the traditional boundaries and fault lines of educational departments can represent a type of danger zone where an interdisciplinary scholar's work and worth is often viewed as suspect. What is essential to understand about these brief descriptions of elements of our professional positioning in academic departments is that a CRT paradigm or interpretive framework informs our work and helps us see, interpret, and act in ways that might not fit neatly into the dominant narratives of education faculty. For us, CRT is not a fad, or methodological "flavor of the month"; it represents one of the main perspectives that inform what we do, and how we do it. By its very core nature, CRT is indeed disruptive to the dominant, master narratives of education such as the mythology of colorblindness and researcher neutrality. One of the key tenets of CRT is providing a critique of Liberalism, which includes notions of colorblindness, meritocracy, and assumptions of neutrality of educational policies.

Within the spirit and purpose of CRT lies the power and importance of critique to speak truth to power and to identify issues, historical contexts, and assumptions that often go overlooked or under-theorized. Not everything has a nice, neat outcome like a well-scripted 30-minute television show that resolves one or more major problems during each broadcast. Over the years, we have begun to reflect on and question ways to articulate the importance of paradigm, process, and resultant work when using CRT. This led us to begin developing an idea we call CRiT walking. We envision it as a flexible metaphor based on legal and education CRT tenets. It requires a paradigm grounded in CRT, rather than conducting research and writing based exclusively on dominant approaches and assumptions, which traditionally often discount and devalue the experiences of people of color, topped off with a few colorful CRT sprinkles.

We understand our work through multiple lenses that acknowledge racism as prevalent and "normal" to the mythology and operating principles of American life. These lenses inform our beliefs, perspectives, and actions as faculty. With this in mind, it follows that a certain mindset as well as appropriate tools are required for doing our work in education. CRT provides the overarching framework for us, and we have sought to complement those ideas with our own vision to articulate the conceptual process of viewing and moving through assumptions, arguments, analysis of data, field observations, documents, and perceived realities. This work has resulted in the development of CRiT walking, a metaphorical lens to describe the underlying conceptual paradigm informed by CRT and a creative narrative expression of moving (i.e., walking) through the racialized landscapes of American education.

As CRiT walkers, challenging master narrative assumptions in educational and qualitative research means an acknowledgment of the premise that normative dynamics exist based on white, middle-class cultural ways of knowing and living in the world and the need to confront those norms with equally valuable perspectives from "non-white" or other racial-ethnic orientations. To disrupt the master-dominant narratives that form and guide most traditional forms of research approaches, scholars must adopt a core critical consciousness guided by ways of knowing designed to question the essence of how and why they are engaged in the process in the first place. To claim actions as disruption and simultaneously perpetuate the master narratives of deficit thinking, racist, sexist, or elitist assumptions of what methods and methodology are most valuable, who should benefit from the research act and its findings, for example, suggests nothing more than paying lip service to the notion of changing the status quo. At the heart of the notion of disrupting the status quo in education is an anti-racist, social-justice-oriented goal. To achieve this type of work, what could guide a prospective educator-scholar in this endeavor? This chapter incorporates Critical Race Theory (CRT) and CRiT walking (Giles & Hughes, 2009; Hughes & Giles, 2010), to comment on the predominance of white, middle-class norms, mythical colorblindness, racially codified language, and culturally deficit paradigms of darker complexioned "others" as central tropes in the master narratives of "American" education.

Critical Race Theory (Bell, 1992; Solórzano & Yosso, 2002; Taylor, Gillborn, & Ladson-Billings, 2009) and CRiT walking (Giles & Hughes, 2009; Hughes & Giles, 2010) offer interconnected theoretical frameworks through which to challenge and disrupt hegemonic, ill informed, and blatantly racially biased epistemologies, policies, and practices. Racialized educational settings represent potential sites of empowering counter-narratives and discourses on systemic problems that plague the national educational landscape. Founded in legal studies and adapted by educational scholarship, Critical Race Theory offers a valuable lens through which to understand and analyze systemic racism and its effects on the lives of individuals and influence on at-large society.

The concept of CRiT walking derived directly and specifically from the tenets and ideological spirit of Critical Race Theory as a creative allegory and metaphor of moving (i.e., walking) through various conceptual paradigms and real-world settings to deconstruct systemic racism and bias that impedes progressive social justice change processes (Hughes & Giles, 2010). Derrick Bell (2009) explained,

> Critical Race Theory writing and lecturing is characterized by frequent use of the first person, storytelling, narrative, allegory, interdisciplinary treatment of law, and the unapologetic use of creativity. The work is often disruptive because its commitment to anti-racism goes well beyond civil rights, integration, affirmative action, and other liberal measures. (p. 41)

By adopting Critical Race Theory, educational scholars who use CRT should commit to incorporate the characteristics Derrick Bell modeled with his ground-breaking, storytelling, counter-narrative approach to examinations of American race relations and legal issues (Bell, 1987; 1992). CRiT walking, as an additional conceptual tool intended to challenge traditional ways of thinking and writing, could enhance how scholars might conceive of and articulate their critical consciousness regardless of the particular focus of their research topic. One goal of CRiT walking is to encourage anti-racist scholars to ground themselves in a CRT-based paradigm and think creatively about the application of their analysis. Following the established leads of CRT scholars such as Derrick Bell (1987), Richard Delgado (1989), and Gloria Ladson Billings (2009) in the ways they use various narrative formats proves instructive. CRiT walking does not and cannot exist outside of CRT. Therefore, if someone is not familiar and fluent with the substantive breadth and depth of CRT literature, then what we (Giles & Hughes, 2009; Hughes & Giles, 2010) offer as CRiT walking will not resonate.

According to founding CRT legal scholars (Matsuda et. al. 1993), the six foundational tenets of CRT include:

> Critical Race Theory recognizes that racism is endemic to American life....Critical Race Theory expresses skepticism toward dominant legal claims of neutrality, objectivity, color blindness, and meritocracy....Critical Race Theory challenges ahistoricism and insists on a contextual/historical analysis of the law....Critical Race Theory insists on recognition of the experiential knowledge of people of color and our communities of origin in analyzing law and society....Critical Race Theory is interdisciplinary and eclectic....Critical Race Theory works toward the end of eliminating racial oppression as part of the broader goal of ending all forms of oppression. (p. 6)

These tenets, slightly altered and adopted for use by education scholars (Ladson Billings & Tate, 1995; Solórzano & Yosso, 2002), constitute the foundational premises from which the CRT movement emerged. Over the years, CRT has continually evolved and taken on various iterations focused on particular group perspectives and experiences, such as LatCrit (Solórzano & Yosso, 2001; Trucios-Haynes, 2001), which focuses on the experiences and concerns of Latino/a groups, and TribalCrit (Brayboy, 2005), which focuses on the experiences and interests of indigenous (e.g., Native American) groups. These extensions and branches of CRT allow a broader and culturally inclusive focus that goes beyond a black-white binary that characterizes the original CRT framework and writings. In a similar vein, we hoped to contribute to the evolution of CRT theorizing by offering CRiT walking, which focuses on the conceptual and metaphorical application of using those powerful CRT perspectives and principles in deconstructing multiple educational environments. Doing Critical Race Theory work must be an intentional choice, a form of "radical teaching" that challenges the dehumanization of oppression and presents opportunities for hope of change by first seeing the operational spaces of our lives through lenses that exposes aspects of that oppression (Matsuda et. al. 1993).

We intentionally decided to spell "CRiT" in a unique way in order to distinguish our emerging concept, to emphasize Critical Race Theory with the lower case i representing the individuality that scholars might bring to it. We envision the term as a creative expression of non-dominant thinking about a non-standard word that many CRT scholars apply to themselves with the term "crits" (Delgado, 2011). For example, Delgado and Stefancic (2001) in their widely read book, *Critical Race Theory: An Introduction,* used the term "crits" in several places to refer to critical race theorists (pp. 22, 23, 31). To our thinking, the term represents a multi-leveled concept, inseparable from Critical Race Theory, encapsulating the individual and collective identities of those who claim CRT as a primary lens and/or epistemological construct for praxis. In that sense, "crit" becomes a type of shorthand for some critical race theorists. It signals a distinctive signature word for our developing work using the idea of embracing a Critical Race Theory paradigm as a primary interpretive framework to conceptually walk through any series of incidents, situations, or contexts that have race and racism as central elements. In that way, the phrase serves as a metaphor of application for CRT analysis. Lastly, with CRiT walking we seek to question and challenge master narrative discourses on educational policies and practices that limit people of color in narrowly constructed majoritarian paradigms.

These majoritarian paradigms often cast non-white students, teachers, and college faculty as either potentially or conclusively deficient based on dubious assumptions and evidence such as racial or ethnic prejudice, social or cultural differences, or divergent intellectual/scholarly interests. Our individual and collective experiences give testimony to the racially constructed politics of assumed deficiency within educational settings (McCarthy, Crichlow, Dimitriadis, & Dolby, 2005; McLaren & Kincheloe, 2007; Wing, 1997). The language and word choices used to communicate any set of ideas reflect and shape a person's philosophy, worldview, and potential action. Noted poet and author Audre Lorde said it best: "The master's tools will never dismantle the master's house" (Lorde, 1984). Our experimentation with the phrase and concept of CRiT walking is offered in a similar spirit. The "tools" of language and conceptual models, such as ways of knowing and seeing, and paradigms or interpretive frameworks that represent and reinforce dominant/master narratives, will not make the change many anti-racist educational scholars wish to see. We (Mark Giles & Robin Hughes) claim positionality as anti-racist, CRiT-walking scholars and wish to advance tools (i.e., language, paradigm) shaped directly, but not exclusively, by CRT as part of the ongoing struggle to challenge dominant narratives that cleverly hide the oppressive nature of dynamics and policies such as standardized high-stakes testing, which we briefly touch upon in this chapter.

Educational theorizing using CRiT walking is an exploratory extension of Critical Race Theory. It should contain elements of CRT tenets including interdisciplinary methodology, historical/contextual grounding, and storytelling as counternarratives to signify intentional challenges to systemic norms. These combined elements represent an additional disruption to dominant educational ideologies and practices. In 2010, we (Hughes & Giles) wrote,

> CRiT walking is the method of strategically thinking and talking through various institutional norms, policies, and procedures to re-interpret and re-connect our understanding of the intersections of race, racism, power, and praxis. As CRiT walkers, we challenge the usual ways in which higher education operates through the use of allegory, metaphor and counter-stories, to turn upside down the dominant, racist, patriarchal, academic life where most of us live. (p. 48)

To ignore the basic racial deficit assumptions deeply embedded in so-called "mainstream" qualitative methodologies, and much of traditional educational research, requires blindly accepting the assumed universalistic epistemology (ways of thinking and knowing) and ontology (ways of being/existing) associated with Euro-American cultural and social norms, which historically do not represent or emerge from the culturally grounded, community-cultural wealth-based (Ani, 1995; Yosso, 2005) experiences of people of color. Marimba Ani (1995) stated, "As Europeans present their culture to the world, they do so consistently in universalistic terms. This representation takes the form of a relentless command to universalize" (p. 511). The focus on universalizing a particular paradigm forms the dominant or "master" narrative that often marginalizes and oppresses people and perspectives deemed "other" as by the same measure, subordinate and less than.

The concept of race is socially constructed through uneven relations of power dynamics between groups of people, and notions of race matter in educational research and practice. Angela James (2008) offered an interesting description of the inherent conundrum,

> while race is a dynamic phenomenon rooted in political struggle, it is commonly observed as a fixed characteristic of human populations; while it does not exist in terms of human biology, people routinely look to the human body for evidence about racial identity; while it is a biological fiction, it is nonetheless a social fact. (p. 32)

Evidence of how "race" became a determining factor in viewing the worth, value, or potential of certain groups, we should remember how early European colonization of native peoples around the world led to the creation of many racial, cultural, and social distinctions that shaped so-called scientific classifications of groups and the "accepted" knowledge about whites as superior and non-whites as inferior (Zinn, 2005). For example, the history of qualitative methods such as Ethnography includes assumptions about not only how best to observe, describe, and document the "other," but also the asymmetrical relationship between the observer (all powerful positionality in the process), the observed-object (less powerful in the process and valued only as whatever meaning is assigned by the observer-researcher), to the production of the study (benefiting the observers, their peers, and future observers) and its intended audience/ consumers (not the objects) (Denzin & Lincoln, 2011; Erickson, 2011; Young, 2008). In this respect, the use of language and the particular word choices of early white ethnographers to describe and categorize the universal-norm from the other-subordinate reveal the power inherent in the perspectives of those who craft the narratives of what is, and what is not, knowledge worth knowing.

Alfred Young (2008) wrote,

> White ethnographers advanced the idea that subcultures were created by members of subordinate social groups contending with the difficulty of achieving the goals and desires that the larger social system considered legitimate. These goals and desires were either beyond

the means of members of the lower echelon group to achieve, or not attainable in the ways that they were for those in more privileged positions. (p. 182)

The power to claim a thing "true," label it, have it accepted and acknowledged as universal/norm/standard, and then analyze and categorize all alternative perspectives and experiences as "sub" or less than, demonstrates the dangerous nature of master narrative ideology regarding research methodology, which deserves confrontation and disruption. Many progressive educators often seek alternative epistemological and methodological ways of seeing, thinking, and acting, which can result in the disruption of oppressive political-corporate-factory models of knowledge construction and dissemination, and toward equitable learning experiences for students across the K-20 continuum (Zuberi & Bonilla-Silva, 2008).

The notion of challenging or disrupting the norms and status quo of educational narratives is needed because of the false assumptions and subsequent policies and practices that flow from so-called standards of excellence that often do not include the voices, experiences, or cultural relevance of non-white groups, and limit the perspectives of females. The raced and gendered aspects of educational norms present a flawed reality that is presented as universal, unassailable, unquestionable truth, which it ain't.

We accept and agree that a progressive, activist, critical consciousness drives our research, teaching, and service perspectives, processes, and relationships with the academy. This evolved into our development of CRiT walking as an attempt to push the language and thinking of how the legal and educational tenets of CRT and the radical, renegade, critical consciousness must go along with someone claiming the mantle of CRT scholar. Using CRT in this way highlights, as Cynthia Tyson (2003) aptly noted, "counterstories and storytelling...as a type of counterdiscourse...to examine the epistemologies of racially oppressed peoples" (p. 20). For many years, we have engaged each other as friends and colleagues in sincere conversations not only about how to conduct research and improve our teaching, but also about the much more important questions regarding why and for what purpose. We have attempted to reject the versions of superficial professional values that guide some scholars and their approach to publishing, reasons for presenting at conferences, and how some position themselves as experts for purely self-serving purposes. The values that should guide CRT scholars center on activism for collective/societal transformation and anti-racist, anti-oppressive praxis. As part of the process of collaboration, we questioned the individualistic, self-serving nature of academe that values a publication record more than the transformation of the students we teach and mentor. We have questioned how to make an impact on pushing the thinking of others to view their environments and their work in educational settings through lenses that disrupt the master narratives of the profession that often go unquestioned.

The politics of challenging faculty-related norms represent dangers that have hindered and injured both of us in various ways. For example, we have been confronted by versions of comments such as "do not get too involved with students of color because they will soak up our time" and "(y)our focus should be on getting tenure." On one level, some people might see this as good advice, yet it smacks of a false choice, as if one thing cannot exist without sacrificing the other. College students of color seek out and need role models of color and the mentoring of faculty of color. To ignore the students' needs and think we can simply return to a focus on them post-tenure adds insult to injury and contributes to the students being under-served at those institutions.

For us, broadly ignoring the needs of any student with the ready-made excuse of pursuing tenure flies in the face of what CRT represents in practice. Tyson (2003) stated, "if we are to engage in emancipatory research, we must stop trying to benefit ourselves, and engage in the process of researching for the greater good of our communities" (p. 23). The comments, assumptions, and implications to ignore students of color for faculty self-serving goals are the types of things worthy of a CRiT walk, or, in other words, systemically and metaphorically employing a counter-narrative with race as a center point of analysis, using Critical Race Theory perspectives as the central and guiding premise. By way of a short illustration of CRiT walking informed by a CRT paradigm and using storytelling, we briefly examine a few aspects of standardized testing.

## A BRIEF CRIT WALK ON STANDARDIZED TESTING

If we CRiT walk the modern landscape of high stakes, standardized testing, it is imperative to view the history of this movement, and more importantly the people behind the building of this widely accepted educational assessment. What is important to the concept of CRiT walking is to approach the topic with a CRT paradigm and interpretive framework. That means the scholar must consider CRT tenets and intentions of that approach to inherently disrupt and challenge the dominant narrative established in over 30 years of literature. Someone unfamiliar with CRT literature and without a CRT operating principle will not take into consideration the essential importance of applying the lenses of race, racism, and power toward analyzing something like the testing industrial complex.

We could stroll over to "Money Trail Drive," where the big houses of the corporate test makers and state and federal pro-privatizing education lobbyists reside. This relatively new, exclusive gated sub-division represents the bounty from windfall profits made by the standardized-testing political-industrial complex. However, instead of that interesting street, let us take a quick shortcut into the basement of the guard tower of the sub-division, called Unquestioned Educational Norms.

We go to the blueprint room of this building, looking for the history of standardized testing, and find information on Lewis M. Terman, who is considered to be the father of IQ testing. He was a professor of educational psychology at Stanford University in the early twentieth century, and advanced the work of Alfred Binet and Theodore Simon. Terman's work became known as the Stanford-Binet test and was used early on to classify children with learning disabilities. The first large-scale use of the IQ test was on American soldiers in WWI. Terman held a particular interest in "gifted" children.

Of importance to our brief afternoon CRiT walk is to notice that Terman was also an avid Eugenicist. Eugenics is a highly controversial social philosophy, used to support some of the Nazi racial ideologies, which advocates the promotion of those deemed superior and the constraints of opportunities for those deemed inferior. For example, in his book, *The Measurement of Intelligence*, published in 1916, Terman wrote:

> High-grade or border-line deficiency ... is very, very common among Spanish-Indian and Mexican families of the Southwest and also among Negroes. Their dullness seems to be racial, or at least inherent in the family from which they come .... Children of this group should be segregated into separate classes .... They cannot master abstractions but they can often be made into efficient workers ... from a eugenic point of view they constitute a grave problem because of their unusually prolific breeding. (pp. 91–92)

Upon those early foundations, other scholars, including social and psychology scientists, built most of the subsequent standardized educational measurement tests used to measure, evaluate, and classify people; their intelligence, ability to succeed, and the opportunities they deserve. In 2013, as we walk down the lanes and pathways of our schoolyards and college campuses, possibly thinking standardized testing is racially neutral and not culturally biased, it helps us to have observed some of the racial blueprints of the purpose and aims of most standardized testing processes.

To assume the processes and outcomes of standardized testing, and the profit-making industry around it, are colorblind and racially neutral helps perpetuate the dominant narratives of education and educational policies that disproportionately marginalize people of color and those from under-funded backgrounds. To understand the origins and purposes of any system (human manufactured or natural) is to shed light on how it will typically operate over time. The CRT paradigm that informs our approaches and perspectives shapes how we "see" situations (i.e., it does not have to be about standardized testing) and how we might analyze ways to discuss, deconstruct, disrupt, challenge, or perhaps value whatever is under investigation. The idea of CRiT walking is what we call this deconstruction process, and multiple storytelling approaches (e.g., vignettes, parables, poems) could represent the writing demonstration of it. In other words, it is less a specific method with rigid steps, and more an expression of the thinking (informed by paradigm) and descriptive sharing (using a range of tenets and techniques grounded in CRT).

We believe that many educational researchers have little knowledge about the racial roots of standardized testing. This is where having a CRT paradigm is critical. How can a self-proclaimed social justice educator "disrupt" the inequity inherent in the philosophy, politics, and design of the testing industrial complex, if they fail to have adequate tools to go beyond the traditional assumptions of colorblindness and researcher neutrality? What will happen in the name of disruption, if that person is perpetuating the very thing they claim to oppose? Yes, they might be doing it unconsciously, but that is the point. By naming the process CRiT walking, we are arguing that if someone adopts and accepts CRT as their paradigm, it potentially offers conscious, intentional, useful tools to problematize ways of knowing and conducting educational research that can disrupt dominant, oppressive traditions and narratives.

## PERSONAL NOTE

Sharing a CRT paradigm is a core element of our professional collaboration. Co-authoring any piece of work requires compromise, patience, humor, and the willingness to disagree in order to achieve the desired result. Because our personal lives and situations are very different, we have learned how to communicate, and sometimes not communicate, with the priority of friendship and balance of professional collaborations in mind. For both of us, our long-standing friendship is more important and valuable than any piece of writing or publication and ultimately our respect and caring for each other represents the glue that brought us together as friends and sustains our willingness to engage in co-authoring academic work.

Robin first mentioned CRiT walking many years ago in a conference talk. The earliest ideas for CRiT walking were developed in a hotel room the night before the presentation. Part of the idea came from watching a Snoop Dogg (now known as Snoop Lion) music video that highlighted "Crip walking," which is a type of dance step used by the street gang known as the Crips that originated in Compton, California. It seemed highly challenging and disruptive to the social status quo, yet was a creative expression of that particular group of young, urban males. In thinking about the academy and its elitist norms through a critical race theoretical lens and the many structurally flawed, racist origins of that system, it seemed interesting to try and blend something of the "street" with a critique of how the normative systems of the academy operate toward people of color. It became a way to theorize about dominant and master narrative approaches to research, service, teaching, mentoring, policy, and the value assigned to certain intellectual work.

The talk was provocative and was well received by the audience. The idea caught hold for us as something we could develop together. Over the years, it has gone from a few lines in a conference presentation to two publications in top-rated peer-reviewed journals. One goal we share is to continue developing the concept and finding creative applications for counter-narrative storytelling in additional publications.

My (Robin) professional experience is often wrought with encounters that re-frame and de-construct often tightly knit Eurocentric discourse and professional practice that make it impossible for me to thrive. I have often been bothered by the notion of "playing the game," which tends to imply "shut up until tenure." I have purposely chosen NOT to play "the game," and to interrupt and re-script what one might consider "the game." Since crits take seriously our commitment to communities of color and activism, I would argue, the work that any of us does is hardly considered to be a playful game. However, when one is narrowly, individually focused on self, then perhaps referencing a metaphorical game may be the appropriate terminology. More specifically, when I went up for tenure, I thought more about what I wanted to look like as a critical scholar of color. Many of the institutional indicators used to measure those productions of my research and writing that were considered scholarly or worthy of tenure had nothing to do with meaningful work that might impact communities of color. I received con-siderable pushback when I mentioned this to faculty colleagues and even more pushback when I refused to take the usual route towards tenure. Eventually, sev-eral of my colleagues and I worked intensively for more than a year to put forth a statement of scholarly values that more clearly articulated scholarship, service, and teaching in our discipline and our intentional work with communities of color. My work specifically included direct collaboration with government agencies, black community-based organizations, and local non-profit educational-oriented com-munity organizations. It was and remains important that I engage in work that is important to and connected with the communities in which I live. If the tenure guidelines exclude such work, then it is up to us (critically conscious scholars) to turn that policy on its head, wrestle with new policy that indeed rebukes systemic racism and institutional bias, and rewrite an exclusive, elitist academic script.

The broader ideas of critical race studies, CRT, and CRiT walking have di-rectly informed Mark's journey as a faculty member. The concepts help me con-nect the dots between the importance of mentoring students, especially students of color, even when "advised" by well-meaning white senior colleagues that doing so could hinder professional progress. The concepts consistently inform my ap-proach to teaching, service choices, and scholarship interests. What those senior colleagues fail to see is the essential, and historical, responsibility I accept as a critically consciousness faculty member of color to find ways to balance giving back to others. I am constantly recognizing how I stand on the shoulders of those who paved the way for me, grounding my teaching and research in the African American experience, and my own professional aspirations and expectations. The paradigm that informs my actions permits me to look for and walk my professional path with the recognition of the racial context of being a black man in academic spaces where people who look like me and who are from my working class background are not well-represented. I use that interpretive framework to bring creativity into my teaching and writing as much as possible, and to remain aware of and vigilant against systemic racism.

## CONCLUSION

CRiT walking can evoke a word-picture and creative metaphors aligned with the counter-narrative storytelling elements advocated by CRT. It can promote conceptual thinking through complex educational issues and situations, while avoiding the master narrative trappings of colorblind, race-neutral research assumptions and methodologies. For example, in a university classroom, faculty (who are grounded in CRT and critical-race-studies perspectives) could use the concept of CRiT walking to help students understand the connective roadmap and/or steps of the school-to-prison pipeline. That could be accomplished by using CRT as a primary guiding lens to review and understand data, and examining the social and cultural stages of biased treatment, racist and punitive actions, and eventual consequences that repeatedly push many black males into and through a school's disciplinary system, which often has a devastating impact on their lives and psyches. Those early school experiences can also lead toward a juvenile criminal record and, possibly, encounters with adult criminal court systems. Another brief example is relevant to how educational researchers might use CRiT walking.

What happens when a researcher who considers themselves a proponent of social justice principles fails to connect the dots between systemic racism and their work on student achievement, retention, financial aid, or effective teaching strategies? Because they might not have the paradigm to see the importance of racial dynamics, they fail to provide the conceptual thinking, or CRiT walking, to deconstruct the historical context that shapes the current condition or situation under investigation. Another example is if an educational researcher who studied African American males used and applied CRT and CRiT walking, they could understand more context and cover the landscape of law enforcement policies such as stop-and-frisk to examine the ripple effect of racial stigma and the impact criminalization has on school- or college-age black males. It is not always obvious to connect the dots on historical and cultural contexts, and how incidents that happen in the community and in people's daily lives are directly tied to the educational enterprise. We name the thinking and writing as CRiT walking to make those connections, and demonstrate them in creative ways. It could apply to any number of areas of research foci for education scholars, such as the connections between stop-and-frisk, racialized criminalization, and educational performance. It is difficult to see the connections, let alone write about them in ways that are inherently disruptive to master educational narratives, unless the researchers are equipped with the paradigm and tools that lend themselves to that work.

Disrupting master narratives regarding issues around race and racism in educational contexts requires persistent activism, including resistance to oppressive norms and advocacy for people whose "faces are at the bottom of the well" (Bell, 1992). Most of that activism, maybe the hardest kind, is the work we must do on ourselves as educators-scholars. Critical Race Theory and its many progressive, evolving, related perspectives represent such activism. This work lends itself to the work of change agents inside and outside of (K-20) classrooms. We suggest that anyone who wishes to claim CRT positionality do so beyond his or her words but also with their deeds (i.e., reflected in their teaching, research, and writing,). Disruption of dominant, hegemonic systems requires activism that often extends beyond a robust publication record. It requires levels of faith and fearlessness, not necessarily recklessness, in the name of making change. Educational scholars cannot proclaim ourselves as change-agents but never risk anything, never venture outside of assigned spaces that traditionally hamper change, and not seek ways to engage in direct action through critical pedagogy, community service, mentoring, and speaking truth to power. However, the challenge for many engaged in this work in the foreseeable future is to not become complacent or seduced by the rewards and trappings of "acceptance" and "affirmation" by the majoritarian forces and/or institutional structures and systems that stand firmly by old biases dressed up in new-fangled, technologically driven, or superficial pronouncements, programs, or policies.

We should remain vigilant with those who regularly use the language, ideology, and tools that have traditionally blocked change along the lines of racial, ethnic, or gender representation in academic departments or administrative ranks, and blocked change in the curriculum, policies, and practices that might help the masses of students, especially students of color (K-20). Critical Race Theory represents one tool of disruption to that master-dominant paradigm in education and legal studies. We have witnessed the cooptation and appropriation of this transformative work and perspectives by some who quickly proclaim that "they" are not racist, sexist, or against meaningful and substantive "diversity," yet they maintain the status quo as if it is equitable, unbiased, and colorblind. We wish to echo the warning of Audre Lorde (1984) regarding the master's tools not created to dismantle the master's house. In addition, we should remember the lessons from so many children's stories about the inherent dangers of accepting and eating the apples, cookies, or candy given by those who might appear nice and beautiful, but who otherwise cause harm, even though they promise the rewards of entering "their" house (i.e., ways of knowing, seeing, and thinking). We must apply critical consciousness to our work, to our settings, and to the larger goals of social justice.

CRiT walking is about understanding and applying CRT-grounded perspectives and interpretive frameworks and techniques, especially into storytelling as counter-narrative, to research endeavors that focus on race, racism, and power. In this way, it is accessible to those who have a solid understanding of what CRT represents for educational scholars who wish to disrupt master narratives in a variety of settings.

A few years ago, at a Critical Race Studies in Education Conference, the issue of fear came up in a large group discussion. Several scholars noted how they agreed with the ideas represented in CRT and wanted to use them. However, they feared repercussions from mentors, journal editors, and faculty colleagues. Some of them mentioned that after they earned tenure, they would advocate for racial justice using perspectives such as CRT, but until then, they felt it was safer to "go along to get along." As a few others echoed that same sentiment, several noted CRT scholars began speaking up and stated that if anyone was looking for or trusting the mythology of being safe, they should avoid CRT.

CRT is not focused on being safe, but on speaking truth to power, which has inherent dangers because it is inherently disruptive to the dominant, master narratives of educational systems and the institutionalized racism, sexism, and classism that represents the status quo. The civil rights movement advanced tremendous positive changes in American life. Activists who did not always agree on method, outcome, or pace of results, marched and protested in different ways. They raised their voices for justice even when scared, standing up for their dignity only to get fired from jobs. They marched, held sit-ins, and suffered being kicked out of school, confronted arrest, bodily injury, and possible death in order to make change for the generations that followed.

We (Mark and Robin), as representative of the generation born in the early 1960s who benefited from the social justice soldiers' sacrifice, regularly discuss our work and professional lives within a larger context of American history, especially its racial history. How could we possibly compartmentalize ourselves from it? Without a paradigm that includes those complex elements, maybe we would not see the obligations and responsibilities to contribute to the larger project of making change, disrupting the master narratives created from systems of oppression and bias. Perhaps to research and write about issues related to race and racism does require a certain amount of courage, and maybe it requires a certain amount of critical consciousness too? We encourage undergraduate and graduate students, faculty, and administrators to have the courage of their convictions to advance social and racial justice, bring light to hidden or less investigated topics, walk with confidence across campuses, into the classroom, into controversial research areas, and demonstrate that walk in the work we do.

## REFERENCES

Alexander, M. (2010). *The new Jim Crow: Mass incarceration in the age of colorblindness*. New York, NY: The New Press.

Anderson, S. L., Attwood, P. F., & Howard, L. C. (Eds.). (2004). *Facing racism in education.* Cambridge, MA: Harvard Education Publishing Group.

Ani, M. (1995). *Yurugu: An African-centered critique of European cultural thought and behavior.* Trenton, NJ: Africa World Press.

Bell, D. (1987). *And we are not saved: The Elusive quest for racial justice.* New York, NY: Basic Books.

Bell, D. (1992). *Faces at the bottom of the well: The permanence of racism.* New York, NY: Basic Books.

Bell, D. A. (2009). Who's afraid of Critical Race Theory? In E. Taylor, D. Gillborn, & G. Ladson-Billings (Eds.). *Foundations of Critical Race Theory in education* (pp. 37–50). New York, NY: Routledge.

Brayboy, B. M. J. (2005). Toward a tribal Critical Race Theory in education. *The Urban Review, 37*(5), 425–446.

Carter, M. (2003). Telling tales out of school: "What's the fate of a black story in a white world of white stories?" In G. R. Lopez & L. Parker (Eds.). *Interrogating racism in qualitative research methodology* (pp. 29–48). New York, NY: Peter Lang.

Darling-Hammond, L. (2010). *The flat world and education: How America's commitment to equity will determine our future.* New York, NY: Teachers College Press.

Delgado, R., & Stefancic, J. (2001). Critical Race Theory: An introduction. New York, NY: New York University Press.

Delgado, R. (2011). Rodrigo's reconsideration: Intersectionality and the future of Critical Race Theory. *Iowa Law Review, 96*(4), 1247–1288.

Denzin, N. K., Lincoln, Y. S. (Eds.). (2011). *The Sage handbook of qualitative research* (4th ed.). Thousand Oaks, CA: Sage.

Dixson, A. D., & Rousseau, C. K. (Eds.). (2006). *Critical Race Theory in education: All God's children got a song.* New York, NY: Routledge.

Erickson, F. (2011). A history of qualitative inquiry in social and educational research. In N. K. Denzin, Y. S. Lincoln (Eds.), *The Sage handbook of qualitative research* (4th ed.). (pp. 43–60).

Feagin, J. R. (2006). *Systemic racism: A theory of oppression.* New York, NY: Routledge.

Giles, M. S., & Hughes, R. L. (2009). CRiT walking race, place, and space in the academy. *International Journal of Qualitative Studies in Education, 22*(6), 687–696.

Hale, J. E. (2001). *Learning while black: Creating educational excellence for African American children.* Baltimore, MD: The Johns Hopkins University Press.

Hughes, R. L., & Giles, M. S. (2010). CRiT walking in higher education: Activating Critical Race Theory in the academy. *Race, Ethnicity & Education, 13*(1), 41–57.

James, A. (2008). Making sense of race and racial classification. In T. Zuberi & E. Bonilla-Silva (Eds.), *White logic, white methods: Racism and methodology* (pp. 31–45). Lanham, MD: Rowman & Littlefield.

Kunjufu, J. (2005). *Keeping black boys out of special education.* Chicago, IL: African American Images.

Ladson-Billings, G., & Tate, W. F. (1995). Towards a Critical Race Theory of education. *Teachers College Record, 97*(1), 47–68.

Lazos Vargas, S. R. (2003). Critical Race Theory in education: Theory, praxis, and recommendations. In G. R. Lopez & L. Parker (Eds.), *Interrogating racism in qualitative research methodology*
(pp. 1–18). New York, NY: Peter Lang.

Lorde, A. (1984). *Sister outsider: Essays and speeches by Audre Lorde.* Freedom, CA: Crossing Press.

Matsuda, M. J., Lawrence, C. R., Delgado, R., & Williams Crenshaw, K. (1993). *Words that wound:
Critical Race Theory, assaultive speech, and the First Amendment.* Boulder, CO: Westview Press.

McCarthy, C., Crichlow, W., Dimitriadia, G., & Dolby, N. (2005). *Race identity, and representation in
education* (2nd ed.). New York, NY: Taylor & Francis Group.

McLaren, P., & Kincheloe, J. L. (2007). *Critical pedagogy: Where are we now?* New York, NY:
Peter Lang.

Noguera, P. A. (2008). *The trouble with black boys: And other reflections on race, equity, and the future of
public education.* San Francisco, CA: Jossey-Bass.

Obakeng-Mabokela, R., & Green, A. L. (Eds.). (2001). *Sisters of the academy: Emergent black women
scholars in higher education.* Sterling, VA: Stylus.

Roithmayr, D. (1999). Introduction to Critical Race Theory in educational research and praxis. In
L. Parker, D. Deyhle, & S. Villenas (Eds.), *Race is...race isn't: Critical Race Theory and qualitative
studies in education.* Boulder, CO: Westview Press.

Shabazz, A. (2004). *Advancing democracy: African Americans and the struggle for access and equity in
higher education in Texas.* Chapel Hill, NC: The University of North Carolina Press.

Solórzano, D. G., & Yosso, T. J. (2001). Critical Race Theory and LatCrit theory and method: Counter-
storytelling. *International Journal of Qualitative Studies in Education, 14*(4), 471–495.

Solórzano, D. G., & Yosso, T. J. (2002). Critical race methodology: Counter-storytelling as an analytical
framework for education research. *Qualitative Inquiry, 8*(1), 23–44.

Taylor, E., Gillborn, D., & Ladson-Billings, G. (Eds.). (2009). *Foundations of Critical Race Theory in
education.* New York, NY: Routledge.

Trucios-Haynes, E. (2001). Why "Race matters:" LatCrit theory and Latina/o racial identity. *La Raza
Law Journal, 12*(1), 1–42.

Tyson, C. (2003). Research, race, and an epistemology of emancipation. In G. R. Lopez & L. Parker
(Eds.), *Interrogating racism in qualitative research methodology* (19–28). New York, NY: Peter Lang.

Washington, H. A. (2008). *Medical apartheid: The dark history of medical experimentation on black
Americans from colonial times to the present.* New York, NY: Knopf Doubleday.

Wing, A. K. (Ed.). (1997). *Critical race feminism: A reader.* New York, NY: New York University Press.

Wise, T. J. (2005). *Affirmative action: Racial preference in black and white.* New York, NY: Routledge.

Yosso, T. J. (March 2005). Whose culture has capital? A Critical Race Theory discussion of community cultural wealth. *Race Ethnicity and Education, 8*(1), 69–91.

Young, A. A. (2008). White ethnographers on the experiences of African American men. In T. Zuberi
& E. Bonilla-Silva (Eds.), *White logic, white methods: Racism and methodology* (pp. 179–200).
Lanham, MD: Rowman & Littlefield.

Zinn, H. (2005). *A people's history of the United States, 1492–present.* New York, NY: Harper Perennial
Modern Classics.

Zuberi, T., & Bonilla-Silva, E. (Eds.). (2008). *White logic, white methods: Racism and methodology.*
Lanham, MD: Rowman & Littlefield.

## ADDITIONAL RESOURCES

Center for the Study of Race and Democracy
 http://as.tufts.edu/csrd/
Centre for Research in Race and Education
www.birmingham.ac.uk
Critical Race Studies in Education Association
www.crseassoc.org
Race Ethnicity and Education Journal
www.tandfonline.com

# CHAPTER FIVE

# Always Already Inquiry

## A/r/tography as a Disruptive Methodology

NICOLE M. POURCHIER AND TERI HOLBROOK

> To engage in a living inquiry is to learn to let go, to leave the spurious safety of Research—
> that crumbling roof over Education that often separated us from life and rarely protected
> us anyway—and to enter an open field, ears and wings bristling. (Neilsen, 2008, p. xvi.)

As qualitative researchers engaged in living inquiry, we have a felt sense of Lorri Neilsen's[1] bristling wings. When we read her words, the pores in our skin tighten, the muscles in our shoulder blades contract, the hairs on our arms lift; we are ready to take flight. And yet, the word *bristling* conjures up more than the excitement of threshing over an open field. Bristling is also to fume and to agitate. In its subtext is the need to mourn and yearn. When, as educational researchers, we take flight in the manner in which which Neilsen urged, we move aloft while also steeling ourselves for what we will see from the air.

What we will see—as Neilsen inferred, and others (e.g., St. Pierre & Pillow, 2000) have evoked—are the ruins of research-as-usual. Within the education field, certain research methods have attained a privileged status through their claims to produce valid, generalizable, and replicable results, despite oppositional efforts to question what is lost in the processes of measuring, normalizing, and reporting. The very notion of measuring implies stasis, containment, stillness, concepts that do not fit well with the human experiences of learning. As (Neilsen, 2008) further noted, "the basis of [research and teaching] is change; to arrest these processes is to reject their *duende*, their spirit" (p. xv).

In this chapter, we present how a/r/tography—an approach to being and in-quiring in the world as artist/researcher/teacher—offers to us as bristling scholars new possibilities for constructing and disseminating knowledge about educational phenomena. A/r/tographic inquirers embrace multiple identities, and the slashes in a/r/tography recognize that an identity cannot be parsed and bracketed. Instead, multiple aspects fold into each other to create a/r/tographers who understand the world through their individual and collective experiences as artists, researchers, and teachers. A/r/tography defies a concise definition; instead, it is "arts-based research as enacted living inquiry" in which an artist/researcher/teacher

> inquire[s] in the world through a process of art making and writing. It is a process of double imaging that includes the creation of art and words that are not separate or illustrative of each other but instead, as interconnected and woven through each other to create addition-al meanings. (Springgay, Irwin, & Kind, 2005, p. 899)

We begin with the philosophical underpinnings of a/r/tography, situated within the larger movement of an arts-based educational research (ABER) field that seeks to incorporate art—comprising such expressive practices as image-making, dance, drama, music, poetry, creative writing, and multime-dia—into how research is conducted and represented. Next, we discuss how we see a/r/tography as a disruptive move in the construction and dissemination of educational research. We share how we use a/r/tography in our work through specific examples of our own living inquiries as a/r/tists. In closing, we issue an invitation to others to take up methods of inquiry that allow for "reflectiv-ity, insightfulness, and imaginative aesthetic transaction" (Gouzouasis, 2008, p. 231) in an effort "to learn to let go" (Neilsen, 2008, p. xvi.) and make possible other ways of producing and using knowledge constructed through educational research.

## THEORETICAL UNDERPINNINGS

Researchers have grappled with how best to conceptualize the various stances and perspectives exhibited within qualitative research. Carolyn Ellis and Arthur Bochner (2009) depicted the field of qualitative research as a continuum with a span of perspectives that range from concepts based on objectivity, validity, replication, and generalizability to postmodern/poststructural arguments that question these concepts and the researcher's ability to know. Within the spectrum, qualitative theories compete, overtake, merge, and evolve as they operate between poles of extremes. Patti Lather (2006) called for a complicated construction of research perspectives, maintaining that a welcomed "profusion" of paradigms made for a "less comfortable social science" with spaces for alternative research practices

(p. 52). She and Elizabeth St. Pierre offered a "paradigm mapping" that situated research theories and discourses within the broad paradigmatic practices of *predict, understand, emancipate, deconstruct* and *next?* Within this model, qualitative research occurs in and across paradigms, from mixed methods approaches that *predict,* to participatory action research that works across *understanding* and *emancipating* paradigms, to citizen inquiry practices currently emerging as *next?* The aim of mappings, Lather maintained, is to "trouble tidy binaries" and push against progressive (with a small p) desire for "'consensus' approaches" to research. Thus, mappings illuminate the "play" between existing, dominant knowledges and those that are emerging, thus recognizing the intellectual and creative possibilities—and accompanying wariness—to be found among a variety of "epistemological homes" (pp. 36–41).

Arts-based educational research is itself a field of/in play, holding as it does research practices and perspectives that span and transgress epistemological homes. Art education scholar Elliot Eisner (1997) advocated for an early vision of "knowledge as process" (p. 7) in opposition to the emphasis on hard data and facts associated with scientific research in education. The arts, Eisner (2008) wrote, provide "an approach to educational research that rely upon the imaginative and expressive crafting of a form in ways that enlarge our understanding of what [is] going on" (p. 18). This stance, common within arts-based educational research, situates the arts as ways of making sense of and meaning from the world. In keeping with Lather's (2006) notions of paradigmatic proliferation, the field of arts-based educational research contains a variety of practices supported by varying and shifting epistemologies. Examples include research studies in which art-making practices are the focus of study (e.g., Albers, Frederick, & Cowan, 2009); visual art techniques are used to capture data (e.g., Emmison & Smith, 2000; Pink, 2007); art-making techniques are used to represent findings (e.g., Glesne, 1997; Richardson, 1997); and art is seen as a method of inquiry through which researchers articulate tentative, partial, and contingent understandings of their worlds. This last category describes a/r/tography, where we situate our own work.

As an approach to inquiry, a/r/tography emerges amidst theoretical underpinnings that take up St. Pierre's (1997) call to "produce different knowledge and to produce knowledge differently" (p. 175). William Pinar (2004) noted that a/r/tography takes up both phenomenological and poststructural aspects in its pursuit of "deep meaning" within aesthetic practices that "[integrate] knowing, doing, and making" (p. 9). In conceptualizing a/r/tography, Rita Irwin and Stephanie Springgay (2008a) noted that it draws upon "philosophy, phenomenology, educational action research, feminist theories, and contemporary art criticism"; it operates in the "in-between" of these discourses and in the juxtaposed and "simultaneous use of language, images, materials, situations, space, and time" (pp. 105–106). As a methodology, they continued, a/r/tography is rhizomatic in the Deleuzian sense, taking place in mutating and interstitial spaces where binaries are nonsensical and where disruption, rupture, interrogation are normative rites. The goal of a/r/tography is not to interpret theory and data as objects to be named and described but rather to complicate understandings. Located in the in-between, a/r/tography "intentionally unsettles perception and knowing" (p. 107).

This unsettling occurs within what Irwin and Springgay (2008b) emphasized as a kind of understanding that is relational, embodied, and contingent. Therefore, a/r/tographers draw upon personal experiences as they work through the arts to question, ponder, and theorize new questions and possibilities. Much a/r/tographic work is autoethnographic in some fashion, adhering to a stance of "research [as] storytelling, thus the more stories told, the greater our fullness of understanding" (Sameshima, 2008, p. 52). Although a/r/tography is open to multiple theoretical perspectives, it supports several pertinent stances about how humans experience the world and generate and communicate knowledge through these experiences. We hesitate to label specific underpinnings that are accepted by all a/r/tographers, but rather acknowledge three theoretical positions that have been put forth by a/r/tographers and that we take up in our work.

## Embodiment

Springgay (2008) posited that a/r/tography "constructs the very materiality it attempts to represent" (p. 159), making artistic practices forms of research. Therefore, a/r/tography conceptualizes knowledge as emerging through the body's senses as it interacts with others and the world. Whereas, "'I see' is commonly understood to mean 'I know'" a/r/tography offers an "approach to understanding through touch [that] reconfigures the ways in which we perceive objects, providing access to depth and surface, inside and outside" (Irwin & Springgay, 2008b, p. xxi). As artists use art as a method to understand their worlds, a/r/tography becomes both a "methodological and ontological strategy—one that is reflective of the ongoing practices of identification" (Springgay, 2008, p. 160) that occur through the processes of using bodies/minds to create a/r/t. But a/r/tography also maintains that meaning resides between things, which leads to a second theoretical position from which a/r/tists understand the world.

## Relationality

Irwin and Springgay (2008) explained that "a/r/tography resides in this intercorporeal space, and attends to the forms and folds of living bodies" (p. xxii). These bodies are not isolated, but connected, which leads to "thinking that reflects on inter-embodiment, on being(s)-in-relation, and communities of practice" (p. xxii). Thus, a/r/tography is an approach to inquiry that understands meaning making as relational encounters between bodies and things. It follows that "research becomes a process of exchange that is not separated from the body but emerges through an intertwining of mind and body, self and other, and through our interactions with the world" (p. xxii). A/r/tographers theorize to understand through their a/r/t and share these understandings with others, but they acknowledge these understandings as contingent ideas that feed an artistic desire for proliferate questioning. These positions lead to a third assumption about how knowledge works: contingency.

## Contingency

A/r/tography takes on an "active stance to knowledge creation through questioning [that] informs practices" (Irwin & Springgay, 2008b, p. xxiii) and this active stance entails an understanding of knowledge as contingent. Elizabeth Ellsworth (2005) described knowledge as constantly "in the making" (p. 2), and a/r/tographers take up this perspective as they maintain that meaning must be both celebrated and interrogated (Irwin & Springgay, 2008b, p. xxix). A/r/tographic meaning is "created as contradictions and resistances are faced, even interfaced with other knowledge. Meanings are negotiated by, with, and among a/r/tographers as well as with their audiences" (p. xxx). When knowledge is understood as contingent, research becomes an always unsettled site where findings cannot be named or even desired. Instead, through imagination and conjecture, the work of a/r/tographic research is "to provoke, to generate, and to un/do meaning" (Springgay, 2008, p. 161). The aim of a/r/tography, then, is not to produce texts where "thought is stored" but instead to convey inquiry as "an embodied, living space" where meaning-making is in an ongoing state of hesitancy and displacement (p. 160).

In addition to its notions of embodiment, relationality, and contingency, a/r/tography offers other concepts, known as renderings, through which a/r/tographers make other (contingent) understandings. These renderings are preferred over the prescribed criteria associated with *methods* (Irwin & Springgay, 2008b, p. xxviii):

- *Contiguity* references the in-between spaces of folded identities of artist-researcher-teacher and forms of expression that include art forms and theoretical writing. Contiguity places a/r/tographers in relation to others through their questions, experiences, and understandings.
- *Living inquiry* describes a way of being in the world through a life of questing, questioning, and inquiring.
- *Openings* are often accessed through questions that enable artists to confront what is known and not known.

- *Metaphor/metonymy* speaks to how artists understand by making connections between concepts through metaphors, which offer new frameworks for understandings.
- *Reverberations* are movements that materialize within and from a/r/tographic works and lead a/r/tographers toward deeper, tentative meanings.
- *Excess* speaks of practices that are outside the commonplace and are intended to be provocative, often leading to transformations. (pp. xxvii–xxxi)

Artists, researchers, and teachers interested in a/r/tography should understand that renderings are not required criteria for a/r/tographic works but instead offer multiple possibilities for inquiries situated within notions of *unstable, ongoing,* and *in-between.* These theoretical positions and renderings vibrate through a/r/tographic work and provide the motif through which a/r/tography becomes a disruptive methodology.

## A STORY OF A/R/TOGRAPHIC RESEARCH

As qualitative researchers, we came to a/r/tography gradually. We met as a new assistant professor (Teri) and doctoral student (Nicole), seeing ourselves as literacy scholars in the making with a focus on multi-genre, multimodal composition. In our work, we used art-making and creative writing produced by and with participants as data and included multi-genre writing and original images in our published articles (e.g., Holbrook, 2010). Nevertheless, we felt a quiet pressure to minimize such research, or at least to limit our focus to participant-produced creative texts that would be the object of our inquiries. We heard the message that in order to be recognized as educational researchers, we needed to turn away from ourselves, objectify the work of others, and produce traditionally crafted research reports—albeit about art and literacy—in conventionally recognized academic structures.

We were restless. Reared by parents who were visual artists—we are both the daughters of painters—we grew up in homes in which art-making constituted everyday practices. Nicole took up collage as a child, using it early in life to communicate her understanding of her world, and Teri was a creative writer from first grade on; she can still remember the day when, as a six-year-old, she decided to "become" a novelist, and the heady confidence the announcement gave her. When we entered the field of educational research, the expectation that we would put aside our artistic tools did not make (embodied) *sense.* What we "knew" as creative writers and artists about the meaning we made conflicted with what we practiced as qualitative researchers, even qualitative researchers using arts-based methods. What we knew as writers and artists was what anthropologist Clifford Geertz (1973) termed the fictions of social science writings—"fictions, in the sense that they are 'something made,' 'something fashioned'—the original meaning of *ficti*—not that they are false, unfactual, or merely 'as if' thought experiments" (p. 15). Culture, Geertz noted, may exist in the actions and products of a people, but "anthropology exists in the book, the article, the lecture, the museum display, or, sometimes nowadays, the film" (1973, p. 16). That is, texts are constructed through a variety of discursive languages, with researchers and their teams as the designers and builders.

But Geertz's (1973) remedy—thick description of research data—also left us discontented. We wondered with St. Pierre's (1997) questions: "Yet how can language, which regularly falls apart, secure meaning and truth? How can language provide the evidentiary warrant for the production of knowledge in a postmodern world?" (p. 179). St. Pierre may have pointed to words in her critique, but we stretched language to mean any communicative and expressive mode and found the same questions applied. Words/images/sounds/gestures: as communicative means they regularly fell apart. We wondered if our carefully collected data based on study participants—the transcripts, field notes, memos, photographs, drawings—that we cut up, coded, collapsed, and categorized in the conventional practices of our field had limited tensile strength. Through neither our words nor our images could we create "one-to-one correspondence between lives lived and lives represented" (Cole & Knowles, 2001, pp. 212–213). Instead of ignoring our discontent, we decided to move into it. Eisner (2008) described research tensions as "a feeling of mild discomfort … that can be temporarily relieved through inquiry … a sense of uncertainty about one's work." These tensions, he reminded, while uncomfortable, "can also be motivating, and … evoke a sense of vitality." The aim for the arts-based researcher is to work with and through tensions to create work that is "either theoretically cogent or practically useful" (Eisner, 2008, p. 17). But for us, the tensions—arising from ideas about researching others and the myths of an objective, reliable, and replicable science—were not mild, and they could not be relieved through the kinds of inquiry we found ourselves tasked with as early career academics. We recognized in our work elements of fictions, factions, and frictions (Gouzouasis, 2008). We found ourselves pushing against commonplace notions in our field—the design of research projects that cordoned off the researcher and the researched, the assertion that researchers could comprehend the experiences of an other and lend voice to those perspectives, conceptions of knowledge as information that could be discovered or found. We also challenged practices that would have us create boundaries within ourselves, separating as a matter of assumption the artist, researcher, and teacher roles that were inseparable within us (Holbrook & Pourchier, 2012). We troubled our own practices of conventional qualitative research—techniques of interviewing, observing, coding, representing that we did as a matter of course and training—recognizing in them what St. Pierre (2011) has called "conventional humanist qualitative methodology" that circulates among dominant notions of research design and data analysis (p. 211). In addition, we called into question institutional structures that pushed us as researchers toward single authorship at the expense of collaboration; privileged print, expository texts over other expressive forms; sought generalizable knowledge at the expense of knowledge constructed around the singular and specific; and promoted sanctioned over what Foucault (1980) termed "disqualified knowledges"—those knowledges that are "particular, local, regional, … incapable of unanimity" (p. 82).

As we worked through and with these tensions, we committed ourselves to reading arts-based educational research, and thus came to a/r/tography, which opened up possibilities that did indeed evoke for us Eisner's sense of vitality. A/r/tography positioned research as living inquiry, where tentative knowledge was made through "theory-as-practice-as-process-as-complication" (Irwin & Springgay, 2008a, p. 107) and where a variety of materials and mediums were valued as both expressive and investigative instruments. Thinking and practicing with a/r/tography, we found space and theoretical support for operating as artist/researcher/teacher in the expression of contingent knowledge, developed over time and across locations, in relation with others, and derived through and communicated in multiple modes.

Irwin and Springgay (2008b) cautioned against "a linear [or] rigid structure through which one could define a/r/tography," arguing instead that "a/r/tographical research is not subject to standardized criteria, rather it remains dynamic, fluid, and in constant motion" (p. xix). Similarly, St. Pierre (2011), writing about post philosophies in general, noted that such perspectives do not offer "a recipe, an outline, a structure … another handy 'research design' in which one can safely secure oneself and one's work" (p. 613). Since a/r/tography is a form of action research, it necessarily includes researcher reflection and is often narrative. What we offer next, therefore, is a narrative of how we came to see our work as a/r/tography—relational and ethical living inquiry that is "concerned with self-study, being in community" (Irwin & Springgay, 2008b, p. xix). We cannot offer a recipe, a pattern to follow or a design to mimic. Instead, we offer the ongoing "story" of our questing—rhizomatic, in-between, both singular and collaborative.

## TWO A/R/TOGRAPHERS' BEGINNINGS

Our encounters with a/r/tography began when our paths crossed at Georgia State University in 2008. Teri was a newly hired assistant professor with a focus on multimodal and digital literacy, and Nicole was a doctoral student just beginning to explore the role of her artistic practices in pedagogy and research. We had not yet named what we were doing, but we were engaged in the sort of "relational learning" that Irwin and Springgay (2008) described as constitutive of an approach to inquiry where a/r/tists "are able to engage in independent and socially transforma-tive activities by theorizing practice" (p. xxiv). We met regularly to talk about ped-agogy; as visual artists, writers, and literacy researchers, much of our discussions had to do with the relationships between the arts and how language is learned, practiced and taught. Looking back on these discussions, we were "always already" (Derrida, 1976/1997) a/r/tographers engaged in living inquiry and were asking questions about how our artistic practices informed our theories about how stu-dents learn and how we should be teaching them. These early questions led us to collaborate in writing staff developments where we invited inservice teachers into multimodal writing experiences, and on to other endeavors to craft opportunities for our preservice teachers to engage in literacy practices that reached beyond stan-dard notions of reading and writing words.

Uncounted hours passed at local coffee shops as we reflected on our teach-ing, asking questions about how our theoretical perspectives inform our peda-gogy and how we theorized through both our teaching and artistic practices. During this same time, we were taking classes at a local art college, immersing ourselves in the discourse of visual expressive forms and developing our skills. Two questions permeated and continue to drive our discussions around the im-portance of what we do as artists within the context of our roles as researchers and teachers:

> What is it about the practices of art-making, teaching, and research that informs how we think and act as each and all of those positions?

> How can our research be conceptualized as a/r/tistic spaces?

We never anticipated nailing down a solid answer to either of these questions but rather recognized (and still recognize) them as a/r/tographic openings that enable us to "give [our] attention to what is seen and known and what is not seen and not known" (Irwin & Springgay, 2008b, p. xxx). Each time we attempt to answer these questions, or dare to put these answers into writing, we experience "at once a loss of meaning, a realization of meaning, or neither" (p. xxx). In lieu of nailing down an answer, we each briefly provide illustrations of work we've created in the process of a/r/tographic research in hopes of articulating a value we see in our work as artist/researcher/teacher.

## BREACHES OF NARRATIVE ORDER—TERI

For more than a decade, I've made regular visits to Eastern State Penitentiary, a nineteenth-century historical prison in Philadelphia. I went there first as a tourist, children and spouse in tow, but was drawn back as an inquirer. It truly was a calling of space-to-body, as if the very paint peeled/pealed out my name. I see this space as an architectural metaphor through which to explore how poststructural theory plays out in the world around me, specifically at the intersections of education, disabilities, and text creation. As a member of a family with learning disabilities, I've taken up architectural elements and imagery—doors, windows, walls, roofs, floors, pipes, bricks, plaster, etc.,—to help theorize the disciplining forces active in educational and other institutional settings that make it possible to label some people disabled and others not. During photography trips to Eastern State Penitentiary and other historical institutional sites, I make images of architectural elements. I later create collages by layering whole and partial photos with fragments of various print texts—old letters, official documents—and my research journals, which include autoethnographic interview transcripts; notes on my text creation processes; reflective notes about art making, research, and teaching; written commentary about readings of Foucault, Deleuze and other poststructural theorists, as well as researchers in the fields of literacy, disability studies, art theory, and geography. The purpose of these juxtapositions is to expand and alter my ongoing conceptions of "normal," including the normative constructions of qualitative research and academic texts.

Figure 5.1 uses the following data: photographs from Eastern State Penitentiary and the Carlisle Indian Industrial School (a historic site where Native American children from 1879–1918 were relocated with the intent, according to the wall text at the Cumberland County PA Historical Society, of erasing their "indianness"; prints of photos from national archives and public domain sites; old documents; and excerpts from my research journals. Working within a grid, I segmented a 6'×3' sheet of wood into even sections or "cells." Each cell contains a separate collage, juxtaposing data related to authority, discipline, time, space, and flight. The title of this piece is "Cells as perverse breach" in reference to art theorist Thomas Brockelman's discussion of the work by twentieth-century collagist Kurt Schwitters as "a kind of perverse breach in narrative order" (Brockelman, 2001, p. 51). By exploring the role of written texts and other writerly constructs in the creation of categories related to ability, I see my inquiries as perverse breaches that impact my thinking about literacy and education at my own cellular level.

## INTO THE DARKROOM—NICOLE

I spent a year volunteering at a mission center in a low-income community, a place where I felt drawn to confront issues of difference, power, and privilege. During this time, I worked with children and teenagers in various ways: tutoring, mentoring, and doing art. I quickly became known as the "the art lady," and the children were always anxious to see what we would be making next. As a literacy researcher my mind was immediately drawn to the mission center as a potential research site,

Fig 5.1 Cells as perverse breach.

but the thought of shifting my role from "art lady" to researcher made me uncomfortable. The mission center and its role in the community was a researcher's dream, ripe with questions and data, not to mention the access I had obtained. But when I recognized that I could not bring myself to collect data in that space, I turned inward and focused on my art.

Immediately, I enrolled in a photography course at a local art college and started taking pictures. I didn't photograph the people I met or worked with at the mission center because my lens was drawn to objects—the things around me that I missed when I was constantly zoomed in on others. I spent several months photographing the objects and textures that surrounded me on the paths I frequently traveled at work, at home, and at the mission center. Slowly, the photographic process became a metaphor that enabled me to theorize about the tensions I felt when I thought about researching in a space where I had developed personal relationships with others.

Figure 5.2 is an excerpt from a short film I crafted to develop the metaphor of research as art. I created and photographed a mock darkroom where I staged and manipulated scenes that represented the photographic process. This collection of images became materials that I drew upon to craft a film that I titled "Into the Darkroom." The film—a series of photographs inscribed with pieces of my creative writing—was my representation of how I understand research as art. Thinking through this space pushed me to use different language to articulate the sense of voyeurism I felt when researching others, as well as a creative way to represent how knowledge is fabricated in pursuit of scientism. When I allowed my research practices to be filtered through my artistic perspectives, I found that I was able to capture exposures: images that I edited, cropped, processed, and developed into a/r/tistic knowledge.

Through our ongoing, always already quests, the renderings of a/r/tography become apparent. As we work in our university classrooms, create art, or travel to other places with our cameras, we live in inquiry: constantly questioning, moving in the directions and spaces in which our queries propel us. We experience contiguity as we fold our lives as artists, researchers, and teachers onto themselves, thinking about how our everyday experiences relate to our teaching and art and how our experiences in the classroom and with art are carried into our everyday lives, all the while striving to make sense through felt and articulated embodiment. We contemplate and develop metaphorical frameworks, whether it be understanding research as an exquisite corpse (Holbrook & Pourchier, 2012) or writing as a guided wandering (Pourchier, 2012), that push us to struggle to conceptualize differently, to think differently, to express differently. We seek out, make space for, and actively create openings—taking up ideas, experiences, and metaphors that might be considered outside the norm—that make new questions and quests possible. We ride large and small reverberations, clutching them as a

things about stuff

The thing
about stuff
is that
you need
it to make
stuff.
The other
thing
about stuff is that it grows, spreads, piles,
collects, and gathers. But the main thing
about stuff is that it follows what it makes.

Fig 5.2 Stuff

means to deeper and wider wonderings as we experience connections between our personal art, research, and teaching practices and those articulated by others. And we search for and value excess, the work that provokes, transforms, and beckons us to take on what traditional research has labeled unacceptable, creating energy that keeps us afoot.

## LIVING IN THE TENSIONS AND POSSIBILITIES AS PRACTICING A/R/TOGRAPHERS

We see our inquiries as tentative and contingent, and while we recognize the rigor in them, we also know that they do not resemble more established forms of qualitative research. Therefore, working as literacy researchers who are also a/r/tographers puts us in professional and personal spaces of both possibility and tension. As we write this chapter, neither of us has tenure; more to the point, we are aware of national discourses within education that strive to privilege conventional scientific practices and diminish or discredit research located within a poststructural paradigm. Those discourses become part of what drives our inquiries; we take the stance that good research includes developing spaces for counter-narratives, counter-theories, counter-work.

## Possibilities and Tensions With Research Language

How to develop such spaces becomes an active quest, and a/r/tographers and arts-based scholars in general take up that quest in multiple ways. Many researchers working in ABER trouble concepts traditionally ascribed to quantitative and qualitative research, such as generalizability, validity, reliability, clarity. Richard Siegesmund and Melisa Cahnmann-Taylor (2008) wrote, "Arts-based research offers the layered versus the linear, the cacophonous versus the discursive, and the ambiguous versus the aphoristic" (p. 232). A field with such offerings strains against concepts grounded in what has been termed "scientifically-based educational research" guided by requirements that "theories, hypotheses, or conjectures must be stated in clear, unambiguous, and empirically testable terms" with corroborating evidence "linked to them through a clear chain of reasoning" (National Research Council, 2002, p. 18). Similarly, a/r/tographers push back against these concepts, committed as many of them are to do their work as nomadic researchers, engaging in a "particular non-linear journeying and border crossing" that positions them in "the frontier, the margin, the border between one thing and another, between this and that, known and unknown, knowable and unknowable" (Pryer, 2004, pp. 201–204).

For example, Peter Gouzouasis (2008) problematized the concepts of validity, assessment, and interpretation, arguing that "all research is story telling" (p. 222). Conventional qualitative research criteria are derived from the language of "positivist, scientific storytellers" and taken up by early qualitative researchers who composed "realist stories in an attempt to make their writing seem more objective, academic, and scholarly" (p. 231). Such language and criteria are insufficient for researchers engaged in a/r/tography. Gouzouasis asked, "Why should we expect a set of unified criteria to assess and validate all [arts-based] research?" He offered a litany of terms and concepts that a/r/tographers may take up in lieu of outdated and out-of-paradigm language:

> We acknowledge the interpretive nature and nurture of our work, and revel in its strength, durability, malleability, tensility, reflectivity, reflexivity, applicability, imaginativity, and tangibility, as well as its verisimilitude, width, coherence, insightfulness, parsimony, various kinds and forms of truth, fairness, ontological and educative authenticity, catalytic and tactical authenticity, comprehensiveness, substantive contribution, aesthetic merit, impact, expression of a reality ... plausibility, imaginative aesthetic transaction, empathy ....Those are all criteria by which we may access a/r/tography in a contemporary, meaningful manner. (Gouzouasis, 2008, p. 231)

Rather than the commonplace concepts by which scientific research is evaluated, a/r/tography requires new language, new norms based on its ontological and epistemological understandings, which are, in part, a call to "seek transformational change that leads to the unfolding of something new, substantially different, and novel" (Gouzouasis, 2008, p. 231).

## Possibilities and Tensions With Researcher Qualifications

As the children of artists, we confess to our own reluctance to call ourselves practicing artists. While we grew up immersed in discourses of visual art, we always saw ourselves as amateurs at the knees of our accomplished parents. Teri, who made a career as a fiction writer, nevertheless hesitated to move toward visual art in her research, aware that the 10,000 hours she had long ago exceeded in her move toward becoming a novelist was still being collected as a visual artist. Nicole, who spent her early years as a "closet artist," was hesitant to share or seriously pursue her interests in drawing and painting because of the sheer mastery of her father's work. Instead, she was drawn to other mediums to establish her own artistic identity and since childhood has practiced collage. These hesitancies point to another tension within arts-based research as a whole: Who can do this work? What are the criteria used to determine not only the quality of a work but also the qualifications of the researcher? We recognize this question as critical in fields that circulate disruptive methodologies. To disrupt is also to propose alternatives that perforce will be scrutinized on the way to legitimacy.

A number of arts-based researchers have proposed criteria within the field. Monica Prendergast (Prendergast & Belliveau, 2012), in discussing poetic-based qualitative inquiry, maintained that while researchers using this form do not need to be practicing literary poets, they do need to articulate their reasons for using the methodology and their own relationship with poetry as a means by which readers can evaluate the aptness of their approach. Kent Maynard and Melisa Cahmann-Taylor (2010), writing about ethnographic poetry, asserted that such works "must aspire and ascribe to the same high standards as poetry more widely" (p. 13). To achieve such goals, ethnographers should "immerse [themselves] in the culture of poetry" by becoming participant-observers within poetry communities and "engaging in [their] rigorous practices of writing and revisioning" (p. 13).

The question of "who" is also taken up among practitioners of a/r/tography. Within the field, artists, researchers, and teachers are conceptualized from a broad perspective. A/r/t is not confined to professionally trained artists, PhD researchers, and certified classroom teachers. Instead, "artists are committed to acts of creation, transformation, and resistance … [and] are committed to artistic engagement in ongoing living inquiry (Irwin & Springgay, 2008b, p. xxv). Teachers are not always classroom educators or higher education professors but rather educators "committed to educational engagement that is rooted in learning and learning communities through ongoing living inquiry" (Irwin & Springgay, 2008b, p. xxv). As researchers, a/r/tographers are committed to inquiry, "a way of living, inquiring, and being that is relations" through the making of and expressing through art (Irwin & Springgay, 2008b, p. xxxi). Such a stance delineates a/r/tography from other forms of arts-based research that describe texts or employ artistic forms to represent data.

We have taken up these questions, possibilities, and tensions in our own arts-based work. While we cannot offer explicit advice about how to navigate through existing academic systems, we can say that we look to other a/r/tographers for alternative approaches. For example, we consider how we might follow other a/r/tographers to think about presenting our work as a/r/tistic installations (see Beer & Grauer, 2012); we think about engaging others in communities of a/r/tographic practice (see Bickel, 2008; Donoghue, 2008; Irwin, 2008). To disseminate our work, we present at conferences and seek out the work of other a/r/tographers. We think broadly about the kinds of academic journals that might serve as venues for our work, looking not only to the journals in our own field of literacy education but also journals in other fields, such as qualitative research, women's studies, and art. As we continue to navigate these systems, we approach this process as a question we pursue through living inquiry. We do not seek definite answers, recognizing that every researcher's context is specific, but instead seek out a/r/tistic and insightful ways to re-imagine the shape of our academic work and ways in which to share it.

## A/r/tography and the Disruption of Dominant Methodological Norms

The concept of a disruptive methodology not only implies a set of practices intended to unsettle research norms, but it also involves a sense of disruption for the a/r/tographer. As a disruptive methodology, a/r/tography cannot be slipped in and out of. Instead, it must be encountered, experienced, and reckoned with by an a/r/tist. It is a way of being in the world that demands that a/r/tists figure out how it is at work within the context of their own lives. A/r/tography cannot provide its own examples because a/r/tography is the "never yet known" (Springgay, 2008, p. 160), and the unknown is rarely comfortable. As qualitative researchers who have "always already" been a/r/tographers, we invite consideration of the possibilities for a/r/tography and the understanding of it as a way of being that can allow for contraries to coexist—contraries that push and shove, but create openings for something new. Something that will set ears and wings bristling.

## NOTES

1. In keeping with other scholars working within feminist-informed theoretical frameworks, we use first and last names of referenced authors when they are introduced in the text.

# REFERENCES

Albers, P., Frederick, T., Cowan, K. (2009). Features of gender: An analysis of the visual texts of third grade children. *Journal of Early Childhood Literacy, 9*(2), 234–260.

Beer, R. S., & Grauer, K. M. (2012, April). *Disrupting currents: Interdisciplinary pedagogical encounters with interactive new media/artwork within cultural/history museums as learning sites.* Paper presented at the meeting of American Educational Research Association, Vancouver, Canada.

Bickel, B. (2008). Unveiling a sacred aesthetic: A/r/tography as ritual. In S. Springgay, R. Irwin, C. Leggo, & P. Gouzouasis (Eds.), *Being with a/r/tography* (pp. 81–94). Rotterdam, The Netherlands: Sense.

Brockelman, T. P. (2001). *The frame and the mirror: On collage and the postmodern.* Evanston, IL: Northwestern University Press.

Cole, A. & Knowles, G. (2001). Qualities of inquiry: Process, form, and 'goodness.' In L. Neilsen, A. L. Cole & J. G. Knowles (Eds.), *The art of writing inquiry* (211–219). Halifax, Nova Scotia: Backalong Books.

Derrida, J. (1997). Of grammatology (G. Spivak, Trans.). Baltimore, MD: The Johns Hopkins University Press. (Original work published 1976)

Donoghue, D. (2008). "That stayed with me until I was an adult": Making visible the experiences of men who teach. In S. Springgay, R. Irwin, C. Leggo, & P. Gouzouasis (Eds.), *Being with a/r/tography* (pp. 109–124). Rotterdam, The Netherlands: Sense.

Eisner, E. (1997). The promise and perils of alternative forms of data representation. *Educational Researcher, (26)*6, 4–10.

Eisner, E. (2008). Persistent tensions in arts-based research. In M. Cahnmann-Taylor & R. Siegesmund, *Arts-based research in education: Foundations for practice* (pp. 16–27). New York, NY: Routledge.

Ellis, C., & Bochner, A. (2009, May). *Writing autoethnography and narrative in qualitative research.* Workshop conducted at the Fifth International Congress of Qualitative Inquiry, University of Illinois at Urbana-Champaign.

Ellsworth, E. (2005). *Places of learning: Media, architecture, pedagogy.* New York, NY: Routledge.

Emmison, M., & Smith, P. (2000). *Researching the visual: Images, objects, contexts and interactions in social and cultural inquiry.* Thousand Oaks, CA: Sage.

Foucault, M. (1980). *Power/knowledge: Selected interviews and other writings 1972–1977* (C. Gordon, L. Marshall, J. Mepham, & K. Soper, Trans.). New York, NY: Pantheon Books.

Geertz, C. (1973). *The interpretation of cultures.* New York, NY: Basic Books.

Glesne, C. (1997). That rare feeling: Re-presenting research through poetic transcription. *Qualitative Inquiry, 3*(2), 202–221.

Gouzouasis, P. (2008). Toccata on assessment, validity and interpretation. In S. Springgay, R. Irwin, C. Leggo, & P. Gouzouasis (Eds.), *Being with a/r/tography* (pp. 221–232). Rotterdam, The Netherlands: Sense.

Holbrook, T. (2010). An ability traitor at work: A treasonous call to subvert writing from within. *Qualitative Inquiry, 16*(3), 171–183.

Holbrook, T., & Pourchier, N. (2012). The Exquisite Corpse as a/r/t: Bodied troubling of qualitative research-as-usual. *Visual Arts Research, 38*(2), 41–55.

Irwin, R. (2008). Communities of a/r/tographic practice. In S. Springgay, R. Irwin, C. Leggo, & P. Gouzouasis (Eds.), *Being with a/r/tography* (pp. 71–80). Rotterdam, The Netherlands: Sense.

Irwin, R. L., & Springgay, S. (2008a). A/r/tography as practice-based research. In M. Cahnmann-Taylor & R. Siegesmund (Eds.), *Arts-based research in education: Foundations for practice* (pp. 103–124). New York, NY: Routledge.

Irwin, R. L., & Springgay, S. (2008b). A/r/tography as practice-based research. In S. Springgay, R. Irwin, C. Leggo, & P. Gouzouasis (Eds.), *Being with a/r/tography* (pp. xix–xxxiii). Rotterdam, The Netherlands: Sense.

Lather, P. (2006). Paradigm proliferation as a good thing to think with: Teaching research in education as a wild profusion. *International Journal of Qualitative Studies in Education, 19*(1), 35–57.

Maynard, K., & Cahnmann-Taylor, M. (2010). Anthropology at the edge of words: Where poetry and ethnography meet. *Anthropology and Humanism, 35*(1), 2–19.

National Research Council. (2002). *Scientific research in education.* R. J. Shavelson & L. Towne (Eds.). Washington, DC: National Academy Press.

Neilsen, L. (2008). Foreword. In S. Springgay, R. Irwin, C. Leggo, & P. Gouzouasis (Eds.), Being with a/r/tography (pp. xv–xvii). Rotterdam, The Netherlands: Sense.

Pinar, W. F. (2004). Foreword. In R. L. Irwin & A. de Cosson (Eds.), *a/r/tography: Rendering self through arts-based living inquiry* (pp. 9–25). Vancouver, Canada: Pacific Educational Press.

Pink, S. (2007). *Doing visual ethnography* (2nd ed.). Los Angeles, CA: Sage.

Pourchier, N. (2012). *Guided wanderings: An a/r/tographic inquiry into postmodern picturebooks, Bourdieusian theory, and writing* (Unpublished doctoral dissertation). Georgia State University, Atlanta, GA.

Prendergast, M., & Belliveau, G. (2012). Poetics and performance. In A. Trainor & E. Graue (Eds.), *Reviewing qualitative research in the social sciences* (pp. 197–210). New York, NY: Routledge.

Pryer, A. (2004). Living with/in marginal spaces: Intellectual nomadism and artist/researcher/teacher praxis. In R. L. Irwin & A. de Cosson (Eds.), *a/r/tography: Rendering self through arts-based living inquiry* (pp. 198–211). Vancouver, Canada: Pacific Educational Press.

Richardson, L. (1997). Louisa May's story of her life. In L. Richardson (Ed.), *Fields of play: Constructing an academic life* (pp. 131–137). New Brunswick, NJ: Rutgers University Press.

Sameshima, P. (2008). Autoethnographic relationality through paradox, parallax, and metaphor. In S. Springgay, R. Irwin, C. Leggo, & P. Gouzouasis (Eds.), *Being with a/r/tography* (pp. 45–56). Rotterdam, The Netherlands: Sense.

Siegesmund, R., & Cahnmann-Taylor, M. (2008). The tensions of arts-based research in education reconsidered: The promise for practice. In M. Cahnmann-Taylor & R. Siegesmund (Eds.), *Arts-based research in education: Foundations for practice* (pp. 232–246). New York, NY: Routledge.

Springgay, S. (2008). An ethics of embodiment. In S. Springgay, R. Irwin, C. Leggo, & P. Gouzouasis (Eds.), *Being with a/r/tography* (pp. 153–166). Rotterdam, The Netherlands: Sense.

Springgay, S., Irwin, R., & Kind, S. (2005). A/r/tography as living inquiry through art and text. *Qualitative Inquiry, 11*(6), 897–912.

St. Pierre, E. A. (1997). Methodology in the fold and the irruption of transgressive data. *Qualitative Studies in Education, 10*(2), 175–189.

St. Pierre, E. A. (2011). Post qualitative research: The critique and the coming after. In N. Denzin & Y. S. Lincoln (Eds.), *The Sage handbook of qualitative research* (pp. 611–625). Los Angeles, CA: Sage.

St. Pierre, E. A., & Pillow, W. S. (2000). Introduction: Inquiry among the ruins. In E. A. St. Pierre & W. S. Pillow (Eds.), *Working the ruins: Feminist poststructural theory and methods in education* (pp. 1–24). New York, NY: Routledge.

## ADDITIONAL RESOURCES

## Printed Materials

Bickel, B. (2008b). Who will read this body? An a/r/tographic statement. In M. Cahnmann-Taylor & R. Siegesmund (Eds.), *Arts-based research in education: Foundations for practice* (pp. 125–136). New York, NY: Routledge.

La Jevic, L. & Springgay, S. (2008). A/r/tography as an ethics of embodiment: Visual journals in preservice education. *Qualitative Inquiry, 14*(1), 67–89.

Leavy, P. (2009). *Method meets art: Arts-based research practice*. New York, NY: Guilford Press.

Leggo, C. (2008). Astonishing silence: Knowing in poetry. In A. L. Cole & J. G. Knowles (Eds.), *Handbook of the arts in qualitative social science research* (pp. 165–174). Thousand Oaks, CA: Sage.

Springgay, S. (2001). Inside the visible: Youth understandings of body knowledge through touch (Unpublished doctoral dissertation). Vancouver, BC: The University of British Columbia.

Springgay, S. (2008). Nurse-in: Breastfeeding and a/r/tographical research. In M. Cahnmann-Taylor & R. Siegesmund (Eds.), *Arts-based research in education: Foundations for practice* (pp. 137–141). New York, NY: Routledge.

Springgay, S., & Irwin, R. (2004). Women making art: Aesthetic inquiry as political performance. In A. Cole, L. Neilsen, G. Knowles, & T. Luciani (Eds.), *Provoked by art: Theorizing arts-informed research* (pp. 71–83). Halifax, Nova Scotia: Backalong Books.

## Website

*A/r/tography*
http://m1.cust.educ.ubc.ca/Artography/

# CHAPTER SIX

# Crystallization AS A Methodology

## Disrupting Traditional Ways of Analyzing and (Re)presenting Through Multiple Genres

CANDACE R. KUBY

Walking down the staircase, to a brown, dark basement, I felt a sense of wonderment. I had not been to this part of the building before and was curious as to what I'd find. My elementary school was a citywide magnet school, whereby students had to meet particular requirements to attend. The building was near the downtown area of our medium-size southern city. The neighborhood was full of old houses and businesses; some might consider it "run down." Most all of my peers were White[1] and had reasonably comfortable lives with their needs (and wants) being met. Since our school was not in our neighborhoods, students were bussed-in from all over the city to attend.

On this day, I cannot remember the reason for walking down this staircase, but I vividly remember what I found. I discovered classrooms. Several classrooms. Full of children I did not recall seeing before. Children who did not ride my bus. Children who did not attend school assemblies with me. Children who did not eat lunch with me. Children who were mostly Black. Are they always down here, I wondered? Who are they? By their size, I could tell that they were younger, not in an upper elementary grade like me. It was confusing to me that their classrooms were … in the basement … away from everybody else. Isolated.[2]

This opening vignette draws upon a memory from a childhood event that I am still processing 20 years later. Through writing, I have wrestled with this experience in relation to who I am as a White, middle-class educator. I have spent time thinking about how this moment of walking down the basement stairs shapes my evolving beliefs and ideologies on race and class, which in turn influence my teaching (and researching) practices with young children. Writings such as these, along with poetry and analysis of photographs, helped me sort out this experience. The process of drawing upon multiple genres for writing and analysis, defined as crystallization, enables researchers to disrupt more traditional processes of analysis and styles of (re)presentation.

The aim of this chapter is to demonstrate crystallization as a methodology, drawing on my dissertation research that studied critical inquiry in an early childhood classroom (Kuby, 2010). Crystallization as discussed by Richardson and St. Pierre (2005) deconstructs traditional views of validity and (post)positivist notions of triangulation. Their concept of qualitative crystallization is a counter response to the idea that by drawing on multiple sources of data, one can know or have an answer to a research question.

Crystallization as a methodology (Ellingson, 2009) embraces a multigenre approach to analysis and (re)presentation that blurs the boundaries of art and science. It brings together artistic ways of analyzing and communicating research with rigorous methods from a potential range of paradigms, including but not limited to, critical, feminist, and poststructural. To demonstrate how crystallization disrupts traditional processes of inquiry, I discuss three fluid and recursive aspects of my dissertation research: 1) autoethnography to unpack ideologies that influenced teaching/researching; 2) practitioner inquiry while teaching children; and 3) a critical performative analysis of emotion. This chapter demonstrates how multiple genres can be used for analysis and (re)presentation of writing, for example: multi-voice poetry, pro/epilogue with narrative vignettes, images, and embodied conversations (attempted to be) captured in transcripts. This chapter offers qualitative researchers one example of how crystallization could look in practice and insights into the paradigmatic roots that support this type of methodology. There is value in adopting this type of methodological framework because it embraces multiple ways of seeing the world and acknowledges that knowledge and reality are neither static nor fixed. Crystallization enables the researcher(s) and reader(s) of the texts (i.e., words, images, performance, art, and so forth) to encounter the texts in new, shifting ways each time they are experienced.

The example of crystallization as a methodology demonstrated in this chapter disrupts dominant approaches to data collection and the process of analysis by using writing as a method of inquiry. This study also disrupts traditional (re)presentation through multiple genres (i.e., poetry, narrative vignettes, images, and embodied conversations with young children).

## CRYSTALLIZATION AS A METHODOLOGY

> "[Researchers] do jump across traditions, we do straddle metatheoretical camps, and (unfortunately) we do let paradigmatic 'definitions' constrain our work ... [I want to] allow for comfortable jumps and straddles and to loosen some of these constraints."
>
> (K. I. MILLER, 2000, P. 48)

Richardson and St. Pierre (2005) discussed crystallization as a counter to post-positivist notions of triangulation in qualitative research. They stated that triangulation "carries the ... assumption that there is a 'fixed point' or 'object' that can be triangulated" (p. 963). This notion of validity assumes there is one truth that can be found as long as multiple types of data demonstrate the same point. However, not all qualitative research rests on the assumption that a singular truth is possible or even desirable. Instead, Richardson and St. Pierre argued that crystallization, as a way to think about the prevailing concept of validity, embraces multiple realities, truths, and ways of knowing:

> Crystals are prisms that reflect externalities and refract within themselves, creating different colors, patterns, and arrays casting off in different directions ... crystallization, without losing structure, deconstructs the traditional idea of "validity" ... Crystallization provides us with a deepened, complex, and thoroughly partial understanding of the topic. (p. 963)

Crystallization embraces the idea that truth is made up of multiple perspectives, which are connected to specific contexts and points in time. Richardson and St. Pierre (2005) wrote that what we see in research depends on our angle of repose each time we approach data. This problematizes the notion of findings because the angle of repose that one brings to conducting and reading research will shape what individuals "find." Researchers' backgrounds, ideologies, and life experiences shape how they approach all phases of a study: design, data collection, analysis, and (re)presentation. Research is not neutral. Therefore, the angle of repose we bring to our research shapes what we look for and find, so to speak, in the data.

Ellingson (2009) moved the notion of crystallization forward by positing that crystallization is a methodology, an approach to inquiry, not simply a different way of moving beyond traditional notions of validity. Ellingson argued that she "needed a framework, a methodological path that [she] could follow that would enable [her] to construct and articulate multiple lived truths, rather than force [her] to choose among them" (p. xi). Ellingson built upon another concept by Richardson and St. Pierre (2005), writing as a method of inquiry, and extended that to include a wide array of artistic (re)presentations (i.e., video, poetry, music, painting, narrative, and so forth). Ellingson defined crystallization as a methodology in the following way:

> Crystallization combines multiple forms of analysis and multiple genres of representation into a coherent text or series of related texts, building a rich and openly partial account of a phenomenon that problematizes its own construction, highlights researchers' vulnerabilities and positionality, makes claims about socially constructed meanings, and reveals the indeterminacy of knowledge claims even as it makes them. (p. 4)

This type of methodology rests on assumptions that knowledge, truth, and reality are constructed and have potential to change each time they are encountered.

Crystallization allows researchers to embrace the marriage of arts and science and see value in both for data, analysis, and (re)presentation. Crystallization is an art as it embraces multiple forms of (re)presentations such as various genres of writing, art, and performance but is also a science as it provides the opportunity for closely examining the social through various approaches of qualitative analysis.

Ellingson (2009) outlined five principles of crystallization as a methodology, which are useful guidelines for researchers who are considering this approach to inquiry. Crystallization

1.  Seeks to produce knowledge about a particular phenomenon through generating a deepened, complex interpretation.
2.  Utilizes forms of analysis or ways of producing knowledge across multiple points of the qualitative continuum [ranging from art/impressionist, middle-ground approaches, and science/realist; see pages 8 and 9 of Ellingson's book for continuum], generally including at least one middle-ground (constructivist) or middle-to-right (postpositivist) analytic method and one interpretive, artistic, performative, or otherwise creative analytic approach.
3.  Includes more than one genre of writing or representation [art, movies, performances, etc.].
4.  Features a significant degree of reflexive consideration of the researcher's self in the process of research design, data collection, and representation.
5.  Eschews positivist claims to objectivity and a singular, discoverable truth and embraces, reveals, and even *celebrates* knowledge as inevitably situated, partial, constructed, multiple, and embodied. (pp. 10–13)

These five principles are a starting place for researchers interested in using crystallization as a methodology to consider how their research design includes each of these aspects. Beyond more traditional data analysis processes such as ethnography and grounded theory, Ellingson (2009) built on Richardson's (Richardson & St. Pierre, 2005) notion of creative analytic process (CAP), a type of ethnography that "displays the writing process and the writing product as deeply intertwined; both are privileged" (p. 962). CAP embraces other forms of analysis and (re)presentation such as autoethnography, poetry and poetic transcription, narratives, fiction, video representations, and performance. These forms of analysis and (re)presentation embody crystallization because they enable researchers to marry both art and science through multiple ways of knowing and encountering the world.

Crystallization's position on knowledge, truth, reality, and values means that when using this methodology, research questions need to embrace the fluidity of ideas. The purpose of research is not to find one singular meaning or truth. Instead, research questions and designs embrace experiences of individuals within social contexts. This research stance positions the researcher as a co-constructor. How the researcher sees the data, based on personal experiences, influences data collection, analysis, and writing. (Re)presentation departs from the traditional research genre (i.e., academic papers with typically ordered sections or dissertations that follow traditional chapter formats) and instead embraces a variety of genres not only for (re)presentation but also for analysis. A researcher using crystallization as a methodology acknowledges that choices in data collection, analysis, and (re)presentation are always value judgments; something is always left out. Crystallization thus disrupts typical ways of doing qualitative research. Crystallization acknowledges that decisions in the research process are never neutral and thus a researcher's ideologies influence analysis and (re)presenting research. This disrupts the idea of objective research. Who we are as people shapes the research questions we ask, the way we go about collecting data, how we interact with participants, which theories we draw upon to make sense of data, the methods we employ for analysis, and how we decide to disseminate insights. Each of these decisions along the way is influenced by our belief systems, prior experiences, and ways of knowing and being. Crystallization enables researchers to embrace the messy, complex, and fluid in all aspects of research that disrupt more stable, fixed, and singular notions of research.

## DEMONSTRATION OF CRYSTALLIZATION AS A METHODOLOGY

Below is an excerpt of crystallization as a methodology taken from my dissertation (Kuby, 2010). It demonstrates multiple ways of analyzing and (re)presenting research through various genres. First, I provide a visual framework that captures my research design of crystallization. Next, I describe the context for the teacher research (Cochran-Smith & Lytle, 1993, 2009) I participated in with five-and-six-year-olds during a summer program. Then, I share several genres of writing from the research process: an autoethnographic multi-voiced poem, flashbacks written in the form of pro/epilogues that book-ended the analysis chapters of the dissertation, and embodied conversations with children captured in transcripts. Finally, I describe the insights I gained from using crystallization, discuss possibilities and tensions of this methodology, and wrestle with issues related to macro, micro, and meso research discourses discussed in the introduction to this volume. Readers are encouraged to encounter the (re)presentations, connecting them to their own lives and experiences. There is no one right interpretation. Each time someone approaches the (re)presentations, different poems or experiences are evoked, so to speak (Rosenblatt, 1978).

The content of the multi-voiced poetry and narratives are sensitive in nature. Sharing these are not intended to hurt feelings or point fingers at others but are used as a way to raise consciousness about my perspective of events and life experiences. All student, teacher, and school names are pseudonyms to protect anonymity.[3]

## Process of Analysis and (Re)presentation

I spent a semester in a graduate course embarking on an autoethnographic journey. I knew the following summer I would return to a city in the southern United States and teach students in an enrichment program. I was excited to return to the classroom with children and try out teaching from a critical inquiry stance, something I was reading about in graduate courses. At some level, I believe I was in the process of becoming a critical inquiry teacher without knowing it or having the label, even before reading about critical inquiry with young children (Comber & Simpson, 2001; Sahni, 2001; Vasquez, 2004). I resonated with these readings and immediately felt a connection to the underlying philosophy. Critical inquiry is a way of living (Vasquez, 2004) that deconstructs the word and world for power, position, and privilege (Freire, 1970/2005). With children, this means listening to their inquiries about injustices they witness or experience and opening up curricular spaces for dialogue and social action in order to make their communities and lives more just places. Most often, critical inquiry scholarship discusses the need for this type of pedagogy with children viewed as marginalized because of race, economic status, gender, disabilities, and so forth. However, I believe that critical conversations need to also take place with children who are relatively affluent and privileged in society. Therefore, as I knew I would be teaching in a relatively affluent school during the summer, I wanted to explore from a teacher-researcher perspective what a critical inquiry curriculum might look like. Before intentionally teaching from this perspective in the summer program, I decided to examine my own childhood experiences, biases, and ideologies, so I embarked on an autoethnographic journey.

Going into teaching that summer, I did not know that the data collected would end up as my dissertation. The chair of my doctoral committee encouraged me to get IRB (ethics review board at the university) consent forms for the children just in case the data was rich enough for a dissertation study. Since my interests were in critical inquiry in early childhood education, a stance not many educators of young children adopt, I found it difficult to find a teacher's classroom near the university to conduct dissertation research because the view of children as innocent and protecting them from injustices permeates. Therefore, using the opportunity in a summer program to teach children myself, exploring a critical inquiry curriculum seemed promising for research. We were right! There was a lot of data, which I spent several years analyzing and thinking about in relation to critical inquiry. As I used writing as a method of inquiry for analysis, I knew I wanted to use multiple genres for (re)presentation and break away from the traditional chapter structure of a dissertation. In the midst of writing, I stumbled across Ellingson's (2009) book on crystallization as a methodology. A label for what I was already exploring! Figure 6.1 is a visual representation of my research design drawing upon crystallization as a methodology. There were three aspects or "phases" to my dissertation research; however, in actuality they were more fluid than what is represented on paper.

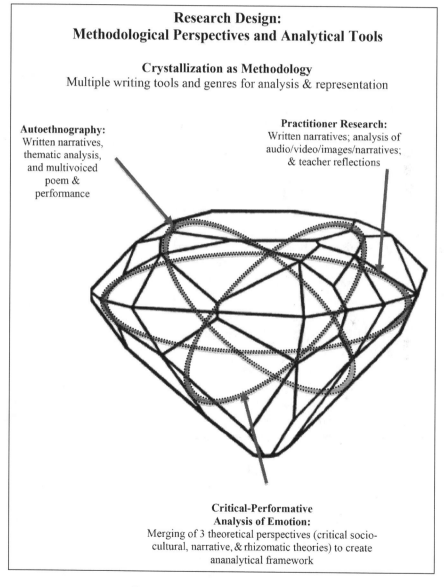

Fig 6.1 Crystallization research design.

On the left hand side of the figure is the aspect of intentionally writing and analyzing my own biases and ideologies in relation to communities and cultures I am a part of, an autoethnography. Spry (2001) defined autoethnography as a self-narrative that critiques the situatedness of self with others in social contexts. Some describe autoethnography as using yourself to interrogate culture (Humphreys, 2005; Wall, 2006). An overarching theme from various scholars is that context is crucial (Cole & Knowles, 2001), because narratives are embedded in interactions (Atkinson & Delamont, 2006; Cole & Knowles, 2001; Jones, 2008; Muncey, 2005). A purpose of autoethnography is critical agency in attempting to know oneself through critiquing and sharing one's own experience (Duncan, 2004; Spry, 2001). A key understanding I have about autoethnography is that it is not self-serving but is purposeful in putting into conversation personal experiences with culture and the world as a way to move towards social action and awareness. I was intentional on wanting to unpack my life experiences, especially growing up in the South, knowing that I would be traveling back home to teach from a critical perspective. In the United States, the South has a long history of racial prejudice and poverty reinforced through systematic, legislative, religious, and political means. I used multiple narrative writings and poetry as a performance to analyze and (re)present the autoethnographic process. Although the autoethnography started before the other two aspects of the dissertation, I found myself over the years circling back to the autoethnographic experiences and writings as a teacher researcher. The autoethnography seeped (and rightly so) into teaching and analysis of data from the summer program.

The right side of the figure represents summer teaching experiences with young children. I used more traditional forms of data collection, such as audio and video recordings in the classroom, a teacher journal at the end of each day, photographs of interactions and student-made artifacts (i.e., drawing, writing), newsletters to parents, and parental questionnaires. However, I also continued to write narratives and think about the autoethnography I had begun in the spring.

The bottom of the research design illustrates the years I spent focusing on analysis and writing after teaching in the summer program. Through analysis of my writings and teaching data, the emotionality of critical inquiry conversations materialized. Looking at emotions within critical inquiry curriculum was not my intention or focus before teaching; however, I felt and lived out emotional encounters with children as we discussed injustices in our lives and historical examples we read in books. Drawing upon poststructural, narrative, and critical sociocultural ideas about emotions as a verb (emotions are performed in relation to others), I sought to create an analytical tool to better understand the emotional collisions between people specifically in critical inquiry experiences. This process led to intentionally juxtaposing the autoethnography and teaching experiences with a specific focus on the performance of my emotions with the children (Kuby, 2013c; in press).

## Context for Teaching and Researching

The university-sponsored summer program that served as my dissertation research site was advertised as enrichment, where students who had completed kindergarten to fifth grades learned through hands on/minds on experiences. My responsibility was to provide learning opportunities in reading, writing, math, arts, and the inquiry of science and social studies to students who had just finished kindergarten. I had eight female and 13 male students (with consent to be a part of the study) identified by parents as African American, Caucasian, Asian, and biracial. Eight students came from families making $51,000–100,000 annually, seven from $101,000–200,000 incomes, and five from above $201,000.

As a critical inquiry teacher, I looked for situations where children discussed or lived-out injustices, in order to bring into the curriculum conversations about their lives and ways to take action. I witnessed a situation on the playground, which appeared to make some of the children uncomfortable. I too found the interaction to be disturbing, but was not sure how to respond in the moment. As we entered an empty playground each day, my students searched for a spot of shade. There was one bench under the shade of a large tree. This is where my students and I gravitated to eat snacks. As other classes came outside, teachers would yell at my students, stating the bench was for adults only. I watched in a state of disbelief and was uncomfortable with how I might respond to this demand. I was not aware of a rule that only adults could sit on benches. Drawing on the notion that critical inquiry should come from the lives of children (Comber & Simpson, 2001; Vasquez, 2001, 2004), I chose to focus our inquiry on the conversations and experiences the children had related to the playground incident. The children being asked to move reminded me of what Rosa Parks might have felt when she was told to move from her seat on a Montgomery, Alabama bus during the civil rights movement of the 1950s and 1960s in the United States. In sharing this with the children, their questions about Rosa Parks helped to guide our explorations about segregation and injustices (see Kuby, 2010, 2011a, 2011b, 2013a, 2013b for more details about the critical inquiry curriculum).

While I realize the connection to Rosa Parks might be viewed as essentializing and minimizing the struggle of civil rights for African Americans, this was not my intention. Scholars (Evans, 2007; Lewison, Leland, & Harste, 2007; Jones, 2006) encourage teachers to use children's literature and history as an entry point into critical inquiry conversations, so I thought discussing the inequality and power relations in Parks's life might open a space for us to discuss what happened on the playground, to nuance how the situations are different, yet each causes us to ask questions and dialogue about social issues.

Building upon the playground bench incident and Parks's story, crystallization was the method of inquiry used to analyze and (re)present my learning, juxtaposed with autoethnographic experiences. Crystallization enabled me to weave together photographic images, memoir writings, classroom interactions (through transcripts), and lived experiences into a coherent text (broadly speaking). Below is a snippet of how crystallization materialized. I invite you to encounter these texts in relation to your own identities and experiences.

## Multivoiced Poetry

### An Autoethnographic Journey to Understand Myself:

A Poem for Two Voices[4]
*Participants read in unison*
Read by Candace

*Father*
Grew up in New Orleans
Sisters: poor, working class, nomadic, many men
"Candace don't be like that"
Doctorate degree
Southern Baptist Minister
Man of few words, but deep emotions

*Mother*
Grew up in New Orleans
Father a Southern Baptist Minister
"No pants, only dresses"
Doctorate degree
Professor of Early Childhood Education

*Father and Mother*
Waited 10 years to have three children
Mom stayed at home; Dad worked at church

*Older Sister*
Shy, private, reserved
Tennessee, Texas, Connecticut, California—for school and work
Pursuing doctoral degree as an orchestral conductor
Liberal

*Younger Brother*
Crocheter, Paintballer, Barracuda Restorer
Repairs commercial dishwashers; in school to be a secondary math teacher
Built a house near parents
Married
Conservative

*Small Alabama city*
Where the "ghettos" and "little Vietnam" are distinct

A household where only Whites have entered through the doors
A family that did not discuss race, class, gender, or other "controversial" issues

*Bussed to a city-wide elementary magnet school where the neighborhood kids were bussed out.*
*Criteria to enter? "Teacher recommendation, leadership skills, and/or intelligence."*
(Read: White and relatively affluent with power, position, and privilege in the community)

I can count on one hand classmates who were Black and/or poor.
By design of the magnet school I had a "gifted" curriculum, I was positioned as privileged in my community, which resulted in power.
It all seemed natural.

*Middle school*
My only two Black teachers (ever)
Images of cafeteria, locker room, and hallway fights between Blacks.
I was left in fear and unable to focus or eat lunch on those days.

*High school*
Interracial dating was (is) taboo
"Stacking the (White) votes" for the Homecoming Court

*Privilege and Power Growing Up*
Routine library visits, kitchen art cabinet,
Dance, piano, gymnastics, tennis, swimming, and baton lessons,
Sculpture days,
Chorus and band
Varsity cheerleading captain,
Honor societies and clubs,
AHS "A Club Sweetheart"

*Positioned*
By mother's choice to return to school for doctorate degree,
Shift in parents' gender roles,
Conflict and lack of support in church over this decision.
*Immediate result*—I became more independent.
*Long-term result*—still developing.

*Shocked*
To discover Black neighborhood kindergarten children in the basement of my elementary school.

*Uncomfortable*
To take gymnastic lessons in a moldy, run-down gym in a small, poor town.

*Strange*
To attend middle and high school with Blacks and people of less economic standing.

*Mom trapped in ideologies.*
PhD program: Jerry and Lynn all contributed to her mind "opening up."

*Candace trapped in ideologies?*
What has opened my mind?

*Bachelor of Science in Early Childhood Education,*
*First teaching job in an inner-city elementary school of Birmingham,*
*Ranked one of the four poorest schools out of 89 schools in the city.*

*Dontrell*
A fish flopping on the floor as mother beats him with a belt.

*Treshaun*
Role-plays having sex on the floor and around poles in the lunchroom,
Outcome—labeled ED[5] like older brother.

*Darnel*
Rolls pencil shavings into joints, pretends to smoke them.

*Anthony*
In contrast, grandson of city councilman.
Only voluntary parent conference all year.

*Charles*
The only White kindergarten student,
Fetal Alcohol Syndrome?

*Reading Curriculum (according to the school district):*
Voyager.

*Master's of Art in Early Childhood Education,*
*Ruby Payne juxtaposed with Peter McLaren,*
*Teacher in "over the mountain," suburban schools.*

*Manuel*
Crying, clinched to grandmother on first day of school in the U.S.

*Stephanie*
Living from motel to trailer to motel,
Kidnapped by father because her "mother is dead."

*Jessica*
Repeating first grade, recognizes few letters and their sounds,
Although Dad said she reads books to him every night.
Could this be because he can't read? (Is she "reading" the pictures?)

*Fellow Faculty, School Board, and City Council Members*
Discussing those "other children" from HUD[6] housing.

City decides to level their apartment complex—for businesses—eviction notices—families displaced once again.

*Lauren*
Whose mom has never said "No."

*"The First Baptist Church"*
*A Southern Baptist Church*
*Dad a minister*
*Gymnastic coach a Pentecostal preacher*

This is what I heard...

*Women are to be submissive.*
*Whites only in the church.*
*Divorce is wrong.*
*Homosexuals* (Tyree) *aren't going to heaven.*
*Christianity is the only way.*
*Actions speak louder than words.*
*Don't ask questions.*

I hear(d) a small voice in my head as a youth questioning...

Recently...
*B. E. (Beginning Experience)*
*Nick*
*Japan*
*Sarah*
*First United Church*
*Caela*
*Jack*
*Ask questions.*

...it is getting louder and louder.

*Once married to a man who wore a mask.*
I will not be a doormat anymore.

*Living in Japan for one year to teach English and professional development about holistic literacy practices in four nursery schools and one university.*
Internal conflicts around religious upbringing. Who am I? What do I believe?

*PhD program focusing on early literacy and policy studies.*
Critical Social Theories
Feminist Methodologies
Critical Discourse Analysis
Gender, Education, and Development
Critical Literacy

*Assumptions*
*Black* equals violence.
*Poor White elderly* equals creepy.
*White* equals wealth.
*Black* equals poor.
*Poor* equals wrong.
*Black* equals fear.
*Why* do we label people as "that *Black* woman" or "that *Hispanic* man?"
But never "that *White* woman?"
*Hard* to break.

*It takes time*
To come to peace in my own skin.

*"It ought to be* revelatory."

*Still* processing.
*Still* evolving.

(Everyone reads:)
*"Sometimes we don't see or notice things happening in our lives until we look back after the fact."*

The process of creating the multivoiced poetry enabled me to closely examine events, memories, relationships, and ideologies not only from my childhood but also as an adult. All of these aspects make up my multiple identities, which influence interactions and decisions in teaching and researching. The genre of a multivoiced poem enabled me to perform it initially with colleagues in a graduate class and since then with educators at conferences. Each enactment of the poetry speaks to me—the meanings and my feelings shift.

## Images: Yearbook Photographs

Spending time flipping through pages in childhood yearbooks, analyzing the images in conjunction with memoir writings I was doing, helped to visualize and relive moments in my childhood. While I do not have permission to publish and want to protect the identities of people in the yearbook images, I looked closely at numerous class photographs across several years. The kindergarten classes were composed of all African American children. The students in the first to fifth grade photographs were mainly Caucasian with a few African American children. These examples confirmed my experiences walking down the basement stairs. Through visual analysis, I was able to see stark differences in privilege materialized through eyeglasses, designer clothes, large hair bows, braces, and smocked outfits.

## Memoirs: Reflective Narrative Writings

I wonder if I was the only student in my school that realized how different the kindergarten classes were. Did other students walk down the back staircase to the basement? Did anyone else question this but not have a space in class to discuss it? While the discovery in the basement puzzled me at the time, I don't remember asking someone else about this as a child. It was not until years later as a graduate student that I began to reflect on this moment and the ways it influenced me, even if I was not conscious of it. Why? I wondered. Why would someone separate all these African American children from the rest of the students at school, not only physically but also in school-wide events? I wonder what my thoughts and beliefs would be today if I had a "safe" space to talk with my teacher and friends about my discovery.

Memoir writing such as this and the vignette at the opening of the chapter were ways for me to (re)present, analyze, and process experiences as a child. Through writing, I was able to closely examine my upbringing—relationships, experiences, ideologies—which shapes who I am today. Writing provided an avenue to tell my story and invite readers to do the same with their lives.

## Embodied Interactions: Conversations With Children

While teaching, I had the Rosa Parks biography book (Schaefer, 2000), and notes about her printed from the Internet on the floor in front of me. I shared with the class a question from Annie, a Caucasian student in the class, about why a law was created to segregate people on buses. For the most part, the conversation happened as a dialogue; not many children raised their hands. The discussion appeared more open than previous days, maybe because I was sitting with them at eye level, not above them in a chair. The conversation had a problem-solving feel to it (see Appendix A for transcription markings).

| | |
|---|---|
| **Ellie:** | It's a pattern |
| **Candace:** | It's a pattern? ↑ What do you mean by that? |
| **Ellie:** | Everyday it could be a pattern. |
| **Candace:** | What do you mean? {*looking at Ellie*} |
| **Ellie:** | Like the Black people could sit in the front and then the White people could sit in the front. |
| **Candace:** | {*look of understanding, clarity*} So, you're thinking it might have been **fair** if they had made a rule that they switch everyday {*motioning back and forth with hands*} = |
| **Derrick:** | =like= |
| **Candace:** | =so the Whites are in the front and then the Blacks and then you swap back and forth everyday. That could be a fair way to handle that? ↑= {*arms stretched out, offering*} |

| Derrick: | =Like, like this, um, um, the White people can sit by Brown people in the **front** and that's how you do it in the bus. {*playing with his socks and shoes; looking up at Candace*} |
| Candace: | See, Derrick's thinking we should all just sit together. {*Put hands out and opened up—looking at the rest of the group—as if posing a question*} = |

The students began to wrestle with what fairness means. Ellie began by posing one possible fair scenario for riding the bus. Here, she articulated that by taking turns, "a pattern," both groups of people would have a chance to sit in the front of the bus and therefore experience fairness. She used this verbal role-play as a way to think about both groups of people, and took on various perspectives.

I found it problematic that by using words such as "the Whites" and "the Blacks" I modeled to the children a homogenizing and essentializing way of thinking of people and various races. In my mind, I remember catching myself in the moment and not feeling comfortable with which terms to use. I felt that by using color words for races, I reinforced race as "color" and "biological" instead of viewing race as a social construction tied to systematic issues (Kuby, 2013a, 2013b).

The conversation shifted to Joey offering the idea that people should sit on the bus like a group hug, meaning all people should get along and race should not matter. This conversation was evident of the social nature of processing the injustice of segregation. Together, the students bounced ideas off each other for wrestling with this topic. Then, children shared the ways they ride busses at their schools. Drawing upon personal experiences they tried to make sense of why and how a law would be created that separated people on busses, since that was not their experience.

| Ellie: | It doesn't matter the color of their skin. |
| Candace: | It doesn't matter? ↑ Oh, well it seemed like it mattered {*looking at whole group—hands out in question*} to the people who made the law.↑ {*looking at Ellie*} Why do you think it mattered to them? {*look of puzzlement*} |
| Joey: | They were sorry. They were so sorry. |
| Candace: | They were sorry to make that law? {*tilt head in suspicion*} |
| Joey: | Yeah, so they won't do it again. |

Joey's comment at the time seemed cute and what someone might expect from a young child. One might expect an early childhood teacher to praise him and agree that they were sorry in order to steer clear of this topic. However, I continued to ask questions. Joey's comment appeared robotically performed, giving me what he thought I might want to hear. Joey knew that when you do something wrong you are supposed to say you are sorry. Especially for children in the early childhood years, adults often condition students to apologize when there is conflict, even if they do not understand what they have done "wrong," and many times when they really are not sorry (Wohlwend, 2007). By stating this, it appeared Joey was positioning himself as the "good" student telling me what he thought I wanted to hear. The conversation continued as children offered more ideas on fair ways to ride on a bus.

Using transcripts, as a genre, enabled me to capture as best I could the embodied interactions lived out in the classroom. This type of genre, perhaps not used often in crystallization, enables researchers to demonstrate interactions between people in a different way than written memoirs or images. By capturing intonation, turns in speech, non-verbal gestures, and paralinguistic features, I could examine the emotionality and power dynamics related to conversations about injustices.

## Narrative Writings: Juxtaposing Childhood Memories With Teaching

On a deeper emotional level, while teaching I saw myself in the students from the summer. Were the discussions really about Rosa Parks for me? Probably not, as the law has already been changed. It was more about acknowledging and allowing a curricular space for young children to verbally wrestle with this injustice.

In the opening lines of the class conversation the children responded, "I don't know," when I asked them why a law would be created that separates people. Really? Should I have been really surprised that they didn't know why that law was created? Do we as adults really understand segregation either? Sure, we can understand it based on studying power and hegemony, but understanding racism and segregation is not easy. I found myself, as a child, in this conversation. I too was questioning why people were segregated in my elementary school basement much like these students were questioning bus segregation. How different might my beliefs be today if I had an experience or space to "problem solve" about the kindergarten children in my school the way these children began to think about bus segregation? How might having a space to dialogue and verbally role-play about what I saw in the basement have helped me as a child to process the situation as well?

Even though I had a funny feeling about my discovery, it seemed normal to me to separate children because nobody, the adults I trusted, talked about it. I probably felt that if nobody else was talking about it, then it must be all right. I pondered the same question that the students did: why would a group of people make a rule that separates another group of people, in this case kindergarten children? Even though I was not consciously thinking about this childhood moment while I was teaching during the summer, I believe on a deeper level it influenced how I taught.

## REFLECTIONS ON USING CRYSTALLIZATION AS A METHODOLOGY

Examples in this chapter demonstrate that crystallization as a methodology disrupts dominant approaches to data collection and analysis by using writing as a method of inquiry, and disrupts dominant notions of (re)presenting research findings through the use of poetry, narrative vignettes, images, and embodied conversations. I found crystallization to be a joyous and richly complex process that enabled me to know myself better through autoethnography, to better understand myself as a teacher and researcher, and stretched me artistically to tinker with various ways of communicating and (re)presenting. The process of crystallization gave me space and permission to acknowledge my privilege, position, and power in society, examining closely the various communities and cultures I am a part of and the multiple identities I embody.

Tensions of using crystallization as a methodology include finding outlets for publication recognized in the academy. Many times, the space limitations and traditional structures of academic journals do not support crystallization. Some journals and reviewers request more traditional section headings and layout of texts. Perhaps pursuing online journals as venues that allow more images, non-traditional writing forms, and more space enables researchers to use creative forms of research. However, as an academy we must reconcile if these online journals are valued just as much as more traditional or dominant ones, especially in the standards for tenure and promotion. I encountered tensions as I searched for publication venues that might be open to multivoiced poetry or images. Many top-tiered research journals in the field of early childhood education seem to value postpositivist research written up in traditional ways that draw on developmental theories (not feminist, critical, or poststructural perspectives) (Cohen & Johnson, 2011). I began to search for journals in reflective practice and qualitative journals; these have proven to provide some space for disruptive approaches. However, word limitations make it difficult to capture research through multivoiced poetry and narratives. I found that performing poetry or sharing memoirs at conferences is a better way to communicate or live out research. However, in a "publish or perish" academic environment these human interactions are not valued as much as publications in peer-reviewed research journals.

As a doctoral student, I was privileged to have had a committee that encouraged me to think of a dissertation in a non-traditional way. The committee members supported my interests in using various genres for analysis and writing. My advice to students is to seek out committee members, even if they are outside your department, that will support and advocate on your behalf to try out disruptive forms of research such as crystallization. While it might be difficult to identify these individuals initially, take time to study people's curriculam vitae. Look for the types of publications and presentations they are involved with and read anything of theirs you can. Notice the kinds of courses taught and service activities they dedicate their time to in/outside the university. Have conversations with potential committee members, asking if they are comfortable supporting you in disruptive practices. Give them examples and a rationale for *why* particular disruptive practices fit your desires as a researcher. Ask questions about policies at the university that might be stumbling blocks and see if the faculty member has ideas for how to navigate them and be supportive of you in the process. Request that you have an outside committee member, a faculty from another university, whose scholarship supports your process as a disruptive researcher. For faculty, even if you are not familiar with crystallization, view advising a student who wants to use this methodology as a learning process for you. How can advising stretch you as a scholar?

These tensions illuminate the interplay of macro/meso/micro levels of politics as described in the introduction to this book. For myself, as a newer scholar, looking ahead for tenure and promotion, it is not easy to navigate the field of educational research at these levels. Many times, conflicting messages are sent. At a macro level, peer-reviewed publications following more traditional ways of research (quantitative and post-positivist qualitative) are valued. Being explicit about the self in research is sometimes frowned upon and does not meet the criteria for objective research.

At a meso level, the institution I work at has tenure and promotion policy documents, but as I talk more to different players in that process (i.e., faculty who already have tenure and vote on my tenure and promotion), I receive mixed messages. For example, I have been told that a book does not count the same as one peer-reviewed journal article—the journal article holds more value. Basically, get the number of journal articles you need, then do whatever else you want (write a book). Or, even within a department that focuses on teacher education, "practitioner-" based articles are not esteemed as highly as "research" articles. This belief perpetuates the idea that teaching and researching are separate or on opposite ends of a spectrum. Or, that articles written for practitioners are not based on rigorous data collection and analysis. This type of policy does not support the belief of theory *and* practice as one or that teachers *are* researchers (some of the best we have, as they are interacting and reflecting daily on teaching decisions and encounters). This is problematic for me on a micro level as I resonate with feminist and critical perspectives. I approach research sites through relationships established over time with teachers (not a top-down approach beginning with a superintendent or principal) and view participants (both teachers and students) as co-researchers, inviting the teacher(s) I work with to have as much (or little) input into the type of data we collect, the process of analysis, and co-authoring and presenting with me (Gutshall & Kuby, 2013). However, when having to assign percentages to author contributions, this proves tricky. Are the percentages based on the number of words written in the article or the overarching contribution of thinking? For example, if a teacher and I spend several hours each week discussing and analyzing what we see in a classroom, but I write most of the words in the manuscript, it devalues the rich conversations and shaping of ideas in the moments of dialogue before writing. These are all tensions I live among at macro/meso/micro levels as I attempt to embark on qualitative approaches to inquiry that support my beliefs. Many times I find friction as I rub against and disrupt more traditional values and expectations in academia.

However, even with these tensions, there are numerous possibilities and joys of engaging in disruptive methods of inquiry such as crystallization. Crystallization adds an aesthetic, embodied aspect to analysis and writing. During the process of research, I felt alive with the data. I felt more in-tune with my identities and who I was becoming. It is more engaging to read a variety of genres than just traditional academic writing. Crystallization invites readers into a text (broadly defined to include visual and embodied texts) at different points and has the potential to connect and pull readers into the experience. Crystallization moves beyond simply having a variety of data sources, to embracing a variety of genres for analysis and (re)presenting. While in the moment it might not seem like joy, disrupting traditional ideas of what counts as a dissertation is beneficial. The process of dissertating became more than just fulfilling a requirement to graduate, it became a process of knowing myself, exploring disruptive ways of researching, and discovering how I want to situate myself in the field of education.

By including autoethnography in the nature of my study, I was purposefully seeking to understand my identities in relation to teaching and researching. However, not all crystallized studies are that explicit. As Ellingson (2009) mentioned in her five principles of crystallization, reflexivity is a crucial tenet of the methodology. Researchers need to be explicit in how their multiple, shifting identities (i.e., race, gender, class, sexuality, ability, nation, religion, and so forth) matter in the process and (re)presentation of crystallization. Research is not neutral. Our identities shape the decisions we make in data collection, analysis, and (re)presenting. We study what is personal in that we do not invest years of time researching qualitatively about topics and inquiries that do not matter to us. We need to examine why we are spending time researching the topics we do. How do cultural influences, personal experiences, and/or historical events play a part in generating ideas for the research?

## CLOSING THOUGHTS

As a group of doctoral students sat in my home to share final projects and celebrate the end of our semester-long narrative inquiry course, I sat amazed at the final products students shared: a play in three acts, creative narrative representations constructed from autoethnographic writings and visual analyses of photographs, and even a modern-day kimono as a text to (re)present analysis of interviews with a textile artist. After students left, I asked my husband what he thought. He responded with a question: What has happened to academic freedom? He was referring to the discourse that permeated the graduate students' discussion on what they thought of the course and how it might shape them as researchers. Most conveyed that while it was great to be in a course that explored multiple genres for analysis and writing, that this type of research would never be accepted by their dissertation committee or academic journals in their fields. Sadly, I understand the tensions graduate students have when they articulate that they want to try out something different, whether that is introducing new theoretical and methodological ideas to their disciplines or creating a play script for their dissertation format. I hear the fear in their voices expressing that their committees will not let them try new research techniques, and a fear that disrupting the academy will not secure them tenure and promotion one day. I am not naïve to this reality, but wonder how change will ever come about if newer scholars do not have support to push boundaries and try out innovative research practices.

My hope is that examples such as my dissertation and this chapter (along with others in this book) will encourage graduate students and faculty to "try out" or "play around with" methodological and theoretical possibilities of using multiple genres for analysis and writing. I also hope that by sharing the experience I had as a graduate student, in disrupting the traditional dissertation processes, it will encourage other doctoral students and perhaps faculty to be bold and take risks. This is my hope for educational research—moving beyond what has already been done—in order to understand and notice innovative ways of researching, learning, and teaching. Specifically, how might crystallization help you to better understand particular phenomena of interest and to share that with others, knowing that each person will experience the research differently? Crystallization as a methodology has potential to transform the academy by embracing an endless array of possibilities for data, analysis, and (re)presentation.

## NOTES

1. I acknowledge that words such as "White" and "Black" reinforce the idea that race is biological and perhaps synonymous with skin color. However, I have chosen to use these terms in memoir-writing because it is true to the language I heard growing up. I now understand race to be a social construction tied to oppression, power, position, and privileges in a culture.

2. Versions of the vignettes and analysis of the segregation of students in the school basement are included in: Kuby (2013a), *Critical Literacy in Early Childhood Classrooms: Unpacking Histories, Unlearning Privilege*. New York, NY: Teachers College Press.

3. Some adult friends in the poem gave permission to use their first names.

4. The poem was originally written in spring 2008.

5. Emotionally disturbed.

6. Government assisted housing.

## Appendix A: Adaptation of Jeffersonian Transcription Markings

Pauses counted by seconds in parentheses—(1)
Up and down arrows for rise/fall of pitch—↑
Colons to show word sounds stretched out—wo:rd
Words that were not clear inside parentheses—(inaudible)
Bold words to show emphasis, louder speech—**word**
Equal sign to show interruption—=word
Brackets to show overlap of speech—[word]
Laughter shown by "h" in parentheses—(h)
In-hale breath—.hh
Exhale breath—hh
Nonverbal movements written in parentheses and italicized—{*nods*}

## REFERENCES

Atkinson, P., & Delamont, S. (2006). Rescuing narrative from qualitative research. *Narrative Inquiry, 16*(1), 164–172.

Cochran-Smith, M., & Lytle, S. (Eds.). (1993). *Inside/outside: Teacher research and knowledge.* New York, NY: Teachers College Press.

Cochran-Smith, M., & Lytle, S. (Eds.). (2009). *Inquiry as stance: Practitioner research for the next generation.* New York, NY: Teachers College Press.

Cohen, L. E., & Johnson, J. E. (2011, April). *Reconceptualizing research methods in early childhood.* Roundtable session at the annual meeting of the American Educational Research Association. New Orleans, LA.

Cole, A. L., & Knowles, J. G. (2001). *Lives in context: The art of life history research.* Lanham, MD: Rowman & Littlefield.

Comber, B., & Simpson, A. (Ed.). (2001). *Negotiating critical literacies in classrooms.* Mahwah, NJ: Lawrence Erlbaum.

Duncan, M. (2004). Autoethnography: Critical appreciation of an emerging art. *International Journal of Qualitative Methods, 3*(4), 1–14.

Ellingson, L. L. (2009). *Engaging in crystallization in qualitative research: An introduction.* Los Angeles, CA: Sage.

Evans, J. (2007). War and peas in the 21st century: Young children responding critically to picture story texts. In Y. Goodman & P. Martens. (Eds.), *Critical issues in early literacy: Research and pedagogy* (pp. 235–250). Mahwah, NJ: Lawrence Erlbaum.

Freire, P. (1970/2005). *Pedagogy of the oppressed* (30th anniversary ed.). New York, NY: Continuum.

Gutshall, T. L., & Kuby, C. R. (2013). Students as integral contributors to teacher research. *Talking Points, 25*(1), 2–8.

Humphreys, M. (2005). Getting personal: Reflexivity and autoethnographic vignettes. *Qualitative Inquiry, 11,* 840–860.

Jones, S. (2006). *Girls, social class, and literacy: What teachers can do to make a difference.* Portsmouth, NH: Heinemann.

Jones, S. H. (Ed.) (2008). *Blackwell encyclopedia of sociology.* Boston, MA: Blackwell.

Kuby, C. R. (2010). *Understanding an early childhood inquiry curriculum through crystallizing autoethnography, practitioner research, and a performative analysis of emotion* (Dissertation). Retrieved from Indiana University Proquest.

Kuby, C. R. (2011a). Kidwatching with a critical eye: The power of observation and reflexive practice. *Talking Points, 22*(2), 22–28.

Kuby, C. R. (2011b). Humpty Dumpty and Rosa Parks: Making space for critical dialogue with 5 and 6 year olds. *Young Children, 66*(5), 36–43.

Kuby, C. R. (2013). "OK this is hard": Doing emotions in social justice dialogue. *Education, Citizenship and Social Justice. 8*(1), 29–42.

Kuby, C. R. (2013a). *Critical literacy in the early childhood classroom: Unpacking histories, unlearning privilege.* New York, NY: Teachers College Press.

Kuby, C. R. (2013b). Critical inquiry in early childhood education: A teacher's exploration. *Voices of Practitioners, 8*(1), 1–15.

Kuby, C. R. (in press). Understanding emotions as situated, embodied, and fissured: Thinking with theory to create an analytical tool. *International Journal for Qualitative Studies in Education.* Online version available as of October 14, 2013: http://dx.doi.org/10.1080/09518398.2013.834390.

Lewison, M., Leland, C., & Harste, J. (2007). *Creating critical classrooms.* Mahwah, NJ: Lawrence Erlbaum.

Miller, K. I. (2000). Common ground from the post-positivist perspective: From "straw-person" argument to collaborative coexistence. In S. R. Corman & M. S. Poole. (Eds.), *Perspectives on organizational communication: Finding common ground* (pp. 47–67). New York, NY: Guilford Press.

Muncey, T. (2005). Doing autoethnography. *International Journal of Qualitative Research, 4*(3), 1–12.

Richardson, L., & St. Pierre, E. A. (2005). Writing: A method of inquiry. In N. Denzin & Y. Lincoln (Eds.), *The Sage handbook of qualitative research* (3rd ed., pp. 959–978). Thousand Oaks, CA: Sage.

Rosenblatt, L. M. (1978). *The reader the text the poem: The transactional theory of the literary work*: Carbondale, IL: Southern Illinois University Press.

Sahni, U. (2001). Children appropriating literacy: Empowerment pedagogy from young children's perspective. In B. Comber & A. Simpson (Eds.), *Negotiating critical literacies in classrooms* (pp.19–36). Mahwah, NJ: Laurence Erlbaum.

Schaefer, L. (2000). *Rosa Parks (first biographies).* North Mankato, MN: Capstone Press.

Spry, T. (2001). Performing autoethnography: An embodied methodological praxis. *Qualitative Inquiry, 7*(6), 706–732.

Vasquez, V. M. (2001). Constructing a critical curriculum with young children. In B. Comber & A. Simpson (Eds.), *Negotiating critical literacies in classrooms* (pp. 55–68). Mahwah, NJ: Lawrence Erlbaum.

Vasquez, V. M. (2004). *Negotiating critical literacies with young children.* Mahwah, NJ: Lawrence Erlbaum.

Wall, S. (2006). An autoethnography on learning about autoethnography. *International Journal of Qualitative Methods, 5*(2), 1–12.

Wohlwend, K. (2007). Friendship meeting or blocking circle: Identities in the laminated spaces of a playground conflict. *Contemporary Issues in Early Childhood, 8*(1), 73–88.

## ADDITIONAL RESOURCES ON CRYSTALLIZATION

Ellingson, L. L. (2009). *Engaging in crystallization in qualitative research: An introduction.* Los Angeles, CA: Sage.

*Ellingson references many of her own publications in book length and article format that are crystallization examples.

Janesick, V. J. (2000). The choreography of qualitative research design: Minuets, improvisations, and crystallization. In N. Denzin & Y. Lincoln (Eds.), *Handbook of qualitative research* (2nd ed.) (pp. 379–399). Thousand Oaks, CA: Sage.

Kuby, C. R. (2010). *Understanding an early childhood inquiry curriculum through crystallizing autoethnography, practitioner research, and a performative analysis of emotion* (Dissertation). Retrieved from Indiana University Proquest.

Richardson, L., & St. Pierre, E. A. (2005). Writing: A method of inquiry. In N. Denzin & Y. Lincoln (Eds.), *The Sage handbook of qualitative research* (3rd ed., pp. 959–978). Thousand Oaks, CA: Sage. *Ideas in the last pages of the chapter on writing activities/exercises that could be used for analysis and representations.

## Examples of Crystallization Referenced in Ellingson's Book, Some From Beyond the Field of Education

### Book length examples

Bach, H. (2007). *A visual narrative concerning curriculum, girls, photography, etc.* Walnut Creek, CA: Left Coast Press.

Ellis, C. (2008). *Revisions: Autoethnographic stories of life and work.* Walnut Creek, CA: Left Coast Press.

Lather, P., & Smithies, C. (1997). *Troubling the angels: Women living with HIV/AIDS.* Boulder, CO: Westview Press.

Richardson, L. (1997). *Fields of play: Constructing an academic life.* New Brunswick, NJ: Rutgers University Press.

### Article-length examples

Clark/Keefe. (2006). Degrees of separation. *Qualitative Inquiry, 12,* 1180–1197.

Hirschman, K. (1999). Blood, vomit, and communication: The days and nights of an intern on call. *Health Communication, 11,* 35–57.

López, E., Eng, E., Randall-David, E., & Robinson, N. (2005). Quality of life concerns of African American breast cancer survivors within rural North Carolina: Blending the techniques of photovoice and grounded theory. *Qualitative Health Research, 15,* 99–115.

Miller, D. L., Creswell, J. W., & Olander, L. S. (1998). Writing and retelling multiple ethnographic tales of a soup kitchen for the homeless. *Qualitative Inquiry, 4,* 469–491.

Minge, J. M. (2007). The stained body: A fusion of embodied art on rape and love. *Journal of Contemporary Ethnography, 36,* 252–280.

# CHAPTER SEVEN

# Beyond Scientific "Facts"

## Choosing to Honor and Make Visible a Variety of Knowledge Systems

CASSIE F. QUIGLEY AND NICOLE BEEMAN-CADWALLADER

For several centuries, *the* definition of science consisted of only one particular view—a view that originated primarily in Western societies, from middle- and upper-class white men (often called Western Modern Science, WMS, in the literature). Grande (2004) called the foundation of WMS the "deep colonialist consciousness," whereby "objective 'expert' knowledge is elicited to solve problems and address crises and traditional knowledge (defined by its non-rational, subjective nature) is viewed as irrelevant or distortional to the objective understanding of the world" (p. 69). Hence, the "deep colonial consciousness" embedded within WMS influences whose knowledge is legitimized in the scientific community (Harding, 1991), and, we argue, from *where* knowledge can be legitimized.

Focusing attention on specific places potentially broadens the scope of whose knowledge garners value in the scientific and science education communities. Place as a concept attracts attention from scholars in a range of academic disciplines, and, hence, carries different meanings. For example, some focus on the psychological dimensions of place (Chawla, 1992), whereas others focus on the geographic features (Tuan, 1977) or cultural and natural landscapes of a specific region (Jackson, 1997). In our research, we seek to value the scientific knowledge that emerges from the interactions between the sociocultural, biophysical, political/economic, and psychological dimensions of specific places. Doing so directly disrupts the dominant view that science is objective, value neutral, and placeless.

While our conception of valuing local places is still considered disruptive to science and science education research, scholars in other fields, namely the sociology of science, study the role of place in scientific knowledge production (Turnbull, 2000; Watson-Veran & Turnbull, 1994). Furthermore, the context-rich, place-contingent knowledge of marginalized and indigenous peoples continues to attract attention in the scientific community. For example, scientists trained in Western Modern Science documented that groups of people indigenous to the Amazon rainforest have a cultural practice of smashing used pottery, along with other "waste materials," then burning and burying them. This practice leaves behind biomass and charcoal that neutralize and enrich the soil, making it viable for agriculture; the soil is known locally as *terra preta* (Mann, 2002). This cultural practice contains valuable scientific knowledge. This knowledge is not only valuable to science; it is also valuable to the cultural life and livelihood of the indigenous group. Preservation and continuation of this knowledge is crucial for the preservation and continuation of this culture. Still, it is only when this knowledge is passed to someone with accepted "expert" credentials that it becomes something of value for legitimized scientific knowledge (Rist & Dahdouh-Guebas, 2006; Zent, 2009).

The notion that scientific knowledge transforms as it migrates from its origin carries importance. We share goals for the integration of traditional indigenous knowledge in science education, but we do so with caution. Nadasdy (2004) outlined problems with utilizing indigenous knowledge in science education. Knowledge integration runs the risk of homogenizing, romanticizing, and subsuming into Western modern science traditional, local knowledge of indigenous peoples. This not only threatens to affect the production of it, but also the production of knowledge in science education research. If the very act of researching the integration of knowledge systems in science education is problematic, then its inclusion in science education will also be fraught with problems. Unless the way we conceive of research in science education changes, the prospects for true integration of indigenous and local scientific knowledge into science education will remain submerged and at the fringe.

Nadasdy (2004) illustrated the issues of Western scientific and traditional ecological knowledge integration in his ethnography among the Kluane First Nations and wildlife biologists in Canada. At the root of these issues is his concern about what applying the term "knowledge" does to the ways of knowing and being of Kluane people. Nadasdy argues that the term "indigenous knowledge" is culturally loaded, and that "applying this term to First Nations peoples' lived experiences has the effect of imposing on their lives a set of 'foreign' assumptions about the nature of the world and how humans can relate to and 'know' it" (2004, pp. 94–95). Furthermore, power relations between Kluane and non-Kluane people are unequal, which has a "direct bearing on what qualifies as knowledge" (p. 113), and forces everyone involved in the efforts to "compartmentalize and distill Aboriginal peoples' beliefs, values, and experience according to external criteria of relevance, seriously distorting them in the process" (p. 183).

As science education researchers, we are motivated and challenged by contested terrains of what and whose knowledge counts as legitimate knowledge. In the dominant view in our field, people trained in a field of science, using the tools of science, produce scientific knowledge. In our epistemological view, we see scientific knowledge embedded in the everyday lives, practices, and contexts of people who have remained all but undetected by formal science. Ontologically, we dare to assert that such knowledge can not only be viewed as scientific, but also that the ways in which it has been generated need not fit the norms of formal, Western science. Furthermore, our axiological stance is that, as a science education community, we must value and honor the knowledge generated, and the way it was generated, by marginalized people as scientific, or we risk losing it.

In this chapter, we share stories and analyses from our own experiences navigating the tensions between desires to have our research accepted by the scientific community as valid and wanting to best serve the communities with whom we work. During these stories, we outline the ways in which we are disrupting qualitative work in science education by disrupting traditional notions of research roles and relationships, the dominant approaches to collecting data, traditional notions of representing and disseminating research findings, and rigid epistemological and methodological boundaries. Then, commonalities from our stories are unearthed. Finally, we discuss insights for science education research and potential paths forward that may be forged.

## STORIES FROM OUR WORK

In each of the examples that follow, we seek to show how our actions and thoughts while conducting research function to put disruptive methodologies to work. Additionally, acknowledging our own backgrounds and subjectivities is also essential. Nicole, a doctoral candidate at Indiana University, identifies as a Caucasian American who grew up in a lower-middle-class family in the Midwest. She researches place-based education in international and domestic higher education, utilizing both decolonizing and critical methodologies. Cassie, a fourth-year assistant professor at Clemson University, identifies as a Caucasian American from an upper-middle-class family. She grew up in the Midwest, although spent several years living abroad in Europe and Southeast Asia. She researches international environmental perspectives using decolonizing methodologies, often with photo-based methodological tools. As both of our studies are contextualized in Kenya and focus on environmental issues, understanding the major ecosystems is important. The United Nations Environment Programme (2009) provided excellent maps illustrating these ecosystems and the cities Eldoret and Narok where we conducted our work (see Figure 5 on p. 5 in the UNEP 2009 document and the pictures of the changing landscape of the Narok district from the years 1975 to 2007 on p. 98 and p. 99).

## DEFENDING FUZZY BOUNDARIES: USING ETHNOGRAPHY TO DISRUPT SCIENCE EDUCATION RESEARCH

Since 2007, the year Cassie and I (Nicole) began our graduate studies, science educators in our field have questioned our work. "How is this science education research?" "Where is the science in this education research?" "This isn't science education, is it?" These questions haunt us in our efforts to push the boundaries and disrupt the equilibrium of science education research. We say that the questions "haunt" us because they directly mark our consciousnesses in that they deeply influence what we choose to study in our research and how we go about studying it. At a surface level, we often feel as though we have to explain our particular methodological choices. In a paradigm where lines are drawn between valid and invalid, significant and insignificant, efficient and inefficient methods and/or findings, the process of explaining such methodologies is incredibly complex; as if we are unveiling a secret. Instead of the clear lines demarcating what and whose knowledge is of most worth to study for science education, we see fuzzy boundaries. At a more complex level, we constantly feel as though we are fighting on behalf of alternative ways of experiencing, documenting, and interpreting reality. It also leaves us wondering about the persistent determination of science and science education to maintain clearly defined disciplinary boundaries.

As a doctoral candidate six years into my degree, I am far more confident pushing boundaries in my field. Gaining this confidence required much struggle, however, and my confidence does not mean that my work always proceeds unquestioned. Here, I tell the story of three phases of a project I did earlier in my graduate work, which both challenged and afforded me opportunities to build confidence through grappling with the "haunting" questions.

### Phase One: Project Development

During the middle of my graduate program, in spring and summer of 2009, I designed and conducted my first independent research project, an ethnography of place in Kenya. I planned to solicit grant funding for my research proposal but before submitting the document for external review I had to generate three different versions of my proposal to get feedback from three different faculty members. The reasons I created three versions illuminate some of the insecurities I faced about my research. On previous occasions, some faculty asked me to isolate science from other ways of knowing (i.e., culture, politics, etc.,). For reasons discussed earlier in this section, this task increasingly felt at odds with my conceptions of knowledge production, yet I still carried fear that my efforts to disrupt would be thwarted. As such, I tailored my writing to what I thought each of these particular faculty members, all from different disciplines in education, would want to see. In doing so, I hoped to get a sense of the degree to which I could disrupt science education research norms and still secure funding. Reflecting on *how* I tailored the proposals revealed interesting patterns. What did I include or exclude in each of the versions, and why? How did the disciplinary homes of the faculty members influence what I thought appropriate for a research proposal, and what does this uncover about rigid epistemological and methodological boundaries in science education?

As I alluded to, the faculty members with whom I shared the proposal have three different disciplinary homes in education: science education; literacy, culture, and language education; and art education. Until I looked back at the versions of the proposals, I did not realize their differences. Yet, some of these differences illustrate my first attempts at disrupting rigid epistemological and methodological, as well as disciplinary, boundaries in science education. The proposal I handed to the science education faculty member contained a lengthy section that was not included in the other two versions. In it, I tried to depolarize notions of Western and indigenous scientific knowledge because I assumed this faculty member from science education held the notion that Western and indigenous scientific knowledge are incommensurable. The final sections of each proposal also differed significantly. For the science education faculty member, I offered proposed findings and limitations, as well as emphasized the role of using the findings from this study to build frameworks for future studies. For the literacy, culture, and language education faculty member, who studies indigenous education, I offered final thoughts on how ethnography of place contributes to the idea of "survivance," or continuation and regeneration of cultural ways of knowing and being, in indigenous education (Villegas, Neugebauer, & Venegas, 2008). For the art education faculty member, who also teaches classes in qualitative research methodology, I focused much more on my role as a researcher, the ethical considerations I needed to make, and how I planned to monitor my subjective lens.

These differences pose interesting questions for me, which reveal some of the struggle of disrupting science education research. I find it encouraging that I dedicated space in the "science education" version of the proposal to a discussion of attempts at depolarizing Western and indigenous scientific knowledge. Too often, scholars present Western and indigenous knowledge systems as diametrically opposed to each other, at polar ends of the knowledge spectrum, and in my work I seek to challenge that presentation. Indeed, this points to a major goal of mine: for science education research to begin to value other ways of knowing as a part

of science education. Likewise, some of the other differences in the three proposals, which ultimately became integral processes in this research, show attempts
at disrupting science education research. For example, my attention to potential
contributions this ethnography could have to "survivance" of indigenous scientific
knowledge, and my focus on keeping my researcher lens visible in my writing, both
push disruption of traditional notions of research roles and relationships in science
education. Still, some of the differences in the proposal I gave the science education faculty member illustrate the tensions in such disruptive work. For example,
why did I find it necessary to state that a major goal was to build frameworks
(universal and generalizable) as opposed to identify alternative ways of knowing
about the scientific world (particular and context-bound)? Furthermore, why did
I state proposed findings and limitations in the version for the science education
faculty, but focus more on the role the study would play for indigenous education
and my role as a researcher in the other versions?

## Phase Two: In the Field

Despite my concerns in the proposal stage, I secured a small grant specifically for
science education graduate students early in their programs. Through conducting an ethnography of place, I sought to understand the interactions between
people and nature in Eldoret, Kenya; the ways those interactions shape their
livelihoods; and the ways local science is embedded in those interactions. I also
sought to build partnerships with science educators in Eldoret. While in Kenya,
I experienced both internal and external struggles about my role as a researcher
and the relevance of the study to science education. Throughout the study,
I felt insecure about how to explain my study to others. I stayed in a boarding
house traditionally used by United States medical residents and researchers, and
wondered how I could make the case that my study would be meaningful for science education. Building partnerships with the regional university and teachers'
colleges seemed defensibly relevant. But, what about observing at the produce
market and non-profit artisan organization? Or just wandering through town
observing and talking with the taxi drivers? How could I make the case, even to
myself, that these activities were going to reveal relevant understandings for how
to approach teaching and learning science in this community? The last phrase
*in this community* provides the clue. I believed then, and continue to believe,
that what and how we learn should be contextual, particularly in non-Western
communities that embody worldviews different from Western Modern Science.
Nonetheless, the doubt I experienced was fierce.

The findings of my study reveal the complicated nature of examining local
knowledge in this community. I interacted with and interviewed several Kenyan-born
scholars in fields either in or related to science, who had trained in "the West" and

then returned to Kenya to work. Doing so raised tensions for them. They expressed the difficult pressure they felt to categorize their traditional cultural knowledge into Western academic disciplines. The following excerpt from field notes illustrates this:

> Michael is a doctor that does a lot of work both in Indiana and here in Kenya. He went to medical school at Harvard. I went to lunch with him. After lunch we were walking around and he told us, "Look at all those diseases (or, did you see) that she [a Maasai woman] can cure from that little box?" I think she was an elder, and she showed us a list of ailments with prices for curing to the right. The prices were in Ugandan shillings, but converted they ranged in price from 1,500 Kenyan shillings to 6,000. The ailments that she listed that she could cure ranged from Menopause to tuberculosis.... I asked Michael, "How do they make all the remedies from so few powders, do they mix them together?" He said, "You know, there is a lot of medicinal plant knowledge here in Kenya ... the problem is that none of it is classified [pharmacologically].... So, a patient may tell me that they used a tree bark to cure an ailment but which tree bark?" (Field notes, 16 June 2009)

Michael communicated important information to me about Kenyan indigenous scientific knowledge through this interaction. First, by drawing my attention to the Maasai healer, he encouraged me to recognize that Kenyan indigenous plant knowledge exists and carries value for many Kenyans. Second, he highlighted the tensions he faces as a Kenyan-born, Western-trained physician. He values the indigenous medicinal plant knowledge and wants to draw on it in his practice, but has difficulty forcing it into the Western pharmacological classification system. Documenting field notes while out in town may be standard practice in ethnographies in many fields. And field notes are certainly common in science education. However, the documentation of field notes in town rather than in a science classroom or a locale of formal scientific practice disrupts dominant approaches to data collection in science education.

## Phase Three: Back Home

When I returned home, my personal doubt about the value and validity of my place-based ethnography quelled. I began writing proposals and manuscripts to share my work with the wider science education community. Shortly, though, doubts crept back into my consciousness. Although I used systematic methods for centering the concerns and realities of Kenyans about their place, such as iterative, participant-directed data collection, I wondered about my authority to speak on issues of science education from an African nation as a Westerner. Mostly, however, I anticipated that my peers would question how the findings relate to science education, or not take their validity seriously. I contemplated how to represent my findings in writing in a way that would simultaneously suit the norms of science education and honor the richness and wholeness of the findings.

The problems I actually encountered surprised me. When I submitted a proposal for presenting this work at a science education conference, I received a request from the organization to remove the geographic indicators and contextual information as an effort to maintain "masked" proposals. Achieving an objective review process, to fit with the rigors of scientific practice, was the intent of the "masking." As I read this request, I felt my face flush and anger rise in the pit of my stomach. The implications of this act seemed grave. I felt that removing the context would render the meanings garnered from the study meaningless. Although I cringed while doing so, I removed the contextual information, but added a footnote that explained my concerns.

This proposal was accepted for presentation in the conference. When I actually did present this work, I chose to disrupt conventional notions of this science education community by including all contextual information, details about the ways I challenged my role as a researcher, and techniques I used to ensure my methods honored the community with whom I worked. To my surprise, responses from listeners at this presentation were overwhelmingly positive. However, I was asked if I was attempting to fuse incommensurate knowledge systems. While this is a valid question and concern, as illustrated by the previous discussion of Nadasdy's (2004) work, my experiences were not consistent with this question. What I found is that the people with whom I worked in Kenya did not delineate their operative knowledge into disciplinary categories. They drew on indigenous knowledge, Western scientific knowledge, and other forms and disciplines of knowledge as the situation saw fit. This made me wonder about the seeming preoccupation with disciplinary boundaries in science/science education. What if the very act of dividing knowledge up into disciplines renders it inaccessible in local contexts? Furthermore, what do we, as Westerners, lose when we attempt to understand knowledge only categorized into its appropriate discipline?

## Final Notes on the Importance of Fuzzy Boundaries

In an interview with a Kenyan science educator, I asked about how environmental issues are addressed in school and how that conflates with Kenyans' understanding of environmental issues. I asked this question because I had noticed how frequently people and the news media addressed environmental issues. Specifically, we talked about deforestation. The science educator explained,

> So the moment we are told, we say, this is an environmental issue, communities now say, no ... you know, in Kenya we have so many communities, sub-communities, so you may find [that] maybe in one community, because they enjoyed the politics of that time, they are the ones that are benefitted the land. So when other people are asking [questioning the actions of others] this is not correct because many people are suffering out of this activity, they say, no, you are trying to target our people. You want to target our people. This is land

we have been given. Now … [rather] than being an environmental issue, it becomes an ethnic tension, and people don't reason well. (Kennedy, Interview, 6 July 2009)

I learned from this explanation that deforestation in Kenya is an incredibly complex issue. From a Westerner's perspective, environmental education might seem like a viable approach to addressing deforestation. I believe that it is, as does the educator whom I interviewed. However, if educators only address the ecological, scientific aspects of deforestation, then deforestation may never abate. This educator made evident that ignorance of the implications of deforestation is not its major cause. Sociopolitical and cultural tensions drive deforestation. I think that the only reason my study revealed those tensions is because I chose to disrupt. I disrupted traditional notions of research roles and approaches to data collection when I observed outside places of formal science/science education and allowed my participants to direct my focus. I also disrupted rigid epistemological and methodological boundaries when I allowed what happens outside places of formal science/science education to be important. For example, focusing my attention on observing in places such as the produce market, suggested by participants, disrupted the epistemological boundary of where legitimate scientific knowledge can be produced. Further, through observing in the markets, I disrupted methodological boundaries of places where science education happens and where science education should be studied. Finally, I disrupted disciplinary boundaries when I included knowledge and concerns outside of science in consideration of science education.

## RE-OPENING CLOSED DOORS: RESPONDING TO HEGEMONIC VIEWS OF SCIENCE

There's a tribe, it's called Ogiek or Dorobo, who live in the forest … their main source of income is honey, wild roots, wild fruits. They know the trees hold their life by hanging their beehives on top … so they don't destroy the forest but unfortunately, the government is affecting them [by adjudicating their land for cattle grazing] and then they're exposed to activities they don't know. They don't know how to raise livestock. They don't know livestock. But they are prohibited from practicing their main activities. Their life is like … changed. (Paul, Interview, 19 October 2013)

In the fall of 2012, my (Cassie's) research group, which consisted of four faculty members, participated in an existing project in Narok, Kenya. The purpose of the research group's study was to listen to the Kenyan participants like Paul, and to listen to the local communities by creating an interdisciplinary, integrative approach to the construct of sustainability and sustainability education. We outlined our exploratory approach to understanding their perspectives of the environment but asked them to take charge of the types of data to collect and to decide what data to share with us. We provided them with technology to capture their environmental perspectives through video, photographs, and audio recording and written descriptions. In this way, we disrupted the traditional notion of the science education research of controlling the type and content of data to collect. Instead, we forged meaningful relationships with the participants and encouraged them to lead us to the ways in which they defined sustainability and sustainability education.

Narok District is endowed with natural resources such as the Mau Forest and the Maasai Mara National Reserve. However, it faces the results of destructive environmental practices such as deforestation, insufficient waste management, and water pollution, which have contributed to drought and hardship in the surrounding valleys (UNEP, 2009). In the Mau forest and Maasai Mara National Reserve, more than one million acres of forest have been cleared for land development and fuel. This deforestation destroyed crucial watersheds, ecosystems, and wildlife as well as sacred lands of the Maasai people. These changes caused disruption of Maasai livelihood and wildlife habitat. This destruction is echoed in the voice of one participant:

> [Because] of all this deforestation—due to cutting down of trees.... Water catchment areas are going to reduce. It is affected in the Mau Forest when there was so much cutting down of trees because of charcoal and farming and we saw the migration in 2009, the wildebeest migration from Serengeti to the Mara was affected because there was so much water in Mara River .... human settlements are affected. This brings about the issue of people fighting for natural resources ... maybe [they] have a little in my own piece of land and so many other people who need water they come and fetch that water [from someone else's land], conflict starts. So lack of all [the trees], is going to result in trouble. (Susan, Interview, 17 October 2012)

Although the government attempted to limit conflict over water through land adjudication practices, these practices limited grazing to small plots of land and constrained the indigenous ways of pastoral living by the Maasai. The government forced the Maasai to change their practices of grazing cattle as a way to reduce deforestation. However, this top-down enforcement did not attempt to understand the indigenous practices, which led to disengagement towards sustainability and sustainability education from the Maasai. Daniel, a Maasai, described these challenges of the land adjudication practices:

> Cattle are the most important Maasai asset, source of food and pride. Cattle are also often blamed for causing soil erosion and at high density may cause wildlife declines. Grazing management is perhaps the biggest challenge to pastoralists, conservationists and government officials working to secure livelihoods in pastoral lands, but just how do we strike the viable optimal level of cattle numbers and grazing arrangement? (Daniel, Interview, 17 October 2012)

Daniel acknowledged the challenges of grazing management while understanding the cultural issues that need to be understood in order to achieve a successful management plan.

## Participants as Co-Researchers

One of the dangers of assuming that all practices of a community have negative impacts on the environment is that one then has little chance of uncovering practices that are sustainable. For the research team, understanding perspectives was particularly important because of the history of excluding the Maasai from the conversations—we did not want to repeat this mistake. As all of the project personnel were qualitative researchers, a priority for us was to first understand the current environmental perspectives of the community members with whom we were working, before making suggestions about initiating behavioral change. As this is an approach not typically used in science education, it is an example of a disruptive act.

Efforts to conserve and preserve the environment in developing or marginalized communities frequently involve a one-way transfer of knowledge and materials from a source in a more developed location to the marginalized community. This situation often results in a short-term donor project, which promises little-to-no long-term impact on local or indigenous relationships with the environment. Not only do such projects promise little, they are potentially damaging. Often times, the "solution" to the environmental issue is not constructed (or even co-constructed) in concert with local people. Ultimately, these solutions are embedded in outsiders perspectives, thus limitations ensue. In other words, the process of creating solutions for issues faced in significantly different geopolitical and social contexts is often itself unsustainable. Our aim was for the Maasai community to construct their own meanings of local environmental hazards and conservation. In this way, even our aim of the study was a disrupting act—it involved the participants in ways that do not readily occur in science education. However, by positioning the participants as researchers, the Maasai transformed their relationship with their environment. In turn, they constructed and enacted sustainable alternatives to destructive environmental practices—that *they* developed. Below, I provide examples of this. Attaining this objective, the research team surmised, contributed towards our long-term goal of increasing access for local and diverse populations to the field and discourse of environmental sustainability *and* disrupted rigid methodological boundaries in science education that typically involves a planned intervention and a pre/post test to determine effectiveness.

## Tensions in Writing-Up Disruptive Research

One way we disrupted science education methodology was exposing our intention in our writing. Even though a manuscript was accepted after working with a journal through two revision cycles, we first received some dispiriting reviews from a different journal that we initially submitted the manuscript to. Below, you can read how the editor of a well-respected science education journal rejected our manuscript without soliciting peer reviews. Interestingly, in 2001, the same journal published a special issue on indigenous knowledge systems in which it called for the inclusion of knowledge types other than Western Modern Science in science classrooms:

> The primary issue, in my mind, is a lack of fit with the mission of the journal and expectations of our readers. Although you situate your study in the debates over whether indigenous knowledge should or should not be considered or included in what gets taught in a typical school science course, the substance of your work is clearly aimed at eliciting Kenyan students' ideas about environmental issues and concerns as they relate to questions of sustainability, economic development, and globalization. You assert that their perspectives on these matters are important in making decisions about how to live and prosper in their local social, political, and cultural environment. That is to say that the questions and points at issue are primarily those—social, political, economic, and cultural—and these are not materially or essentially concerned with science or even alternative knowledge systems that primarily relate to our understanding of the natural world. (Personal communication with journal editor, 29 October 2012)

This editor's response surprised me. The most powerful (and disappointing) part is the final sentence. As a research team, we sought to disrupt the traditional ways in which science is depicted in the research. Although we understood the risk (in this case, rejection), we were surprised at some of the tensions. For us, social, political, economic, and cultural issues inherently influence understanding of the natural world. What would understanding the natural world look like if we asked people to remove these other areas related to these issues? What would the research methods look like if we were not concerned with the social, political, economic, and cultural issues? To navigate these tensions, we submitted the manuscript to another journal that was supportive of the integration of the social, political, economic, and cultural aspects of science (Quigley, Dogbey, Che, & Hallo, in press).

Because our writing included the participants' views of the environment that incorporated a broad definition of science (including social, political, economic, and cultural components), critics told us to wait until we had "real data" and then publish it in the traditional ways. However, if we did that we would not only continue the current trajectory of science education research, we would also not be valuing the work of seeking to understand perspectives as science education research. In this way, we are pushing the boundaries and disrupting what is currently permitted as publishable in science education research. I understand when I disrupt science education research, I am taking risks, and so I come across closed doors. However, the question is what to do and how to react to those closed doors? In this section, I presented the closed door as journal rejection. There are other types of closed doors: unfunded proposals because of lack of control groups and testable hypotheses, de-valuing our work as not rigorous because of who we position as researchers, and challenges to the validity of our work because of our broadened epistemological views of science education. However, I find promise in re-opening closed doors; by having my work published by peer-reviewed journals in our field, I am broadening the boundaries of what counts as legitimate science. Thus, I am disrupting the notions of what is science education research.

## Honoring Indigenous Ways of Knowing

As the ultimate goal of the work was to enhance environmental sustainability efforts, we felt it only ethical to first understand the ways in which the participants viewed the environment to avoid the common pitfall of creating another short-term donor project that ultimately has little to no use. Despite our intentionality towards avoiding these short-term donor projects, we found it necessary to remain vigilant with respect to enacting these aims throughout our research. For example, a U.S. biology professor, who was a part of the initial planning and research team, insisted that solar cookers be a part of our efforts. She wanted to purchase solar cookers to bring to Kenya and teach them about deforestation due to cooking with charcoal (here, charcoal is made by burning pieces of wood). We persisted in our efforts to document the perspectives of Kenyans and found that they were well-versed in the issues of deforestation and the need for alternative fuels. In fact, a European environmental action group purchased several solar cookers for the Maasai; however, the food tasted "strange," and the rainy season posed tech-nological difficulties that extended beyond problem-solving. Instead, they already employed the Kenyan traditional envirostove, called a "jiko." Jikos are very popular in Kenya, and with good reason, as they require very little wood to function.

> Rural household charcoal burning is one of the ways of deforestation. Many people in the community depend on charcoal burning and selling as a source of income. As much as they depend on charcoal burning and selling, there is an impact of it as they contribute to environmental degradation. Cutting down of trees for charcoal production exposes the soil to the agents of erosion (water and wind), increases emission of green house gases leading to global warming, and increases drudgery on women and child labor. Educating the community on the impact of charcoal burning and the importance of conserving for-est can reduce these challenges. The community should also be educated on importance of education to their children and alternative source of income such as practicing dairy forming, poultry keeping, and garden farming for production of vegetables and fruits. (James, Interview, 15 May 2012)

James, a Kenyan teacher, clearly implicated the economic issues when talking about how charcoal is a source of income. He also addressed the environmental is-sues when discussing the agents of erosion and increased emissions of green house gases, as well as the social and cultural issues with the mention of women's rights and child labor.

Similarly to James, Esther, another Kenyan teacher, offered a solution that dramatically reduces the quantity of charcoal, thus attending to the cultural needs of the community (the desire for food cooked with charcoal) and the environmental issues.

> I got interested in jikos because of its conservative nature. Since most people in Kenya uses firewood or charcoal for cooking, this jiko uses very few pieces of firewood to cook hence avoiding felling down of trees thus conserving the environment while still allowing them to cook in the ways that they are accustomed to. (Esther, Interview, 5 June 2012)

Here, Esther, described how jikos are a more sustainable approach to cooking while attending to the cultural ways of open-fire cooking. If we had ignored the perspectives of our participants and launched into an intervention, we would have wasted money and resources, and discounted the environmental knowledge of the community.

Overall, throughout the documentation of the participants' perceptions of environmental issues in their community, we discovered the environmental issues they discussed were not unique to Narok. The issues—deforestation, water quality, waste disposal, and erosion— are found in other areas of the world. However, what is important to note is that we did not name these issues, the local community did. We believed that our participants were co-researchers and their ways of knowing valuable. By documenting local perspectives, we were enacting disrupting methodologies by disrupting the traditional notions of participants' roles in research. As we move from understanding environmental perspectives to fostering sustainable actions co-imagined with the community, we situated the participants as knowers. To quote Smith (1999):

> Indigenous people across the world have other stories to tell which not only question the assumed nature of those [common sense/taken for granted western academic] ideas and the practices they generate, but also to serve to tell an alternative story: the history of Western research through the eyes of the colonized. These counter-stories are powerful forms of resistance, which are repeated and shared across diverse indigenous communities. (p. 2)

In this way, through prioritizing the knowledge of the participants, we de-centered Western modern science and engaged with the narratives of the participants. A de-centering that incorporates the social, economic, and cultural environment. What if we had listened to the first "closed door" from the journal editor and reframed our work according to their requirements of hegemonic science? We would not have valued the stories, the knowledge, and the practices. Instead, we would have perpetuated the progression of what is defined as science through Western, academic ideas and the ways in which those closing the doors view participants.

## COMMONALITIES ACROSS OUR WORK

We discovered two commonalities across our work. Throughout this discussion, we point to the ways in which we disrupt the traditional roles of researchers, our disruption of traditional approaches to data collection and representation of findings, and, ultimately, how these disruptions serve to disturb rigid epistemological boundaries.

### More Than Just the "Scientific Facts"

Across both projects, we noted the need for positioning the participants as contributors of knowledge or understanding their funds of knowledge. Funds of knowledge acknowledge and honor the abundant historically accumulated and culturally developed knowledge that a household or family possesses (Moje, Tehani, Carrillo, & Marx, 2004). The knowledges constructed by the communities in which we worked are complex and holistic. The scientific knowledge of the communities in which we worked is embedded in their lived experiences. It encompasses more than what traditional scientists would call science, by necessity. We argue that anything less would fail at truly valuing local knowledge. In our work and research, we both included local knowledges and lived experience in our conception of scientific knowledge.

In Nicole's research, she consistently expanded her scope beyond the science classroom to better understand science education in Eldoret, Kenya. Taxicabs, the town market, *and* science classrooms all became sites for understanding science education. In Cassie's research, she challenged the dismissive assumptions by U.S.-based scientists and researchers towards the rich, experiential knowledge they had of their own ecosystems. By doing so, she garnered traditional technologies for energy production that she and her research team would have otherwise missed.

From these examples, we show that expanded scopes and open ears are crucial to pushing the boundaries of what counts as science education research. Looking beyond the science classroom and listening intently to our participants has revealed knowledge essential to include in meaningful science education with the communities that we worked with.

### Struggles, Tensions, and Defending Our Choices

We struggle throughout our work disrupting dominant approaches for how science is defined, how knowledge is constructed, and how research is shared. However, ultimately, we make the choices of what to include, what to publish, which leads to what is valued. Even though our participants are involved throughout the research process, we initiated the work. Is it, then, a disrupting act? We believe it is; however, we acknowledge that another layer to this disrupting act is to support the participants in work they initiate. Complicating this challenge in supporting indigenous participants in initiating the research is the unapologetic history of research in/on indigenous communities (Smith, 1999). We intentionally tried to disrupt colonizing practices of researching *about* indigenous people and instead attempted to research *with* indigenous people. Cassie described ways in which she prioritized participants' knowledge. Nicole described her struggle with becoming viewed as an authority figure on science education issues in an African nation. We had opportunities to work with indigenous communities and value their knowledge, but we wonder if it is enough to simply move their knowledge to the forefront. Although we both initiated our work, the power was shared with each of the communities. In Nicole's example, she expanded her idea of an educational community to include the Kenyans' views. This expansion enabled her to incorporate data sources she probably would have missed. Through ethnography of place, she focused on Kenyans' views, which shifted the power towards the participants. In Cassie's example, she legitimized the knowledge of the participants from the outset of her study by disrupting the data collection tools to support the participants, in order to be in control of the data that would be collected and shared with the researchers. Without this legitimization, she could have fallen prey to the mistakes of many environmental educators that had worked with this community before her. Throughout our work, we find power and promise in both our successes *and* our struggles. Without these struggles, we believe we would not reflect on our work in the same ways.

Our tensions often pulled us between challenging, and resigning to, dominant science education research perspectives. Through Nicole's work, she described these tensions. At times, she felt she was conducting research in meaningful and effective ways, but at other times she worried about the reactions of her colleagues and her peers in science education. As she stated,

> Just wandering through town observing and talking with the taxi drivers? How could I make the case, even to myself, that these activities were going to reveal relevant understandings for how to approach teaching and learning science in this community? (Nicole's reflective journal, 6 June 2009)

Would it be easier to dilute her work into a series of organized data sources with boundaries for defining community and education? Similarly, Cassie describes her tensions with the peer-review process and gate-keeping editors. It certainly would have been easier to listen to the editor and change the manuscript so that it would fit the editor's view of science. It is in these moments we find ourselves disrupting science education research. We listen to the critics and even understand their issues and dilemmas with our work—as their questions are often the same ones we continually ask ourselves. Then, our attention goes back to our participants, and the type of work we want to embody. We resist temptations to maintain the status quo and continue to disrupt, even if it is only for those we work with.

Often we find ourselves defending our work to the point where we become overly distrustful and cynical of our critics. This is depicted clearly in Nicole's description of differentiating her proposal for her committee members. On the one hand, it is viewed as smart—she tailored her work for her different audiences. But upon further examination, she is accommodating the sensibilities of those who are more comfortable with normative ways of conducting research (and hold power over her completing her PhD degree). The problem results when we move from defending our work to becoming completely cynical of all other types of work. The risk is that we become researchers who throw our hands up in the air and state, "they just don't get it," without explanation. In Cassie's work, she could have taken the time to respond to the editor to help make the connections for him. That is part of our work as well, is it not? In this way, we have learned to be more intentional about the ways we describe our methods. When our work is critiqued, we take the time to deconstruct the criticism to the salient points that will improve our work by trying to help the critic see our rationale for disrupting science education. Thus, we feel the naysayers enhance our work.

## INSIGHTS FOR SCIENCE EDUCATION RESEARCHERS

We are not the only scholars attempting to disrupt science education research, and we are hardly experts. However, our work illuminates insights that may serve as guidance for other science education researchers. We distill the insights into four recommendations described below.

### Sharing a Vision With the Communities and Participants You Work With

Even when every bit of our Western Modern Science trained sensibilities questioned it, our ethical intuition led us to release the reigns of control on our research and share them with our participants. Nicole did this through her use of iterative data collection, informed by her participants and their context. In interviews, participants often directed her to places in and around town to observe, and what she observed and read about in newspapers informed questions she would ask in future interviews. Cassie and her research team resisted the urge from U.S. scientists to provide education on using solar cooking, and instead listened to participants, who revealed local sustainable cooking practices (using a jiko) already in use.

## Practice Brave Research

Conducting and communicating disruptive research carries the risk of questioning or rejection. It also brings potential for promoting diverse ways of knowing in science education. As such, pursuing a disruptive research project often requires bravery. Nicole described how she included disruptive methods, those outside the norm in science education research, even when it did not always make sense to some in her field. While at times difficult to justify to others in her field, she knew that observing in the produce markets, on public buses, etc., would reveal broadened understandings *for* science education. Convicted by the importance of communicating her participants' narratives to the wider science education community, Cassie persevered to find a journal that welcomed doing so.

## Prepare for Surprise

We anticipated and worried about the ways our field might question or reject our work. Still, we found ourselves surprised. Requests to remove the contextual information from a proposal about her study, information she felt made it meaningful, surprised and angered Nicole. The broad support she received when she eventually presented the study with all of the contextual information surprised her even more. Cassie submitted her research group's manuscript to a journal, which, just a few years prior, published an issue about the need to value diverse ways of knowing in science education. To her shock, she received a letter back from the editor refusing its review, due to what this editor saw as a "lack of fit" between the manuscript and the aims and scope of the journal.

## Promote Diverse Ways of Knowing in Science Education Research

There is much to learn about science education by looking outside of science classrooms and/or locales of formal science practices. However, our field currently focuses narrowly on these places. Through observing in places outside those expected in science education, Nicole revealed how ways of knowing and being outside of science influence science education, such as the complex issues surrounding deforestation in Kenya. Cassie and her colleagues consistently de-centered Western Modern Science, and engaged the narratives of participants, which allowed space to share local scientific knowledge that promotes sustainability (e.g., the jiko). We find inspiration by disrupting science education research through these actions. We hope these insights and stories provide support for other science education researchers striving to disrupt.

# REFERENCES

Chawla, L. (1992). Childhood place attachments. In I. Altman & S. M. Low (Eds.), *Place attachment* (pp. 63–86). New York, NY: Plenum Press.

Grande, S. (2004). *Red pedagogy*. Lanham, MD: Rowman & Littlefield.

Harding, S. (1991). *Whose science? Whose knowledge?* Ithaca, NY: Cornell University Press.

Jackson, J. B. (1997). *Landscape in sight: Looking at America*. New Haven, CT: Yale University Press.

Mann, C. C. (2002). The real dirt on rainforest fertility. *Science, 297*(5583), 921–923.

Moje, E. B., Ciechanowski, K. M., Kramer, K., Ellis, L., Carrillo, R., & Collazo, T. (2004). Working toward third space in content area literacy: An examination of everyday funds of knowledge and discourse. *Reading Research Quarterly, 39*(1), 38–72.

Nadasdy, P. (2004). *Hunters and bureaucrats: Power, knowledge, and Aboriginal-state relations in the southwest Yukon*. Vancouver, Canada: UBC Press.

Quigley, C. F, Dogbey, J., Che, M., & Hallo, J. (in press). Kenyan perspectives of environmental sustainability. *Cultural Studies of Science Education*.

Rist, S., & Dahdouh-Guebas, F. (2006). Ethnosciences—A step towards the integration of scientific and indigenous forms of knowledge in the management of natural resources for the future. *Environmental Development and Sustainability, 8*(4), 467–493.

Smith, L. T. (1999). *Decolonizing methodologies*. London, England: Zed Books.

Tuan, Y-F. (1977). *Space and place: The perspective of experience*. Minneapolis, MN: University of Minnesota Press.

Turnbull, D. (2000). *Masons, tricksters and cartographers: Comparative studies in the sociology of scientific and indigenous knowledge*. Abingdon, England: Taylor & Francis.

United Nations Environment Programme (UNEP). (2009). *Kenya: Atlas of our changing environment*. Nairobi, Kenya. Retrieved from: http://www.unep.org/dewa/africa/kenyaatlas/ on November 30, 2013.

Villegas, M., Neugebauer, S. R., & Venegas, K. R. (2008). Part three introduction: sites of survivance. In M. Villegas, S. R. Neugebauer, & K. R. Venegas. (Eds.), *Indigenous knowledge and education: Sites of struggle, strength, and survivance* (pp. 209–210). Cambridge, MA: Harvard Educational Review. (Reprint Series No. 44).

Watson-Veran, H., & Turnbull, D. (1994). Science and other indigenous knowledge systems. *Knowledge: Critical Concepts*, 345–346.

Zent, S. (2009). A genealogy of scientific representations of indigenous knowledge. In S. Hecker (Ed.), *Landscape, process and power: Re-evaluating traditional environmental knowledge* (pp. 19–62). Oxford, England: Berghahn Books.

# ADDITIONAL RESOURCES

## Place in Education

Aikenhead, G., Calabrese, A. B., & Chinn, P. W. (2006). Forum: Toward a politics of place-based science education. *Cultural Studies of Science Education, 1*(2), 403–416.

Gruenewald, D. A. (2003). Foundations of place: A multidisciplinary framework for place-conscious education. *American Educational Research Journal, 40*(3), 619–654.

Orr, D. W. (1992). *Ecological literacy: Education and the transition to a postmodern world.* New York, NY: SUNY Press.

## Diversity in Science Education

Carter, L. (2004). Thinking differently about cultural diversity: Using postcolonial theory to (re) read science education. *Science Education, 88*(6), 819–836.
Carter, L. (2008). Globalization and science education: The implications of science in a new economy. *Journal of Research in Science Education, 45(5)*, 617–623. doi:10.1002/tea.20189

## Funds of Knowledge

González, N., & Moll, L. C. (2002). Cruzando el puente: Building bridges to funds of knowledge. *Educational Policy, 16*(4), 623–641

## Decolonizing Methodologies

Paris, D., & Winn, M. T. (2013). *Humanizing research: Decolonizing qualitative inquiry with youth and communities.* London, England: Sage Publications.
Smith, L. T. (1999). *Decolonizing methodologies.* London, England: Zed Books.

# CHAPTER EIGHT

# "Bringing A Little Bit OF Heaven TO Humanity"

## Raising Hell While Interrupting Traditional Methods for the Purpose of Justice

DAVID STOVALL

The quote in the title of this chapter is taken from a conversation with a colleague on the intention of interrupting the status quo in community-based educational research.[1] During our interaction, I mentioned how "raising hell" is often a precondition in the radical tradition of engaged, activist research. Often, community-engaged, activist researchers are tagged with the moniker, "hell-raiser" or "difficult" when they make conscious attempts to challenge traditional research paradigms that are not sanguine to the needs of communities that are working towards just solutions to address their conditions. Because we ourselves have been tagged in such a way, my colleague was explaining to me that we are not raising hell, but are instead "bringing a little bit of heaven to humanity." The interruption of traditional methods is the "heaven" the humanity of researchers needs to engage to refute the colonial relationship often engendered in traditional research methods. Integral to the process of methodological interruption is the realization that despite the unpopularity of authentic community engagement, it often serves as a recruitment tool for students and like-minded faculty at the university level. Using the city of Chicago as the site, this chapter highlights the author's experience in a local public school, as the central office of Chicago Public Schools (CPS) attempted to close the institution because it was deemed "too expensive" and "underperforming." Returning to the concept of "raising hell," this chapter engages in the truth-telling of what is needed to understand our work in higher education institutions as intentional and uncompromisingly political. Despite perceived and real limitations, such work remains necessary if we are to make any claims towards justice.

As a descriptive, analytical essay, the chapter is divided into four sections. The first explains the current moment in U.S. educational policy through a discussion of Chicago. This section highlights why it is absolutely necessary to work in solidarity with communities during times such as these, where public education is threatened. Section two describes the intersection in which I operate as a concerned community member and researcher. Critical to this discussion is the constellation of research methods I incorporate in my current work. The third section continues the discussion to include the necessity of doing research for the purpose of justice. Included in this section are my offerings about how to create a cadre of researchers equipped to work in solidarity with communities, intentionally interrupting and challenging the colonial project inherent in traditional approaches to research methods. The last section contains my reflections on the "slow" but intentional nature of the task of community-based research as protracted struggle.

## CHICAGO IN CONTEXT: WHY I WORK IN THIS WAY

As public education is challenged by corporate entities in conjunction with local, state, and federal arms of government, the current political moment is of particular significance to the constellation of students, families, teachers, community organizers, and concerned citizens who believe in student-centered, justice-focused education. As epicenter of large-city educational reform, the political economy of Chicago intimately shapes the way in which I engage research. As the city currently seeks to close 49 schools in predomiantly African-American neighborhoods for supposed "under-utilization," it should also be understood as reflective of the massive displacement/gentrification project that has removed almost 200,000 African-American residents from the city (Lipman et al., 2012). Documented extensively in the works of Lipman (2003, 2004, 2011), Saltman (2007, 2010), and Fine and Fabricant (2012), Chicago has been a hotbed for said initiatives. Because these changes have largely resulted in the further marginalization of low-income, working-class communities of color, as a concerned community member, I cannot pass over the current trends as being simply in the natural order of educational progression. More importantly, as an African-American male who is also a native Chicagoan, if I stood by and did nothing I could never claim to be part of any larger justice project seeking to reframe, re-imagine, and create viable public schools for families of color that have historically been subject to the worst delivery of resources and infrastructure. For these reasons (and countless others), I attempt to perpetually challenge myself to understand the political economy, with the intention of working in solidarity with communities.

Neoliberal policy reform is an accurate description of school reform policies and implementation in Chicago. Largely rooted in the belief that free market economies provide solutions for the vast majority of social concerns, neoliberal reform is centered in the rights of the individual (Lipman, 2011). For low-income families of color, this often results in a rhetorical charge that the market can solve the vast majority of political, economic, and social issues. Because these resources (i.e., access to quality health care, education, and gainful employment, etc.) are falsely positioned as available to all, low-income working-class families of color are often blamed for not accessing said means.

The neoliberal project in education and housing has been most evident in Chicago since 1995. Beginning with the educational policy shift resulting in mayoral control of Chicago Public Schools (CPS), the mayor is the sole authority in appointing the school board, which is responsible for final approval of school-related issues (e.g., fiduciary matters, curricular shifts, contract procurement, approval of new schools, etc.). In addition to the mayor's ability to appoint members of the school board, as part of the policy, s/he has the ability to overturn any decision made by the board. Facilitated under the 22-year mayoral tenure of Richard M. Daley, the city has laid a blueprint for numerous cities in the U.S. desiring to centralize control of their school systems. Currently, the board membership consists largely of people from the business, legal, and philanthropic sectors (Lipman, 2003). The centralized board appointment process fosters a reciprocal relationship between the board and the mayor's office as board members are usually individuals or employees of entities that have contributed significantly to the mayor's re-election campaign.

Sections of the Chicago model of reform have been duplicated in cities such as New York, Los Angeles, and Houston (Fine & Fabricant, 2012). Officials from all three cities have come to Chicago to study mayoral control (of the school board) and how to connect education and business, with the intent to foster long-term development. Internationally, Chicago has been cited for its improvements in business, housing, and education (Lipman, 2003). As a central hub for global finance, informational technological advancements, and management for systems of production, Chicago has fashioned itself as a viable competitor for investment from transnational global firms in business, industry, and entertainment (Smith & Stovall, 2008).

In 2003, the Civic Committee of the Commercial Club of Chicago, a collaborative of business interests, developed a report known as "Left Behind." A central premise of this report was that students in the U.S. were falling behind internationally in reading, math, and science. The committee's suggested solution was to retool the public educational landscape by infusing "innovation" from the business sector. Said innovations would be for the purposes of strengthening the U.S. workforce and returning the U.S. economy to supremacy in the global marketplace.

The people best suited for this direction were those who possessed an intimate knowledge of free-market strategies to boost competition amongst education providers (Civic Committee of the Commercial Club of Chicago, 2003). Key to this strategy is the idea that competition is a means of boosting academic performance. Under free-market capitalism the belief is that if one school is performing well, it will push others to improve due to the competitive interests of all institutions for students. Contrary to this understanding is the idea that each school serves a different set of students, requiring a unique set of resources germane to that particular population. The competition strategy becomes ridiculous and absurd when accounting for the unique needs of students in a particular school.

Nevertheless, the city moved forward and rolled out a plan in the summer of 2004 to implement the suggestions of the Civic Committee. In the plan called Renaissance 2010, CPS proposed to target up to 70 "chronically underperforming" schools for "transformation" into 100 schools with the distinction of either charter, contract, or performance school. Where charters are granted by the state, contract schools are a designation for individuals or groups that have secured individual contracts with the city to create schools. The Academy of Urban School Leadership (AUSL) is currently the largest contract institution in Chicago. Schools in the performance category intended to provide principals and teachers some levels of autonomy regarding curriculum and schedule. Simultaneously, the internal understanding was to lessen the city's financial commitment to education through the use of partners that could in turn use their contributions to education as tax subsidies (through the federal tax code's provision for charitable donations). Returning to the public sphere, Renaissance 2010 was posited to community residents as CPS moving to provide "choice" and "options" in the "education marketplace," as repositioned schools were offered as "new" options for families (www.cps.edu/NewSchools/Pages/ONS.aspx).

Since the rollout of Renaissance 2010 in 2004, CPS has closed 101 schools. Over 97% of these schools were either serving African-American or Latino/a students and families, with the majority being African-American families (Lipman et al., 2012). Under the tenure of recently elected mayor Rahm Emanuel, Chicago has engaged in the largest single set of school closings in the U.S., with 49 schools scheduled to close in June of 2013. The argument is that the city has lost over 100,000 students, and many schools are "underutilized." CPS claims that keeping under-enrolled schools open will deepen the school system's budgetary hole. Compounding this rhetoric is the idea that this new set of school closures fills a budget deficit of almost $700 million. However, through the work of a forward-thinking set of researchers known as Chicagoland Researchers and Advocates for Transformative Education (CReATE), CPS has been challenged on its budget rationale. As members of CReATE, we are discovering that this new set of closings should be considered part of a larger plan to further isolate and disinvest in schools that serve African-American and Latino/a students in low-income communities. Additionally, instead of claiming these schools as underutilized, many neighborhood public school populations have been depleted by a neighboring charter or contract school (www.createchicago.org). As new charter schools are erected in proximity to neighborhood public schools, the population of the neighborhood schools decrease, enabling CPS to claim them as "underutilized."

Critical to these reforms is the intimate relationship to the housing market. Cited extensively in Arrastia (2007), Lipman (2003, 2011, 2012) and Smith et al. (2006), because housing stock is key in attracting business interests in the city, schooling becomes an important conduit in solidifying long-term investment in schools. As the schools in a prospective neighborhood are the main determinant of a family's home purchase, neighborhoods close to the central business district have become a hotbed for gentrification, most notably through the mass destruction of public housing through the Chicago Housing Authority's (CHA) Plan for Transformation (Lipman, 2011). Touted as a $1.6-billion endeavor, the Plan for Transformation aims to redevelop areas once occupied by high-rise public housing as mixed-income communities. As housing stock in the redeveloped areas will be distributed in thirds amongst very low-income, moderate-income, and market-rate homes, questions arise, as dubious qualifications have been placed on the low-income group (*Chicago Tribune*, September 22, 2004). To receive any of the homes in the recent developments, public housing families have to go through a battery of screenings for health (specifically for substance abuse), employment (applicants must now work at least 30 hours per week unless they are unable to, or are in a training/educational program), and criminal activity (a person cannot rent an apartment if anyone in the household has a felony conviction). In the Plan for Transformation, schools are framed as an important part of the plan, and the change in housing has been projected to mean an increase in families of moderate and affluent incomes. Because the paring of housing and education requires strategic planning on the part of the City of Chicago, the converging of Renaissance 2010 and the Plan for Transformation was critical in bringing the larger neoliberal plan of forced displacement of low-income African-American and Latino/a families and the redevelopment of the central business district into fruition. Despite the provisions for low-income families in the new mixed-income communities, the aforementioned health, employment, and criminal compliances help to carefully sanitize the community marketed to newcomers. Schools, as the final frontier, provide the necessary push for the aforementioned homebuyers to take the final step in securing life in the city. Fortunately for the low-income African-American and Latino/a families that remain in some of the targeted areas, a collective of community organizations have developed strategies to contest the efforts of CPS. In a humble attempt to join such efforts, this contextual analysis enables me to situate my research within the larger justice project in education.

## GETTING CLOSE, MESSY, AND CONTRADICTORY:
## METHODOLOGY THAT INTERRUPTS

As a concerned resident of Chicago trained as a researcher and seeking to support community-driven efforts in education, I offer the following to describe the theoretical frameworks that inform my methodological approach. Currently, my methods sit at the intersection of Critical Race Theory, Youth Participatory Action Research, Activist Scholarship, and Critical Urban Studies. Informed significantly by Critical Race Theory (CRT), I seek to position my work as an interdisciplinary effort to bridge the aforementioned disciplines through methods that specifically challenge the notion of researcher as objective or impartial. Instead, I subscribe to the notion that understanding my biases and shortcomings is key to the collaborative process. Because my intention is not to be objective, the purpose of my work seeks to highlight the inconsistencies of local, state, and federal agencies while working with young people and community residents to engage tangible methods by which to investigate and transform education on their own terms. As will be discussed later in this section, inherent to these research relationships are the "messiness" often equated with qualitative research and the contradictions that are inherent to any justice-driven process. Instead of shying away from the contradictions, my research includes engaging my shortcomings and inconsistencies directly, with the understanding that my own viewpoints need to be challenged, interrupted, and revisited. As method, I borrow heavily from the work of Tuhiwai-Smith (2012) who asserted that decolonization is a "long term process involving the bureaucratic, cultural, linguistic, and psychological divesting of colonial power" (p. 101). For myself, this long-term process includes working with people and organizations in communities with the intent of supporting their efforts at self-determination.

For these reasons, research with students and families in school and community spaces is important to engage from the perspective of co-constructor or co-collaborator. Doing so requires us to work at the intersection of multiple theoretical and methodological approaches that coalesce in our work on the ground in/with communities (Cammarota & Fine, 2008; Ibanez-Carrasco & Meiners, 2004; Jennings & Lynn, 2006; Lynn & Parker, 2002). By interrupting the traditional research paradigm suggesting "objectivity" and "validity," Critical Race Praxis (CRP), like grounded theory, engaged scholarship, youth participatory action research (YPAR), critical ethnography, and community-based participatory research before it, encourages scholars to get "close" to our work (Yammamoto & Su, 2002). Encapsulated in this approach is the understanding that any work towards the larger justice project in education will sometimes require making tough, uncomfortable decisions that often have the potential to isolate scholars from the groups they work with (Tuhiwai-Smith, 2012). As Yamamoto (1999) has offered a working definition of CRP in legal scholarship, I am posing a combination of existing tenets of CRT in education, and CRP from legal studies, to propose working tenets for Critical Race Praxis in Education. I am noting the term "working" because I do not contend that my working definition provides a comprehensive explanation of the concept. Instead, my offering of a working definition invites malleability as needed to address conditions in the spaces we have chosen to actively engage said communities.

From critical race praxis in legal studies I incorporate the tenets of Yamamoto's (1999) working definition of race praxis from the *Interracial Justice* text.

- *Conceptual:* Examining the racialization of a controversy and the interconnecting influences of heterosexism, patriarchy, and class while locating that examination in a critique of the political economy (p. 130).
- *Performative:* Answering the question as to what practical steps are responsive to the specific claim and who should act on that claim (p. 131).
- *Material:* Inquiring into changes, both socio-structural and the remaking of the democratic structure of public institutions, in the material conditions of racial oppression. Examples would include access to fair housing, health care, quality education, employment, etc. (p. 132).
- *Reflexive:* Commitment to the continual rebuilding of theory in light of the practical experiences of racial groups engaged in particular antiracist struggles (p. 132).

The aforementioned tenets are useful in my work as I attempt to move from the conceptual to the material and reflexive. For example, if there is a theoretical concept, the first question I ask of it is "what does this mean on the ground with people who are experiencing injustice?" I use the performative and material to put the theory into concrete action. The reflexive component operates as an evaluative component in that I am looking to improve the work I engage in with people and organizations in communities according to their stated issues and concerns.

From *CRT in Education*, I utilize the tenets suggested by Yosso and Solorzano (2005) in their chapter on creating a framework for a Critical Race Theory of sociology. Similar to the tenets of Yamamoto (1999), Solorzano and Yosso's framework speaks to the current concerns of scholars in the educational disciplines. In the attempt to coalesce the Yosso, Solorzano, and Yamamoto tenets, I offer the following to be considered in developing CRP in education.

- *Commitment to on-the-ground work:* Our theorizing and methods should deal less with abstract concepts and should be rooted in a tangible commitment to the physical/material, social, and intellectual support of communities that are experiencing educational injustice. An explicit understanding of the political economy of the moment is critical to perform said tasks, while working with communities to unpack how the realities of the current political economy are relevant to the situation at hand.

- *Social justice as an experienced phenomenon:* Social justice requires a material commitment by scholars to work with communities in reaching tangible goals, while understanding that the spaces in which we work are "grounded in concrete and often messy and conflictual racial realities" (Yamamoto, 1999, p. 129).
- *Utilization of interdisciplinary approaches:* A commitment to continue to utilize theoretical and methodological approaches (e.g., ethnic studies, humanities, social sciences, gender and women's studies, public health, medicine, urban planning, etc.) to specifically address the racial, social, political, and economic concerns of the communities with whom we work.
- *Training others to move beyond the intellectual exercise of challenging dominant ideologies:* Continuing the work of CRT scholars such as Solorzano (1997) and Ladson-Billings (1995), CRP requires a commitment to develop the capacity of up-and- coming scholars (e.g., graduate students, new faculty, etc.) to engage communities and groups working for educational justice.
- *Commitment to self-care:* In order to engage the larger project of justice in education, it is imperative to commit ourselves to physical, mental, and spiritual well-being. Because justice work in education can be extremely taxing to our minds and bodies, we must engage individual and collective efforts aimed at taking care of ourselves (Rager, 2005).

Where the first four tenets operate as a revisionist interpretation of the Yamamoto (1999) and Yosso and Solorzano (2005) tenets, critical to the discussion of CRP in education is the necessity of self-care. Refuting the unspoken expectation of academics who are "serious" about their work, our physical, mental, and social well-being need not be compromised. Instead, if we focus on our health as part of the justice project in education, we would have greater potential to provide a holistic approach to justice work in education. Noted by Rager (2005) in her seminal account of research with breast cancer patients, the work we are concerned with can be taxing due to its intense nature. In Rager's situation, the participants in her study were living in the throws of a potentially deadly disease. In the case of educational justice in low-income/working-class communities of color, our work rests in the realities of communities losing their neighborhood schools or being wrongfully displaced due to gentrification, imminent domain, or other state-sanctioned policies with long-term negative effects. In both instances, taking care of oneself can be a daunting task. Late nights, early mornings, travel schedules, faculty responsibilities (i.e., teaching load, committee work, student support, support of new faculty, research/writing, promotion and tenure), and family concerns should not be considered outside of the realm of justice work in education. Adding to the "messiness" of qualitative work, paying attention to our physical, mental, and spiritual selves is critical if we are to remain fully present in our participation with communities.

After explicating the context and construct of these methods, many would ask, *so what does this work look like on the ground?* For my own work, this manifests itself in numerous examples, but the one most germane to this chapter would be my work at the Greater Lawndale High School for Social Justice (SOJO). Because SOJO was developed as the result of a community-driven initiative to create a high school (i.e., a 19-day hunger strike), my research methodology was largely informed by the initiative, in my attempt to be accountable to the terms and conditions set by the hunger-strikers. Where some might consider this a grounded approach, myself and another researcher/professor comrade worked in tangent with teachers, administrators, community organizers, and youth workers to support the development of the school. As a faculty member at an urban public university, the hope was to engage theory and method from an experiential/participatory standpoint, to develop relevance for myself and pose a viable option to the problematic status quo of distanced, objective research. Instead of engaging the "liberal rhetoric" of helping the downtrodden, my idea is to engage on the ground, understanding that working in this way is the most viable way for me to make sense of what I'm supposed to be doing as a concerned community member, teacher educator, and researcher.

As a member of the school design team I have worked with community members in numerous capacities, including membership of the local school council (responsible for principal hiring and budget approval) and as a classroom teacher. Regarding issues of method, there are a number of ways in which the tenets of CRP in education have manifested themselves. Taking a critical stance on traditional methods, the key to my engagement is the moniker "critical." From this perspective, it is my belief that critical ethnography, critical policy analysis, and participatory action research operate for the purposes of *transparency, responsibility, accountability,* and *consistency.* Each tenet pushes my understanding of methodology in community-based research from a critical perspective.

## Transparency

The group of teachers, community members, parents, and hunger-strikers participating in the school design team agreed to the practice of transparency. Every document developed in creating the school proposal had to be shared and approved by members of the design team. When myself, my colleague, and the person designated for the principal position were given the responsibility of drafting the proposal, we had to share drafts of each section with the design team. The process included the three of us gathering research on social justice education and incorporating it into the proposal. Often described as member-checking in qualitative methodology, ours was different in that it was directly linked to the process of bringing the school to fruition.

## Responsibility

By posing an alternative model to the traditional colonial researcher-subject relationship, work beyond the initial school design team has been central to work in relationship between myself and community stakeholders at SOJO. Since 2002, as university researchers we have presented at numerous conferences with SOJO students (Stovall, Calderon, Carrera, & King, 2009) and teachers (Stovall & Morales-Doyle, 2010). Borrowing from the work of Derrick Bell (1980), we have also produced an article for publication with 29 authors (Stovall et al., 2009). Moving forward, this has also included writing letters of recommendation for SOJO students for college and SOJO teachers for graduate school.

## Accountability

For myself, this concept simply means matching words with actions. When the proposal for the school was first drafted, the university researchers wrote a clause into the document promising that we would teach at the high school. From this promise, we created three courses that provided students with dual credit (high school and college), making the college credit transferrable to the university of their choice (through general education requirements). We have begun to document this process with our students, seeking to engage the promise we made at the beginning of the design-team process.

## Consistency

In opposition to "helicopter research" where university faculty "drop down" on communities and leave once they have collected their data, we have engaged a long-term process of inquiry and collaboration. Since our 2003 experiences with the design team, we have consistently worked with the social studies and math departments to create curricular units, lesson plans, and new courses. As method, this includes documentation of our practice as teachers through theoretical inquiry, video analysis of each other's teaching, and evaluation of our practices for the purpose of improvement.

Where these tenets may not be considered methodology in the traditional sense, such reframing is necessary to challenge the traditional notion of research as a solitary exercise. If we begin to think of methods as the practice by which we engage communities for the purpose of addressing their expressed needs, we are less prone to attempt to override community concerns with research agendas. Although not a perfect process, this work best lends itself to the practice of humility.

## TRAINING A NEW CADRE: WORK BEYOND OURSELVES

Where the work of a university professor often requires lots of reading, writing, and theorizing, I am perpetually questioning whether or not traditional methods challenge and propose new paradigms or continue to perpetuate the colonial project in education. Noting that the later takes the stance that low-income communities of color offer a perspective lacking in deep, research-based inquiry, I unequivocally reject this assumption. Simultaneously, my experiences have also shown that many schools of education reject such positioning due to its lack of "results-driven" or "value-added" stance. Words such as "reflection" come off as weak, sing-songy approaches that don't improve the assumed "bottom line" of student performance. Evaluation becomes the sole quantifiable measure associated with test performance. For these reasons, and countless others, many colleges of education continue to exist most comfortably as compartmentalized fiefdoms, rejecting interdisciplinary approaches or collaborations to engage the contested and political spaces of education (hooks, 1994).

As policies become more arcane in function (i.e., "No Child Left Behind," school vouchers, charter schools, Educational Management Organizations, teacher performance assessments, etc.), those who profess their concern for social justice find themselves at a crossroads. Unfortunately, neoliberal educational policy interprets engaging the lives of young people as an outcome-based endeavor that regulates the life-chances of young people through a scantron sheet. Conversely, those who find the aforementioned policies counterproductive must engage and struggle in a process that names the dysfunctional nature of current policies while creating critical and productive spaces for young people to process their lives. Such practice of resistance is participatory in that students and teachers are engaged in producing thoughts and actions that address the issues and concerns of the day. Coupled with a historical context, the social project of education becomes one that challenges all parties involved to challenge commonly shared assumptions on how things should be.

Many would argue that my particular position in the high school as volunteer social studies teacher, professional development collaborator, and local school council member is still that of an outsider. In terms of my employment at the university, this argument may appear to be more salient. However, in recognizing the racialized contexts of education, I understand that at any given moment, the realities of the young people I work with have been and could be my own. As an African-American male, my experiences have taught me that my current position is the combination of choice and circumstance. I could have been suspected of a crime, deemed unruly in a class-room, or improperly placed in a program that could have stifled my learning capacity. Knowledge of this fact returns me to a statement I share with my close comrades, that "your PhD will not save you from oppression." It may give you the illusion of utiliz-ing the accouterments that come with the occupation, but as a person of color you are far from the first-class citizen you have fooled yourself into believing. A terminal academic degree alone will not equip you with the skill set to critically assess and ac-tively engage the work you live. It can assist in the process of whatever, but it should never be considered the sole determinant for liberatory practice. Similar to texts or articles, the degree is best used as a reference and for access to resources. From here, the option for myself was to engage a process that refutes the claim of "PhD equals privilege for all," while placing the issues and concerns of students, families, teachers, and community members at the forefront of the argument.

If we understand this reframing of methods as part and parcel of a process designated to challenge orthodoxy in academia, there is an added response in sup-porting those who will continue this work during our time on this planet and after we are gone. Often, the individualistic nature of academia would have us believe that our research is solely ours and we have no responsibility to shepherd a new generation of scholars willing to engage communities on the ground. Because the aforementioned policies are real and are drastically affecting urban communities of color, it is irresponsible to stand by and pity the situation. Instead of viewing this position as extreme, I count it in the lineage of researchers who have taken the mantra of freedom fighter Assata Shakur (2001) in that "we have nothing to lose but our chains" (p. 2).

Taking comrade Shakur's (2001) statement in context, it is critically important for mid-career scholars such as myself to support the efforts of graduate students and new faculty. Their ability to navigate and challenge the academy continues to be a critical cog in the wheel of leveraging resources for communities that are ex-periencing injustice. In addition to supporting their research, teaching, and service endeavors through the simple acts of sharing syllabi, supporting them through the tenure process, making them first authors on articles and chapters, and providing them with our contacts at manuscript publishing companies, we must recognize another set of work. These are the tasks rooted in understanding the academy as hostile territory where talk is cheap, and the ability to make your words match your actions as the most valuable currency to possess.

At the same time, a multi-lingualism is critical to this endeavor. Graduate stu-dents and new faculty must be able to know the language of mainstream research ideology for the specific purposes of deconstructing and challenging its merits. This requires the extra work of knowing the rationales of the oppressor while working with others to develop alternatives to research that has historically mar-ginalized, isolated, and exploited communities of color. It should be considered multi-lingual because the language of status quo research methodology has to be challenged by the language of alternative positionings that are reflective of working on the ground in communities. This may require looking across disciplines to excavate tangible examples of authentic community engagement. This edited volume is a step in such a direction.

It is also important for these graduate students and new faculty to know that sometimes the aforementioned people are few and far between, depending on the context in which you operate. Much of the support may come through virtual means, written form, or will be carried out in meetings at conferences and community gatherings. This current political moment in education requires us to think creatively to ensure that the ability to think and create is preserved in K-12 public education. Because we are perpetually challenged by testing companies, Educational Management Organizations (EMOs), and state and local governments as to what counts as quality education, we have a serious task ahead. It continues to be my opinion that these tasks are best addressed through collective efforts instead of individualized attempts.

## CONCLUSION: SLOW WORK IN TOUGH TIMES

Through numerous conversations with colleagues who engage communities in similar fashion, a colleague of mine refers to research in this mode as "slow work."[2] The reference is not to the rapid rate at which policies are enforced to the detriment of our communities, but instead to the protracted nature of the struggle for justice in education in very challenging times. Because there is no singular answer to address oppression via educational policy, it would behoove us as critically conscious scholars to build community with fellow travelers (i.e., community members, students, teachers, families, critical scholars) who understand the seriousness of the situation in our urban centers. If we do not, we are commiserating with the corporate entities that continue to devastate families and neighborhoods under the false premise of "choice" and "competition." For reasons expressed throughout this chapter, I understand the later to be unacceptable.

## NOTES

1. I would like to thank Cheryl Matias, Assistant Professor of Teacher Education at the University of Colorado, Denver for her contributions to this project through countless conversations concerning methodology and alternative framings.
2. I would like to thank Erica Meiners, Professor of Educational Policy and Community Studies and Latino/a Studies at Northeastern Illinois University for her conversations with me in developing this project.

## REFERENCES

Arrastia, L. (2007). Capital's daisy chain: Exposing Chicago's corporate coalition. *Journal of Critical Education Policy Studies, 5*(1), 121–155.

Bell, D. (1980). Brown v. Board of Education and the interest convergence dilemma. *Harvard Law Review, 93*, 518–533.

Cammarota, J., & Fine, M. (2008). *Revolutionizing education: Youth participatory action research in motion.* New York, NY: Routledge.

Civic Committee of the Commercial Club of Chicago (2003). *Left behind: Student achievement in Chicago's public schools.* Chicago, IL: Commercial Club of Chicago.

Editorial: The small schools express. (2005, Summer). *Rethinking Schools, 19*(4), 4–6. Retrieved from http://www.rethinkingschools.org/ProdDetails.asp?ID=RTSVOL19N4&d=toc

Fine, M., & Fabricant, M. (2012). *Charter schools and the corporate makeover of public education: What's at stake?* New York, NY: Teachers College Press.

hooks, b. (1994). *Teaching to transgress: Education as the practice of freedom.* New York, NY: Routledge.

Ibanez-Carasco, F., & Meiners, M. (Eds.). (2004). *Public acts: Disruptive readings on making curriculum public.* New York, NY: RoutledgeFarmer.

Jennings, M., & Lynn, M. (2005). The house that race built: Critical pedagogy, African-American education and the re-conceptualization of a critical race pedagogy. *Educational Foundations, 19*(3–4), 15–32.

Ladson-Billings, G. (1995). Just what is Critical Race Theory and what's it doing in a "nice" field like education. *International Journal of Qualitative Studies in Education 11*(1), 7–24.

Lipman, P. (2003). Chicago school policy: Regulating black and Latino youth in the global city. *Race, Ethnicity, and Education, 6*(4), 331–355.

Lipman, P. (2004). *High stakes education: Inequality, globalization, and urban school reform.* New York, NY: Routledge.

Lipman, P. (2011). *The new political economy of urban education: Neoliberalism, race, and the right to the city.* New York, NY: Routledge.

Lipman, P., Smith, J., Gutstein, E., & Dallacqua, L. (2012, February). Examining CPS' plan to close, turnaround, or phase out 17 schools. Retrieved from http://www.uic.edu/educ/ceje/articles/D&D%20final%20draft%202012%202-29-12.pdf

Lynn, M., & Parker, L. (2002). What's race got to do with it? Critical Race Theory's conflicts with and connections to qualitative research methodology and epistemology. *Qualitative Inquiry, 8*(1), 7–22.

Rager, K. B. (2005). Self-care and the qualitative researcher: When collecting data can break your heart. *Educational Researcher, 34*(4), 23–27.

Saltman, K. (2007). *Capitalizing on disaster: Taking and breaking public schools.* Boulder, CO: Paradigm.

Saltman, K. (2010). *The gift of education: Public education and venture philanthropy.* New York, NY: Palgrave Macmillan.

Shakur, A. (2001). *Assata: An autobiography.* New York, NY: Lawrence Hill.

Smith, J., Bennett, M., & Wright, P. (2006). (Eds.). *Where are poor people to live? Transforming public housing communities.* New York, NY: M. E. Sharpe.

Smith, J., & Stovall, D. (2008). Coming home to new homes and new schools: Critical Race Theory and the new politics of containment. *Journal of Education Policy, 23*(2), 135–152.

Solorzano D. (1997). Images and words that wound: Critical Race Theory, racial stereotyping, and teacher education. *Teacher Education Quarterly, 24*(3), 186–215.

Stovall, D., Calderon, A., Carrera, L., & King, S. (2009). Youth, media and justice: Lessons from the Chicago doc your block project. *Radical Teacher, 86*, 50–58.

Stovall, D., & Morales-Doyle, M. (2010). Critical media inequity as high school social studies for social justice: Doc your block. In T. Chapman & N. Hobbel (Eds.), *Social justice pedagogy: The practice of freedom.* New York, NY: Routledge.

Tuhiwai-Smith, L. T. (2012). *Decolonizing methodologies: Research and indigenous peoples.* New York, NY: Zed Books.

Yamamoto, E. (1999). *Interracial justice: Conflict and reconciliation in post-civil-rights America.* New York, NY: New York University Press.

Yammamoto, E., & Su, J. (2002). Critical coalitions: Theory and practice. In F. Valdez, J. McCristal Culp, & A. P. Harris. (Eds), *Crossroads, directions, and a new Critical Race Theory* (pp. 379–392). Philadelphia, PA: Temple University Press.

Yosso, T. (2005). Whose culture has capital? A Critical Race Theory discussion of community cultural wealth. *Race, ethnicity and education, 8*(1), 69–91.

Yosso, T., & Solorzano, D. (2005). Conceptualizing a Critical Race Theory in sociology. In M. Romero & E. Margolis (Eds.), *Blackwell companion to social inequalities.* New York, NY: Blackwell.

## RESOURCES

www.coreteachers.org
www.pureparents.org

# CHAPTER NINE

# Picture This

## Using Photography to Tell a Black Girl's Truth

CLAUDINE CANDY TAAFFE

Fig 9.1 Picture This!

The photo above (Figure 9.1) was taken during a Saving Our Lives, Hear Our Truths (SOLHOT) session when the girls decorated mirrors to document how they wanted others to see them. Often projected back to Black girls from a mirror is a result of what they project onto it. Black girls are often thought to be just the consumers of the images projected onto mirrors in society. However, in an attempt to create a disruption in those kinds of narratives, Black girl spaces are encouraged to engage school and community-based work where the genius of Black girls is showcased and thus, they become known as producers of mirror images and not only consumers. In this chapter, I provide an overview of a visual ethnography in the making. For the purpose of this discussion, I consider how the methods of data collection, analysis, and representation are used to disrupt status quo expectations of how photography is normally engaged with within academic research. Currently, I am writing my dissertation, which continues to be an overwhelming and yet incredibly satisfying feat. I argue that when photography is used as a data-collection tool and put in the hands of Black girls, what results are necessary counter-narratives to the stereotypical images of Black girls within popular culture. As a way to investigate their own lives and disrupt the stereotypes about Black girls in popular culture, girls in SOLHOT use photography and create collective meaning through the utilization of photovoice as a qualitative method.

SOLHOT is a space where the life experiences of middle-school-aged Black girls are shared and documented. SOLHOT, as a site of praxis, is where I conduct my dissertation research in both of my roles of Black woman researcher and Black girl participant. In the research that is conducted and created, ownership is fluid and based upon context. For this reason, I go between the use of "I" and "we" throughout this chapter. It is not my intention, however, to take away from the fact that SOLHOT is a collective process. As a doctoral student, I feel pressure to extract meaning, produce knowledge, share insights, and all the while remain sane. The pressure manifests a circular process as I find myself involved in an endless search for "the" book that will answer questions roaming my mind concerning my work with Black girls. I suppose my doctoral process is an attempt to write the book that I'm searching for. I also recognize the complexity involved in that task as echoed by Alice Walker (1983):

> In my own work I write not only what I want to read—understanding fully and indelibly that if I don't do it no one else is so vitally interested, or capable of doing it to my satisfaction—I write all the things I should have been able to read. (p. 13)

The goal of my research is to create a visually liberating, Black-girl-centered political project collectively facilitated for the purpose of countering dominant narratives about Black girls. The meta-narrative about Black girls being sexually deviant, loud, and not interested in education continues to be a negative source of the stories that are placed onto the bodies of Black girls. SOLHOT as an active and living space rises up to interrupt the process of mislabeling Black girls and, thereby, disrupts the intentional process of endangering the lives of Black girls.

In SOLHOT, Black girls share their life stories with each other, using cameras as tools for interrogating notions of power, voice, representation and stereotypes. Photovoice is a participatory research method through which individuals use photography to document their lives, capture aspects of their communities they consider important, and leverage the sharing of those images publicly to ignite social change. In this chapter, I discuss the disruptive methods of data collection, analysis, and representation used in visual ethnography. In my dissertation, I explore how photography is used to document the counter-narratives of Black girls, where a value is intentionally placed upon collective voice and analysis over individually produced research. This process of collective data collection, analysis, and representation is in line with legacies of Black women's self-determination.

## THE SETTING: SOLHOT AS SACRED SPACE

SOLHOT is an arts-based, after-school space for Black girls in central Illinois where Black girls can speak out loud the stories of their lives in text, photography, dance, song, and performance.[1] The creation of SOLHOT is a necessary attempt to bridge theory and practice for Black girls and women who are committed to having their voices heard and carried inside and outside of the walls of the academy and other institutions of importance in their lives.

The SOLHOT site, which also doubles as my site of research, operates out of a public middle school on a weekly basis. During my two years of conducting research at the school, Black girls work in partnership with mostly college-aged women in the engagement of an arts-based curriculum centered on themes the girls deem most important. The women involved in SOLHOT facilitate activities for, and with, the girls, utilizing a critical pedagogical approach. Critical pedagogy enables us to ask how and why knowledge is constructed and why some knowledge is given more currency over other types of knowledge and whose interests that type of prioritizing serves (McLaren, 2003). The intention behind the conversations facilitated in SOLHOT is to encourage Black girls to serve as visible witnesses to the stories created about them, and to author their own stories. Once documented, those stories are deconstructed by the girls through group dialogue, re-imagined with Black girls at the center of the narrative (as opposed to the margins), and disseminated through text, photography, performance, song, and dance. Whereas there is an importance placed on the dissemination of those re-constructed narratives within the general public (more specifically, among the key people and institutions in the lives of Black girls), our creations are for us first. We prioritize having our selves be the focus of our creations first because we acknowledge the level of deconditioning that is necessary for us before we engage any kind of social change work within the communities in which we live. We believe in Black girl authored stories and photography because we believe the stories created by others about Black girls leave labels imposed on our bodies that, in turn, contribute to stereotypes. In no way do we claim that the removal of those imposed-upon, deficit-based labels marked on our bodies is a neat and organized process. It's hard. It's ugly, chaotic, and loud, yet necessary, liberating, and, most importantly, possible. There is a kind of doing in the space of SOLHOT that encourages Black girls and women to act boldly with no fear of repercussions for being loud in our articulation of what is most important to us. We embrace fully that our silence will not save us (Lorde, 2007). Because Black girls are not heard above the loudness of their voices, their truths are ignored or dismissed.

In SOLHOT, our space is sacred. We live in it. We allow ourselves the vulnerability to feel our feelings inside of it. We love each other and we give each other attitude. We always tell the truth. We don't apologize. We question the rules and we ask the right questions—the questions that matter to us. The womanhood of the women in SOLHOT is not dependent upon the girls being "good" and the girlhood of the girls in SOLHOT is not dependent upon the women being "all knowing" adults (Brown, 2009). In the same way that Black women theorists rely heavily on the remembering of their own Black girlhoods in the articulation of their Black womanhood, so too do we see that same transparency at work in SOLHOT. In our space, the learning and teaching are bi-directional—at all times we are teaching and learning with each other and collectively creating new pedagogies, methodologies, and research findings. Together, we construct a kind of Black girl wisdom that emerges from the sharing of our thoughts about our day, our week, and our lives.

## THE STORYTELLER: AN AFRO-LATINA'S TESTIMONY

I believe that Saving Our Lives, Hear Our Truths (SOLHOT) is a verb, an adjective, a noun, a call to action, and an experience that surpasses every binary ever created about Black girls and women. In SOLHOT we are always negotiating back and forth between being Black girls and being Black women depending on the moment at hand. When you truly "get it" about SOLHOT, you keep coming back in whatever ways you know how. And because there is no space in SOLHOT to lean back and serve only as a witness, when someone doesn't "get it" about SOLHOT, the girls will let them know—all the while still offering their love to Black women freely.

I am beyond humbled by what Black girls have taught me about surviving and thriving and in the ways they have taught me. They have shown me how to keep love at the center of the survival of self when others who are not interested in your life story stack the odds against you. In giving themselves the permission to be free, they have also given me the permission to be free. In having no fear to grab hold of a camera, they have strengthened my courage to document in words what we do and how we do it. They have taught me a language through which to connect not only with them but to also re-connect with my father.

Only in my work with the girls have I come to understand how important it is to own this gift of photography, recognize its potential to disrupt paradigms and binaries, trust in it and share it freely. Since this recognition, I find my photography of, and with Black girls to be about finding freedom, to serve as our way to let the world know we are here and we are looking at you looking at us. When asked about the choices I make when I take photographs in SOLHOT my answer is always very simple and short—I take photos of Black girls and women as my way of saying, I see you and I believe in your beauty, your brilliance and your right to be here in all the ways you know how. I have come to realize that when Black girls take photos, it is their way of contributing to the production of knowledge concerning the real questions that should be asked of Black girls. In many ways, they become the creator of the methodology and no longer the object of it.

Taking photos in SOLHOT has been my way to dance, to be loud, to sing, to be beautiful, to be bold, to be courageous and to be right here. It is my hope that through our collective photography the girls can see the reflections of just how incredibly beautiful and strong they are. I will be forever grateful for their permission to have me and a camera share in their world. They have given me a gift that is truly beyond measure! (Taaffe Artist Statement, SOLHOT Photo Exhibit, Spring 2009)

In February 2009, we premiered a SOLHOT photo exhibit at the Krannert Art Museum on the University of Illinois campus. The above artist statement accompanied the photos collectively taken by myself and the girls and women in SOLHOT. This is who I am. More specifically, within academic spaces, I am an Afro-Latina activist scholar hungry for opportunities to challenge and re-imagine status-quo theoretical frameworks, while simultaneously manifesting spaces of praxis, as called for by Paulo Freire (2006), who suggested that educational praxis should combine both action (practice) and reflection (theory) as part of the educational process. I believe in the power of young people and the courage of the most marginalized among us. I believe in communicating in all the ways necessary in order to connect with others in a genuine spirit of humanity. I believe contradictions show us where we hurt as well as the ways through which we can learn how to love and be free. As a researcher, I believe that the contradictions existing within educational research can either bind my work with a tone of status quo co-conspirator or free me to fully engage with the complexities involved in reigniting the seeds of humanity within the academy. I argue that putting a visual method such as photography in the hands of young people (in this case, Black girls) allows for a re-articulation of humanity in research about Black girlhood that centers them as producers of knowledge and not just consumers.

I am currently in the preliminary writing stages of my dissertation and am using the following question to guide my work: What are the counter-narratives that Black girls document (speak, write down, photograph) in response to the stereotypes about them in education and society? I rely on an intentional combination of critical/active listening (on the part of the researcher), critical group dialogue, digital photography (in the hands of the girls), and the engagement of activities that focus on the celebration (and not investigation) of Black girls' experiences to produce a unique and liberating visual ethnography project that manifests the contribution of Black-girl-authored counter-narratives in response to much of the current deficit-based literature about Black girls. What characterizes deficit-based literature about Black girls is a suggested tone (whether subtle or intentional) of a need for Black girls to be saved (and saved in a very missionary type of way that depends on no recognition of the strength Black girls have to save themselves). My methods of data collection include participant observation, critical group dialogue, digital photography, interviews, and Black-girl-authored texts.

194 CLAUDINE CANDY TAAFFE

In the specific academic work I engage in with Black girls in SOLHOT, I rely primarily on the definition of education as argued by Paulo Freire (2006, 1998) and supported by the work of critical theorists (Darder, 2002; hooks, 1994). Learning is a process where knowledge is presented to us, then shaped through understanding, discussion, and reflection. I bring my voice into SOLHOT through my role of participant observer. However, as an insider/outsider my observations are rarely objective. I, as an activist-researcher, am always interrogating the constructs that I bring to the table in my work with Black girls. Similar to Deborah Willis (2009), an African-American photographer and scholar, who admitted, "In my own photography and writings, I've struggled with the continuing challenges surrounding visual images of Black people" (p. xiii), I too am in a perpetual state of unlearning, re-learning, sharing, listening, and questioning. Insomuch as this work is not about me, my voice is never far from speaking alongside the voices of the girls. As the girls take photos, I take photos of them taking photos. As they bring their opinions to what they see through the lens of a camera, so do I. I do not argue that our voices are one and the same, but I do argue that the uniqueness, celebratory nature, and transformative aspect of SOLHOT allows for the voices of the girls and my voice to be dependent upon each other—the kind of interdependence that brings visual storytelling alive.

## NECESSARY TRUTHS: THE SIGNIFICANCE OF FOCUSING ON BLACK GIRLHOOD STORIES

In the creation of traditional research projects with young people, some stories are placed at the center, while other stories remain on the margins. Those stories situated at the center, more often than not, are considered "the norm," and other stories that might differ are considered a "departure from the norm." Therefore, standards often arise based on this norm, and stories that differ, or depart from that norm, are devalued and subordinated (Delgado-Bernal, 2002). In the field of research about Black girls, what typically constitutes the story at the center is more often than not, the story of White, middle-class girls (Leadbeater & Way, 2007). As a consequence, the ways of being a Black girl are compared to standards created for White girls. This kind of thinking enables Black girls to be labeled deficient, thereby divorcing the choices of Black girls from the structural issues of racism, sexism, patriarchy, and heterosexism at play in their lives. While the personal narratives lifted up in a space of praxis offer a description of the lens through which Black girls view and attempt to understand the different worlds they inhabit, they also provide researchers an opportunity to deconstruct the deficit-based measurements used to define Black girlhood. Still, their stories are just a mere portion of the complex existence that Black girls perform and deconstruct in a society entrenched in a patriarchal, capitalistic, heterosexist, and racist legacy.

In this focused work on Black girlhood stories, photos are used as evidence of how Black girls can investigate and create an analysis of their own lived experiences. Through the use of photography and text, Black girls come to know, perform, and interrogate their reality as they see it, and as they frame it. It is my intention to use the text and images created collectively by Black girls and women to make the stories about Black girls' experiences live beyond the researched moments I am afforded and privileged to be a part of.

## OUR PHOTOS ARE FOR US FIRST: THE DISRUPTION

Visual methods have historically been used as a research tool within the field of qualitative inquiry. Overall, there are two dominant intentions behind the use of visual methods. One, with regard to the creation of images by the researcher for the purpose of documentation and/or two, the collection of images for the purpose of analysis (Banks, 2007; Pink, 2007; Collier, 1986). These two uses are not separate from each other and often work in conjunction with a researcher's attempt to extract meaning about the lives of the participants they are researching. In either case, photos are often used to derive meaning—whether that meaning results from the use of photographs in interviews (photo elicitation) or the creation and use of images for participants to better elaborate on their lived lives (documentary photography).

With the rise in use of digital cameras (and disposable cameras as well), qualitative researchers are witnessing an emergence of using photovoice as a tool in the creation of visual ethnographies. Photovoice is a process by which people can identify, represent, and enhance their community through a specific photographic technique. It entrusts the cameras in the hands of research participants to enable them to act as recorders and potential catalysts for change in their own communities (Wang & Burris, 1997). Whereas visual ethnography alludes to the kind of research being undertaken and the method of data collection and analysis, photovoice gives rise to the purpose of the method. In other words, the use of photovoice as a method serves as the foundation of a research project to be political in nature, to have a social justice intent, and to have stories be documented and constructed by the very people not just living the stories but also negotiating the realities of those lived experiences, particularly in marginalized communities. In SOLHOT, our use of photography enhances our collective voice. Different from documentary photography, in SOLHOT our voice is fluid and less static than it might be in stand-alone photos. As well, the use of photography enables us to produce meaning and ask and answer questions about our lives. This is different from photo elicitation where the asking of questions and the production of meaning is solely in the hands of the researcher.

Initially, I hesitated to think about the use of photography in SOLHOT as a method. Photography itself seemed disruptive to the systematic methods of data collection and analysis I was taught about in methodology courses. However, as I write my dissertation I realize that the photographs are OUR data, OUR evidence that WE are here. Douglass Harper (1998) reminded us of Howard Becker (1974) warning that photographs are often thought of as truth, though they are more precisely reflections of the photographer's point of view, biases, and knowledge (or lack of knowledge). If the research design is one in which deficit-based assumptions exist of the youth involved in the project, this warning rings true. If a researcher enters a space already consciously or unconsciously with negative ideas concerning the potential of the youth involved to construct critical opinions of the world they inhabit, then that same researcher might attach little worthwhile meaning to photographs taken/created/or given text to by the youth. This is a risk I was aware of before the beginning of my research and one that I continue to actively work against in considering the photographs taken by the girls in SOLHOT.

Photovoice allows for research participants to enact and demonstrate an enormous amount of agency in being the creators of the images and not only the subjects. Normally, the use of photovoice is based upon three main goals: (1) to enable people to record and reflect their community's strengths and concerns, (2) to promote critical dialogue and knowledge about important community issues through large and small group discussion of photographs, and (3) to reach policymakers (Wang & Burris, 1997). Photovoice serves as an appropriate site of entry for working with Black girls, as the method enables Black girls to determine what issues about their lives are examined and the ways in which those issues are discussed. However, different than photovoice, SOLHOT's use of photography as method prioritizes how the girls see themselves. Moreover, as a tool for civic engagement, photovoice is often cited as a method for empowering youth to become more invested in the communities in which they live. In SOLHOT, our first priority is placed on the stories attached to the photos we take, and this is yet another disruption to traditional photovoice method. We are committed to articulating out loud that we see how you see us and we affirm our power in countering negative stories. In SOLHOT, Black girls often feel as though they are being investigated by the outside world (by social workers, teachers, administrators, etc.). Through our disruptive way of using photovoice, we investigate our own lives and find ways to present back to the outside world positive and true representations of what we learn.

We craft the exploration of our lives in our exchange of visual stories about what it means to be a daughter, a friend, a cousin, a mother, and a student—all the while remaining whole as Black girls becoming Black women and as Black women re-remembering what it means to be a Black girl. Of use to this process of becoming a Black woman and of re-remembering our Black girlhood is photography. Every week, girls and women in SOLHOT are taking photos, constructing collages of images and adding to them the necessary text that transforms the messages these images send to the general public about us—messages that are socially constructed with a tone of negative assumptions about Black girls.

Our photos intentionally document how we think the world sees us in contrast to how we see ourselves. We share our narratives unapologetically with the world and if there is but one thing we are sure of, it is that every space in which we stand—at any given moment—is the space in which we are the most proud of being a Black girl! Inherent to SOLHOT is a call for imagining a new world, for creating freedom dreams while also recognizing the inspirational caution spoken by activist-scholar Andrea Smith (2005),

> From our position of growing up in a patriarchal, colonial, and white supremacist world, we cannot fully imagine how a world that is not based on structures of oppression might operate. Nevertheless, we can be part of a collective, creative process that can bring us closer to a society not based on domination. (p. 191)

I continue to believe that the ability to imagine is freeing, necessary, and needs to be considered a political project when spaces with Black girls are engaged as revolutionary movement work. We constantly own the process of using photographs as our messaging tool to the world. And I, as an activist scholar, am always living within the tensions attached to my choice to rely on the transformative power of images alongside the transformative power attached to text within the academy.

The long-term goal of my work with Black girls is to name the unique and creative ways Black girls and women use methods of visual ethnography to tell our stories. Given that the examination of Black girls utilizing visual research strategies is ongoing and potentially breaking new methodological ground within qualitative inquiry, I present my emerging thoughts in the next section with an intention of "writing to know." "Writing to know" means to me that as I write—and stay centered in the tensions that often arise in the writing up of research—more of what I want to say and how I want to say it will be revealed. It is my hope that what comes across to the reader most is the incredible insight that Black girls have to offer to the world of educational research. However, I remain cognizant of Ruth Behar's (1996) assertion that, "When you write vulnerably, others respond vulnerably. A different set of problems and predicaments arise that would never surface in response to more detached writing" (p. 16). Although in large part this work forces me to be humble, there is also an inherent spirit that challenges me to own my gifts and greatness in the same way that I challenge the girls to own their gifts and greatness.

Visual methods applied by Black girls and women engaged in collective work remains a field rich of disruptive potential. While we must continue to negotiate the dilemma of the gaze of those who view the photos taken by the girls and the negative constructs about Black girlhood viewers might bring to the photos, I believe that in many ways, a photograph taken by a Black girl is her way of talking back to those negative constructs. Photography is one way that allows her to be heard above the so-called "loudness" many people so often see in her and refer to as evidence for many of the stereotypes about Black girls.

## PICTURE THIS: THE FRAMING OF MIYA'S TRUTH

Fig 9.2 Standing in the Path of Black Women's Self-Determination.

In SOLHOT, each girl is given a disposable camera to take home in order to capture images (both of people and symbols) that represent home, love, beauty, community, and what it looks like to be a Black girl growing up in central Illinois. We also work with digital cameras during our time together and document people, places, and things about school that bring us joy, pain or need to be changed. The cameras are always present in our space. They are an integral part of our investigation into what we know, what we don't know, and how we know what we know about the communities we live in. We come together each week to discuss the meanings of the photos we take and write about them as individuals and as a group. Along with documenting what we see, we have very honest conversations about how we would like things to change. We discuss the changes we are willing to make as Black girls and make suggestions about how people in decision-making positions can do things differently in order to create a more positive impact in our lives. Our photos and our words show the outside world what we believe in and embody what we would like to change in our worlds so that the lives of Black girls can be better understood and honored. This kind of work, we believe, lies at the center of a legacy of Black women's work in self-determination.

At the beginning of our work with the girls in SOLHOT, we asked that they take home disposable cameras and photograph people, places, and things that they believed represented their lives as Black girls. The photo at the beginning of this section (Figure 9.2) is a photograph taken by Miya (pseudonym). This photo was in answer to the prompt given to the girls in SOLHOT requesting that they photograph things that they believed represented their life as a Black girl. Miya's mother is a hair stylist and owns her own hair salon. What is so gripping and speaks loudly to my argument that the work of SOLHOT exists within the legacy of Black women's self-determination work is how Miya's body is situated in the photo, in the shadow of the hot combs. As a student of Black history, I think back to stories about Madame CJ Walker and her visionary contributions to the development of hair products for Black women, particularly after the invention of the hot comb. Miya and her mother stand in the center of that history. In our conversation about the photograph, Miya shares an excitement about her mother's work and I share the history about hot combs in a historical conversation about Black women's hair. Embedded in the creation of collective meaning is the legacy of Black women's self-determination manifested with Miya's photograph.

## CONCLUSION

In this chapter, I provided an overview of a visual ethnography in the making. I addressed the methods I used for data collection, analysis, and representation for my dissertation that I consider a disruption to the status quo. I argued that when photography is used as a data-collection tool and put in the hands of Black girls, what results are necessary counternarratives to the negative and stereotypical images of Black girls within popular culture. As a way to investigate their own lives and disrupt stereotypical images of Black girls in popular culture, girls in SOLHOT use photography to create collective meaning. In SOLHOT, we are committed to the transformation of the negative stories told (or thought about) regarding Black girls. Our work continues!

## NOTES

1. The idea of SOLHOT was a gift to Black girls and women from Dr. Ruth Nicole Brown in the fall of 2006. She put out a call to other women of color to work with her on an effort to engage Black girls and I answered.

## REFERENCES

Banks, M. (2007). *Using visual data in qualitative research*. Los Angeles, CA: Sage.

Becker, H. S. (1974). Photography and sociology. *Studies in the Anthropology of Visual Communication*, *1*, 3–26.

Behar, R. (1996). *The vulnerable observer: Anthropology that breaks your heart.* Boston, MA: Beacon Press.

Brown, R. N. (2009). *Black girlhood celebration: Toward a hip-hop feminist pedagogy.* New York, NY: Peter Lang.

Collier, J., & Collier, M. (1986). *Visual anthropology: Photography as a research method.* Albuquerque, NM: University of New Mexico Press.

Darder, A. (2002). *Reinventing Paulo Freire: A pedagogy of love.* Boulder, CO: Westview Press.

Delgado-Bernal, D. (2002). Critical Race Theory, Latino critical theory, and critical race-gendered epistemologies: Recognizing students of color as holders and creators of knowledge. *Qualitative Inquiry, 8*(1), 105–126.

Freire, P. (1998). *Pedagogy of freedom.* Lanham, MD: Rowman & Littlefield.

Freire, P. (2006). *Pedagogy of the oppressed.* New York, NY: Herder and Herder.

Harper, D. (1998). Visual sociology: Expanding sociological vision. *The American Sociologist, 19*(1), 54–70.

hooks, b. (1994). *Teaching to transgress: Education as the practice of freedom.* New York, NY: Routledge.

Leadbeater, B., & Way, N. (2007). *Urban girls revisited: Building strengths.* New York, NY: New York University Press.

Lorde, A. (2007). *Sister outsider.* Trumansburg, NY: Crossing Press.

McLaren, P. (2003). Critical pedagogy: A look at the major concepts. In A. Darder, M. Baltodano, & R. Torres (Eds.), *The critical pedagogy reader.* New York, NY: Routledge.

Pink, S. (2007). *Doing visual ethnography: Images, media and representation in research.* London, England: Sage.

Smith, A. (2005). *Conquest: Sexual violence and American Indian genocide.* Cambridge, MA: South End Press.

Walker, A. (1983). *In search of our mothers' gardens.* New York, NY: Harcourt Brace Jovanovich.

Wang, C., & Burris, M. A. (1997). Photovoice: Concept, methodology, and use for participatory needs assessment. *Health, Education and Behavior, 24*(3), 369–387.

Willis, D. (2009). *Posing beauty: African American images from the 1890s to the present.* New York, NY: W. W. Norton & Company.

## ADDITIONAL RESOURCES

The following list contains some of the websites, books, and articles that helped me in my thinking through the use of photography with Black girls (and young people, in general). A few items speak to photography and the politics of its use, specifically—all providing me with either inspiration or challenge in my thinking through organic and disruptive ways of creating collective photographic memory in SOLHOT.

http://www.photovoice.org — This group is based in London, UK. Much of the great and most community-based work with Photovoice has been done internationally.

http://www.youth.society.uvic.ca/node/286 — The center provides examples of youth-driven Photovoice projects in Canada.

Bach, H. (1998). *A visual narrative concerning curriculum, girls, photography etc.* Edmonton, Canada: Qual Insitute Press.

Ducre, A. K. (2012). *A place we call home: Gender, race, and justice in Syracuse.* Syracuse, NY: Syracuse University Press.

Moletsane, R., Mitchell, C., Smith, A., & Chisholm, L. (2008). *Methodologies for mapping a Southern African girlhood in the age of AIDS.* Rotterdam, The Netherlands: Sense.

Sontag, S. (1977). *On photography.* New York, NY: Picador USA.

Wallace, M., & Smith, S. (Eds). (2012). *Pictures and progress: Early photography and the making of African American identity.* Durham, NC: Duke University Press.

Wang, C., & Burris M. A. (1997). Photovoice: Concept, methodology, and use for participatory needs assessment. *Health, Education and Behavior, 24*(3), 369–387.

I discussed in my chapter how Photovoice served as an entry point to using photography with Black girls. It was a way to satisfy my doctoral student paranoia about using a "credible" qualitative method. As I dug further into the literature about the use of visual methods within African American communities, it is the work of photographer and scholar Deborah Willis that continues to motivate and inspire me! If you are not familiar with her work, please get familiar! Black girls' photos exist within a legacy of her work!

Willis, D. (2009). *Posing beauty: African American images from the 1890s to the present.* New York, NY: W. W. Norton & Company.

http://nmaahc.si.edu/Events/envisioningemancipation — Museum director Lonnie Bunch discusses with Deborah Willis, PhD, her latest work, *Envisioning Emancipation: Black Americans and the End of Slavery.* Through rare photographs and documents, the book focuses on Black enslavement, emancipation, and life from 1850–1930.

# Living IT Out: Disrupting Politics AND Practices in THE Academy

# CHAPTER TEN

# Identity AS Inquiry

## Living and Researching from the Borderlands

Z. NICOLAZZO

*This feels risky.*
*(This is risky.)*
*This feels dangerous.*
*(This is dangerous.)*
*This feels scary.*
*(This is scary.)*
*This feels important.*
*(This is important.)*

As a white, queer, able-bodied, culturally Jewish, atheist, middle-class, trans*[1] individual, I live in the borderlands: between privileged and marginalized identities, between visible and invisible identities, and between the culturally (re)enforced gender binary. Originally conceptualized by Anzaldúa (2007),

> A borderland is a vague and undetermined place created by the emotional residue of an unnatural boundary. It is in a constant state of transition. The prohibited and forbidden are its inhabitants. *Los atravesados* live here: the squint-eyed, the perverse, the queer, the troublesome, the mongrel, the mulato [sic], the half-breed, the half dead. In short, those who cross over, pass over, or go through the confines of the "normal." (p. 25)

Not only do I live in the borderlands, but as a trans* scholar researching with trans* college students, my work is deeply entrenched in the borderlands. Participants, data collection and analysis, and the very process of research shape and define me as much as I shape and define my research. My research "bruises" me (Mazzei, 2013), leaving its traces on my mind as it makes me recall past emotions and experiences. There have even been times when I have wondered where I end, and my research begins, as if there should be a neat and tidy divide between my life and my research. However, I have known this was never the case. Instead, I have come to recognize that I am researching trans* students in postsecondary education into existence, including myself.

When I entered the Student Affairs in Higher Education doctoral program at Miami University in the fall of 2011, I had recently "come out" as trans*. I did not really know what this meant for my life, both personally and professionally, but I knew I had to get out of my current job, which was not a supportive environment in which to explore my gender. I also knew I needed to get out of Arizona. During my time living there, the state increasingly became a dangerous place for many people with marginalized identities, especially those with subordinated racial identities (e.g., indigenous peoples, migrants, Latin@ people). Additionally, after five years of working in higher education administration, I was ready to make changes in both my life and work. Little did I know when I decided to go to Miami how closely entwined these changes would be.

When I made the choice to focus my research on the experiences of trans* college students, I was aware that I would have to dissolve boundaries between my research agenda and myself, viewing the two as informing and enriching each other. Rather than erecting false borders between the culture I study and myself, or believing I can bracket my experiences (Jones, Torres, & Arminio, 2006) from my research, I prefer to locate the "I" (Ellis, 2004) in my research. Who I am and how I show up in space has effects (Butler, 2006) on the broader culture in which I live and work. Therefore, the way I dress and walk, the things I research, write, and talk about, and the company I keep influence my environment and those around me just as they influence me. To deny this connection and interplay seems myopic at best.

The connections between my work, my research, and myself have led to—and will likely continue to lead to—a tempestuous journey. Even in my young career, I can think back to the opportunities I was given, only to have them taken away without adequate explanation. Most notably, a previous mentor had encouraged me to submit a proposal for a special issue journal for educators working in the areas of college housing and residence life that he was co-editing. After talking about some options with him, I settled on an option I found compelling—challenging the illogical idea of sex-segregated housing on college campuses—wrote the proposal, and submitted it. The next month, I saw my mentor at a professional conference, where he congratulated me, letting me know my proposal had been accepted.

After four months of work, one round of editing, and two drafts of my manuscript, my mentor and his co-editor stopped communicating with me about the status of my submission. One evening, someone who was also writing a manuscript for the same special issue journal asked me if I had received the author agreement paperwork for my manuscript. He had received an email with this paperwork earlier in the week, and had noticed all the other authors writing articles for the publication were included on the email, except me. After seeking an explanation from the co-editors of the publication, and not receiving even a confirmation of communication for over a month, my mentor finally emailed me to let me know my article would not be included in the publication after all. Despite my proposal being accepted and getting positive feedback through the review process, I was told my manuscript was "not empirical enough." I was also told the Executive Editor of the journal questioned how well my article on trans* students fit within the theme of the special issue, which was defined as being about "men's issues."

I was suspicious that the topic of my manuscript, and its critical approach—the very reasons my mentor told me my proposal had originally been accepted—led to the last-minute decision to deny its publication. When I mentioned this, and suggested the silencing of my voice and perspective was a manifestation of transphobia, I was met with extreme and direct resistance. My mentor told me that he, a cisgender[2] man who, by his own admission, "had every privilege in the book," would never support transphobia and, thus, the decision not to publish my manuscript was not based in genderist assumptions. My mentor then took the opportunity to remind me again that the piece was not accepted due to it being "non-empirical." Although the original call for proposals had not mandated all pieces be empirical—a point I made clear in my communication with my mentor, his co-editor, and the Executive Editor of the publication, all of whom are cisgender men—I was told the decision was final. However, they did tell me my piece could run as a "point of view" piece, which to me seemed to diminish the overall significance of its (research-based) argument. Instead, I pulled my manuscript and pulled back from my mentor. I still have not published my manuscript, and it has been over a year since I last spoke with my mentor, who at the time had meant so much to me.

I can also clearly see in my mind the people from whom I have distanced myself because they told me I was "overly sensitive about all that gender stuff," or I was "too angry." In these moments, I am reminded of Anne Lamott's (1994) assertion, "This is a difficult country to look different in … and if you are too skinny or too tall or dark or weird or short or frizzy or homely or poor or nearsighted, you get crucified" (p. xvi). Although Lamott wrote this about the United States broadly, I hold the same to be true of the educational research community—it is a difficult place to look, be, and research differently. If you are "too angry," engage in scholarship that seeks to uncover and interrogate power dynamics, recognize yourself as a provocative source for data collection, or are from a marginalized community that informs your research agenda, you run the risk of the orthodoxy labeling you as one of "those scholars." One of the angry ones: the ones who read power into situations (as if it was not always already present); the ones who need to give up on alternative methodologies and seek "truth" in significance and generalizability.

*Because my work is so personal, I need to give consideration to what the consequences of this all may be. How can the rawness and proximity to my work be dangerous? What opportunities, people, and conversations may be "off limits" due to my (personal) work? Do I care? How do I cope? What are the possibilities of this all? In essence, I am left wondering: what are the effects of locating myself in my work? Do I even have the ability not to do this?*

With these questions as a backdrop, I use the remainder of this chapter to explore the connections between the dimensions of my personal identity and the scope, methodologies, and representation of my research as a young scholar. Utilizing an autoethnographic approach[3]—itself a disruptive form of data collection and knowledge representation—I examine how living in the borderlands has influenced who I am personally and professionally. Specifically, I explore concerns encountered in my doctoral program about how I present both myself and my research in a higher education environment that is increasingly ambivalent to disruptive formations of identity and inquiry (Pasque, Carducci, Kuntz, & Gildersleeve, 2012). I describe advising and mentoring relationships that encouraged me to explore alternative issues, methodologies, and representations of research as a way to counteract assimilationist research practices. I close by advocating for the proliferation of research agendas and lines of inquiry situated intimately in one's personal identities and experiences. Although such an approach is laced with tensions related to issues of power and privilege, it has the potential to expand who we are, who we come to know, and the populations and communities who become known to us.

As I have already done in this chapter, I will continue to star the text (Barthes, 1974) with reflections from my own personal journal. As Barthes (1974) stated:

We shall therefore star the text, separating, in the manner of a minor earthquake, the blocks of signification of which reading grasps only the smooth surface, imperceptibly soldered by the movement of sentences, the flowing discourse of narration, the "naturalness" of ordinary language.... This cutting up, admittedly, will be arbitrary in the extreme; it will imply no methodological responsibility ... it will be a matter of convenience ... variable according to the moments of the text.... The text, in its mass, is comparable to a sky, at once flat and smooth, deep, without edges and without landmarks; like the soothsayer drawing on it with the tip of his [sic] staff an imaginary rectangle wherein to consult, according to certain principles the flight of birds, the commentator traces through the text certain zones of reading, in order to observe therein the migration of meanings. (pp. 13–14)

My starring of the text, seen in the right-justified italicized passages throughout this chapter, represents my cutting up and blending multiple personal narratives together. I chose to adopt Barthes's (1974) method of "starring the text" as a way to highlight how my personal identities mediate and change my identity as an educational researcher. Therefore, my starring of the text serves not only as an interruption to the chapter itself, but also surfaces critical questions, confluences, tensions, and possibilities of living and researching in the borderlands. Starring the text also provides me a reminder of why I use disruptive methodologies. For example, when I write

*This feels risky.*
*(This is risky.)*
*This feels dangerous.*
*(This is dangerous.)*
*This feels scary.*
*(This is scary.)*
*This feels important.*
*(This is important.)*

I am both elucidating the difficulty in using disruptive methodologies—it feels, and is, risky, dangerous, and scary—while also reminding myself why I continue to use them—because it feels and is important to who I am and the research I do. In this sense, starring the text enables me to highlight how the borders of my personal identities invariably leak into my research, and vice versa.

## DANGERS, CONCERNS, AND PITFALLS OF BLURRING THE (SUPPOSED) PERSONAL/PROFESSIONAL DIVIDE

I do not like to talk much about loss. I do not mean the loss of a relationship or loved one so much as the loss of opportunities and people in my life because of who I am. As a trans* scholar, I know all too well the media-based tropes depicting trans* people as pathetic (Serano, 2007) and freakish (Siebler, 2010). Furthermore, there continues to be scholarship written about the social ostracism, harassment, and violence we face, both broadly (Grant et al., 2011) and in the collegiate setting (Rankin, Weber, Blumenfeld, & Frazer, 2010). However, while I find this research to be important work, I am keenly aware that I and other trans* people are more than just victims of transgender oppression (Catalano, McCarthy, & Shlasko, 2007). Similar to our cisgender peers, we have mundane lives and get lost in the banal details of friendships, work, and family. We thrive, celebrate successes, mourn, cry, smile, and laugh. In many ways, we bask in the sheer everydayness of our lives. And it is because this everydayness is occluded from view that I try not to talk about loss. Because I want to be seen as more than a tragic figure, as someone to be pitied or told "you poor thing" by those who exclaim, "It must be so tough to be you!" while in the same breath they ask, "How do you do it?" Admittedly, loss and the threat of loss are part of our story as marginalized people. However, despite not wanting to start here for fear of loss consuming how others see me and other trans* people, I feel I must.

> *Yesterday, I remembered how I have been punished for my scholarship being too personal. While I thought I had moved past this, I still felt pain and anger in my writing about this experience. Although this experience was painful—it led to a rift between me and my (former) academic mentor that has yet to be bridged—I also realized something important about myself. I am unwilling to cordon off my voice, perspective, and self (in whatever way I want to show up) so my work will be "more palatable" or "less angry" in order for it to be considered more publishable. I am unwilling to do this because my work is an extension of me and of those participants with whom I am collaborating.* (Bhattacharya, 2008)*

> *My work is for us, not merely for publications. If I have to defend my work and my choices as I progress in my career, so be it; those are fights I am willing to undertake in order to do justice to the voices of myself and the participants with whom I am researching.*

Have I experienced loss? Yes. I have lost mentors, publication opportunities, relationships with people whom I make uncomfortable with the stares and looks I garner, deeper connections with people who do not see me as I want to be seen. I have lost places I want to return to, but cannot, unless I choose to cover (Yoshino, 2006), or hide, my transness, both personally as well as through my own research and scholarship, so others might "accept" me. Ironically, if I were to comply by covering who I am as a trans* person and scholar in order to gain acceptance from other educators and scholars, they would be accepting who they *want me to be* rather than accepting me for who I am and am becoming as a person, researcher, and scholar.

I have also felt the struggle of losing my past as I look to create my present and future. For example, I have shied away from using my given name, replacing it with phrases like "my legal name." At times, it feels good. I am choosing my own name and setting the rules by which other people refer to me. However, it also has the effect of distancing me from people and a past I cherish. I have chosen not to "come out" to my grandmother, a 98-year-old first-generation Sicilian-American for whom I would do anything. Because of this, she will never know me as, or call me by, my chosen name. Additionally, I still feel a twinge of guilt whenever my mother calls me Z, as she is the person who gave me my legal name. In fact, the reason I have chosen not to legally change my name is due in large part to realizing her naming me is one of the many connections between us.

Questions over my name have also created barriers between myself and my brother, who must know there is something different about his younger sibling, but has chosen not to ask, because perhaps actively *unknowing* may be less difficult in the long run. Moreover, countless friends who cannot get it, will not get it, or do not want to get it, struggle with my identity and research, sometimes fading into spectral associations from my past. These are but a few of the people who I have loved and still love, but with whom I feel guarded or who have left my life in relation to my shifting understanding of my gender identity and expression. So yes, I have experienced loss. You can count me among the pantheon of trans* people who live with loss; I am reminded of it whenever I receive bills in the mail addressed to "Mr. Zachary D. Nicolazzo," get an email from my Aunt that starts off with "Hi, Zach," or pack for the sojourn to my childhood home and must leave behind as many traces of my femininity as I can while also preparing for the questions that will inevitably arise regarding those signs and symbols I choose not to hide (e.g., my shaved legs). These are reminders of who I am, who I was, and how I have struggled—and oftentimes failed—to hold onto my past as I continue living and researching from the borderlands.

*But I am more than that. Can you see that I am more than that? Let me show you.*

My experiences of negotiating the loss I have felt by living in the borderlands have played a crucial role in shaping my research. By focusing my dissertation on trans* student resilience, I am seeking to complicate the "trans* as pathetic" narrative that is so pervasive through the public sphere. I have also chosen a methodology, Critical Collaborative Ethnography (Bhattacharya, 2008), that foregrounds collaboration and connection between and amongst participants and researcher. Additionally, I have proposed to write sections of my dissertation with participants, and am working on ways to use their words and their writing to "star the text" of my dissertation. I recognize the choices I am making will not completely shift the balance of power inherent in the researcher-participant relationship. However, my decisions come from a desire to focus on and create connections rather than dealing wholly in loss. I want to work with trans* participants to share their self-efficacy, talents, and abilities rather than just portraying them as individuals who lose friends, loved ones, or connections to campus. For so long I felt as though I struggled to find a home, in both a physical and emotional sense. This was further compounded by not feeling like I had a community of my own that I could connect with and lean on during times of struggle and loss. Therefore, the choices I have made about my research, epistemology, methodology, and representation of the knowledge we create together is a way for all of us (myself as the researcher and the participants with whom I am working) to generate a sense of kinship and of home together.

"Home" had been an elusive concept to me prior to starting my doctoral work. Before coming to Miami University, I lived in Tucson, Arizona, a place I thought would be my home for the foreseeable future when I first arrived. As I drove away in the Arizona heat, plastic wrap clinging to the fresh tattoo of my grandparents I had gotten over my heart the day before, I wept. I wept for me, for those I was leaving behind, and for the weight of living a life that had become untenable, precarious, and risky over my four-year tenure in the Southwest. I had gone to Arizona for a partner, a marriage, a family, an academic program, and a career, but things did not turn out as I had anticipated. My marriage crumbled, I put off going back to school, and felt stuck in a professional position that I began to think detracted more than it benefitted the mission and values of higher education. Furthermore, along the way, I realized I could no longer deny the desires I had to—

> *This feels risky.*
> *This feels dangerous.*
> *This feels scary.*
> *This feels important.*

—wear women's clothing, modify my bodily appearance, and live openly as trans*. Arizona had become—and still remains—a dangerous place to exist for subaltern communities, be it along the vectors of race, ethnicity, sex, sexual orientation, or gender identity. Laws such as SB 1070,[4] which other state legislatures throughout the country have copied (Lacayo, 2011) and HB 2281,[5] sent a clear signal that I, and others like me, were not welcome. For these reasons, I left. On the surface, it could seem like I left one dangerous place—the neoconservative Southwest— for another—the desolate landscape of a highly conservative county in Southwest Ohio. Even after two years, some of the same concerns greet me as I wake up for the day,

> *Will today be the day? The day I stop being able to say, "No—I've never been attacked or assaulted because of my gender identity."*

as I walk into my closet to decide what I will wear each day,

> *Is this too obvious? Is this not obvious enough? I hate my clothes; they are too boyish ... but what does that even mean?*

and as I walk around campus. I have gotten into the habit of wearing dark sunglasses to spare me from the looks, the staring, the gawking, the head turns I garner. Sometimes I smirk—I am glad to confuse and fuck with people. I am glad people do not know what to do with me, where to place me, how to codify me. However, other times, I worry. Despite my questioning if I am just playing (I am not) and feeling like an imposter on days when I cover (do we not all feel this way at times?), this is more than a game. This is my life, and there are potential consequences for how I live it that I must contend with.

My concerns also translate to my work. I worry my work will be overlooked due to my researching a highly marginalized and largely invisible student population. In the past two years, I have received several responses to manuscripts I have submitted for publication that state something to the effect of, "the research you are doing on trans* students is very important, but this topic does not fit within the scope of our journal." I have begun to wonder what it means for research with trans* college students to not "fit" into educational journals, especially those focusing on postsecondary education, college students, and student identity development. Furthermore, *why* does this research not "fit"? I cannot help but think it has something to do with the discomfort and unease cisgender people feel when confronted with a student population that uncovers the deep flaws inherent in the cultural presumption of gender as a dichotomous construct.

Additionally, colleagues and fellow students have also asked me, "just how many trans* college students *are* there?" more times than I care to remember. In response to this question, I have taken to inquiring why it matters. If there were to be a certain critical mass of trans* college students, would it make the population—and by extension, my research—more "reliable," "important," or "meaningful"? Also, as Dean Spade (2010) pointed out, "the process of creating an administrable category of transness would no doubt do the same violence that other forms of identity categorization do, establishing criteria that inevitably fail in their universality as all such criteria do" (p. 74). By establishing norms around who counts as trans* in an attempt to determine how many trans* college students exist, one invariably creates a standard that is limiting, constrictive, and defines who people are and can be rather than allowing each individual trans* person to have agency in defining their lives, experiences, and transness themselves. One also runs the risk of reifying a hierarchy within the category of "trans*," where those who are publicly "out" and/or are transitioning[6] are seen as "trans* enough," and all other trans* people—those of us who cross-dress, are gender-non-conforming, choose not to have medical interventions, are stealth,[7] and/or seek to fuck with the gender binary—are not. In this sense, the very asking of the question perpetuates violence against trans* people.

I also worry that being a critical trans* scholar doing research with trans* students will mark me as someone who reads things into hir[8] research. For example, people might think my work is "too personal," and therefore is undeserving of publication. There still exists the notion that research and data are things outside of us, which we must hold at a distance to discover an objective "Truth" (e.g., Smith, 2008). While there are some who are making inroads to repurpose the way research is performed, analyzed, and understood (e.g., Hesse-Biber & Leavy, 2008), empiricism and methodological conservatism still rule the day (Pasque, Carducci, Kuntz, & Gildersleeve, 2012). I also worry that due to my gender identity and my desire to focus on trans* student resilience, others may shrug off my research as forwarding my own voice and ideas rather than those of my fellow participants. My concerns about my work and how it will be accepted—or not—have only increased as I get closer to searching for tenure-track faculty positions, think about acculturating myself to a new location and department, and begin the process of securing tenure.

> *My advisor told me I should not go into a job search tentatively, as this will make me nervous and defensive about my methods. I know she is right, but I am not sure how to feel comfortable given an environment focused so intently on forcing my hand toward "being normal." I keep searching for, scrapping for an answer. A ledge to rest on and become settled. Maybe this isn't the point, though. Maybe it will always feel risky, dangerous, scary. But it will also always feel important, for me and for others.*

But I am more than the aforementioned concerns, worries, and questions, brought about by my living and researching in the borderlands. Can you see I am more than this? Let me show you.

## MY GUIDES IN THE BORDERLANDS: THE IMPORTANCE OF ADVISORS AND MENTORS

In *The Electric Kool-Aid Acid Test*, Tom Wolfe (1968) wrote about spending time with a group of beatniks who rallied around Ken Kesey, the author of *One Flew Over the Cuckoo's Nest*, and called themselves the Merry Pranksters. Slipping in and out of hallucinogenic states, the Merry Pranksters traversed the country in a bus with the word "Furthur" painted on the side. As Wolfe (1968) wrote, "The manifest, the destination sign in the front, read: 'Furthur,' with two *u*'s" (p. 61). The word, a misspelling of further, symbolized both the distance the Merry Pranksters had yet to travel as well as their state of being while traveling, that of being further, or transcending, their current state of consciousness through the use of LSD. In a similarly transcendent vein, the word further has come to embody the consultation and advising I have received from advisors and mentors since entering my doctoral program. Far from being unsatisfied with my work, my mentors have encouraged me to explore new areas of interest, try alternative ways of knowing and representing knowledge, and transgress the boundaries of my own previously held rationalizations for the phenomena I experience and research, all in an effort to push my work further than where it previously had been. In this sense, mentors have advocated that I set up camp in the borderlands by exploring disruptive epistemologies, methodologies, and representations of knowledge.

I have never felt more supported as an intellectual and scholar as I do at Miami University. Specifically, the program that I'm a part of (Student Affairs in Higher Education) has been an exceedingly patient and caring place for me to grow as an emerging scholar. While several mentors have cautioned me that I will need to work hard for recognition in the academy, a product both of the youth of the program I am in[9] as well as the anomalous research and scholarship I do, no one has ever told me to forego pursuing my interests or using disruptive method-ologies and epistemologies. In fact, mentors have told me that my work has sev-eral benefits. One of these benefits is the ability to highlight an underrepresented population in higher education (i.e., trans* students) through collaborative-based and cultural studies approaches, which are misunderstood and underappreciated. Becoming comfortable with the unorthodoxy of my gender identity and expres-sion, as well as the alternative ways in which I think, research, write, and practice education, has been an ongoing process of embracing that which others see as weird, bizarre, and unusual. For me, the process of becoming comfortable with who I am as a person and a scholar has become a personal practice borne partially from necessity. Exploring these two intersecting identities—my personal identity and my scholarly identity—also speaks to the way in which I desire to promote radically divergent understandings of who people are, how we live, and how we make sense of our worlds. However, I view such self-exploration as more than personally enriching. I see this process as being politically and ethically motivated, resulting in my ability to advocate for the increased visibility of the various ways subaltern communities, such as trans* college students, are already living, working, and engaging in the world.

When I was applying to doctoral programs, I looked for specific scholars that I wanted to work with. It was important for me to find scholars who not only excited my intellectual curiosities, but who would also serve as positive mentors. This meant I needed to feel comfortable talking with them. Furthermore, because my work and my life were—and still are—so intimately connected, I needed to know I had the space to be, share, and discuss myself with them. Admittedly, this is a tall order for anyone to sort through during the application and admissions process. However, because I knew I wanted to pursue a terminal degree years be-fore I actually applied, it gave me additional time to sort through the complexities involved in finding scholarly and mentoring matches. I reached out to peers who had attended the institutions I was considering, seeking their input on their overall experiences with the faculty. I also began developing relationships with scholars at the doctoral programs I was considering, keeping in regular contact with several of these people throughout the two years prior to and during my applying to their programs.

As a current student, I have continued to build relationships with faculty. The time we spend together extends beyond the classroom, as we co-construct a community of scholars. I have continued to reach out to faculty whose work I find insightful, meaningful, and personally moving. Although I am fortunate to have a number of critically minded scholars who study issues of personal identity, I have also taken risks when building rapport, sharing my personal writing, seek-ing advice, and confiding personal/professional anxieties. These moments of vul-nerability have sometimes been difficult and, at times, incredibly uncomfortable.

However, whenever I feel self-conscious, I remind myself that such rawness and vulnerability are the very same things I seek and value from others, especially faculty, staff, students, and research participants. Thus, for me to hold back would seem to be disingenuous.

Moreover, I have recognized that my relationships with each of my faculty members are not the same. For example, what I look for in a relationship with my advisor (e.g., someone to challenge me intellectually and push me further)—

> *There it is again.*
> *Think deeper. Stretch yourself. Explore more. Be playful in your approach.*
> *Go further.*

—is different from the methodological conversations I have with another faculty member or the deeply personal questions about power, privilege, and difference that I explore with yet another faculty member. It was liberating for me to realize I did not need to have the same type of relationship with all my faculty and committee members. Furthermore, I was also able to understand my relationships with faculty were different from the relationships my fellow doctoral peers had with them. Instead of creating resentment, animosity, or competition with other doctoral students for faculty attention, I felt free to develop relationships with faculty members that were natural, meaningful, and organic.

> *There are times when I wonder how I fell into a program and am surrounded by people who encourage me to follow whatever lines of thought and inquiry I desire. But then I remember I was intentional in searching for a program like this; a program that would push me to do my work in the way I wanted to do it. I also have continued to create a network of peers and colleagues who believe in the radical nature of disruptive dialogue, research, and scholarship.*
>
> *Although I feel fortunate to be here, I know my being here is not based in luck. Additionally, I have taken care to develop a queer and radical community of scholars who also push the boundaries. Whenever I am tired or feel cynical, these are the people who remind me of the transformative power of being disruptive. They give me the strength to continue being a "border denizen" (Hale, 1998). It is in them where I find the home I have been searching for.*

Who I am as a person and scholar will likely always feel risky, dangerous, and scary to some degree. Whether it is being made to feel uncomfortable as a trans* person in a rigidly gender dichotomous world, or the potential difficulties in securing employment upon attaining my doctoral degree, risks abound. However, who I am and the work I do have always been, and continue to be important.

Of course, there have been times when I have questioned my abilities as well as the support of my advisor and mentors. I have wondered if the faculty in my program doubt my abilities to teach and have been unsettled by how they may (or may not) make sense of my trans* identity. There have also been moments when I have wondered if the difficulty some faculty had using my preferred pronouns (ze and hir) was a reflection of their commitment (or lack thereof) to me as a person and a scholar. Although these feelings were real, I also know they were cynical and largely predicated on my own insecurities. There is likely some truth to my faculty not always understanding my scholarship or me. However, this is unreflective of a lack of commitment or a lack of desire to be good company (Baxter Magolda, 2002) for me as I make my way through my doctoral process and enter into the academy. My faculty continue to be with me in my journey, regardless of if they "get" what it is like for me to be trans* or to be a disruptive scholar researching with trans* students. I have learned that who I am as a person and a scholar is different from many people who are in or have been a part of the doctoral program that I'm a part of. Because of this, I have developed patience, for myself, my fellow doctoral students and candidates, and for the faculty that I'm in community with. Although we may not always "get" each other, I have never once felt unwelcome or concluded that I should walk away.

Creating and maintaining a sense of community with my advisor and faculty has been an ongoing work in progress. I have had to do some educating about trans* people, identities, and terminology. I have also had to overcome some of my fears that current mentors would treat me the same way previous mentors had. However, I owe much of my resolve and ability to continue moving forward in my personal and professional journey to the queer and radical community I have developed over the past several years, including my advisor and current mentors at Miami University. Whether it has been connecting with fellow queer, trans*, and radical educators at conferences, emailing questions to authors about their writing and thinking, or asking mentors if they can intentionally connect me to other like-minded individuals, I have worked hard to cultivate and maintain my community. It is people like this who truly make me feel like I may have finally found a home in the academy and, just as importantly, in my life.

## RETHINKING HOME

*The word home has me thinking a lot lately. What counts as my home? There seem to be multiple different definitions of home. There is a geographic definition, as in the place I am from and/or currently reside. Although where I live now feels more like home than where I have lived in the past or where I grew up, the geographic limitations of this understanding of home sometimes feel suffocating and isolating.*

*A second way I have begun to think of home extends beyond the boundaries of geography. Instead, it foregrounds the affective aspects of life. Being at home, or to feel like I have found a home, takes more than a room or a physical space (a yard, a porch, a laundry room). When*

*I think about home as a borderlands space, as being neither here nor there, as being beyond physical geography, I think about what has felt, sounded, smelled, and tasted like home to me in the past.*

*Home is a phone call from a dear friend where I lose track of time; the dim light bouncing off apartment walls where people have gathered to share food, company, and stories; the sound of sharing lives; sitting alone on a rocky outcropping to take in a scenic view; the hugs and encouragement to keep going on my work, my writing, and research when I doubt myself most.*

Lately, the concept of home—where is it? What is it? How do I find and maintain it?—has become something of personal interest to me. Being a border denizen, I have often felt like an oddity. I am the only trans*-identified person in my academic department and have struggled to find other trans* scholars at some of the conferences I attend. Furthermore, the papers and sessions focusing on trans* issues are either relatively few in number, or focus on violence against trans* people or advocate for educators creating accommodations for trans* students. I know I am not "the only one," but I often feel dislocated by my living and researching in the borderlands.

At times, I feel downright nomadic, bouncing from place to place, but without a permanent space I can truly call mine. For example, whenever I have had breaks from classes or work, I head "home" to the Northeast, the area where I grew up and my family still lives. When these visits have ended, I have gone back "home" to where I have been living, which has not always felt like home to me. For me, the concept of a "home" being connected to a physical space has become increasingly problematic, as no space has ever felt wholly comfortable, safe, and inviting to me. No physical space has ever conveyed the sense of warmth and security I have wanted to feel from a home.

On the contrary, I have felt at home when I am in the presence of, am talking to, or thinking of, particular people and memories. The sound of my Italian grandfather's laugh when he told me he fed pasta to his oversized goldfish; the smell of fresh cut grass and the quiet before a big soccer match; listening to the rhythmic cadence of a partner's breath as they sleep; the early morning light piercing through trees of the Grand Canyon; a conversation with a dear colleague who encourages me to continue my work; the satisfied exhaustion felt after spending a day doing fieldwork. These fleeting moments, people, and places provide the feeling of home, despite their brevity. These moments, these people, these places, trapped in the past/present/future of my life, bring me home. They are my foundation, my safety, my lighthouse.

*If my feeling at home transcends borders and locations, then how am I to find and hold onto it? Where do I even begin to look for my home in the borderlands? Is looking for home, a process of seeking locations and spaces, even going to help me ever feel at home, something that is tied neither to here nor there?*

If home is not merely a place, neither here nor there, then how do I look for it? If I live and research in the borderlands, can I even find a home? Or am I always already destined to wander from place to place epistemologically, methodologically, and personally? Contemplating the affective dimensionality of home as a concept is liberating; it also provides a conundrum when thinking about how to find, maintain, and nurture a home of one's own, especially for those of us who are border denizens.

Despite the slipperiness of home, I have found it multiple times. I found it when I first moved to the Midwest, where I completed my master's degree. I found it again in the snowy Upper Valley of New Hampshire during my first professional position, and followed it to Arizona, where I learned to seek solace in the mountains I used to climb and descend on my bike. Now, as a doctoral student, I have never before felt such a deep sense of home. I can feel its warmth, the comfort it provides, and the way it encourages and challenges me to go further. Home exists, of that I have no doubt. I have been able to find it and build upon it throughout the years of my professional practice and study. However, how it comes to be, or how I came to find it, have been difficult questions for me to answer.

*The year before I left Arizona, I remember feeling defeated. I felt like I had moved to the Southwest for a life that no longer existed; I felt like I had failed. I was ready to just pack up and move out. The upcoming year weighed heavily on my mind. In sharing my trepidations with a friend one day, I told her I just needed to get through the coming year so I could move on with my life. There was a pause on the other end of the phone.*

*"Baby, you have got to find your people," she told me. "You can't wait for a year—go out and find them now. Volunteer, join groups outside of work, go to events; do what you need to do to find your people."*

*Her words struck a chord with me. She was right; I needed to find my people. I needed to reach out to those meaningful people I already had in my life and seek out others who would becoming meaningful. I felt a sense of urgency after that phone call, and went about the task of finding my people. I have continued to do this ever since.*

Numerous researchers have studied the isolating nature of doctoral work, pointing out that such isolation leads to doctoral student attrition (Ali & Kohun, 2006, 2007). However, throughout my experience, I have found a sense of home in the solidarity I share with other queer and radical faculty, staff, and students in disparate departments and institutions, as a way to significantly decrease my own feelings of isolation. Even in those moments when I feel fearful or nervous about my work and my ability to achieve my goals, I remember that I am not alone, but am part of a larger network of peers, comrades, and colleagues.

*My fear is not enough to stop my moving forward. I am more than my fear. And when I am
not, we are, together.*

I began to develop my support network before I entered my doctoral program.
At the time, I had been an active member of an affinity group in an international association for postsecondary educators for a few years, and was encouraged
to run for the chair position. The membership elected me to a two-year term
as chair, which enabled me to network with others in the association at large,
as well as people who were in other affinity groups. I do not mean to suggest,
however, that one needs to become a chair of an international committee to
build a community of like-minded peers and colleagues. In fact, just finding
and becoming a part of these affinity groups was encouraging to me. As a natural introvert, large groups have always overwhelmed me. However, in smaller
groups, I was able to get to know others who had come to talk about the same
issues I cared about: gender, trans* identities, radical thought, and critical education. It also gave me the time and space to develop connections that I nurtured throughout the year, despite my not being in the same physical location
as many of the people I interacted with.

Once I entered my doctoral program, I began searching for other scholars doing trans* research. At conferences, I would go to any sessions or paper presentations related to trans* students. Although there were not many sessions or papers,
I was able to survey what was being done while also getting to know some of the
people producing trans* scholarship. I also made sure to attend sessions on critical
and disruptive inquiry, as this was an important aspect of my growing scholarly
identity. Lastly, I also made sure to take courses outside of my program and department at Miami. I took great care to ensure my doctoral program allowed me
to take courses in other areas, which I used to my benefit. For example, I ended
up receiving a graduate certificate in Women's, Gender, and Sexuality Studies,
which was integrated into my doctoral curriculum. Through my interactions with
the faculty teaching these courses, I was able to secure teaching opportunities and
set myself up for the potential of teaching in the fields of gender and/or sexuality
studies when I graduate.

True to the borderlands concept, the connections I have made traverse disciplines, departments, and campuses, defying easy categorization or a sense of fixity.
For example, the opportunity to write this chapter is an example of my borderlands
network, stemming from a connection with one of the editors (Rozana) on the
issue of critical qualitative inquiry and alternative methodologies. The educators
and scholars that I am in community with have provided good company (Baxter
Magolda, 2002) as I seek to explore, extend, and transgress boundaries. They provide the support and encouragement for me to do so, but they also provide a sense
of safety. It is this notion of a network that transcends geographical boundaries,

of finding a home within a scholarly community, that I use to ground my call for more critically minded and activist scholars to engage with and proliferate more alternative, radical, and disruptive research.

## A CALL TO SET UP CAMP IN THE BORDERLANDS

*So, if you want to really hurt me, talk badly about my language. Ethnic identity is twin skin to linguistic identity—I am my language. Until I can take pride in my language, I cannot take pride in myself…. I will no longer be made to feel ashamed of existing. I will have my voice: Indian, Spanish, white. I will have my serpent's tongue—my woman's voice, my sexual voice, my poet's voice. I will overcome the tradition of silence.* (Anzaldúa, 2007, p. 81)

She sat across from me at a circular table next to a metal bookcase teeming with volumes of *Ms.* magazine and literature texts. In the background, her desk held a mountain of work—I knew she had other things to do yet she was making time to help me through my own insecurities. She was patient as she stirred her coffee and made affirming eye contact with me. I was nervous. I did not really know her well, but she had granted me the opportunity to teach an Intro to GLBT Studies class the following semester. I did not want to show weakness, but I was scared of what the students may say, how they may react, what they might do when they saw me walk into the room. I was not "normal." I was not "right." I did not comply with the role of "teacher" very well. I wanted so desperately for her to validate me, which made me feel ashamed. I should be beyond this point, I thought. I should not need someone to tell me I am good enough. Was her offering the opportunity for me to teach next semester not validation enough? I felt messy and undone.

"I am worried … I guess I just … I don't know. How do you manage how people read you in the classroom? I mean, how do you manage how they make sense of who you are and how you teach?" There it was. I sat there wringing my hands. This was it. She would take this opportunity away from me. I was too immature, too silly, not self-assured enough to teach. I had exposed myself and the house of cards was about to come crashing down before I even set foot in the classroom.

"That's an important question," she started. She paused, reached for her coffee cup, took a sip. I did not take a breath. "These students may not have been confronted by a lot of difference in their lives, but remember that at least one of those students just needs you to be you." She went on to say more, but there it was. Someone always just needs me to be me.

*Undone or put together, messy or refined, butch, femme, or gender-blended, someone just needs me to be me.*

These words have continued to stay with me and have provided me the strength to continue when, at my lowest points, I wonder if I, my research, or my writing, are good enough. Despite the risks I run, along with others from subaltern populations, it is imperative to be myself in my work, my research, and my scholarship. However I show up at that moment. Saying this does not negate the intense pressures that encourage conformity, normality, and covering, both from a methodological and lived practice perspective. The intricate politics of job searches, promotion and tenure committees, the publication process, and the many ways in which I am evaluated—both formally and informally—by students, colleagues, supervisors, community members, and administrative institutions, is a reality that I have already had to contend with. The cumulative effect of these overlapping systems of managerialism (Tuchman, 2009) and administrative surveillance (Spade, 2011) is to move me toward normalcy. To somehow get me to become less radical, less "angry," less "hostile," and less focused on all the "gender stuff" those critics of mine have been saying in hushed (or perhaps not so hushed) tones. Capturing the question facing all critical, radical, activist, and otherwise disruptive scholars seeking to transgress the aforementioned normalizing effect, hooks (1990) wrote:

> Within complex and ever shifting realms of power relations, do we position ourselves on the side of the colonizing mentality? Or do we continue to stand in political resistance with the oppressed, ready to offer our ways of seeing and theorizing, of making culture, towards that revolutionary effort which seeks to create space where there is unlimited access to the pleasure and power of knowing, where transformation is possible? (p. 145)

These questions are challenging for anyone to answer, let alone those who have already felt the sting of marginalization due to the identities they embody.

The work I and other disruptive scholars do is aimed at making the transformative space hooks (1990) evoked a reality. By unsettling normative ways of being, knowing, and researching, we are forwarding new visions for personal and professional identity and praxis. By thinking beyond the limits of what has been deemed "acceptable" or "appropriate" in terms of subject matter, methodologies, and writing styles, we create space for future disruptive scholars. By living and researching in the borderlands, we create new knowledge, make visible those populations previously invisible, and provide personal and research exemplars for future disruptive scholars. By openly interrogating the hegemony of "normalcy," other queer and radical scholars and I add to the increasingly vocal call to view the margins, the borderlands, as a site of active resistance.

hooks (1990) proclaimed the margins as, "A site of creativity and power, that inclusive space where we recover ourselves, where we move in solidarity to erase the category colonized/colonizer. Marginality as a site of resistance. Enter that space. Let us meet there. Enter that space" (p. 152). Embodying these words, I have found the resilience to resist through communal networks of radical and disruptive peers and colleagues. It is in these spaces where I feel at home with people who share similar passions, interests, and pursuits. It is in these communities where I am in solidarity with other queer and/or critically minded activist-scholars who are keen to push boundaries, transgress previously held understandings, and go further. I know there may be consequences for my associations, just as there already have been for my work. However, I will not let others take my voice. Echoing the Anzaldúa epigram at the outset of this section, I too will overcome the tradition of silence. In doing so, and with the solidarity and camaraderie of like-minded peers, we will continue to make room for ourselves and other radical, activist, and disruptive scholars waiting to emerge from the borderlands.

## NOTES

1. As Killermann (2012) explained, the use of the asterisk in the word trans* recognizes "all non-cisgender gender identities, including transgender, transsexual, transvestite, genderqueer, gender-fluid, non-binary, genderfuck, genderless, agender, non-gendered, third gender, bigender, and trans man and trans woman." The asterisk, which is used in computer searches to signify searching for a term in addition to any characters after that term (e.g., searching for trans* would yield results for the prefix trans and any letters after it, such as transgender and transsexual), represents an inclusive turn in discussing all who transgress, trouble, and/or resist gender boundaries.

2. Schilt and Westbrook (2009) defined cisgender by stating, "Cis is the Latin prefix for 'on the same side.' It compliments trans, the prefix for 'across' or 'over.' 'Cisgender' replaces the terms 'nontransgender' or 'bio man/bio woman' to refer to individuals who have a match between the gender they were assigned at birth, their bodies, and their personal identity" (p. 461).

3. Chang (2008) described autoethnography as a form of inquiry that honors the intertwined nature of self and culture through the recognition of oneself as a legitimate site of research, learning, and cultural formation. Additionally, Ellis and Bochner (2008) suggested autoethnography was a didactic process of looking within oneself to aid in making sense of the outward cultural context that one is embedded in, and vice versa.

4. Officially named the Support Our Law Enforcement and Safe Neighborhoods Act, SB 1070 gave "state and local law enforcement officials the responsibility to detain persons whom they have 'reasonable suspicion' to believe are unlawfully present" (Campbell, 2011, p. 1). Governor Jan Brewer signed SB 1070 into law in April 2010 and furthered an us/them dynamic by which subaltern communities—in particular, migrant, Mexican, and Latin@ individuals—were unfairly and inappropriately cast as outsiders who were dangerous, were stealing American jobs, and were benefitting from social services such as health care and education.

5. Commonly referred to as the Ethnic Studies Ban, HB 2281, developed by then Superintendent of Public Instruction, Tom Horne, a highly conservative public official, banned ethnic studies programs in K-12 education (Soto & Joseph, 2010). The bill itself states that four types of teaching would be prohibited, including those that "promote the overthrow of the United States government .... Promote resentment toward a race or class of people .... Are

designed primarily for pupils of a particular ethnic group [and] …. Advocate ethnic solidarity instead of the treatment of pupils as individuals" (State of Arizona, House of Representatives, 2010, p. 1). This bill, which is currently in place and has dismantled programs such as the Mexican-American Studies program in the Tucson Unified School District, has spurred John Huppenthal, the current Arizona Superintendent of Public Instruction and an Ex-Officio Regent on the Arizona Board of Regents, to openly question whether ethnic studies and affinity-based programs (e.g., Women's Studies, LGBTQ Studies) should be offered in higher education (Planas, 2012).

6.  "Transitioning" is a term used to denote the process by which transsexuals transition from one sex to another. Many transsexuals transition by using hormone treatments and/or having certain surgeries to change their body morphology.

7.  "Stealth" is a term used to denote those trans* people who "pass," or are recognized publicly, as being the sex and/or gender they prefer. Stealth people may not share their trans* identity with many people, and some may not even identify as trans*. Instead, they live their lives as their preferred sex and/or gender and may not face gender-based violence due to their passing.

8.  The pronouns ze (pronounced zee) and hir (pronounced here) are pronouns many trans* people prefer to use. These pronouns replace the he/she and him/her gender binaries, respectively, and are used by some, but not all, who identify as transgender and gender non-conforming. As these are the pronouns I prefer, I use them when referring to myself throughout this chapter.

9.  When I began my doctoral studies at Miami University in the fall of 2011, I was the sole member of just the third cohort of students accepted into the Student Affairs in Higher Education doctoral program, which was established in 2009.

## REFERENCES

Ali, A., & Kohun, F. (2006). Dealing with isolation feelings in IS doctoral programs. *International Journal of Doctoral Studies, 1*, 21–33.

Ali, A., & Kohun, F. (2007). Dealing with social isolation to minimize doctoral attrition: A four stage framework. *International Journal of Doctoral Studies, 2*, 33–49.

Anzaldúa, G. (2007). *Borderlands/La frontera: The new mestiza* (3rd ed.). San Francisco, CA: Aunt Lute Books.

Barthes, R. (1974). *S/Z*. New York, NY: Hill and Wang.

Baxter Magolda, M. B. (2002). Helping students make their way to adulthood: Good company for the journey. *About Campus, 6*(6), 2–9.

Bhattacharya, H. (2008). New critical collaborative ethnography. In S. N. Hesse-Biber & P. Leavy (Eds.), *Handbook of emergent methods* (pp. 303–322). New York, NY: The Guilford Press.

Butler, J. (2006). *Gender trouble: Feminism and the subversion of identity*. New York, NY: Routledge.

Campbell, K. M. (2011). The road to S. B. 1070: How Arizona became ground zero for the immigrants' rights movement and the continuing struggle for Latino civil rights in America. *Harvard Latino Law Review, 14*, 1–21.

Catalano, C., McCarthy, L., & Shlasko, D. (2007). Transgender oppression curriculum design. In M. Adams, L. A. Bell, & P. Griffin (Eds.), *Teaching for diversity and social justice* (2nd ed.) (pp. 219–246). New York, NY: Routledge.

Chang, H. (2008). *Autoethnography as method*. Walnut Creek, CA: Left Coast Press.

Ellis, C. (2004). *The ethnographic I: A methodological novel about autoethnography*. Walnut Creek, CA: AltaMira Press.

Ellis, C., & Bochner, A. P. (2000). Autoethnography, personal narrative, reflexivity: Researcher as subject. In N. K. Denzin & Y. S. Lincoln (Eds.), *The Sage handbook of qualitative research* (2nd ed.) (pp. 733–768). Thousand Oaks, CA: Sage.

Grant, J. M., Mottet, L. A., Tanis, J., Harrison, J., Herman, J. L., & Keisling, M. (2011). *Injustice at every turn: A report of the national transgender discrimination survey*. Washington, DC: National Center for Transgender Equality and National Gay and Lesbian Task Force.

Hale, C. J. (1998). Consuming the living, dis(re)membering the dead in the butch/FTM borderlands. *GLQ: A Journal of Lesbian and Gay Studies, 4*(2), 311–348.

Hesse-Biber, S. N., & Leavy, P. (2008). *Handbook of emergent methods*. New York, NY: The Guilford Press.

hooks, b. (1990). *Yearning: Race, gender, and cultural politics*. Boston, MA: South End Press.

Jones, S. R., Torres, V., & Arminio, J. (2006). *Negotiating the complexities of qualitative research in higher education: Fundamental elements and issues*. New York, NY: Routledge.

Killermann, S. (2012). What does the asterisk in "trans*" stand for? [Blog post]. Retrieved from http://itspronouncedmetrosexual.com/2012/05/what-does-the-asterisk-in-trans-stand-for/.

Lacayo, A. E. (2011). *One year later: A look at SB 1070 and copycat legislation*. Washington, DC: National Council of La Raza.

Lamott, A. (1994). *Bird by bird: Some instructions on writing and life*. New York, NY: Anchor Books.

Mazzei, L. A. (2013, April). *Knowing in being: Material feminist productions of ontoepistemology*. Unfinished paper presented at the American Educational Research Association Annual Meeting, San Francisco, CA.

Pasque, P. A., Carducci, R., Gildersleeve, R. E., & Kuntz, A. K. (2012). *Qualitative inquiry for equity in higher education: Methodological innovations, implications, and interventions. ASHE Higher Education Report*. San Francisco, CA: Jossey-Bass.

Planas, R. (2012). *Arizona official considers targeting Mexican American studies in university*. Retrieved from http://latino.foxnews.com/latino/politics/2012/03/28/arizona-official-considers-targeting-mexican-american-studies-in-university/

Rankin, S., Weber, G., Blumenfeld, W., & Frazer, S. (2010). *2010 state of higher education for lesbian, gay, bisexual & transgender people*. Charlotte, NC: Campus Pride.

Schilt, K., & Westbrook, L. (2009). Doing gender, doing heteronormativity: "Gender normals," transgender people, and the social maintenance of heterosexuality. *Gender & Society, 23*(4), 440–464.

Serano, J. (2007). *Whipping girl: A transsexual woman on sexism and the scapegoating of femininity*. Berkeley, CA: Seal Press.

Siebler, K. (2010). Transqueer representations and how we educate. *Journal of LGBT Youth, 7*(4), 320–345.

Smith, L. T. (2008). Research through imperial eyes. In A. M. Jaggar (Ed.), *Just methods: An interdisciplinary feminist reader* (pp. 58–67). Boulder, CO: Paradigm.

Soto, S. K., & Joseph, M. (2010). Neoliberalism and the battle over ethnic studies in Arizona. *Thought & Action: The NEA Higher Education Journal, 26*, 45–56.

Spade, D. (2010). Be professional! *Harvard Journal of Law & Gender, 33*(1), 71–84.

Spade, D. (2011). *Normal life: Administrative violence, critical trans politics, and the limitations of law*. Cambridge, MA: South End Press.

State of Arizona, House of Representatives. (2010). *House bill 2281*. Retrieved from http://www.azleg.gov/legtext/49leg/2r/bills/hb2281s.pdf

Tuchman, G. (2009). *Wannabe u: Inside the corporate university*. Chicago, IL: The University of Chicago Press.

Wolfe, T. (1968). *The electric kool-aid acid test*. New York, NY: Bantam Books.

Yoshino, K. (2006). *Covering: The hidden assault on our civil rights*. New York, NY: Random House.

# CHAPTER ELEVEN

# Advancing Disruptive Methodological Perspectives IN Educational Qualitative Research Through Teaching AND Learning

PENNY A. PASQUE

Colleges and universities are positioned to play an instrumental role in researching and addressing inequities in the world today, including health care, educational and economic inequities, the environment, incarceration rates, drug and human trafficking, food and water sustainability, and other issues of social injustice. However, higher education institutions often fail to foster such needed social change in the current era of neo-liberalism, accountability, privatization, and reduction in state appropriations (Cannella & Miller, 2008; Giroux & Giroux 2004; Pasque, 2010; Rizvi & Engel, 2009). In *Take Back Higher Education*, Henry Giroux and Susan Searls Giroux (2004) conveyed an ethical call to action for individual educators, parents, students, and others to "reclaim" higher education as a democratic public sphere that works toward equality, liberty, and justice (pp. 11–12). One specific way instructors may work toward fostering social justice is through the education of researchers, practitioners, and policy makers.

In this chapter, I argue that educators have the opportunity to disrupt dominant paradigms in educational research by centering dominant *and* non-dominant approaches to qualitative research. For example, while it is important to introduce students to the most common five approaches to qualitative research in education—narrative research, phenomenology, grounded theory, ethnography, and case study (Creswell, 2012), it is imperative that educators expand beyond these five to include non-dominant methodologies, such as critical inquiry, arts-based methodologies, and engaged scholarship, that work toward social justice. This disruption of traditional content expands the methodological approaches available to students and, in turn, expands opportunities for scholars and practitioners to address inequities and injustice. For example, critical research "begins with questions of inequity and disparity [and] holds the most promise for promoting policies and practices that can lead to economic, ecological, and human justice, and a sustainable global future" (Shields, 2012, p. 3). Patricia Leavy (2013) described the appeal of arts-based methodologies as the potential to "transform consciousness, refine the senses, promote autonomy, raise awareness, express the complex feeling-based aspects of social life, jar us into seeing and thinking differently, illuminate the complexity and sometimes paradox of lived experience, and to build empathy and resonance" (p. 23). In a third example, engaged scholarship focuses on the recognition, analysis, and resolution of social injustice and inequity (Chambers & Gopaul, 2010).

Critical, arts-based, and engaged scholarship approaches—along with many other methodologies not often centered in the introductory qualitative research classroom—have the potential to foster individual, collaborative, community, and culture change. As Bobbi Harro (2000) argued, this requires

> a struggle against discrimination based on race, class, gender, sexual identity, ableism and age—those barriers that keep large portions of the population from having access to economic and social justice, from being able to participate fully in the decisions affecting our lives, from having a full share of both the rights and responsibilities of living in a free society. (p. 450)

Beyond identifying injustice and inequity as important topics for research, it is also imperative that qualitative educational scholars adopt research methodologies and methods reflective of their aims to advance educational equity toward social justice. As the editors point out in the introduction of this volume, educational qualitative research is dominated by postpositivist and constructivist approaches and has not—to this point—alleviated individual, institutional, and systemic oppression. Yet, if graduate students are only taught traditional notions of qualitative inquiry, then dominant research paradigms, findings, and implications will continue to perpetuate the status quo and educational inequities (Pasque, Carducci, Kuntz, & Gildersleeve, 2012).

Introducing new educational researchers to non-dominant methodologies through teaching and learning goes beyond simply adding a "special week" on critical theory to the end of a research course or offering special seminars on particular methodological approaches for the few students interested in this type of inquiry. Non-dominant methodologies, including critical methodological perspectives and principles, need to be fully integrated across the entire doctoral curriculum into introductory, intermediate, and advanced methodology courses, foundational studies, and advanced thematic seminars (Pasque, Carducci, Kuntz, & Gildersleeve, 2012). This perspective is consistent with definitions of pedagogy, cultural pedagogy, and critical pedagogy as described by Norman Denzin and Yvonna Lincoln (2008) in the *Handbook of Critical and Indigenous Methodologies*,

| | |
|---|---|
| *Pedagogy:* | To teach in a way that leads. Pedagogy is always ideological and political. |
| *Cultural pedagogy:* | The ways that cultural production functions as a form of education, as it "generates knowledge, shapes values and constructs identity ... cultural pedagogy refers to the ways particular cultural agents produce hegemonic ways of seeing." (Kincheloe & McLaren, 2000, p. 285; McLaren, 1999, p. 441). |
| *Critical pedagogy:* | To performatively disrupt and deconstruct these cultural practices in the name of "more just, democratic and egalitarian society." (Kincheloe & McLaren, 2000, p. 285). (p. 7–8) |

As such, educators have an opportunity to provide content knowledge regarding dominant and non-dominant methodologies while they simultaneously disrupt traditional dominant notions of the classroom by performatively challenging the space and deconstructing cultural practices through the instructors' own pedagogical choices. Stated another way, the content includes dominant and non-dominant approaches to qualitative methodologies and the pedagogical decisions made by the instructor have the opportunity to challenge dominant approaches to teaching qualitative research as well. In this way, critical pedagogy mirrors the course content and vice versa.

Intentional critical pedagogy around qualitative methodologies prepares graduate students to articulate and defend the underlying assumptions and aims that guide their scholarship, such as in questions of epistemology, ontology, axiology, and methodology (beyond simply method). Notably, intentional critical pedagogy around non-dominant qualitative methodologies also prepares students to engage in scholarly dialogues with proponents of methodological conservatism. Failing to prepare students for these conversations serves to "perpetuate the continued marginalization of non-dominant epistemological perspectives and exacerbate conditions of educational inequity" (Pasque, Carducci, Kuntz, & Gildersleeve, 2012, p. 84).

Similarly, Elizabeth St. Pierre (2011) argued in her chapter on "Post Qualitative Research: The Critique and the Coming After" that the first step in deconstruction is to reverse the binary. For example, we are often taught in binary oppositions that can be violent hierarchies because people on the "other side" of the binary can be "brutalized for their difference" (p. 617) (e.g., self/other, identify/*différance*, dominant/non-dominant qualitative methodologies). She argued that educators and students must know the privileged position and "reverse the binary" in order to overturn, open up, and liberate. In the context of this chapter, it would be the non-dominant methodological approaches that should hold the privilege position in order to reverse the binary and move toward deconstruction and liberation.

Further, Patti Lather (2010), in *Engaging Science Policy: From the Side of the Messy*, talked about the possibilities as well as the limits of a "getting lost" research practice where there is a "fussying of the borders between science and philosophy" (p. 15) or doing and knowing, practice and theory. In this approach, it is not the reversing of the binary but the fussying of the borders that gets privileged as a way to consider qualitative research in a non-reductive manner.

As a way to help new graduate students explore the complexities of these arguments by St. Pierre (2011) and Lather (2010), I often turn to popular culture examples that connect with many of the students. For example, in Brad Pitt's real-life romantic drama around 2004, were you "Team Aniston" or "Team Jolie"? Society asked us (the public) to decide—as if it was our decision to make—and some people even sported T-shirts to claim a side of this dichotomous relationship.

In another example, if you read the *Twilight* (Meyers, 2005) books or watched the movies, were you "Team Jacob" or "Team Edward" (if at all)? This example also reflects dichotomous and reductive relationships. The characters and their behaviors were not dichotomous; they were complex as they connected numerous issues across race, ethnicity, nationality, class, gender, gender expression, sexual orientation, indigenous culture, (post)colonialism, appropriation, and other contemporary and historically based issues. Neither Jacob nor Edward necessarily embodied pure good or pure evil, yet Twilighters (not limited to tweens) created a false dichotomy as though one had to choose which man to celebrate and which to reject, each option steeped in notions of hegemonic masculinity (Wilson, 2011). Complexities are present in the book's narrative—but are not often interrogated in a critical or meaningful manner.

To be sure, popular culture is filled with dualistic relationships and false choices, as are traditional and reductive models of qualitative inquiry that limit students to five approaches to research and diminutive methods within those approaches. This is reflective of the "traditional" historical moment (1900–1950) of qualitative research as a field of inquiry associated with the positivist, foundational paradigm (Denzin & Lincoln, 2011). It is also reflective of graduate students' current-day requests for didactic drawings, figures, or condensed representations of qualitative paradigms and approaches to research as they work to understand qualitative research in an entry-level class (I get these requests every year). As an instructor, I work toward expanding student knowledge production (Cheek, 2008) and introducing students to the eight historical moments of qualitative research, including the most recent postmodern (1990–1995), postexperimental inquiry (1995–2000), the methodologically contested present (2000–2010), and the future (2010–) (Denzin & Lincoln, 2011). These later moments confront methodological backlash, involve moral discourse, and engage in critical conversations about "democracy, race, gender, class, nation-states, globalization, freedom and community" (p. 3). *In the eighth moment, critical issues are topics of research but, importantly, researchers also operationalize critical approaches within methodologies and methods that congruently reflect equity and social justice* (also see Pasque, Carducci, Kuntz, & Gildersleeve, 2012).

As a way to help new graduate students explore the complexities of the postmodern turn in qualitative inquiry and understand the argument by St. Pierre (2011) about knowing the privileged position in order to overturn, open up, and liberate—I draw on artist Lady Gaga. She is the epitome of postmodernism in the current moment and has changed the shape of music, culture, and inclusion of non-dominant paradigms related to gender, gender performance and identity, sexual orientation, fashion, ways to listen to and "see" music, and—most recently—the boundaries on the expected size zero clothing for celebrities. Lady Gaga is blurred and fuzzied. Notably, she was classically trained before pushing boundaries in music and performance art on an international stage. She learned privileged positions in music, theatre, and art before/as she overturned, opened up, and liberated them. Student knowledge of the classic qualitative traditions prior to, or in conjunction with, non-dominant perspectives have been argued by many (Lather, 2010; St. Pierre, 2011) and these classics have been centered in qualitative classrooms for generations. To be sure, non-dominant perspectives, including postmodern, arts-based, critical, and indigenous knowledges and arguments, also need to be centered in qualitative classrooms and research experiences (see Denzin, Lincoln, & Smith, 2011; Madison, 2012). Our college-going student population is more diverse across race, ethnicity and gender than in years past, although the degree programs and institution types are still infused with disparities (Allan, 2011; Bergerson, 2009; Lee, Poch, Shaw, & Williams, 2012). Many of our students' epistemological, ontological and axiological perspectives are grounded in critical or indigenous approaches and—even if not—centering all perspectives helps to expand student knowledge and awareness about the diversity of qualitative inquiry and approaches to research.

Lady Gaga and the graduate students of today are living in a different world—so why do researchers and instructors think it is useful to utilize the same old dominant paradigms and pedagogies to explore inequities in a new and ever-changing society, especially when, as mentioned, dominant methodologies do not have a track record for directly addressing educational inequity?

To be sure, the inclusion of non-dominant qualitative methodologies and critical pedagogy in educational inquiry courses is a political act; just as not including them is a political act. As Pallas (2001) noted "the issue of which epistemologies and whose get privileged in doctoral programs is a matter of politics and power" (p. 10). I do not take this statement lightly and acknowledge the complexities of politics and power in the academy. However, disrupting the status quo in terms of research topics, teaching pedagogy, and the centering of non-dominant research methodologies and methods is imperative as we educate ourselves as instructors and emerging scholars. I offer two examples of where I have attempted innovative approaches to teaching and learning in order to deepen student understandings around disruptive methodological perspectives.

## DISRUPTING THE CHAIR: RESEARCHER REFLEXIVITY EXERCISE AND DISCUSSION

Some students seem to find safety in the physical location of their classroom chair, with pen and paper or computers that serve as a barrier between themselves, other students in the classroom, and the professor. This barrier is spatially indicative of the problematic banking model of education where professors deposit knowledge into the open and empty vessels that are student minds (Freire, 1970/2002). It also enables students to intellectualize the issues at hand without actually experiencing them—as they would do if they were engaged in a research setting (i.e., interviews in a coffee shop, in the field with "participants"). This exercise disrupts that familiar spatial pattern while asking students to reflect on their own social identities and the identities of participants in their study (if any).

"Who's Here"[1] is an exercise often used in diversity and social justice courses, but I utilize it in qualitative inquiry courses in order to help students consider issues of researcher positionality, reflexivity, researcher identities, participant identities, privilege, power, and oppression. At the point in the course when I introduce this exercise we have already engaged in discussions about myriad dominant and non-dominant methodologies; admittedly they are initial and inconclusive introductions to the breadth and depth of methodologies. On the day that we read about and discuss researcher positionality and reflexivity, which many critical scholars argue should be done prior to and throughout the research process, students read about "working the hyphens" between participant-researcher by Michelle Fine (1994) and "dangers in educational research" by Richard Milner (2007) on seen, unseen, and unforeseen dangers of research for participants and researchers.

For the Who's Here exercise that pedagogically "disrupts the chair," I ask students to get out of their chairs and stand (or sit in a wheelchair) in a circle. As I call out an identity, students (and I) step in the circle if they claim that identity in the moment. For example, I start with a potentially low-risk question such as "who here LOVES chocolate and just cannot get enough chocolate?" At this point, students who love chocolate step in the center of the circle, stay for about 10–20 seconds, are asked to look around (if a participant is legally blind we will verbally describe what we see), and then move back to the circle. I start with this seemingly low-risk item and then proceed to more in-depth items about social identities and experiences. It is important to note that I also start the exercise by mentioning that if someone does not feel safe to claim an identity here in this room, then that is absolutely okay. I also ask students to only self-identify and not name an identity for a person or friend in the room; don't "out" anyone on any identities (i.e., if someone does not step in when I ask "who here is adopted?" it is not up to a friend to point this identity out for the class, self-identification only).

I mention how identities are often fluid and change over time. Further, students can put only their toe in, their entire leg, or step into the center of the room completely; it is up to them. I ask about gender and name each subcategory separately for people to step in when they identify; who here identifies as a man? Woman? Transgendered, gender transgressive, gender queer, or gender identities that I did not name? I then ask about race, ethnicity, nationality, language, socio-economic status, religion, sexual orientation and ally status, number of siblings, birth order, veteran or member of the armed forces, parent—and the categories, including sub-categories, continue for approximately 20 minutes. I ask that students notice how it feels to be on the inside or outside of the circle as well as how it feels to be the only person who steps in, or with many people who step in together.

At times, students show great excitement to step into the middle of the circle. For example, women will often hug each other or touch each other when they step in the circle as a way to physically connect with each other. At other times, there are snickers or laughter if students are uncomfortable. For example, when I ask about sexual orientation and ally status some students may get uncomfortable, whereas some students are very comfortable. Inevitably there are a number of students who identify as lesbian, gay, bisexual, or an ally, and I explicitly ask for a definition of an ally (Broido, 2000; Broido & Reason, 2005) in case some in the room do not know the term (and share information about the ally training program on campus). It is important to remind students about what voices we have represented in the room, what voices are missing, and that none of us may speak for everyone or anyone who identifies in the same ways. At the end of my list of questions, I open it up for students to ask each other additional questions to the group and they usually add a few questions of interest. To be sure, the students and I discuss how the categories listed in this exercise are bound and that there are complexities and multiple dimensions to identity and identity development (Jones & Abes, 2013).

It has also been useful to participate in this exercise myself, so students have a chance to learn a bit more about me and my own identities now (i.e., white, second-generation Italian American, first-generation college student, no children)—and as I grew up (without enough access to resources). In addition, I'm not asking students to share anything that I am not willing to share with them simultaneously. This is an important concept for a researcher as well as instructors:

Would you ask participants to answer questions that you would not necessarily feel comfortable answering yourself? Why or why not? Would you ask students to share something that you are not necessarily comfortable answering yourself in a course context? Why or why not?

From here, I ask if participants in their research studies (if any) have similar and/or different identities as you, the student researcher? This opens discussions about various identities, privilege, historical and socio-political contexts, power relationships in research situations, and choices in research relationships (including community partners as co-primary investigators on research projects). Specific questions for dyads and large group discussions may include:

- What identities are you aware of most often? Least often? Why?
- How do social identities, researcher positionality, and researcher reflexivity relate to research in your field or discipline?
- What are the social identities of your participants and how might researcher reflexivity be important in your own study? How might these identities and relationships be complex and reflect multiple dimensions?
- In what ways is the chapter on "Working the Hyphens" by Michelle Fine (1994) useful to your approach to qualitative inquiry?
- What are the differences between dangers that are "seen," "unseen," and "unforeseen" by Richard Milner (2007)? How does this relate to your specific research study?
- In what ways do notions of power, privilege, and oppression show up in your current or past research studies?
- What methods might you include in your study if researcher positionality and reflexivity are centered in your approach to qualitative inquiry (if relevant)? Working-the-hyphen? Addressing dangers?
- In what ways did this exercise limit or bind identities? In what ways might you limit or bind identities within your study and what are some strategies that may reduce the reductive nature of research?

My hope is that the questions spark deep discussions and reflections about the readings, theory and research practice, navigating the hyphen, dangers of research, researcher positionality, and researcher reflexivity. The "disruption of the chair" is a risky endeavor because, as an instructor, I'm not certain how this non-traditional pedagogical approach will be perceived in a research course; however, it is often a welcomed activity that interrupts patterns of faculty as knowledge producer and students as knowledge absorbers. It also encourages students to physically participate in the exercise as they intellectually consider how they will physically participate in their study.

## DISRUPTING THE CLASSROOM AGENDA:
## STUDENT RESEARCH

In a Foundations of Qualitative Inquiry course, I ask students to engage in their own pilot research study, which they further in an advanced course. There is only one paper required for this course but an updated version of the paper is due every month in order to reflect the iterative writing and revision process, student thinking and learning, and so that I may ask questions and provide feedback at various stages of the study. In this paper, students speak to their own approaches to epistemology, ontology, axiology, theoretical perspectives, methodology, methods for participant selection, methods for analysis, analysis, findings, implications, and/or any relevant information and perspectives. Stated another way, if a chosen approach does not literally include "participants" (e.g., no people in the study) then none is expected as long as the writing and approach to the research is congruent throughout their paper (Jones, Torres & Arminio, 2006).

Students may choose from the wide array of methodological approaches that exist, which we explore in class (breadth) before they choose one specific methodology for their pilot study (depth). To be sure, issues of breadth vs. depth are a challenge to negotiate as a faculty member; however, the students are able to select from a methodology that sincerely fits with their worldview (beyond five), and each time I teach the course it is different based on the students enrolled. For example, if a student is grounded in a postpositivist worldview, then when they are choosing a methodological approach for their study I remind the student of our methodological conversations regarding case study by Robert Yin (2009) or grounded theory by Juliet Corbin and Anselm Strauss (2008). If a student is more interpretive, they may consider Tami Spry's (2011) approach to performance autoethnography. If a student comes from a critical approach, then perhaps Michelle Salazar Pérez and Gaile Cannella's (2013) situational mapping for critical qualitative research may be of interest. Stated another way, I ask that the students follow a methodological approach that is "congruent with" (Jones, Torres, & Arminio, 2006) their own worldview and to make certain the language, methodology, methods, and all elements of the study are consistent or—if they deviate—that there is an intentional rationale for that deviation.

More specifically, if a student's approach to research is postpositivist, I encourage them to design a study that reflects that perspective and not choose an alternative approach (critical ethnography, for example) because they think it's "cool" or what they think I want to read as the professor. To be clear, I argue that epistemological, ontological, and methodological incongruence may "do harm" and, instead, students should reflect on their own worldviews and select research methodologies and methods congruent with that worldview.

Patrick Miller is an example of a graduate student who thrived in this inclusive methodological environment. Designing an introductory qualitative inquiry seminar that limited Patrick to only five methodologies would have—to paraphrase from Rosalind Russell's *Auntie Mame* (DaCosta, 1958)—put braces on his brain! For his semester-long project, Patrick wrote a fantastic research paper entitled, "One in Six: An Autoethnographic Dramaturgy Exploring a Rural Students Decision Making Process in Regards to Participation in Higher Education," and he is in the process of moving this manuscript to publication. Specifically, Patrick spent time writing his own autoethnographic dramaturgy which included an informed description of his methodological approach; a discussion of Bourdieu's (1986) species of capital (social, cultural, political, and economic); and the literature (and absence of literature) about rural students in colleges and universities. In the full manuscript, he interrogated higher education recruitment and socialization practices as well as implications for those practices.

As Patrick's research unfolded, it became evident that a "table read" of Patrick's manuscript during the last day of the course would enhance his final revisions of the manuscript because he could hear it read out loud by many students/participants/actors, make changes, and incorporate student feedback (a form of triangulation in the postpositivist paradigm). All students in my course and the students in Dr. Courtney Vaughn's naturalistic inquiry course (educational studies) came together to participate in the "table read" of Patrick's piece. The addition of the table read was a disruption to my original plan for the final day of class and was a risk, in that I was not certain how the other faculty members or students would perceive this research process; however, this disruption enhanced the teaching and learning goals of the course and helped educate all the students about the complexities of autoethnography and dramaturgy. I would argue that this table read made far more of a contribution than my originally planned final class period—and featured the deep and complex work of a master's student.

Patrick Miller (2012) graciously gave permission for me to share an excerpt from his scholarship with you in order for me to more clearly show (vs. tell) you about the experience on this final day of class.

Dramaturgy is described as "the analysis of the interactional order of social life ... via the metaphor of theater" (Schwandt, 2007, p. 76). Through dramaturgy, critical issues of society, culture, and politics are presented, analyzed, and critically reflected on through dramatic text and the performance in front of an audience. By incorporating my own autoethnographic experiences I wove together the presentation of dramaturgy, presented here in a traditional theater script form, with the methodology of performative autoethnography (Spry, 2011). Performative autoethnography emerges from the writing of the self/other/culture/language and results in a dramaturgy that critically reflects on the self's negotiations with others in the context of such issues as race, class, gender, and sexual orientation.... Through dramaturgy I wanted to push past the point of not seeing myself reflected in others' research, and critically reflect on my own experiences in the context of the "others" that played a part in these memories. I chose dramaturgy to insert living, breathing voices into the discussion on how rural students make the decision to participate in higher education. Dramaturgy allowed me to bring to life my lived experience and make those experiences "livable" for an audience. (pp. 6–7)

## Cast (in part)

Non-dialogue Part

Patrick

Off-Stage Narrator

## Scene 1

| | |
|---|---|
| *Non-Dialogue Part:* | *The lights come up on a standard student desk, complete with pull-string lamp, stapler, and other desk items. It is not completely disorganized, but has enough books and papers on it to show that it is well used. At the desk sits a young male student, in jeans and a t-shirt, filling out a scholarship application. His name is Patrick.* |
| PATRICK: | (*Reading from application.*) Thank you for your interest in attending [insert name of local university]. Please fill this … (*Patrick's voice trails off as Off-Stage Narrator's voice comes in. There is a slight overlap.*) |
| OFF-STAGE NARRATOR (OSN): | Please fill this form out in its entirety. This form will be used as your application for general scholarships for which you may qualify. Please print or type. Please use dark ink. Question 1: Please state your legal name. |
| PATRICK: | Patrick Michael Miller |
| OSN: Legacy Status: | Please list the name and date of graduation of any parent, grandparent, or other family member that graduated from State University? |
| *Non-Dialogue Part:* | *As Patrick begins his aside the lights come on a scene behind him. Appearing behind Patrick to his right and left are two tables set for a family meal. It appears that Patrick is positioned in the middle of the two tables. They are two distinct settings and the only connection they have to one another is Patrick. The left-hand table is set with paper plates, the meal coming from casserole dishes. At the left-hand table there are gathered Virginia, Teddy, and Clarissa. Virginia and Clarissa are in various styles of "blue collar" or working class clothes (jeans, t-shirts) in bright colors. Teddy is in a police officer's uniform to imply he just got home* |

*from work. The right-hand table is set with black table cloth,*
*matching dishes and stemware. Sylvia and Howard are seated at*
*the table. They are dressed in formal clothes (dress shirts, slacks,*
*loafers, sweater sets and skirt) that are in a monochromatic color*
*scheme of black and white.* (p. 7)

Patrick's manuscript goes on to uncover the complexities of class, race, and geo-graphically rural student upbringing as well as how these complexities have direct implications for potential and/or invisible college students. His work has the capa-bility to make a strong contribution to the transition from high school to college as he asks us to feel the complexities of the living, breathing voices of rural college students and their families and address issues of educational inequities around class and geography. In this way, the hope is that students feel issues of social jus-tice instead of simply intellectualizing the issues.

At the end of the semester, Patrick posted a picture on Facebook of the two of us when we were at his University of Oklahoma graduation where he received his Master's of Education. In the caption for this picture, Patrick reflected on our time together and how much this course meant to him. He shared,

> Mission: get picture with Dr. Pasque = Success! I cannot even begin to articulate the impact you have had on my life. Thank you for reminding me that it is OK for scholars to talk with their hands, reference pop culture, and be funny. Thank you for "pushing me out of the air-plane" and supporting me when my parachute didn't look like everyone else's (and thanks for introducing me to Performance Ethnography AND Species of Capital). Thank you for believing in me when I didn't believe in myself, listening to my views on higher education, and letting me cry in class when I got overwhelmed!
> —WITH PENNY PASQUE. (PATRICK MILLER, MAY 16, 2012)

Patrick has given me permission to share this (public) post as evidence of how disrupting dominant methodologies through teaching and learning sincerely can make a direct impact on the lives of students. Teaching and learning qualitative in-quiry without adhering to the so-called five dominant methodologies and didactic methods may feel a bit like being "pushed out of an airplane" as we discussed the first day (and many days) of class, but critical pedagogical spaces for hands, pop culture, tears, and non-dominant methodological perspectives have the potential to simultaneously disrupt and deconstruct cultural practices in the name of a more just, democratic, and egalitarian society.

## CONCLUDING THOUGHTS

I have argued that disrupting the traditional paradigms of qualitative research courses is imperative as we educate ourselves and the scholars of tomorrow. Critical pedagogy and the inclusion of non-dominant research methodologies and methods—such as exercises on researcher reflexivity or the curricular space to explore an autoethnographic dramaturgy and a table read—deepens student understandings of methodological perspectives. This disruption expands the methodological approaches available to students and, in turn, expands opportunities for scholars and practitioners to address inequities and injustice.

Gaile Cannella and Yvonna Lincoln (2004) asked scholars committed to advancing critical social science to consider "How is resistance to research placed at the center? How do we continually contest our research practices while at the same time continuing to conduct research" (p. 305)? I continually ask myself these questions and try to reconcile these answers with my approaches to teaching, research, and service with the goals of addressing inequities and fostering individual, collaborative, community, and culture change. As such, I am committed to learning more about—and attempting to infuse—critical pedagogy and non-dominant methodological perspectives in the classroom.

In closing, I leave us all with a few questions for future discussion with ourselves, students, and each other. In what ways do our teaching and learning pedagogical approaches perpetuate dominant paradigms within the academy and within educational research? In what ways may graduate student researchers become cognizant of the complexities in relationships between researchers and community members before establishing a research design? Are we creating spaces where students can display non-dominant modes of masculinity, femininity, and blurred gender expression? In what ways do we take risks with our own careers in order to help end this cycle of perpetuating dominant methodologies in educating the next generation of scholars in order to foster educational equity and social justice through our 1) content (i.e., rural students), 2) research methodologies (i.e., arts-based) and 3) the ways in which we teach and learn (i.e., get out of your chair)? I will continue to ask myself these questions, educate myself, and alter teaching and learning practices on a regular basis.

## NOTE

1. "Who is here" is an exercise that I have seen a number of people present and found in various locations on the internet, but have not been able to determine the original citation. The first time I participated in it was in various sessions around 1993 in Ithaca, NY, with Vivian Relta of Cornell University's ILR program http://www.ilr.cornell.edu/hcd/dm.html and Dr. Maura Cullen http://www.mauracullen.com/. See also, "Who's in" at http://www.dbhds.virginia.gov/2008CLC/documents/clc-Trn-Whos-InDisabGroups.pdf, or "Stand if you're different" at http://www.paulwesselmann.com/resources/pm/diversity_resources

## REFERENCES

Allan, E. J. (2011). *Women's status in higher education: Equity matters. ASHE higher education report, 37*(1). San Francisco, CA: Jossey-Bass.

Bergerson, A. A. (2009). *College choice and access to college: Moving policy, research and practice to the 21st century: ASHE Higher Education Report, 35*(4). San Francisco, CA: Jossey-Bass.

Bourdieu, P. (1986) The forms of capital. In J. Richardson (Ed.), *Handbook of theory and research for the sociology of education* (pp. 241–258). New York, NY: Greenwood.

Broido, E. M. (2000). The development of social justice allies during college: A pheonomenological investigation. *Journal of College Student Development, 41*(1), 3–18.

Broido, E. M., & Reason, R. D. (2005). The development of social justice attitudes and actions: An overview of current understandings. *New Directions for Student Services, 110,* 17–28.

Cannella, G. S., & Lincoln, Y. S. (2004). Epilogue: Claiming a critical public social science—Reconceptualizing and redeploying research. *Qualitative Inquiry, 13*(3), 315–335.

Cannella, G. S., & Miller, L. L. (2008). Constructing corporatist science: Reconstituting the soul of American higher education. *Cultural Studies—Critical Methodologies, 8*(1), 24–38.

Chambers, T., & Gopaul, B. (2010). Toward a social justice-centered engaged scholarship: A public and a private good. In H. E. Fitzgerald, C. Burack, & S. Siefer (Eds.), *Handbook of engaged scholarship: Contemporary landscapes, future directions: Volume I: Institutional change* (pp. 55–70). East Lansing, MI: Michigan State University Press.

Cheek, J. (2008). A fine line: Positioning qualitative inquiry in the wake of the politics of evidence. *International Review of Qualitative Research, 1*(1), 19–32.

Corbin, J., & Strauss, A. (2008). *Basics of qualitative research: Techniques and procedures for developing grounded theory* (3rd ed.). Thousand Oaks, CA: Sage.

Creswell, J. (2012). *Qualitative inquiry and research design: Choosing among five approaches.* Thousand Oaks, CA: Sage.

DaCosta, M. (Director, Producer). (1958). *Auntie Mame* [Motion picture]. Hollywood, CA: Warner Brothers.

Denzin, N. K., & Lincoln, Y. S. (2008). Introduction: Critical methodologies and indigenous inquiry. In N. K. Denzin, Y. S. Lincoln, & L. T. Smith (Eds.), *Handbook of critical and indigenous methodologies* (pp. 1–20). Thousand Oaks, CA: Sage.

Denzin, N. K., & Lincoln, Y. (2011). Introduction: The discipline and practice of qualitative research. In N. K. Denzin & Y. S. Lincoln (Eds.), *The Sage handbook of qualitative research* (4th ed.) (pp. 1–33). Thousand Oaks, CA: Sage.

Denzin, N. K., Lincoln, Y. S., & Smith L. T. (Eds.) (2008). *Handbook of critical and indigenous methodologies.* Thousand Oaks, CA: Sage.

Fine, M. (1994). Working the hyphens: Reinventing self and other in qualitative research. In N. K. Denzin & Y. S. Lincoln (Eds.), *The Sage handbook of qualitative research* (pp. 70–82). Thousand Oaks, CA: Sage.

Freire, P. (1970/2002). *Pedagogy of the oppressed.* New York, NY: Continuum.

Giroux, H. A., & Giroux, S. S. (2004). *Take back higher education: Race, youth, and the crisis of democracy in the post-civil rights era.* New York, NY: Palgrave Macmillan.

Harro, B. (2000). The cycle of liberation. In M. Adams, W. J. Bluenfield, R. Castañeda, H. W. Hackman, M. L. Peters, & X. Zúñiga (Eds.), *Readings for diversity and social justice* (pp. 463–469). New York, NY: Routledge.

Jones, S. R., & Abes, E. S. (2013). *Identity development of college students: Advancing frameworks for multiple dimensions of identity.* San Francisco, CA: Jossey-Bass.

Jones, S. R., Torres, V., & Arminio, J. (2006). *Negotiating the complexities of qualitative research in higher education: Fundamental elements and issues.* New York, NY: Routledge.

Lather, P. (2010). *Engaging science policy: From the side of the messy.* New York, NY: Peter Lang.

Leavy, P. (2013). *Fiction as research practice: Short stories, novellas, and novels.* Walnut Creek, CA: Left Coast Press.

Lee, A., Poch, R., Shaw, M., & Williams, R. D. (2012). *Engaging diversity in undergraduate classrooms: A pedagogy for developing intercultural competence: ASHE higher education report.* San Francisco, CA: Jossey-Bass.

Madison, D. S. (2012). *Critical ethnography: Method, ethics and performance* (2nd ed.). Los Angeles, CA: Sage.

Meyers, S. (2005). *Twilight.* New York, NY: Little, Brown & Company.

Miller, P. (2012). *One in six: An autoethnographic dramaturgy exploring a rural student's decision making process in regards to participation in higher education* (Unpublished paper). Foundations of Qualitative Inquiry in Adult and Higher Education, University of Oklahoma.

Milner, H. R. (2007). Race, culture, and researcher positionality: Working through dangers seen, unseen, and unforeseen. *Educational Researcher, 36*(7), 388–400.

Pallas, A. M. (2001). Preparing education doctoral students for epistemological diversity. *Educational Researcher, 30*(5), 6–11.

Pasque, P. A. (2010). *American higher education, leadership, and policy: Critical issues and the public good.* New York, NY: Palgrave Macmillan.

Pasque, P., Carducci, R., Kuntz, A. K., Gildersleeve, R. E. (2012). *Qualitative inquiry for equity in higher education: Methodological innovations, implications, and interventions. ASHE Higher Education Report. 37*(6). San Francisco, CA: Jossey-Bass.

Pérez, M. S., & Cannella, G. S. (2013). Situational analysis as an avenue for critical qualitative research: Mapping post Katrina New Orleans. *Qualitative Inquiry, 19*(7), 505–517.

Rizvi, F., & Engel, L. C. (2009). Neo-liberal globalization, education policy, and the struggle for social justice. In W. Ayers, T. Quinn, & D. Stovall (Eds.), *Handbook of social justice in education* (pp. 529–541). New York, NY: Routledge.

Schwandt, T. A. (2007). *The Sage dictionary of qualitative inquiry* (3rd ed.). Thousand Oaks, CA: Sage.

Shields, C. M. (2012). Critical advocacy research: An approach whose time has come. In S. R. Steinberg and G. S. Cannella (Eds.), *Critical qualitative research: Reader* (pp. 2–13). New York, NY: Peter Lang.

Spry, T. (2011). *Body, paper, stage: Writing and performing autoethnography.* Walnut Creek, CA: Left Coast Press.

St. Pierre, E. A. (2011). Post qualitative research: The critique and the coming after. In N. K. Denzin & Y. S. Lincoln (Eds.), *The Sage handbook of qualitative research* (4th ed.) (pp. 611–626). Los Angeles, CA: Sage.

Wilson, N. (2011). *Seduced by Twilight: The allure and contradictory messages of the popular saga.* Jefferson, NC: McFarland.

Yin, R. K. (2009). *Case study research: Design and methods* (4th ed.). Thousand Oaks, CA: Sage.

## ADDITIONAL RESOURCES

The Critical Lede www.thecriticallede.com is a series of podcasts designed by Drs. W. Benjamin Myers and Desiree D. Rowe that discuss various qualitative research books, articles, and research concepts. The podcasts have been a strong teaching tool in order to provide a different pedagogical approach to qualitative research courses.

Journal of Critical Thought and Praxis http://www.education.iastate.edu/jctp/ is a peer-reviewed online journal committed to providing a space for critical and progressive scholarship, practice, and activism. It is an accessible and inter/transdisciplinary journal that supports awareness and challenges individuals to move toward advocacy. The journal brings together emerging scholars, educators, and activists with the intention of providing recognition to the work of the social justice community.

International Congress of Qualitative Inquiry http://www.icqi.org/ is an annual conference designed to bring over 1400 scholars together to present and discuss qualitative research. An array of qualitative research approaches, methodologies, and topics are on the program.

Intervention Through the Socialization of New Educational Researchers is a section (pp. 81–85) of a monograph that discusses strategies for educating new researchers in the field of education. See Pasque, P., Carducci, R., Kuntz, A. K., Gildersleeve, R. E. (2012). Special Issue: *Qualitative inquiry for equity in higher education: Methodological innovations, implications, and interventions. ASHE Higher Education Report. 37*(6). San Francisco, CA: Jossey-Bass.

National Conference on Race and Ethnicity http://www.ncore.ou.edu conference series constitutes the leading and most comprehensive national forum on issues of race and ethnicity in American higher education. The conference focuses on the complex task of creating and sustaining comprehensive institutional change designed to improve racial and ethnic relations on campus and expand opportunities for educational access and success by culturally diverse, traditionally underrepresented populations.

Social Justice Training Institute http://www.sjti.org/ provides a forum for the professional and personal development of social justice educators and practitioners to enhance and refine their skills and competencies to create greater inclusion for all members of the campus community.

# CHAPTER TWELVE

# Disrupting THE Dissertation, Phenomenologically Speaking

## A Reflexive Dialogue Between Advisor-Advisee

HILARY E. HUGHES & MARK D. VAGLE

*To seek new epistemological and methodological avenues demands that we chart new paths rather than constantly return to well-worn roads and point out that they will not take us where we want to go.*

TIERNEY, 1998, P. 68

## DISSERTATION DEFENSE: MARCH 2011, ATHENS, GA

"We have time for one more question," my advisor, Mark, says as he looks around the room at the three other members on my dissertation committee and the ten people who have come to support me. I feel my fatigued body slowly releasing into itself. *One more question and all of this will finally be over.*

"I have one last question," a committee member says, "but it will be brief." *Thank God,* I think. *I am freaking exhausted from life and could use* brief *right about now.* I smile big at him as he turns toward me to ask his brief question.

| Him: | This dissertation is, some would say, *radical,* in terms of departure from what we see as a typical dissertation.... In what ways is it *not?*" |
|---|---|
| Me: | |

## RADICAL

Rad-i-cal (adj.) [rad-i-*kuh* l]

1. thoroughgoing or extreme, especially as regards change from accepted or traditional forms[1]
2. seemingly until this moment, my dissertation

I am disoriented and practically stare through my committee member's body as I try to make sense of what he just asked. "In what ways is it *not* radical?" I hear myself repeating out loud, hoping I have heard him incorrectly. My committee member nods his head "Yes" to my repeated question, and I then hear myself attempting to clarify a bit more: "Do you mean in *presentation* or *thinking*?" He crosses one leg over the other and gently interlaces his fingers before resting them on his knee: "However you want to answer."

> He is smiling.
> I am not.

For some untapped reason that I have yet to work out in therapy, I suppress what I *want* to say in that moment and instead hear myself addressing everyone in the room with some sort of stream-of-consciousness babble related to not one, but multiple reasons why my dissertation suddenly mirrors the phenomenon I explored for my study: *bodily-not-enoughness*—those moments in American culture when someone or something tells women and girls we are not enough *of something* in our lived or physical bodies (e.g., not thin-enough, pretty-enough, smart-enough, toned-enough, rich-enough, White-enough, sexy-enough, popular-enough, English-speaking-enough, Christian-enough). And through this incessant babble, I am saying the exact opposite of what the eight 12-year-old girls of color who participated in my study would have said if one of them were confronted in a moment of not-enoughness: RESIST. I hear myself whittling down two years and thousands of hours of incredibly difficult work to something that sounds like defeat. Any one of those girls in my study would have shot one hand up in front of the committee member's face and said something like, "I don't need nobody asking me why my dissertation ain't radical enough, honey! This is as radical as it gets and I don't change nothin' for nobody, baby!"[2] Resistance. Agency. Something I learned from the girls each week during our two to three hour writing group meetings at coffee shops, book stores, or pizza joints, and I heard and observed that resistance and agency come into being when anyone or anything told them they were not enough of something in their lived or physical bodies. In the present moment, however, that was something I unfortunately could not summon.

## *TIME* FOR ONE MORE QUESTION

As the "advisor," I do not have much recollection of the specifics of Hilary's response. However, I do have an acute memory of the phenomenological space in which I found myself dwelling at the moment. I remember feeling this deep ambivalence about the question itself. The ambivalence centered around the irony that we had read a beautiful dissertation and had spent time together working through all sorts of interesting nuances and complexities of the phenomenon of *bodily-not-enoughness*—finding ourselves in implicit and explicit agreement about the profoundly negative effects perpetuating not-enoughness discourses have on young adolescent girls, in particular—and there we were closing the defense with Hilary searching for ways to describe how her "radical" dissertation was, in some way, also not-enough.

As I write this now (quite a few doctoral committees later), I continue to be troubled by the ways in which people with the letters (like me) situate ourselves pedagogically in relation to our doctoral students and THEIR work. It is as though we as the committee must be able to demonstrate how a student's work is not enough, or we run the risk of being perceived as not doing our job. This is not to say, of course, that anyone's writing is beyond reproach—ours and our students' work is never complete and is always a work in progress—and, of course, each faculty member on a committee has the right and responsibility to ask any and all questions she or he sees fit. However, situating our "advising" through not-enough discourses, for lack of a better phrase, can also be read as not-enough—especially when a doctoral student is actively disrupting traditional dissertation forms, in favor of experimenting with forms and genres that open up meanings in ways that are not otherwise possible. So, for me, the question of whether the dissertation was radical enough, is not the question I would pose when there is *time* for one more question—rather, my final question would be something like, *In what ways does the radical dissertation help us see possibilities?*

## PHENOMENOLOGICAL PERSPECTIVES

Phe-nom-e-no-log-i-cal (adj.) [fi-nom-*uh*-nl-**oj**-i-k*uh* l] Per-spec-tives (n.) [per-**spek**-tivs]

1. Self-critical because it continually examines its own goals and methods in an attempt to better understand the strengths and shortcomings of its approaches and realizations.[3]

2. Intersubjective because the researcher needs the other (for example, the reader) in order to develop a dialogic relation with the phenomenon, and thus validate the phenomenon as described.[4]

3. An attempt to accomplish the impossible: attempting to construct a robust interpretive description of some aspect of the lifeworld, while completely aware that lived life is always more complex than any explication of meaning can reveal.[5]

4. The phenomenological reduction teaches us that complete reduction is impossible, that full or final descriptions are unattainable. Rather than giving up on human science research altogether, we pursue its project with extra vigor.[6]

## THE NEED FOR MORE FLUID TEXTS

If one were to conduct a review of dissertations using phenomenological methodologies (mine from back in 2006 included), one would likely see texts that include thick descriptions or interpretations of themes, meaning units, essences, essential meaning structures, invariants, variants, patterns of meaning and/or constituents to name a few. Many, if not most, would also claim to hold true to one or more of the very important phenomenological perspectives Hilary describes here—and perhaps their claims would be defensible. However, I have come to believe that crafting a text that seriously and thoughtfully demonstrates, at once, a methodology *self-critical* of its own commitments; *intersubjective* so as to allow the reader to have an active dialogic relation with the phenomenon; *robust* enough to capture some of the endless complexities; and *vigorous* in its pursuit of the impossibility at arriving at some sort of final description, demands a more fluid text.

Consistent with the theme of this volume, it requires that the text itself (its structure, form, language, genre) disrupts. Having served on a number of dissertation committees (phenomenological and otherwise), I have found committees to be alarmingly (or perhaps predictably) conservative on this front. That is, even some of the most critically oriented (theoretically, that is), poststructural (philosophically, that is) committees have tended to guide (sometimes direct, other times require) students to produce texts that conform to a fairly narrow set of guidelines—most often tending toward the "five-chapter" format or something akin. There are often institutional demands to make sure dissertations adhere to particular guidelines (e.g., must be organized in a particular sequence, have particular headings, able to be archived). Although institutions will need to continue to re-consider such guidelines given the various creative, often multi-modal, forms with which doctoral students are experimenting, what is at issue for me as a scholar and as a research mentor is when these sorts of traditional assumptions of format and structure get in the way of deep and meaningful engagement with the phenomenon under investigation.

## PHILOSOPHICAL DILEMMAS: (BRIDLING JOURNAL, 7.28.10)

Merleau-Ponty (1945/2002) wrote that because we are in the world, we are condemned to meaning. I pretty much concur with that statement whether I like it or not. As a novice phenomenological researcher I am a perpetual beginner. And as a novice researcher studying bodily-not-enoughness, I keep finding myself questioning what this all means anyway. This research thing, this work of trying to make meaning in a world that is so complex and messy and uncertain and seemingly unattainable. MP is running through my head constantly reminding me that the "world is not what I think, but what I live through. I am open to the world, I have no doubt that I am in communication with it, but I do not possess it; it is inexhaustible" (pp. xviii–xix). The world is inexhaustible, and I am indeed condemned to meaning. Awesome. Good times ahead.

At present I do feel condemned to meaning, but not necessarily the kind of meaning I am supposed to be condemned to. I am supposed to embody the role of qualitative researcher/writer/author/meaning-maker/phenomenologist. I am supposed to "interpret my data." I am supposed to read and think and reread and write and think and rewrite and reread and rewrite my way through the data—all while I am constantly checking myself before I wreck myself—Bridling—in order to inscribe some kind of meaning on the phenomenon, to inscribe some kind of meaning onto the girls with whom I spent a year. But I know I am to not *really* inscribe meaning, because phenomenology's aim is not to taxonomize, classify, or abstract the pre-reflective world (van Manen, 1990). No, instead, my charge as a budding phenomenologist is to lay out the tacit structures of bodily-not-enoughness, to unfold the folds in the multilayered constitution of this intentional relationship the girls have with bodily-not-enoughness (Caputo, 1988). But damn. How do I do that?

## TRYING TO *CAPTURE* MULTI-LAYEREDNESS

I recall a number of moments like this throuhout Hilary's dissertation process. That is, I perceived what I would call a productive tension for Hilary. She understood the demands phenomenology makes (as a philosophy and methodology) so deeply that it meant that she could not settle for superficial explanations. She knew too much. Had read too much philosophy; too much methodology. She could not not work desperately to try to capture the multi-layeredness of the phenomenon—and she could not bring herself to force the multi-layeredness (what I am calling the shifting, changing, tentative manifestations of the phenomenon in post-intentional phenomenology) into a five-chapter dissertation.

Hilary's reflections on Merleau-Ponty here are important to the dissertation she crafted as well. Although the word condemn in Merleau-Ponty's *condemned to meaning* seems as though one is being reprimanded or sentenced to something, I read it as an important reminder that we can never escape meaning nor can we ever capture meaning in its fullness, in its contextualities, in its shifting gnarly departures. This also makes the pursuit of saying something *meaningful* about meanings both exhilarating and exhausting, a blessing and a curse. Hilary worked in, through, and along these tensions—always keeping a careful eye on what might be possible in her final textual representation that she "defended." She wrote her way to and through—oftentimes *in the dark,* as van Manen (2001) likes to say—her text(s).

Merleau-Ponty posited that the *real* is supposed to be described—not constructed or formed—which means that I am not supposed to "put perception into the same category as the syntheses represented by judgments, acts or predications" (2002, p. xi). Though, I feel that as a human being, and even more, one who is condemned to meaning because I *am* a sensing, perceiving, judging, acting human being who has a whole history of experiences tethered to my being, I cannot possibly describe the subtle structures of bodily-not-enoughness without being/becoming a part of that construction or formation. And so comes about this problem that my descriptions *cannot exist* without a syntheses infused with judgments, acts, and predications, because, well, is it even humanly possible to do so?

## WORKING *INSIDE* THE PHILOSOPHY

And here is yet another example of Hilary working inside the philosophy and realizing that she wanted to push back a bit. I read this excerpt as an important foreshadowing of what was to come in the teen magazine dissertation she crafted. She realized early—even though she did not yet know what form her alternative dissertation would take—that describing the phenomenon of bodily-not-enoughness could never be about her stepping back and pointing readers to descriptions of the phenomenon. Rather, Hilary intuitively knew that she was/is grafted (Freeman & Vagle, 2013) into this phenomenon, just as her participants were/are—and that in order to draw out this grafting and bring readers into the text she would need to craft a dynamic text that does the infusing she knew was necessary and perhaps even desirable.

*Writing is the way that phenomenology is practised ... Phenomenological research does not merely involve writing: Research is the work of writing—writing is at the very heart of the process.*[7]

I knew when I started conceptualizing my dissertation study that multigenre writing would play a fundamental role in my research process because I had historically relied on that kind of writing in my personal and professional life as a tool for discovery, solace, doubt, therapy, friendship, privacy, wonder, fantasy, and reflexivity. How I had come to understand writing's purpose when conducting phenomenological research also reassured me that using phenomenology as a philosophy and methodology would benefit the ways in which I already used writing as a tool of inquiry. According to van Manen (2011), writing is not a simple step of

> writing up one's conclusions, it is not composing the final research report, it is not something that comes at the end of phenomenological inquiry, as if it were a mere state in the complex set of procedures of the research process. (par. 3)

In the act of research and phenomenological inquiry writing, the "insights achieved depend on the right words and phrases, on styles and traditions, on metaphor and figures of speech, on argument and poetic image" (par. 4). Streams of consciousness, poetry, vignettes, creative nonfiction excerpts, letters that will never be sent, short lists, long lists, narrative journal entries—these are the genres I call upon when I want to find out something new, understand something more deeply, or simply enter into a dialogue with myself on any given day, and I hoped that these genres and many more would help me breathe life into the phenomenon (van Manen, 1990) of bodily-not-enoughness as the girls in the study experienced it.

As for the format of the dissertation, that was a different story—one of uncertain fits and starts. I proposed using an alternative dissertation format in my research proposal because of my multigenre writing style and because of the ways in which van Manen invites human science researchers to construct "animating, evocative descriptions (texts) of human actions, behaviors, intentions, and experiences as we meet them in the lifeworld" (1990, p. 19). I was not surprised when my committee approved (and perhaps expected) my request for an alternative dissertation format because of those same reasons, and it felt very freeing to know I would have some autonomy with my format. That liberating feeling slowly churned its way into angst, however, because with freedom comes great responsibility. I was supposed to be drawing on the quality of language and my processes of writing-as-thinking (Hughes & Bridges-Rhoads, 2013) using that quality of language to construct an example of examples, a "science of examples" (Buytendijk in van Manen, 1990) about bodily-not-enoughness; but as I continued writing I kept finding myself *stuck*.

The more I wrote about the phenomenon the more I realized how important the format would be, because that format—whatever it was to become—would represent the content (Richardson, 1991). I wanted a format that would do justice to the fullness of the girls' experiences (Vagle, 2010a, 2010b; van Manen, 1990) and I did not have one. Within the dozens upon dozens of pages I typed and wrote by hand, there were found poems, shape poems, and short-story excerpts I created from transcripts; creative nonfiction pieces in the voices of the girls; and my research journal rants and ramblings filled with uncertainties, epiphanies, questions, doubts, and wonderment. What had not come to fruition in those pages, however, was a format that would eventually become a metaphor for everything I wanted to communicate: trying to do qualitative research with young adolescent girls while acknowledging just how entangled I was with the phenomenon myself; trying to (re)conceptualize bodies and bodied experiences in ways that were applicable to middle grades education, teacher education, and qualitative inquiry; trying to think outside of traditional and dominant discourses surrounding the body and body image(s), young adolescenTS and young adolescenCE (Vagle, 2012) and girls of color; and trying to find my way as a budding phenomenologist who likes to dabble in other theoretical playgrounds. All fantastically messy.

I continuously asked my writing partners, advisor, committee members, family, and anyone else who would listen how I could expect to keep writing if I didn't know what that writing was supposed to look like at the end of the dissertation process. Several assured me that if I "just kept writing" the format would come, and while that advice infuriated me, I knew it was true. Knowing, however, did not help the mental obstruction that ensued each day as I sat down at the computer. If I had no format, I had nowhere else to go with my writing-as-thinking, and as Richardson (1991) suggested, how writing happens influences what is written. What was a phenomenological dissertation supposed to look like if its purpose as a text, like poetry, was to be implicit as it explicated the subtle structures of bodily-not-enoughness? How could I remain responsible to the philosophy of phenomenology, while still trying to work within the limits of the dissertation genre? And then it was right in front of me on my desk one day, literally.

I received a revise and resubmit on an article I wrote about popular culture magazines and young adolescent bodies, and I remember the anxiety growing as I glanced over at the five teen magazines I used for the article thinking, *I CANNOT look at those magazines one more time.* And there it was. Writing the dissertation as a magazine had never crossed my mind, even as I met with the girls each week for writing group and recorded their conversations that mostly came from the teen magazines I brought, or those they picked up when we wrote at bookstore coffee shops. I had even utilized teen magazines as the central focus for an entire dinner conversation at an all-you-can-eat pizza joint to spark a discussion around the pressures popular culture inscribes on girls' and women's bodies (cf. Hughes-Decatur, 2012). Until that random revise-and-resubmit moment, it never occurred to me that a magazine format would be the perfect metaphor. The magazine would enable me to work within and against the very apparatus of power that regulates and maintains (Walkerdine, 1997) young adolescent girls' bodies in such limited ways (white, middle-class, heterosexual/asexual, abled, and skinny). Once the magazine idea was there, the writing seemed to flow like the wine I drank while dissertating.

---

## GETTING OUT OF THE WAY

As we crafted this chapter my first thoughts based on my initial read were to not add a "pedagogical box" here—to try to avoid doing that thing advisors often do: tidy things up. But, this is a moment in which I think an advisor is well-advised to get out of the way and just say something like:

> *This section is a powerful stretch of writing...*

---

## STUCKNESS: (BRIDLING JOURNAL, JANUARY 2011)

I find myself constantly questioning the convoluted relationship I have developed with writing and it's really pissing me off. I have really tried to remain true to the tenets of phenomenology as I have written my way through all of these processes (conceptualization to dissertation), but in doing that I feel like I am experiencing a very different relationship with writing than I ever have before. How the hell am I supposed to present this magazine as an evocative and animating text? Quite frankly doing this shit makes me doubt myself as a researcher and writer. I should have just written the damned traditional dissertation. So much easier.

----------

Some days I would write myself into places I could not get out of—dead ends, stuck places, nonsensical meaning-making—and I would end up closing or even deleting that document in order to start from scratch. Blank pages can be very detrimental to writers at any stage, and after multiple hours of writing in one day, it sometimes felt like I was playing a joke on myself. Giving a phenomenological nod to other writers' experiences of "the writer's life" that Margaret Atwood (2002) illustrated so beautifully, it was like walking into a labyrinth without knowing what monsters would be inside; like being in a cave when you can see the daylight through the opening, but are, yourself, stuck in the darkness; like wading through a dark river at dawn or twilight; like being in an empty room filled with unspoken words, with a sort of whispering all around you; like grappling with an unseen being or entity; like sitting in an empty theatre before a play or film begins, anxiously waiting for the characters to appear.[8]

On those days, the phenomenon seemed to want something more: perhaps a poetic representation that would contribute to the deeper meaning structures of bodily-not-enoughness. When I felt I could not provide that in the writing, I combed through teen magazines searching for the right genre, *the* one that could coax the writing out of me and onto the page. My writing partners suggested genre after genre hearing me talk through what it was I wanted to say, but on those days the dissertation text, just like the young adolescent bodies of color I was writing about, did not seem to ever *be enough*. But enough for whom? For me? For Mark? For the girls in the study? For education research? Yes. I wanted to make sure I was doing justice to the phenomenon of bodily-not-enoughness, while also following Polkinghorne's call for reformist writers within the community of human science to be "accountable to readers who raise questions about the validity of their conclusions based on the evidence provided" (Goodall, 2008, p. 137). I also had to remember, however, that in phenomenological inquiry writing "no text will ever be perfect, no interpretation ever complete, no explication of meaning ever final, and no insight beyond challenge" (van Manen, 2011, par. 5).

On the days when the ideas and genres came together like beautiful, complex puzzle pieces, it was as if I could viscerally feel what it meant to embody reflexive researcher, moving freely through the processes of bridling (Dahlberg, 2006) and writing my way through the girls' experiences of bodily-not-enoughness. I interrogated my presuppositions and fore-meanings about the phenomenon, the girls, their teachers, my own bodily-not-enoughness, and American popular culture— and I made sure to re-check myself before I wrecked myself. When I found myself "in" that difficult work of bridling, I sometimes felt mocked by my own words on the page as they glaringly reflected back some privileged ignorance I had not yet worked through or some disillusioned meaning I had written onto the girls' experiences that was only there because *I* thought it should be. Of course, it took the work of writing and re-writing my way through those moments, as well as talking with Mark or my writing partners, to realize this, but that is also the work of phenomenological inquiry.

*CALLING FOR* WAYS TO BE WRITTEN

The notion of stuck places is really important, as is the idea that a phenomenon—as the phenomenologist is writing her way to and through the phenomenon—would call for ways to be written. I interpret how Hilary found herself in this (and other) moment(s) to be a vivid and important demonstration of reflexivity (bridling in this brand of phenomenology). And I don't simply mean that she followed through on the methodological commitment to exercise reflexivity—she actively and persistently lived and wrote reflexively. I think the teen magazine dissertation demonstrates this reflexivity in exciting, animating, and engaging ways. Finally, in the moments Hilary came to me *stuck*, I think my default response was something pedagogically rich and eloquent like,

*"Keep going ..."*

## FANTASTICAL (AND FICTIONAL) RE-DOS: A *BREAKFAST CLUB-ESQUE* (1985) RESPONSE

Dear Mr. Vernon,

    I accept the fact that I had to sacrifice an entire weekday to defend my dissertation; after all, that is the way of the normative world within PhDness.[9] But your need to ask me why I think my dissertation is not radical (enough) is perplexing. You see it as you want to see it[10] —and what I have come to understand about phenomenology is something you might not (want to) understand:

> Phenomenology uses practiced methods of reflecting, intuiting, focusing, and questioning; it attempts to illustrate through content and form, as well as through tentative manifestations (Vagle, 2010a, 2010b) embedded in lived experiences. Phenomenology, Mr. Vernon, is self-critical in that it continually examines its own goals and methods in an attempt to come to terms with the strengths and short-comings of its approach and achievements; and it is intersubjective in that the researcher (me) needs the reader (you) in order to develop a dialogic relation with the phenomenon. Although *radical* is the word that we are supposed to be talking about here, there is only one word I would use to characterize phenomenology, Mr. Vernon, and that word is *thoughtfulness*, which is a pretty radical concept when thinking about qualitative research. In the works of great phenomenologists such as Heidegger (1962), thoughtfulness is described as a minding, a heeding, a caring attunement—a heedful, mindful wondering about the project of life, of living, of what it means to live life. (van Manen, 1990, pp. 11–12)

*Does that answer your question?*

Sincerely,
Hilary E. Hughes

## *ENGAGING* DISRUPTION

After some distance from Hilary's defense and after having experienced, as a faculty member, many defenses since, I have found that engaging with the disruption of dissertation form, structure, and purpose to be mighty precarious work. Precarious, in large part, because faculty (we) come to clearly see what we hold (and how deeply we hold) dear (i.e., the dissertation form, structure, and purpose) when we are faced with something that violates that very form, structure, and purpose. In various committee meetings, I have sensed that faculty members *find themselves in* what I would call *pedagogical ambivalence,* between wanting to be responsive to the individual student's desires and wanting to be answerable (Bakhtin, 1922/1993) to dissertation traditions. From my perspective, most faculty members either tend to lean toward the former or the latter, with fewer working along the tensions between student desire and dissertation tradition.

I think I tend to try to follow where students want (seem to want) to go with their work, more than responding to traditions. In Hilary's case, it became clear, early, that a traditional dissertation would not work for her. She had assembled a committee that practiced the sort of pedagogical openness necessary to support disruptive work—and was in consistent communication with committee members throughout her writing process. At the risk of stating the obvious, these two matters are incredibly important.

As an advisor, my following-where-students-want-(seem to want)-to-go ethos ends up in places of "big, bold, radical" disruption, other times more subtle disruption, and yet other times to the traditional. I am fine with all of these. I just want to continue to help students get smarter about what it appears they want to get smarter about—and I want to help them make the disruptive thinkable.

## POST SCRIPT

### Passionate, Questionable Parts: The Disruptive Academic Dissertation

Where might someone's passion for writing find its place in the academy, you ask? Especially when the tradition of "writing up" academic texts such as the dissertation is such "an enduring part of American doctoral training" (Duke & Beck, 1999); and seen as a "strongly disciplined activity" that we have to "gear ourselves up for" (Woods, 1999). According to Woods (1999), research writing is "nothing like writing 'delightful' junior school essays or turning out 'cathartic bits of biography, diary, or magazine articles'" (Badley, 2009, p. 211), so my dissertation-as-magazine—with all of its cathartic bits—did not quite have a place in the traditional spaces of academia. This came to be a reality for me when nearing the end of my dissertating processes I sent my institution's graduate school a few sample pages from the Microsoft Publisher version of my dissertation-as-magazine with a few questions about what they considered acceptable formatting. This is an excerpt from their response:

> I'm sorry, but you are correct that you will not be able to submit the dissertation formatted in [Microsoft Publisher] columns like the "sample page." We don't even allow people using published journal articles as chapters to use this format (it says this in our guidelines under "journal articles"). You are also correct that the table of contents must use the traditional format as in our guide.... The format of the "Talking-Back" section is more acceptable than the "sample page," but still has some questionable parts. If page 1 is the title page for the dissertation, it must meet the formatting guidelines for the title page....You cannot leave large sections of blank space within a chapter, but you can have the sections of notes or quotes in single spacing as long as they are set apart in some way.... Figures are fine, either embedded or on pages alone, but they must be labeled as figures. The "silhouette" figure is quite nice, but it has to be clear what it is. It should either be captioned as a figure to explain it or set out as a separate chapter or at least a section in a chapter. You can't just make unaccountable changes from one genre to another in the text—changes in genre need to be explained somehow.[11]

Tom Romano (1995) posited that passionate writing is often misread, "seen as raw, dangerous emotion with no intellect behind it, no critical stance" (p. 25). I imagine this, too, is how unorthodox dissertations or other unconventional academic texts might sometimes be perceived—as raw, dangerous emotion with no intellect behind it, no critical space, and, I would add for some critics, no "scientific objectivity." But as Fisher (1984) proposed almost 30 years ago, reasoning does not need to be bound to prose, nor does it need to be expressed in clear-cut structures; reasoning can be discovered in all sorts of "symbolic action—nondiscursive as well as discursive" (as cited in Markham, 2005, p. 816). Although scholars have been arguing for alternative ways to write and think about research for at least 15 years,[12] the traditions of how we "write up" dissertations seem to be stuck on the bottom of our academic shoes. Unfortunately, my institution's graduate school was not up for engaging in the messy work of parting with those sticky traditions, so I essentially had to produce two dissertations: one in the format similar to a teen magazine, written in Microsoft Publisher with ads, photos, artwork, shape poems, articles, and letters to the editor, and another in the graduate school's Microsoft Word format with "no extra spaces on the page," a traditional table of contents, appropriate headings for each chapter I had to create for that version, and shape poems and popular culture ads conformed to "Figures," set off from the rest of the text. Entire sections from the original dissertation had to be omitted because I could not figure out how to mold them into the appropriate figures or tables (i.e., non-questionable parts). If Mark and I knew then what we know now, perhaps this would have been different. However, I have no regrets about the original way I chose to write the dissertation. Even though it was an incredibly complex and arduous writing process, the magazine and all of its genres enabled me to honor phenomenology, my own writing styles, and, most importantly, the girls who participated in the study in ways that the traditional five-chapter dissertation simply could not.

## *ASKING* INSTITUTIONAL PERMISSION, *BEGGING* FORGIVENESS, *NEGOTIATING* POSSIBILITIES

Having worked with other students interested in disrupting dissertation form, I remain ambivalent whether first checking with the Graduate School for approval during prospectus is, necessarily, the best course of action. On the one hand, in Hilary's case, asking institutional permission would have saved her a lot of time, effort, and headaches if she wouldn't have had to translate her magazine to the traditional form—or Hilary at least would have known from the start what she was facing, if she decided to proceed. On the other hand, I also wonder whether Hilary would have turned herself over to the phenomenon, to the girls, to the multi-genre text with the same depth and care if she knew what she was facing from the start. In other words, knowing the limitations of the dissertation form doesn't just limit form and structure: it limits thinking, perceiving, writing, creating, intuiting, opening up, and disrupting.

This is not to say, knowing what I know now, that I would suggest students and advisors "roll the dice" and run the risk of either having to produce the dissertation in two dramatically different forms or not have the dissertation accepted. Instead, I would lean toward a careful combination of advocacy and negotiation throughout the process. Another of my students—who defended a year after Hilary—wanted to craft a multi-modal, intertextual website for her dissertation. We worked with the Graduate School throughout the process, advocating for the website to BE the dissertation. In the end, although Graduate School would not accept the website as the final form—stressing concerns about lack of archivability and uncertainty over whether the site's webhost would remain—a Graduate School staff member did work with the student to screen capture each web page, turning each screen-captured page into a PDF, and then sequencing the PDFs congruent with the Graduate School's guidelines. Although the outcome was not outright acceptance of the alternative form, there seemed to be more willingness to negotiate possibilities. I think the only way for significant change to be realized, is for students and advisors to continue to actively and persistently disrupt form and structure—and make the case for alternative, disruptive form.

## IMPLICATIONS: "THE BUTTERFLY EFFECT" OR "A SOUND OF THUNDER" IN THE ACADEMY

In 1952, Ray Bradbury wrote a short science fiction story called "A Sound of Thunder." The story and its concept were later termed, "The Butterfly Effect." It seems that both of these titles, as well as the (general) concepts behind them, are appropriate for the ways in which disruptive dissertations are taken up (or rejected) in the academy. A simplistic gist of Bradbury's story: people from the future go back to the past on a guided safari to hunt and kill a Tyrannosaurus Rex, but in order to do so, they must stay on the path provided by the safari company so they won't disrupt the natural environment. This one hunter basically freaks out and indeed steps off the path; when he returns to the future he finds a crushed butterfly on the bottom of his boot. Basically, because he stepped off the path and consequently killed a butterfly, all hell breaks loose in the future and the guy has to try and fix it.

It only *felt like* I was stuck in time during the days of dissertating—rather than traveling from present to past disrupting the world—but what actually transpired when I stepped off the traditional path has had its own negative and positive butterfly effects, if you will. Even though I have received a few awards for my dissertation and several colleagues have used it as an example in their doctoral seminars at various institutions, there has also been continued push-back from other colleagues at various institutions and conferences who hear about or read my dissertation. Through the "Yes, but" syndrome they conclude that this *kind* of academic writing will not suffice: "This is incredibly insightful work, but our university would never allow that kind of radical thinking here." Or, "This is creative and thoughtful work, but everyone is not like you so we can't expect this from everyone." Or, "I really like this idea, but how would I ever mentor a doc student to do *this* kind of work?"

Arguing over 20 years ago that poetic representation was a viable method for seeing beyond social scientific conventions and discursive practices, Richardson (1991) suggested how we write has consequences for our discipline, the public we serve, and for ourselves. Additionally, how we are expected to write in the academy affects what we can write about, and the form shapes the content. Richardson held that "prose is the form in which social researchers are expected to represent interview material. Prose, however, is simply a literary technique, a convention, and not the sole legitimate carrier of knowledge" (1991, p. 877). I like to think about all academic writing in this same way, and especially with regard to the dissertation: "writing up" research does not have to be eternally bound to traditional scientific/academic prose, because "prose" is a literary technique, a convention or structure of writing that has been repeated in so many journals, textbooks, handbooks, and dissertations over the years, "we now believe it is true and real. *We've forgotten we made it up*" [emphasis original] (St. Pierre, 2011, p. 613).

My suggestions to both the naysayers and those who wish to embark on disruptive journeys such as these? Why can't we (re)create what we know as "normal" for academic texts such as the dissertation in the academy? If we always do what we've always done, then we'll always get what we've always got. So why not, *not* do what we've always done and see what happens? St. Pierre (2011) maintained that "if we don't read the theoretical and philosophical literature, we have nothing much to think with during analysis except normalized discourses that seldom explain the way things are" (p. 614). If you are a doctoral student who has a hankering to disrupt normalized discourses within the academy, I agree with St. Pierre that you must first read, read, read, and become theory-smart, so you can formulate an articulate argument as to why your alternative dissertation format will tell a different kind of story than a traditional format might allow. If you're like me and you're not really interested in turning the academy on its head as much as creating a powerful and thoughtful text that does its best to represent the story you want to tell, and a traditional format might not allow for that to happen, then I suggest the same: read, read, read, and become theory *and* format smart. See what others have done and are doing. Ask questions. Read books by those who *write about writing* both outside the academy and within. Play with and dwell in your data as you write your way through it. If you're mentoring a doc student who wants to step off that path and create her own butterfly effect, think about what Mark did for me: try to be open and remember that you are a guide, a mentor; listen thoughtfully and often, and respond to moments of panic or "stuckness" with evocative statements such as, "Keep going."

## NOTES

1. http://dictionary.reference.com/browse/radical
2. Original quote from "Buttercup": *"Oh, I can model any size I am, honey. They gonna have to pay me or they gonna lose something special .... I don't lose weight for nobody, baby."* —Buttercup, 2009.[1]
3. van Manen, 1990, p. 12
4. van Manen, 1990, p. 12
5. van Manen, 1990, p. 18
6. van Manen, 1990, p. 18
7. van Manen, 2011, par 1.
8. Atwood, 2002, pp. xxii–xxiii
9. Hughes & Bridges-Rhoads (2013)
10. The original lines from the concluding letter in the movie, *The Breakfast Club* (1985):

> **Brian Johnson:** Dear Mr. Vernon, we accept the fact that we had to sacrifice a whole Saturday in detention for whatever it was we did wrong. What we did *was* wrong. But we think you're crazy to make us write an essay telling you who we think we are. You see us as you want to see us.... In the simplest terms, in the most convenient definitions. But what we found out is that each one of us is a brain...

| Andrew Clark: | ...and an athlete... |
| Allison Reynolds: | ...and a basket case... |
| Claire Standish: | ...a princess... |
| John Bender: | ...and a criminal... |
| Brian Johnson: | Does that answer your question? Sincerely yours, the Breakfast Club. |

11. The graduate school ProQuest version of the dissertation can be found under: H. E. Hughes (2011). *Phenomenal Bodies, Phenomenal Girls: How Young Adolescent Girls Experience Being-enough in Their Bodies* (Doctoral dissertation). University of Georgia, Athens, GA.

12. cf. Bridges-Rhoads & Van Cleave, in press, 2013; 2012; Cahnmann-Taylor & Siegesmund, 2008; Duke & Beck, 1999; Holbrook, 2010; Richardson, 1991, 2001; Richardson & St. Pierre, 2005; St. Pierre, 2011.

# REFERENCES

Atwood, M. (2002). *Negotiating with the dead: A writer on writing.* New York, NY: Random House.

Badley, G. (2009). Academic writing as shaping and reshaping. *Teaching in Higher Education, 14*(2), 209–219.

Bakhtin, M. (1993). *Toward a philosophy of the act.* In M. Holquist & V. Liapunov (Eds.) (V. Liapunov, Trans.). Austin, TX: University of Texas Press. (Original work published 1922)

Bradbury, R. (1952, June 28). A sound of thunder. *Collier's Weekly,* 20–21.

Bridges-Rhoads, S., & Van Cleave, J. (in press). Writing the torment: Aporetic data and the possibility of justice. *Cultural Studies: Critical Methodologies, 13*(3). Retrieved from http://csc.sagepub.com/content/early/2013/05/19/1532708613487872

Cahnmann-Taylor, M., & Siegesmund, R. (2008). *Arts-based research in education: Foundations for practice.* New York, NY: Routledge.

Caputo, J. (1988). *Radical hermeneutics: Repetition, deconstruction, and the hermeneutic project.* Bloomington, IN: Indiana University Press.

Dahlberg, K. (2006). The essence of essences—The search for meaning structures in phenomenological analysis of lifeworld phenomena. *International Journal of Qualitative Studies on Health and Well-Being, 1,* 11–19.

Duke, N. K., & Beck, S. W. (1999). Education should consider alternative formats for the dissertation. *Educational Researcher, 28*(3), 31–36.

Fisher, W. R. (1984). Narration as a human communication paradigm: The case of public moral argument. *Communication Monographs, 51,* 1–22.

Freeman, M., & Vagle, M. D. (2013). Grafting the intentional relation of hermeneutics and phenomenology in linguisticality. *Qualitative Inquiry, 19*(9), 725–735.

Goodall, H. L. (2008). *Writing qualitative inquiry: Self, stories, and academic life.* Walnut Creek, CA: Left Coast Press.

Holbrook, T. (2010). An ability traitor at work: A treasonous call to subvert writing from within. *Qualitative Inquiry, 16*(3), 171–183.

Hughes, H. E. (2011). *Phenomenal bodies, phenomenal girls: How young adolescent girls experience being-enough in their bodies* (Doctoral dissertation). University of Georgia, Athens, GA.

Hughes, H. E., & Bridges-Rhoads, S. (2013). Beyond the scope of this paper: Troubling writing across paradigms in education dissertations. *International Review of Qualitative Research, 6*(1), 103–125.

Hughes-Decatur, H. (2012). Always becoming, never enough: Middle school girls talk back. In M. D. Vagle (Ed.), *Not a stage! A critical re-conception of young adolescent education* (pp. 93–117). New York, NY: Peter Lang.

Markham, A. N. (2005). "Go ugly early": Fragmented narrative and bricolage as interpretive method. *Qualitative Inquiry, 11*, 813–839.

Merleau-Ponty, M. (2002). *Phenomenology of perception* (C. Smith, Trans.). London, England; New York, NY: Routledge Classics. (Original work published in 1945)

Richardson, L. (1991). Poetic representation of interviews. In J. F. Gubrium & J. A. Holstein (Eds.), *Handbook of interview research: Contents and methods* (pp. 877–892). Thousand Oaks, CA: Sage.

Richardson, L. (2001). Getting personal: Writing stories. *International Journal of Qualitative Studies in Education, 14*, 33–38. doi: 10.1080/09518390010007647

Richardson, L., & St. Pierre, E. A. (2005). Writing: A method of inquiry. In N. K. Denzin & Y. S. Lincoln (Eds.), *Handbook of qualitative research* (pp. 959–978). Thousand Oaks, CA: Sage.

Romano, T. (1995). *Writing with passion: Life stories, multiple genres.* Portsmouth, NH: Heinemann.

St. Pierre, E. A. (2011). Post qualitative research: The critique and the coming after. In N. K. Denzin & Y. S. Lincoln (Eds.), *The Sage handbook of qualitative research* (pp. 611–625). Los Angeles, CA: Sage.

Tierney, W. G. (1998). Life's history's history: Subjects foretold. *Qualitative Inquiry, 4*(1), 49–70.

Vagle, M. D. (2010a). Re-framing Schon's call for a phenomenology of practice: A "post-intentional approach." *Reflective Practice, 11*(3), 393–407.

Vagle, M. D. (2010b, May). A post-intentional phenomenological research approach. Paper presented at the annual meeting of the American Educational Research Association, Denver, CO.

Vagle, M. D. (Principal Author and Editor). (2012). *Not a stage! A critical re-conception of young adolescent education.* New York, NY: Peter Lang.

van Manen, M. (1990). *Researching lived experience: Human science for an action sensitive pedagogy.* London, Canada: The Althouse Press.

van Manen, M. (2001). *Writing in the dark: Phenomenological studies in interpretive inquiry.* London, Canada: The Althouse Press.

van Manen, M. (2011). Phenomenological inquiry is practiced as phenomenological writing. *Phenomenology Online.* Retrieved from http://www.phenomenologyonline.com/inquiry/writing/.

Walkerdine, V. (1997). *Daddy's girl: Young girls and popular culture.* Cambridge, MA: Harvard University Press.

Woods, P. (1999). *Successful writing for qualitative researchers.* London, England: Routledge.

# CHAPTER THIRTEEN

# Methodological Freedom

## A Journey

NANA OSEI-KOFI

*"As a person of color, I think you are too close to the subject matter, too close to do good research on students of color."*

*"We would like you to apply for our position opening, but we would require that you do traditional empirical work until you are awarded tenure, and at that point you will be able do more conceptual and theoretical work."*

*"We don't want you to do more arts–based work until you get tenure because we don't know how to evaluate it and we don't know of any scholars outside of the institution whom we might ask to do so."*

Fig 13.1  Untitled self-portrait, 2013.

You may wonder why people would say such things, and how it makes me feel about the work I do. I think people say things like this to people like me for different reasons. As I have thought about it over the years, I have come to believe that these people fall into three different groups, broadly speaking. There are those who in many ways may be viewed as supporters. These are people who may or may not be intimately familiar with my work, but they believe in me and want the best for me. They want to protect me and the best way they know to do this is to encourage me to draw within the lines. The second group is made up of those who come from a place of fear. My work is outside of their sphere of familiarity, and if there is something they do not know, it must not be very good. Academic socialization is about the possession of expert knowledge. Therefore, to admit to not knowing something brings with it great fear, and so it is easier to push the unfamiliar away, rather than engage it. The third group is those I think of as the true traditionalists. These are people who believe strongly, whether consciously or not, that the academy has been polluted by women, people of color, GLBTQ-identified individuals, and the working class, and that these groups have brought with them illegitimate forms of knowledge production that need to be squashed. To them my work is of little value or use.

What these groups see as disruptive, I see as simply doing what Audre Lorde (1984) asked of each us, "to find our work and do it." To me, academic work is not an abstract intellectual exercise. To me it is about real people, real lives, and real consequences. As a woman of Ghanaian and Swedish heritage, I understood race as a floating signifier experientially early on in life. As part of a family actively involved in the labor movement, the politics of class was also something that I was very familiar with growing up. And living in a female-led household, gender roles and expectations were something I reflected on frequently as a child and young adult. Additionally, I grew up around educators and activists whose conversations more often than not centered on social justice, which today is at the heart of the academic work I do.

Guided by critical and feminist epistemologies, my work engages with three broad, yet overlapping, areas of inquiry: social contexts of education, inclusive education, and arts-based educational research. In my approach to this work, I strive to engage in the production of transdisciplinary knowledge. Challenging existing discipline-oriented boundaries and combining multiple forms of theory and analysis, I embrace the idea of bricolage, which Joe Kincheloe (2005) described as "new forms of complex, multimethodological, multilogical forms of inquiry into the social, cultural, political, psychological, and educational domains" (p. 323), as a powerful way to gain new insights and imagine new possibilities. My scholarship, which is primarily theoretical/conceptual and qualitative in nature, and emphasizes issues of social and economic justice in education and beyond, is very much part of who I am and that which I care about. And despite the challenges of working at the margins of the field in which I am currently located (the study of higher education), I feel incredibly fortunate to go to work every day and do something that excites me and that is of great importance to me.

As counter-balance to the messages I shared at the beginning of this letter, it is like-minded scholars—who lead by example, who provide encouragement when needed, who stretch my thinking, and with whom I share what Paulo Freire (1970) described as radical love; an enactment of love for the world and for humanity through social action—that sustain me as a scholar. Concomitantly, I also want to acknowledge that at this point and time, I am at a place in my career where I have the privilege of being tenured, which at least on an emotional level, softens the sting of disapproval of disruptive work.

Having said that, the privilege of tenure, for me, is not about *finally* being able to do my "real" work, as it is often described. While not without its challenges, I have continuously tried to stay true to that which I understand as my intellectual project. What tenure means to me is that I now have a certain kind of freedom from the need to negotiate the intricacies of the politics of academic advancement in the way that is often necessary, especially if you are a member of a non-dominant group in society *and* do disruptive work pre-tenure.

To get to this place in my career would not have been possible without champions. I remember in 2000, I had just started my PhD program when Mildred Garcia (2000), who is now the president of California State University, Fullerton, came out with the book, *Succeeding in an Academic Career: A Guide for Faculty of Color*. The one thing I will never forget from this book, because of the ways in which it has rung true in my own life, is that to make it in the academy in the body of a minoritized individual requires champions. When I think of the big moments in my academic career, getting into a graduate program, finishing my dissertation, getting my first job, achieving promotion and tenure, at each turn I see the faces of key individuals that served as champions. Most were women of color.

When I reflect on the road I have traveled, which I tentatively describe as a journey to methodological freedom (which I will say a little bit more about later), there are three key incidents that help mark this journey for me.

## INCIDENT #1

The first incident was in graduate school. I wrote a paper on the digital divide and framed it as a conceptual/theoretical piece informed by critical theory, with particular attention to issues of class and race. I did not know enough at the time to articulate the framing of my paper in this way, I just knew that for me, analytically, this was a very important way to engage with the reality of the digital divide, and that this was a perspective that was largely absent from the literature that I had been exposed to in the class. The feedback I received on the assignment from the faculty member teaching the class was that I needed to include more statistics and engage in more analysis of statistical data. By chance, I happened to mention this feedback to another faculty member whom I met a few days later, and she immediately said to me, and of course I am paraphrasing here,

> that feedback doesn't sound as though it engages with what you were trying to do. What I hear you saying is that your analysis is centered on the ideology and worldview that informs the ways in which the digital divide is framed in dominant discourse.

Wow! I had been heard. Looking back, I am sure I could have articulated my rationale more clearly, but what was important to me at the time was that I had confirmation that I was not losing my mind. The type of analysis I wanted to engage in had value and was important to someone other than me. This is my first memory of beginning to have a sense of the politics of the production of knowledge.

## INCIDENT #2

Fast-forward a few years. I had successfully defended a theoretical dissertation and was on the job market. My dissertation study, grounded in a critique of the logic of capitalism, explored the political economy of higher education and was informed by Marx's method of dialectics. My study placed emphasis on the ways in which both public and private forces, from the time of the industrial revolution, have shaped higher education in the interest of market-driven imperatives. Based on a historical analysis of these conditions, I grappled with the question of what the particulars of the historical moment in which I wrote my dissertation required of members of the academic community committed to struggle for human emancipation. With this work in hand, everywhere I turned, I learned that education departments were looking for mainstream scholars doing quantitative work, with a few mainstream qualitative positions sprinkled in. Theoretical and conceptual work, I learned, was "nice" as an add-on, but not viewed as being in any way at the core of education scholarship. Have you ever heard anything so strange? That thinking about, and engaging with, the ways in which we come to understand education, the way we frame issues, and thus the way we address them, was not viewed as an essential part of a field of study. But I needed a job, so I started to somewhat reluctantly investigate what possible qualitative research projects would satisfy both my interest in critical and feminist analyses of higher education, and respond to the demand, albeit small, for assistant professors doing mainstream qualitative research. Around this time, I attended an AERA roundtable on the then forthcoming release of a new edition of the *Handbook of Complementary Methods in*

*Education Research* (Green, Camili, & Elmore, 2006). One of the presenters, a senior scholar, said to the group around the table where I was seated, "You know, there are more options out there, you don't *have to be* a quant or a qual." That comment hit me like a lightning rod. I did not have to keep trying to force my academic being into one of two narrowly defined boxes externally defined for me. My work, whether it was theoretical/conceptual or arts-based, had a place, it was okay for me to be myself. This may sound like a small thing to you, but to me it was as though a huge weight was lifted from my shoulders. I did not have to perform a role that had been externally defined for me. I did not have to keep my creativity under wraps. I had something to contribute that was of value and I was part of a community of scholars that fell outside the rigid quantitative/qualitative divide, which I did not previously know existed.

## INCIDENT #3

Through experiences such as the aforementioned, I figured out who I was as a scholar and went about my work of critically engaging with issues of social justice in education and broader society. In so doing, there was one thing, though, that I wish I had learned much earlier. It was something I heard Yvonna Lincoln, who is probably best described as one of the most influential higher education scholars writing about qualitative research, say when we were on a panel together about two years ago. An audience member asked Yvonna about publishing and she recounted how hard it had been for her to get qualitative work published in higher education journals in the early years. What she encouraged the questioner to do was to write and publish to her audience. That is to say, we should submit our work to journals familiar and welcoming of the type of scholarship we produce. Yvonna confirmed for me what I had learned the hard way. I tend to describe the process of submitting my work to mainstream outlets, over a period of several years, because that was what I was told was the "gold standard," as "beating my head bloody against a wall." Rather graphic, I know, but my point is that typically the feedback I would receive was similar to the feedback I received on my digital divide paper as a graduate student. I was working within one paradigm, while my work was being evaluated based on a completely different paradigm. Therefore, unless my interest was in shifting paradigms or replacing a focus on subject matter with a focus on the paradigm used to frame the work, what I could do with the feedback was often limited. And I think I use such a violent analogy because of the emotional toll that these types of experiences result in. The feedback does not engage with your work, rather it dismisses it. So, tired of the wall, I expanded my horizon and started submitting my work to journals with editorial boards that were sincerely open to the paradigms I work in. I thought I had entered into another universe of cream and honey! I am not saying that my submissions were now viewed as the greatest thing since sliced bread, but what I am saying is that the feedback I received engaged with my work, it was meaningful, and it pushed and challenged me in ways that were about making my work better, not invalidating it. It felt to me like being in conversation with really smart people that cared deeply about my work. Finding these outlets, for me, reinforced the importance of reading broadly and across artificially constructed disciplinary and sub-disciplinary boundaries in order to allow for deep engagement with the issues as well as with colleagues approaching these issues from multiple and varied perspectives. Figuring this out earlier would have saved me a lot of anxiety and frustration.

As I hope these three experiences convey, what I am calling methodological freedom for now, for me, is about an internal process whereby we remain open to multitudes of ways of coming to know. It is about resisting boundaries on the ways in which we conceive of knowledge production. It is about refusing to get caught up in the false dichotomy of quantitative versus qualitative research. It is about internalizing a freedom in the choices we make in our efforts to understand the issues we explore through our research. Of course, this is not to say that the freedom of which I write can be equated with an absence of barriers, obstacles, and resistance to work that is informed by this mindset, because it cannot. What I am trying to capture, and where I want to place emphasis, is on this as an internal process, as a way of understanding intellectual labor, separate from external conditions. In fact, it may be that it is this very separation that fosters the sense of freedom I am attempting to put into words, because it is grounded in a refusal to accept a dominant narrative of acceptable knowledge production in the field of education.

When I share some of the experiences I discuss here, I am often asked about ways to navigate the promotion and tenure process as someone who may be termed a disruptive scholar. The primary question is typically about how I situated my work in relation to promotion and tenure requirements, so I will say a little bit about that here. Before I do, though, let me preface my comments by stating very clearly that my primary goal as a scholar has always been about the work. This is not to say that tenure and promotion were not important goals when I started out as an assistant professor; however I want to make it clear that the desire to do meaningful work, rather than the quest for institutional recognition, was and is what motivates me. That said, when it came to the particulars of putting together a promotion and tenure dossier, having very specific examples of materials compiled by scholars outside the mainstream was very valuable to my process. In particular, I had access to materials that a colleague at another institution was willing to share with me that dealt with how to explain and present the importance of ethnic studies to members of the academy with little-to-no knowledge or familiarity with the field. Additionally, I had the opportunity to review several successful dossiers from a range of disciplines at my home institution. Once the first version of my dossier was complete, I had senior colleagues from fields as diverse as engineering, psychology, and family and consumer sciences, as well as education, read my dossier and provide feedback. While I focused on explicitly articulating the value of my work in accessible language within the framework of the guidelines for promotion and tenure at my institution, one of my colleagues described the first version of my promotion and tenure narrative as "getting all the anger and frustration out." Looking back, it was in many ways a narrative that sought to respond to the types of comments I shared at the beginning of this letter, with all the emotion that comes with hearing such things. This was not the narrative I submitted! Once I recognized what I had done and got this out of my system, so to speak, I was able to write the accessible and persuasive narrative I had in mind. And yet, I am convinced that separate from any evaluation of the "quality" of my work, without champions willing to advocate for the importance of scholarship that does not fit neatly within the parameters of what I often think of as "the study of higher education proper" (e.g., the senior colleagues who offered to read my draft dossier and the university administrators that knew me from university-wide service projects I engaged in and who believed in my work), the outcome of my promotion and tenure case could easily have been very different.

It is champions who have served as navigators, guides, and advocates as I have journeyed through the academic landscape, and without them, I would not be where I am today. However, there is also another group of people that have served in an equally important role. These are those who have fed my soul as a scholar and as a human being. The shortest way I can describe this group is to say "FMS." FMS, or the Future of Minority Studies Research Project (http://www.fmsproject.cornell.edu) is "a consortium of scholars and academic institutions with a primary interest in minority identity, education, and social transformation." I was first introduced to FMS in 2005, and have been involved ever since, becoming an FMS Fellow in 2006. During the year I was a Fellow, I spent part of the summer at Stanford University as a participant in the FMS Summer Institute, *Theory From the Periphery: Minority Struggles for Social Justice*. During this time as Fellows, in addition to intense study, we had the opportunity to receive one-on-one mentoring related to specific projects we were each working on at the time from the Institute faculty, as well as other senior scholars committed to the work of FMS. FMS meetings, which I have attended over the years as often as possible, no matter the topical focus, are about intergenerational dialogue and deep engagement with interdisciplinary scholarship on social justice. To spend time with a diverse group of people, from undergraduates to graduate students to new faculty to senior scholars such as Chandra Mohanty, Angela Davis, Minnie Bruce Pratt, and Beverly Guy-Shefthall, grappling with difficult questions of research, theory, and practice, energizes me every time I participate in an FMS event! And I have to mention the good food. You may laugh, but to break bread together, to sit across a table talking and sharing good food is something very different than sitting in a sterile classroom. The engagement is more intimate, more open, more honest. To share my work at FMS events is an experience similar to what I shared about submitting work to journals that welcome the paradigms with which I engage. As an interdisciplinary group, not everyone is intimately familiar with the disciplinary frameworks that we employ in the scholarship that we share with one another, but what we share is a commitment to the issues. It is a space where methodological freedom is valued.

I first learned about FMS through my involvement with Women's Studies. I earned an M.A. in Applied Women's Studies while completing my PhD and have always been a Women's Studies affiliate at the institutions where I have worked. Therefore, I see Women's Studies as important in grounding me as a scholar. This affiliation has served as a constant reminder of the value and importance of different ways of knowing, when I have felt the most constricted by the pragmatism and anti-intellectualism that is too often present in the field of education. Don't get me wrong, there are brilliant minds doing diverse types of work in the field of education, but these are rarely the minds whose work is celebrated and recognized for its contributions to the field, whether it is with awards, grants, invitations to give keynote addresses or to edit special issues of journals, etc. In an economic and political climate of neoliberalism and where an obsession with particular and limited notions of accountability is the order of the day, it is scholarship that aligns with these notions that is valued and celebrated as the ideal we should all aspire to.

What is it that I think is going on in the field of education? What is it that has shaped the context within which my journey has taken place and continues to take place? On some level, I think it is important to recognize that methodological conservatism, which rejects "epistemological and methodological perspectives of feminism; postmodernism; poststructuralism; critical, queer, and critical race theories; postcolonialism, and/or indigenous scholarship," (Carducci, Kuntz, Gildersleeve, & Pasque, 2011, n.p.) is not limited to what is happening in the field of education. However, that is a conversation for another time. For now, let me say something about what I think is happening in education and what we can do about it. First of all, if anyone is making an argument that the dominance of methodological conservative scholarship is about lack of knowledge and information, I am not buying it. There is a range of work that engages with the politics of knowledge production in a multitude of ways. Think, for example, about Walter Mignolo's work or Dolores Delgado Bernal, Eduardo Bonilla-Silva, Vandana Shiva, Linda Tuhwai Smith, and the list goes on. What is keeping methodological conservatism in place is that it is reinforced everywhere around us. We see it as common sense whether it is through what we are taught as students in the classroom, what we read in journals, what we hear at conferences, and maybe most of all, in the type of research that gets funded. It is methodologically conservative work that fosters power, privilege, and prestige in the field. The situation is about what Vandana Shiva (1995) described as monocultures of the mind. Using agriculture as a metaphor, Shiva described how "dominant scientific knowledge ... breeds a monoculture of the mind ... alternatives disappear, very much like monocultures of introduced plant varieties lead ... to the displacement and destruction of ... diversity" (p. 12). Not only do we have work on different approaches to knowledge production in education, we also have excellent work that critiques the mess we are in, of which I think Benjamin Baez and Deron Boyles (2009) book *The Politics of Inquiry* is noteworthy as a point of introduction. In short, then, if we are serious about challenging the issue of methodological conservatism, more of us need to engage with the literature available to us in doing so.

Another question, and an important one, is, of course, what we can do about methodological conservatism. How do we cultivate spaces where methodological freedom is valued? There are several things that come to mind as I reflect on this question, with much of what I think of coming from excellent critiques of the current conditions under which we labor. As an example, I think of Monisha das Gupta's (2006) distinction between place taking versus place making, through which she argued that place taking, which may be a situation in which many of us find ourselves in the academy, is informed by a politics of accommodation, whereas space making, which we must struggle for, is instead about a politics of transformation. I also think about the ways in which Baez and Boyles (2009) pointed to the need to resist "gutter utilitarianism" in educational research. That is to say, the need to resist the advancement of narrow, faddish ways of engaging with education based on an economic argument of "what works," which simply results in the crudest forms of analysis. Henry Giroux's (2012) call for collective resistance is never far from my mind. I spend a lot of time thinking about how we can engage critically with oppressive processes of reproduction and create spaces where restrictive practices can be challenged and transformed. Being on the other side of tenure, I believe I have added responsibility to work for change. In ways similar to when I was untenured, I continue to be disappointed by senior scholars with multiple forms of privilege, whose work suggests a commitment to progressive politics and a transformation of methodological conservatism, but who, on the ground, have little interest or concern in radical restructuring of the academy. I aim to do what I can to not fall into this category. As part of this effort to remain vigilant, on an individual level I try to show newer scholars, by example, that it is possible to do disruptive work in the academy. This is not to say that academic politics can or should be ignored, but to recognize that there *are* small pockets of scholars in the academy today that do disruptive work and that there are ways to strategically advance this type of work. I am also deeply committed to involving newer scholars in projects that I'm involved in when such possibilities arise. Frequently, I remind myself of my own experience in the academy, and when I can, serve as a champion for others in ways similar to those who have supported and continue to support me.

On an organizational level, I currently direct a social justice graduate certificate program that I see as creating space for like-minded faculty and students to engage in disruptive scholarship (to read more about the social justice concentration, see Osei-Kofi, Shahjahan, & Patton, 2010). Another example of an effort at creating change is the creation of the *Journal of Critical Thought and Praxis*, which comes out of the Certificate program and is a student-driven initiative that I have been able to support in order to create a space for new and emerging scholars and activists engaged in diverse forms of knowledge production to share their work and enter into conversation with one another. As I put the finishing touches on this letter, I am preparing to move to a new institution to assume a position as the director of a faculty development program that places emphasis on incorporating issues of difference, power, and discrimination into curricula across fields and disciplines. Much like my work with the social justice certificate program, I am hopeful that through this type of work, I can continue to contribute to efforts to foster institutional change. Of course, these efforts are not *the* ultimate answer, but they *are* a part of doing the work, and I continue to always look toward new opportunities, possibilities, and ways of being that I view as in some way advancing a commitment to structural change in the U.S. academy.

To that end, what I have been thinking about lately, and maybe this is a good place to end this letter is about the idea of a critical translational praxis. This is something that has stuck with me following a conversation at the National Women's Studies Association conference with Nancy Naples and several other qualitative scholars at various places in their academic careers (personal communication, 2012). What I took from Naples' comments, or my spin on it, if you will, is that because critical and qualitative scholars want a seat at the table, we often buy into the false binaries that uncritically frame debates and discussions that methodological conservatism sets up. The alternative that was discussed is to develop a critical translational praxis through which we can challenge the premises upon which these debates are structured and break down false binaries/notions of parallel worlds of knowledge creation. Is this the answer? As I have alluded to earlier, I do not think there is "one," answer, nor do I know where the idea of a critical translational praxis may lead, but for now, it is something that is challenging me to think in new and sometimes uncomfortable but productive ways. As an example, I have been thinking a lot recently about points of connection that may exist in the work I do with the work of colleagues whose work I would typically view as having little to do with mine, and recognizing that at times there may be very unlikely connections that advance a shared goal, and ultimately can contribute to shifting the conversation beyond the siloes that so many of us in the academy often find ourselves. Is this part of what it means to practice methodological freedom? I am not yet sure.

Each of us comes to this work with different experiences, and our journeys all unfold in varied ways, but if there is one thought I can leave you with, it is to continue to do the work you believe in and that you have passion for. There is a quote by Charles W. Mills (1997) that seems appropriate to make this point. In *The Racial Contract*, Mills wrote,

> One has to learn to trust one's own cognitive powers, to develop one's own concepts, insights, modes of explanation, overarching theories, and to oppose the epistemic hegemony of conceptual frameworks designed in part to thwart and suppress the exploration of such matters; one has to think against the grain. (p. 119)

To do this and to do it well, I say have great clarity about your work; disruption of the status quo will always garner great scrutiny, and this is something for which you must be prepared. Hence, it is important that you have a clear sense of your work. Once you achieve this, don't censor yourself! This is one of the most valuable things I heard from my advisor Antonia Darder in graduate school, and so I pass it on to you. When you do disruptive work, you can expect others to try and censor you, so at least don't do the censoring for them! Find champions and supporters to guide you along the way. I must admit I have no specific process for identifying guides, but I think it has something to do with sharing your work and your intentions broadly, and that through this process you come in contact with others who believe in your intellectual project. If you can find groups within your scholarly community that offer experiences similar to that which I experienced through the FMS project, I highly recommend getting involved. If you can't find something similar, start your own group. And finally, take care of yourself. I can't say enough about self-care. Give yourself permission to rest, to enjoy your friends and family, to be creative, to experience joy, to live. Your work will benefit.

In solidarity,
Nana

## REFERENCES

Baez, B., & Boyles, D. (2009). *The politics of inquiry: Education research and the "culture of science."* New York, NY: State University of New York.

Carducci, R., Kuntz, A., Gildersleeve, R., & Pasque, P. (2011). The disruptive dialogue project: Crafting critical space in higher education. *InterActions, 72*(2).

das Gupta, M. (2006). *Unruly immigrants: Rights, activism, and transnational South Asian politics in the United States*. Durham, NC: Duke University Press.

Freire, P. (1970). *Pedagogy of the oppressed*. New York, NY: Herder & Herder.

Garcia, M. (2000). *Succeeding in an academic career: A guide for faculty of color*. Westport, CT: Greenwood.

Giroux, H. (2012, October 16). Can democratic society survive a neoliberal society? *Truthout*. Retrieved from http://truth-out.org/opinion/item/12126-can-democratic-education-survive-in-a-neoliberal-society

Green, J. L., Camili, G., & Elmore, P. B. (Eds). (2006). *Handbook of complementary methods in education research*. New York, NY: Routledge.

Kincheloe, J. (2005). On to the next level: Continuing the conceptualization of the bricolage. *Qualitative Inquiry, 11*(3), 323–350.

Lorde, A. (1984). *Sister outsider*. Freedom, CA: The Crossing Press.

Mills, C. W. (1997). *The racial contract*. Ithaca, NY: Cornell University Press.

Osei-Kofi, N., Shahjahan, R., & Patton, L. (2010). Centering social justice in the study of higher education: Strategies and possibilities for institutional change. *Equity & Excellence in Education, 43*(3), 265–278.

Shiva, V. (1995). *Monocultures of the mind: Perspectives on biodiversity and biotechnology*. New York, NY: Zed Books.

# Contributing Authors

**Nicole Beeman-Cadwallader** is a doctoral candidate in Science Education at Indiana University. Her research interests include documenting the unique narratives, rich with traditional ecological knowledge, of traditionally marginalized communities for purposes of broadening the cultural congruency of science and environmental education. Much of her research engages with interrogating environmental education, from pre-Kindergarten through university education, and often beyond school settings. Nicole also has interests in self-study and qualitative research methodologies, particularly those of ethnographic and narrative traditions.

**Ruth Nicole Brown** is an assistant professor of Educational Policy, Organization & Leadership and Gender and Women's Studies at the University of Illinois Urbana-Champaign. She earned her doctoral degree in Political Science from the University of Michigan, Ann Arbor. At Michigan, she also earned certification in gender and women's studies and world performance studies. Her research interests include cultural production, girls' studies, performance, research methodology, and women of color feminisms. She is the author of *Black Girlhood Celebration Toward A Hip-Hop Feminist Pedagogy* (2009) and co-author of *Wish To Live: The Hip-Hop Feminism Pedagogy Reader* (2012), both with Peter Lang Press. Her second single-authored book, *Hear Our*

*Truths The Creative Potential of Black Girlhood*, is forthcoming, published by the University of Illinois Press.

**Rozana Carducci** is an assistant professor of Higher Education in Student Affairs in the Department of Adolescent Education and Leadership at Salem State University. She received her doctorate in Higher Education from UCLA and her Master's degree in College Student Personnel from Miami University. Her research and teaching interests include the politics of inquiry, higher education leadership, and academic capitalism within the context of student affairs. Rozana is co-author of the ASHE Higher Education Report, *Qualitative Inquiry for Equity in Higher Education: Methodological Innovations, Implications, and interventions* (Pasque, Carducci, Kuntz, & Gildersleeve, 2012).

**Rosario Carrillo** is an assistant professor of Literacy Education in the Department of Mexican American Studies at the University of Arizona. Her doctoral degree in Literacy Education is from the University of Michigan, Ann Arbor. She utilizes a critical socio-cultural approach to literacy that centers on power differences and involves ways of reading, writing, knowing, and being. Her areas of research include out-of-school pedagogy and educational cultural production. The *Education of Latinas and Decolonial Chicana Theory* are among the courses she teaches.

**Sara M. Childers**, PhD, is an Independent Scholar living in Dublin, Ohio. She received her doctorate in Social and Cultural Foundations of Education from Ohio State University. Her research focuses on qualitative methodologies, including ethnography, sociocultural policy analysis, feminist and post-structural theories, and urban education.

**Mark S. Giles** is an associate professor in the Department of Educational Leadership and Policy Studies and director of African American Studies at the University of Texas at San Antonio. Dr. Giles received his PhD from Indiana University. His research interests include twentieth-century African-American history, Critical Race Theory, intersections of race, leadership, and spirituality, and the social, cultural, and political contexts of education.

**Teri Holbrook** is an assistant professor of Literacy and Language Arts in the Department of Early Childhood Education at Georgia State University. Her research—including text creation, text analysis, and text use—looks at how digital and arts-infused, multimodal composition alters notions of literacy education, academic and literary writing, and qualitative inquiry.

**Robin L. Hughes** is an associate professor in the Department of Educational Leadership and Policy Studies, and Higher Education Student Affairs program at Indiana University—Indianapolis (IUPUI). Her research focuses on the intersection of race and sports in American culture, student-athletes in revenue-generating sports, and faculty and students of color in higher education. Dr. Hughes is co-editor and co-founder of the Journal for the Study of Sports and Athletes in Education (JSSAE).

**Hilary E. Hughes** is an assistant professor of Curriculum and Instruction in the Department of Teaching and Learning at Virginia Commonwealth University. Her research interests include equity-oriented teacher education, phenomenology as a philosophy and methodology, theories around the body, and young adolescents.

**Candace R. Kuby** is an assistant professor of Early Childhood Education at the University of Missouri. She received her PhD in Literacy, Culture, and Language Education from Indiana University. Her scholarly interests focus on: critical inquiry, multimodal literacies, and qualitative research methodologies such as narrative, feminist, critical, and post-structural approaches. She is the author of *Critical Literacy in the Early Childhood Classroom: Unpacking Histories, Unlearning Privilege* (2013), Teachers College Press. Journals in which her work appears include: *Young Children; Journal of Early Childhood Literacy; Education, Citizenship, and Social Justice; Voices of Practitioners; Talking Points; and Teaching & Learning: The Journal of Natural Inquiry and Reflective Practice.*

**Nana Osei-Kofi** is director of the Difference, Power, and Discrimination Program and associate professor of Women, Gender, and Sexuality Studies at Oregon State University. Previously, Osei-Kofi served as director of the Social Justice Studies Certificate Program in the School of Education at Iowa State University. Her scholarship includes work on critical and feminist theories of education; race and popular culture; the political economy of higher education; and arts-based inquiry. Journals in which her work has appeared include *Discourse: Studies in the Cultural Politics of Education; Latino Studies; Review of Education, Pedagogy, and Cultural Studies; and Feminist Formations.*

**Z Nicolazzo** is a doctoral candidate in the Student Affairs in Higher Education Program at Miami University in Oxford, OH. Ze earned hir M.S. in College Student Personnel from Western Illinois University and hir B.A. in Philosophy from Roger Williams University. Hir dissertation study is an ethnographic study of trans* student resilience at a large public institution in the Midwest and focuses specifically on the ways in which trans* college students navigate, confront, push back, and resist genderism on campus. Z's research interests include trans* college students, activism in higher education, and alternative epistemologies, methodologies, and representations of knowledge.

**Penny A. Pasque** is associate professor in the Department of Educational Leadership and Policy Studies, Women's and Gender Studies, and the Center for Social Justice at the University of Oklahoma. She is also a visiting scholar at the University of Michigan with the Center for the Study of Higher and Postsecondary Education and the Center for the Education of Women. Her research addresses in/equities in higher education, dis/connections between higher education and society, and complexities in critical qualitative inquiry. She is co-author of *Qualitative Inquiry for Equity in Higher Education: Methodological Implications, implications, and interventions* (Carducci, Kuntz, & Gildersleeve), from Jossey-Bass.

**Nicole M. Pourchier** is a clinical assistant professor of Literacy and Language Arts in the Department of Early Childhood Education at Georgia State University. She received her doctorate in Teaching and Learning from Georgia State University. Her research focuses on writing pedagogy and theory, post-structural research methodologies, and a/r/tography.

**Cassie F. Quigley** is an assistant professor of Science Education in the Department of Teacher Education in the Eugene T. Moore School of Education in the College of Health, Education, and Human Development at Clemson University. Her research focuses on equitable practices for science education that extend to research methods.

**David Stovall** is associate professor of Educational Policy Studies and African-American Studies at the University of Illinois at Chicago. His research interests include Critical Race Theory, school/community relationships, youth culture, and the relationship between housing markets and urban school districts. In addition to his duties and responsibilities at the university level, he is also a volunteer social studies teacher at the Greater Lawndale Social Justice High School.

**Claudine Candy Taaffe** is a doctoral student at the University of Illinois Urbana-Champaign in the Department of Education Policy, Organization, and Leadership. Her research interests include visual methodology, youth organizing, and Black girlhood studies. Her dissertation is a two-year-long visual ethnography of middle-school-aged Black girls, who use photography to create counter-narratives to the negative stereotypes about Black girls in schools and popular culture.

**Mark D. Vagle** is an associate professor in the Department of Curriculum and Instruction at the University of Minnesota's College of Education and Human Development. He conducts and teaches doctoral seminars focusing on phenomenological research. In addition, Vagle teaches courses on qualitative research methodologies, as well as philosophies, theories, and pedagogies that inform the schooling of elementary students. Currently, Vagle is using what he has termed post-intentional phenomenology to critically examine various ways in which broad philosophical and social concerns (social class in particular) take concrete (lived) shape in the curriculum and pedagogies of elementary education.

# Index

## critical qualitative research

Shirley R. Steinberg & Gaile S. Cannella, *General Editors*

The Critical Qualitative Research series examines societal structures that oppress and exclude so that transformative actions can be generated. This transformed research is activist in orientation. Because the perspective accepts the notion that nothing is apolitical, research projects themselves are critically examined for power orientations, even as they are used to address curricular, educational, or societal issues.

This methodological work challenges modernist orientations and universalist impositions, asking critical questions like: Who/what is heard? Who/what is silenced? Who is privileged? Who is disqualified? How are forms of inclusion and exclusion being created? How are power relations constructed and managed? How do different forms of privilege and oppression intersect to affect educational, societal, and life possibilities for various individuals and groups?

We are particularly interested in manuscripts that offer critical examinations of curriculum, policy, public communities, and the ways in which language, discourse practices, and power relations prevent more just transformations.

For additional information about this series or for the submission of manuscripts, please contact:
    Shirley R. Steinberg and Gaile S. Cannella
    msgramsci@aol.com | Gaile.Cannella@unt.edu

To order other books in this series, please contact our Customer Service Department:
    (800) 770-LANG (within the U.S.)
    (212) 647-7706 (outside the U.S.)
    (212) 647-7707 FAX

Or browse online by series:
    www.peterlang.com